About This Book

Why is *e-Learning and the Science of Instruction* important?

This is a book about what works in e-learning. Increasingly, organizations are turning to e-learning to save travel costs and instructional time. In fact since our first edition of this book, e-learning in both synchronous and asynchronous formats has risen to account for over one-third of all delivery of workforce instruction. However, dollars saved are only an illusion if the quality of the training does not pay off in improved job performance.

Many books on the market offer useful advice for design and development of e-learning. But unlike these books, the guidelines we present are not based on opinion; but rather on empirical research. Much of this new research is inaccessible to those producing or evaluating online learning because it has been distributed primarily within the academic research community. This book bridges the gap by summarizing research-based answers to questions that practitioners ask about effective e-learning.

What's new in the third edition?

The popularity of the first two editions is testimony to consumer interest in evidence-based guidelines on how to best use visuals, text, audio, practice exercises, and examples in e-learning. In our third edition we have updated all chapters, adding new research, guidelines, and examples. You will also find a new chapter on the basics of evidence-based training. To illustrate our guidelines, we have added new storyboards from an asynchronous lesson on Excel, a synchronous lesson on Excel, and an asynchronous lesson on pharmaceutical sales.

As a result of the popularity of previous editions as a text, we have also added an instructor guide, which is available on the publisher's website. Contact your Pfeiffer representative to access it.

What can you achieve with this book?

If you are a designer, developer, or consumer of e-learning, you can use the guidelines in this book to ensure that your courseware meets human psychological learning requirements. In particular you can learn the best ways to:

- Communicate your content with visuals, audio, and text;
- Avoid overloading learners with extraneous media effects;

- Leverage social presence to encourage deeper learning;

- Design examples and practice exercises that help learners build new skills;

- Use networked collaborative facilities effectively for learning;

- Define the best navigational schemes for your learners;

- Design e-learning to help learners build problem-solving skills; and

- Evaluate simulations and games relevant to your instructional goals.

How is this book organized?

Chapters 1 through 3 lay the foundation for the book by defining e-learning, describing how the methods used in e-learning can promote or defeat learning processes, and summarizing the basics of evidence-based practice.

Chapters 4 through 10 summarize the multimedia principles developed by over twenty-five years of research by Richard Mayer at the University of California. In these chapters you will read the guidelines, the evidence, and examples of how to best use visuals, text, and audio, as well as content segmenting and sequencing in e-learning.

Chapters 11 through 15 focus on guidelines related to important instructional methods and approaches in e-learning, including use of examples, practice and feedback, collaboration facilities, navigation tools, and techniques to help learners build problem-solving skills.

Chapter 16 updates the research and presents issues to consider in use of games and simulations in e-learning.

Chapter 17 integrates all of the book's guidelines into a comprehensive checklist and illustrates how they apply in concert to asynchronous and synchronous e-learning examples.

See the Introduction for a more detailed summary of what is covered in each chapter.

About Pfeiffer

Pfeiffer serves the professional development and hands-on resource needs of training and human resource practitioners and gives them products to do their jobs better. We deliver proven ideas and solutions from experts in HR development and HR management, and we offer effective and customizable tools to improve workplace performance. From novice to seasoned professional, Pfeiffer is the source you can trust to make yourself and your organization more successful.

Essential Knowledge   Pfeiffer produces insightful, practical, and comprehensive materials on topics that matter the most to training and HR professionals. Our Essential Knowledge resources translate the expertise of seasoned professionals into practical, how-to guidance on critical workplace issues and problems. These resources are supported by case studies, worksheets, and job aids and are frequently supplemented with CD-ROMs, websites, and other means of making the content easier to read, understand, and use.

Essential Tools   Pfeiffer's Essential Tools resources save time and expense by offering proven, ready-to-use materials—including exercises, activities, games, instruments, and assessments—for use during a training or team-learning event. These resources are frequently offered in looseleaf or CD-ROM format to facilitate copying and customization of the material.

Pfeiffer also recognizes the remarkable power of new technologies in expanding the reach and effectiveness of training. While e-hype has often created whizbang solutions in search of a problem, we are dedicated to bringing convenience and enhancements to proven training solutions. All our e-tools comply with rigorous functionality standards. The most appropriate technology wrapped around essential content yields the perfect solution for today's on-the-go trainers and human resource professionals.

www.pfeiffer.com

Essential resources for training and HR professionals

e-Learning

and the Science of Instruction

The Instructor's Manual for the third edition of *e-Learning and the Science of Instruction* is available free online. If you would like to download and print out a copy of the manual, please visit: www.wiley.com/college/clark

e-Learning
and the Science of Instruction

Proven Guidelines for Consumers and
Designers of Multimedia Learning
Third Edition

Ruth Colvin Clark • Richard E. Mayer

A Wiley Imprint
www.pfeiffer.com

Published by Pfeiffer

An Imprint of Wiley

989 Market Street, San Francisco, CA 94103-1741 www.pfeiffer.com

For additional copies/bulk purchases of this book in the U.S. please contact 800-274-4434.

Pfeiffer books and products are available through most bookstores. To contact Pfeiffer directly call our Customer Care Department within the U.S. at 800-274-4434, outside the U.S. at 317-572-3985, fax 317-572-4002, or visit www. pfeiffer.com.

Pfeiffer also publishes its books in a variety of electronic formats. Some content that appears in print may not be available in electronic books.

ISBN 978-0-470-87430-1 (cloth); 978-1-118-08616-2 (ebk); 978-1-118-08617-9 (ebk); 978-1-118-08621-6 (ebk)

Library of Congress Cataloging-in-Publication Data

Clark, Ruth Colvin.
    E-learning and the science of instruction : proven guidelines for consumers and designers of multimedia learning / Ruth C. Clark, Richard E. Mayer. — 3rd ed.
        p. cm.
    Includes bibliographical references and index.
    ISBN 978-0-470-87430-1 (hardback)
        1. Business education—Computer-assisted instruction. I. Mayer, Richard E., 1947- II. Title. III. Title:
ELearning and the science of instruction.
    HF1106.C55   2011
    658.3'12402854678–dc22
                                                                                          2011012858

Acquiring Editor: Matthew Davis   Production Editor: Michael Kay
Marketing Manager: Brian Grimm   Editor: Rebecca Taff
Director of Development: Kathleen Dolan-Davies   Editorial Assistant: Michael Zelenko
Developmental Editor: Susan Rachmeler   Manufacturing Supervisor: Becky Morgan

Printed in the United States of America

THIRD EDITION

Printing   10 9 8 7 6 5 4 3 2

CONTENTS

2. How Do People Learn from e-Courses? 29

3. Evidence-Based Practice 49

4. Applying the Multimedia Principle: Use Words and Graphics Rather Than Words Alone 67

5. Applying the Contiguity Principle: Align Words to Corresponding Graphics 91

9. Applying the Personalization Principle: Use Conversational Style and Virtual Coaches 179

ACKNOWLEDGMENTS

IN THIS THIRD EDITION, we have added new sample lessons to illustrate the application and violation of our principles. We are grateful for the talents of Mark Palmer, who created the asynchronous Excel and sales storyboards.

We acknowledge the many instructional researchers throughout the world whose work has contributed to this book. In particular, we thank the following researchers and practitioners who gave us access to their examples and research for inclusion in this third edition:

Robert Atkinson, Arizona State University

Dale Bambrick, Raytheon Professional Services

Lance Dublin, Dublin Consulting

Susanne Lajoie, McGill University

Lloyd Rieber, University of Georgia

Dan Suthers, University of Hawaii

Finally, we are grateful to support we received from the Pfeiffer team, especially to Matt Davis for editorial support.

GETTING THE MOST FROM THIS RESOURCE

Purpose

The training field is undergoing an evolution from a craft based on fads and folk wisdom to a profession that integrates evidence into the design and development of its products. Part of the training revolution has been driven by the use of digital technology to manage and deliver instructional solutions. This book provides you with evidence-based guidelines for both self-study (asynchronous) and virtual classroom (synchronous) forms of e-learning. Here you will learn the guidelines, the evidence, and examples to shape your decisions about the design, development, and evaluation of e-learning.

Audience

If you are a designer, developer, or consumer of e-learning, you can use the guidelines in this book to ensure that your courseware meets human psychological learning requirements. Although most of our examples focus on workforce learning, we believe instructional professionals in the educational and academic arenas can equally benefit from our guidelines.

Package Components

For this third edition we have added an instructor guide that includes many resources. The instructor guide is located on the Pfeiffer website. Contact your Pfeiffer representative for access.

Table I.1 summarizes the content of the book's chapters. We have added a new Chapter 3, which describes the basics of evidence-based practice. We have updated the research in all of the chapters and added new storyboard examples for a lesson on Excel as well as for a more strategic skill of consultative selling.

Table I.1. A Preview of Chapters.

Chapter	Topics
1. e-Learning Promise and Pitfalls	• Our definition of e-learning • Evidence on e-learning effectiveness • The promise and pitfalls of e-Learning • Inform versus perform outcome goals • Three architectures for e-learning design
2. How People Learn from e-Courses	• An overview of human learning processes and how instructional methods can support or disrupt them
3. Evidence-Based Practice	• What is evidence-based practice? • Three approaches to research on instructional effectiveness • The features of effective experimental comparisons • An introduction to the statistical concepts in the book

Table I.1. (Continued).

Chapter	Topics
4. Applying the Multimedia Principle: Use Words and Graphics Rather Than Words Alone	• Evidence for whether learning is improved in e-lessons that include visuals • Types of visuals that best promote learning • Who benefits most from visuals? • Static illustrations Versus animations
5. Applying the Contiguity Principle: Align Words to Corresponding Graphics	• Evidence for the best placement of text and graphics on the screen • Evidence for sequencing of text or audio in conjunction with visuals • Situations in which the contiguity principle is most applicable as well as the psychological basis for this principle
6. Applying the Modality Principle: Present Words as Audio Narration Rather than On-Screen Text	• Evidence for presenting words that describe graphics in audio rather than in text • When the modality principle is and is not applicable as well as the psychological basis for the principle
7. Applying the Redundancy Principle: Explain Visuals with Words in Audio OR Text: Not Both	• Evidence for use of audio to explain graphics rather than text and audio • Situations when adding on-screen text to narration can be helpful to learning
8. Applying the Coherence Principle: Adding Extra Material Can Hurt Learning	• Evidence for omitting distracting graphics and stories, irrelevant audio, and detailed textual explanations • Evidence for using simple rather than complex visuals • Evidence for omitting extraneous words added for interest, to expand on key ideas or for technical depth
9. Applying the Personalization Principle: Use Conversational Style and Virtual Coaches	• Evidence for conversational style, voice quality, and polite speech to improve learning • Situations in which the personalization principle is most applicable • Evidence for best design of computer agents to promote learning • Evidence for making the author visible to the learner through the script

(Continued)

Table 1.1. (Continued).

Chapter	Topics
10. Applying the Segmenting and Pre-Training Principles: Managing Complexity by Breaking a Lesson into Parts	• Evidence for breaking a continuous lesson into bite-size segments and allowing learners to access each segment at their own rate • Evidence for sequencing key concepts in a lesson prior to the main procedure or process of that lesson
11. Leveraging Examples in e-Learning	• Worked examples for well-structured tasks, strategic tasks, and modeling examples • Evidence and guidelines to transition from examples to practice assignments through fading • Ways to ensure examples are processed by adding questions that promote self-explanations or by methods that promote active observation • How to design examples that support learning of strategic skills
12. Does Practice Make Perfect?	• Evidence for the amount and type of practice needed to support learning objectives • Evidence and guidelines for design of effective practice feedback • Evidence for the distribution and grouping of practice within and among your lessons
13. Learning Together Virtually	• Factors proven to promote learning from collaborative assignments • Summary of types of computer-supported collaborative learning • Samples of research studies on computer-supported collaborative learning • Use of structured controversy as one proven collaborative learning method

Table I.1. (Continued).

Chapter	Topics
14. Who's in Control? Guidelines for e-Learning Navigation	• Distinction between learner and program control • When to use learner versus program control • Techniques for dynamically adapting instruction to evolving learner needs • Techniques for navigational aids in hypermedia environments
15. e-Learning to Build Thinking Skills	• Three types of thinking skills • Evidence on the effectiveness of thinking skills training programs • Features of and evidence for whole-task instruction • Guidelines for making thinking processes explicit in e-learning • An introduction to cognitive task analysis to define expert thinking skills
16. Simulations and Games in e-Learning	• What are simulations and games? • Evidence for effectiveness of simulations and games • Techniques to ensure the learning effectiveness of simulations and games
17. Applying the Guidelines	• A checklist and summary of the guidelines in the book • Three discussions of how the guidelines apply to e-learning samples

Glossary

The Glossary provides definitions of the technical terms used throughout the book.

CHAPTER OUTLINE

What Is e-Learning?

Is e-Learning Better?

The Promise of e-Learning

Promise 1: Customized Training

Promise 2: Engagement in Learning

Promise 3: Multimedia

Promise 4: Acceleration of Expertise Through Scenarios

The Pitfalls of e-Learning

Pitfall 1: Too Much of a Good Thing

Pitfall 2: Not Enough of a Good Thing

Pitfall 3: Losing Sight of the Goal

Pitfall 4: Discovery Learning

Inform and Perform e-Learning Goals

Near Versus Far Transfer Perform Goals

e-Learning Architectures

Interactivity in the Architectures

What Is Effective e-Courseware?

Training Goals

Learner Differences

Environment

Learning in e-Learning

1

e-Learning

PROMISE AND PITFALLS

IN THIS CHAPTER we define e-learning as training delivered on a digital device such as a smart phone or a laptop computer that is designed to support individual learning or organizational performance goals. Our scope includes asynchronous forms of e-learning designed for self-study as well as synchronous instructor-led e-learning. Among these two forms of e-learning, we include e-courses developed primarily to provide information (that is, inform courses) as well as those designed to build specific job-related skills (that is, perform courses).

In the five years since we wrote the second edition of *e-Learning and the Science of Instruction*, digital technology has continued to evolve rapidly. Web 2.0 shatters the traditional model of unidirectional instruction by supporting online multilateral exchanges of visuals, text, and audio within and outside of the learning community. Search engines such as Google, coupled with social media such as Facebook and YouTube, make learners receivers, producers, and distributors of knowledge. Technology has also become more immersive in other ways. Three-dimensional worlds made popular by gaming applications offer environments in which learners assume an avatar persona and can move around and interact with objects and other participants. Likewise, platforms have shrunk and diversified, giving birth to a range of mobile learning devices.

However, the benefits gained from these new technologies will depend on the extent to which they are used in ways compatible with human cognitive learning processes. When technophiles become so excited about cutting-edge technology that they ignore human mental limitations, they may not be able to leverage technology in ways that support learning. Instructional methods that support rather than defeat human learning processes are an essential ingredient of all effective e-learning courseware. The most appropriate methods depend on the goals of the training (for example, to inform or to perform); the learners' related skills (for example, whether they are familiar with or new to the skills); and various environmental factors, including technological, cultural, and pragmatic constraints.

In this chapter we lay the groundwork for the book by defining e-learning and identifying both the potential and the pitfalls of digital training. We also distinguish between inform and perform e-learning goals, introduce three e-learning design architectures and summarize key factors associated with effective courseware.

What Is e-Learning?

We define e-learning as instruction delivered on a digital device such as a computer or mobile device that is intended to support learning. The forms of e-learning we examine in this book have the following features:

- Stores and/or transmits lessons on CD-ROM, local internal or external memory, or servers on the Internet or intranet
- Includes content relevant to the learning objective
- Uses media elements such as words and pictures to deliver the content
- Uses instructional methods such as examples, practice, and feedback to promote learning

- May be instructor-led (synchronous e-learning) or designed for self-paced individual study (asynchronous e-learning)

- Helps learners build new knowledge and skills linked to individual learning goals or to improved organizational performance.

As you can see, this definition has several elements concerning the what, how, and why of e-learning.

What. e-learning courses include both content (that is, information) and instructional methods (that is, techniques) that help people learn the content.

How. e-learning courses are delivered via digital devices such as computers and smart phones using words in the form of spoken or printed text and pictures such as illustrations, photos, animation, or video. Some forms of e-learning called asynchronous e-learning are designed for individual self-study. We show a screen shot from an asynchronous class on Excel in Figure 1.1. These courses are typically self-paced, allowing individual learners to access

Figure 1.1. A Screen Capture from an Asynchronous Excel Lesson.

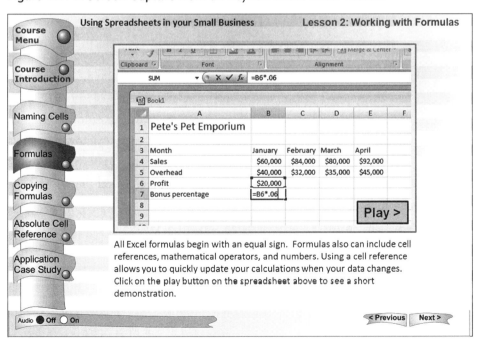

Figure 1.2. A Screen Capture from a Synchronous Excel Lesson.

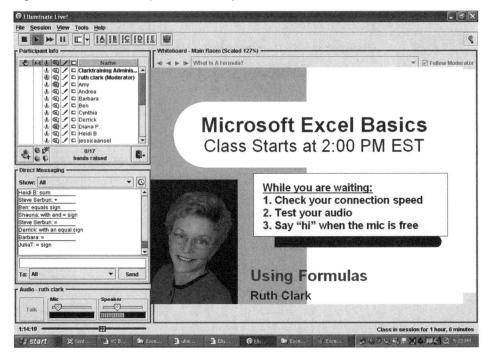

training at any time or any location on their own. Other formats called virtual classrooms, webinars, or synchronous e-learning are designed for real-time instructor-led training. We show a screen shot from a virtual classroom in Figure 1.2. Synchronous e-learning allows students from New York to New Delhi to attend an online class taught by an instructor in real time. However, synchronous sessions are also often recorded, allowing them to be viewed by a single learner in a self-paced manner. Synchronous and asynchronous forms of e-learning may support collaboration with others through tools such as wikis, YouTube, chat, discussion boards and email.

Why. e-learning lessons are intended to help learners reach personal learning objectives or perform their jobs in ways that improve the bottom-line goals of the organization.

In short, the "e" in e-learning refers to the "how"—the course is digitized so it can be stored in electronic form. The "learning" in e-learning refers to the "what"—the course includes content and ways to help people learn it—and the "why"—refers to the purpose: to help individuals achieve educational goals or to help organizations build skills related to improved job performance.

Our definition states that the goal of e-learning is to build job-transferable knowledge and skills linked to organizational performance or to help individuals achieve personal learning goals. Although the guidelines we present throughout the book also apply to lessons designed for educational or general interest learning goals, our emphasis is on instructional programs that are built or purchased for workforce learning. To illustrate our guidelines we draw on actual training courseware from colleagues who have given us permission to use their examples. In addition we have built two sets of storyboards: one with a focus on basic Excel skills intended to illustrate a typical technology training course and a second with a focus on sales skills intended to illustrate instructional techniques that apply to more strategic skills.

Is e-Learning Better?

For many training goals, you may have a choice of several delivery media. One of the least expensive options is a traditional hard-copy book. In-person instructor-led training augmented with slides and the occasional video is another popular option. Finally, e-learning in either self-study or instructor-led formats offers a third choice. As you consider your delivery options you might wonder whether some media are more effective for learning purposes than others.

Although technology is evolving rapidly, much of what we are seeing today under the e-learning label is not new. Training delivered on a computer, known as computer-based training or CBT, has been around for more than forty years. Early examples delivered over mainframe computers were primarily text on a screen with interspersed questions—electronic versions of behaviorist psychologist B.F. Skinner's teaching machine. The computer program evaluated answers to the multiple-choice questions and prewritten feedback was matched to the learner responses. One of the main applications of these early e-lessons was to train workers to use mainframe computer systems. As technology has evolved, acquiring greater capability to deliver true multimedia, the courseware has become more elaborate in terms of realistic graphics, audio, color, animation, and complex simulations. However, as we will see, greater media capabilities do not necessarily ensure more learning.

Each new wave of instructional delivery technology (starting with film in the 1920s) spawned optimistic predictions of massive improvements in learning. For example, in 1947 the U.S. Army conducted one of the first published media comparisons with the hypothesis that film teaches better than classroom instructors (see box for details). Yet after more than sixty years of research attempting to demonstrate that the latest media are better, the outcomes fail to support the superiority of any single delivery medium over another.

THE FIRST MEDIA COMPARISON RESEARCH

In 1947 the U.S. Army conducted research to demonstrate that instruction delivered by film resulted in better learning outcomes than traditional classroom or paper-based versions. Three versions of a lesson on how to read a micrometer were developed. The film version included a narrated demonstration of how to read the micrometer. A second version was taught in a classroom. The instructor used the same script and included a demonstration using actual equipment along with still slide pictures. A third version was a self-study paper lesson in which the text used the same words as the film, along with pictures with arrows to indicate movement. Learners were randomly assigned to a version and after the training session they were tested to see whether they could read the micrometer. Which group learned more? There were no differences in learning among the three groups (Hall & Cushing, 1947).

With few exceptions, hundreds of media comparison studies have shown no differences in learning (Clark, 1994; Dillon & Gabbard, 1998). A meta-analysis by Bernard et al. (2004) integrating research studies that compared learning from electronic distance education to learning from traditional classroom instruction yielded the achievement effect sizes shown in Figure 1.3. (See Chapter 3 for information on meta-analysis and effect sizes). As you can see, the majority of effect sizes in the bar chart are close to zero, indicating no practical differences in learning between face-to-face and electronic distance learning. However, the bars at either end of the graph show that some distance learning courses were much more effective than classroom courses and vice versa. A review of online learning by Tallent-Runnels, Thomas, Lan, Cooper, Ahern, Shaw, and Liu (2006) concurs: "Overwhelming evidence has shown that learning in an online environment can be as effective as that in traditional classrooms. Second, students' learning in the online environment is affected by the quality of online instruction. Not surprisingly, students in well-designed and well-implemented online courses learned significantly more, and more effectively, than those in online courses where teaching and learning activities were not carefully planned and where the delivery and accessibility were impeded by technology problems" (p. 116).

Figure 1.3. Electronic Distance Learning Versus Face-to-Face Instruction: Distribution of Effect Sizes.

Adapted from Bernard et al., 2004.

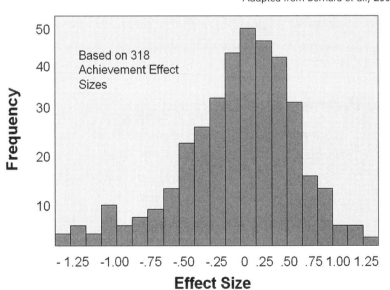

From the plethora of media comparison research conducted over the past sixty years, we have learned that it's not the delivery medium, but rather the instructional methods that cause learning. When the instructional methods remain essentially the same, so does the learning, no matter which medium is used to deliver instruction. Conversely, a course that includes effective instructional methods, will better support learning than a course that fails to use effective methods—no matter what delivery medium is used.

Still, we don't want to leave the impression that all media are equivalent. Each delivery environment has its tradeoffs. Books, for example, are inexpensive, self-paced, and portable but limited to text and still graphics. Classroom instructor-led training offers high social presence and opportunities for hands-on practice, but is instructor-paced and content invariant, requiring all learners to proceed at the same pace and review the same content. Computers represent one of the most flexible media options, as they support media elements of text, graphics (still and animated) and audio. Computers offer opportunities for unique engagement with simulations or with highly immersive environments that in some cases would be impossible to replicate outside a digital environment. In addition, computers offer opportunities to tailor learning—opportunities that are difficult to achieve outside of one-to-one human tutoring. With Web 2.0, computers offer multi-lateral communication channels that span time and space. All of these features offer promise but also harbor pitfalls when not used in ways congruent with human learning processes.

The Promise of e-Learning

How popular is e-learning in workforce learning? The trends in delivery media for the last decade shown in Figure 1.4 reveal a steadily increasing market share for digital learning. In the first edition of *e-Learning and the Science of Instruction*, we reported that in the year 2001, approximately 11 percent of all training was delivered via computer (including the Internet, intranets, and CD-ROM). By the second edition, written at the end of 2006, that figure had risen to 29 percent. As we begin the second decade of the 21st Century, e-learning accounts for 36.5 percent of delivery (ASTD State

Figure 1.4. Percentage of Learning Hours Available Via ILT (Instructor-Led Training) and Technology.

Adapted from ASTD's *State of the Industry Report*, 2010.

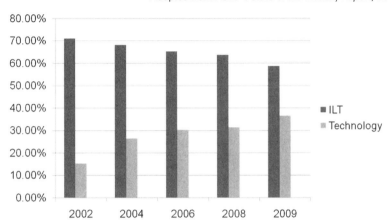

of the Industry Report, 2010). Driven by economic conditions that seek more cost-effective forums for training as well as by continued evolution of computer technology, e-learning now accounts for over one-third of all workforce learning delivery.

Organizations are turning to e-learning to save training time and travel costs associated with traditional face-to-face learning. However, cost savings are only an illusion when e-learning does not effectively build knowledge and skills linked to desired job outcomes. Will you leverage the potential of e-learning to provide relevant and cost-effective learning environments? Part of the answer depends on the quality of the instruction embedded in the e-learning products you are designing, building, or selecting today. We propose that the opportunities to foster learning via digital instruction rely on appropriate leveraging of four unique features that we summarize in the following paragraphs.

Promise 1: Customized Training

Self-study asynchronous e-learning has the potential to customize learning to the unique needs of each learner. By unique needs, *we don't mean learning styles*—a myth still popular among training practitioners in spite of a lack of evidence to support it (Clark, 2010; Pashler, Bain, Bottage, Graesser, Koedinger, McDaniel, & Metcalfe, 2007). By customized training we mean tailoring content and instructional methods based on the work roles and learning needs of individuals (particularly their prior knowledge). In Chapter 14 we review adaptive e-learning in which the program customizes content and training methods dynamically based on learner responses. With adaptive e-learning you can save valuable staff time and ensure consistent learning by providing more practice and examples for those who need them and less for those who don't. Other than one-on-one tutoring with human mentors—an expensive option that often yields inconsistent results—no other delivery environment offers the customization options available in asynchronous e-learning.

Promise 2: Engagement in Learning

Regardless of delivery media, all learning requires engagement. In Figure 1.5 we show our Engagement Matrix, which includes two types of activity: behavioral and psychological. By *behavioral engagement* we mean any overt

Figure 1.5. The Engagement Matrix.

Adapted from Stull and Mayer, 2007.

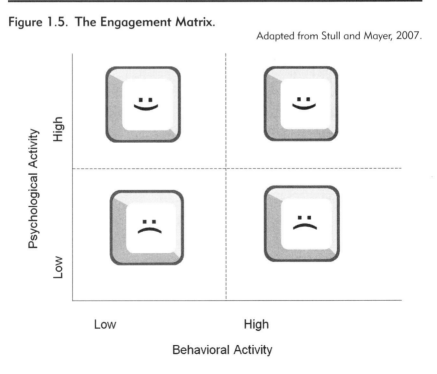

Psychological Activity

High

Low

Low   High

Behavioral Activity

action a learner takes during an instructional episode. Some examples of behavioral activities in e-learning include pressing the forward arrow, typing an answer in a response box, clicking on an option from a multiple-choice menu, verbally responding to an instructor's question, selecting an action from a pull-down menu, or using text chat during a webinar. By *psychological engagement,* we mean cognitive processing of content in ways that lead to acquisition of new knowledge and skills. Some cognitive processes that lead to learning include paying attention to the relevant material, mentally organizing it into a coherent representation, and integrating it with relevant prior knowledge. Some examples of activities in e-learning intended to prime psychological engagement include self-explaining a complex visual, summarizing a portion of a lesson, generating an outline or drawing based on the lesson, or taking a practice test.

As you can see in Figure 1.5, the matrix crosses high and low behavioral activity against high and low psychological activity. Learning occurs in the upper cells of the matrix in the zones of high psychological activity. Note that high levels of behavioral activity do not necessarily correspond with high levels of psychological activity (lower right quadrant). Pressing the forward button in e-learning or playing a computer game such as PacMan involve high levels of behavioral activity but little psychological activity that leads to learning. In contrast, carefully watching an animation explained with audio narration involves little or no behavioral activity but will lead to psychological activity needed for learning. Our point is that high levels of behavioral activity don't necessarily translate into the type of psychological processing that supports learning. Likewise, meaningful learning can occur in the absence of behavioral responses. Your goal is to use media elements and instructional methods that fall into the upper half of the matrix. Throughout this book we will show evidence-based techniques to help you achieve that goal.

Promise 3: Multimedia

In e-Learning, you can use a combination of text and audio, as well as still and motion visuals to communicate your content. Fortunately, we have a healthy arsenal of research to guide your best use of these media elements that we discuss in Chapters 4 through 10.

Promise 4: Acceleration of Expertise Through Scenarios

Studies of experts across a wide variety of domains show that about ten years of experience are needed to reach high levels of proficiency (Ericcson, 2006). In some work settings, getting that experience can take years because situations that require certain skills rarely present themselves. e-Learning, however, offers opportunities to immerse learners in job-realistic environments requiring them to solve infrequent problems or complete tasks in a matter of minutes that could take hours or days to complete in the real world. For example, when troubleshooting equipment, some failures are infrequent and may require considerable time to resolve. A computer simulation, however, can emulate those failures and give learners opportunities to resolve them in a realistic work environment such as the one in Figure 1.6. In Chapter 15 we discuss e-learning programs such as this one designed to build thinking skills.

Figure 1.6. A Simulated Automotive Shop Offers Accelerated Learning Opportunities.

With permission from Raytheon Professional Services.

The Pitfalls of e-Learning

The powerful features of e-learning are a two-edged sword with many potential traps that sabotage learning. Here we summarize some of the major pitfalls that can rob your organization of a return on investment in digital learning:

Pitfall 1: Too Much of a Good Thing

As we will see in Chapter 2, the human cognitive system is limited, and when it comes to instruction, less is almost always more. It's tempting to use an eye-catching mix of animations, sounds, audio, and text to convey your content. However, we have good evidence to support our advice: Don't do it. Read Chapter 8 on the Coherence Principle to learn the details.

Pitfall 2: Not Enough of a Good Thing

At the other end of the spectrum you can find e-learning that, in fact, is minimalist in that it fails to make use of features proven to promote learning. For example, a wall-of-words approach ignores opportunities to leverage relevant visuals by providing explanations that use text and more text. Alternatively, some e-learning, called "page turners," omits interactivity other than the forward and back buttons. These courses may present screen after screen of stunning animations but don't provide the learners with overt opportunities to process the content through practice exercises or simulations.

Pitfall 3: Losing Sight of the Goal

In 2009, $126 billion were invested in workforce learning in the United States alone (ASTD State of the Industry Report, 2010). We suspect there is little evidence of return on that investment—a safe speculation on our part because most organizations don't invest the time or resources to assess outcomes from their training. Regardless of delivery medium, any training development process must identify key skills that promote organizational goals and build training around the tasks that constitute those skills. Be it games, virtual worlds, or social media, technophiles gravitate toward the latest cool trends—sometimes without considering whether and how best to leverage them in ways that support relevant learning.

Pitfall 4: Discovery Learning

Because the metaphor of the Internet is high learner control, allowing users to search, locate, and peruse thousands of Internet sites, a tempting pitfall is to create highly exploratory learning environments that give learners an unrestricted license to navigate and piece together their own unique learning experiences. One lesson we have learned from over fifty years of research on discovery learning is that it rarely works (Mayer, 2004). Instead, as we discuss in Chapter 16, we recommend a structured form of e-learning lesson that provides guidance.

Inform and Perform e-Learning Goals

As summarized in Table 1.1, the guidelines in this book apply to e-learning that is designed to inform as well as e-learning that is designed to improve specific job performance. We classify lessons that are designed primarily to build awareness or provide information as *inform programs,* also known as briefings. A new employee orientation module that reviews the company history and describes the company's organization or a product knowledge update are examples of topics that are often presented as inform programs. The information presented is job relevant, but there may be no specific expectations of new skills to be acquired. The primary goal of these programs is to transmit information.

Table 1.1. Inform and Perform e-Learning Goals.

Goal	Definition	Example
Inform	Lessons that communicate information	• Company history • New product features
Perform Procedure	Lessons that build procedural skills (to promote near transfer)	• How to log on • How to complete an expense report
Perform Tasks	Lessons that build strategic skills (to promote far transfer)	• How to close a sale • How to analyze a loan

In contrast, we classify programs designed to build specific skills as *perform programs.* Some typical examples of perform e-learning are lessons on software use, designing a database, or troubleshooting an automotive failure. Many e-courses contain both inform and perform learning objectives, while some are designed for inform only or perform only.

Near Versus Far Transfer Perform Goals

We distinguish between two types of perform goals: (1) procedural, which promote *near transfer*, and (2) strategic, which promote *far transfer.* Procedural lessons such as the Excel examples in Figures 1.1 and 1.2 are designed to teach step-by-step tasks, which are performed more or less the same way each time. Many end-user computer-skills courses fall into this category. This type of training promotes near transfer because the steps learned in the training are identical or very similar to the steps required in the job environment. Thus, the transfer from training to application is near.

Lessons designed to build strategic skills teach general approaches to tasks that do not have one correct approach or outcome. Thus, the situations presented in the training may not be exactly the same as the situations that occur on the job. These tasks require the worker to adapt guidelines to various job situations. Typically, some element of problem solving is involved. The worker always has to use judgment in performing these tasks because there is no one right approach for all situations. Far transfer lessons include just about all soft-skill training, supervision and management courses, and sales skills. Figure 1.6 illustrates a screen from a far transfer course on troubleshooting. The lesson begins with a work order specifying a high idle problem in the automobile. The learner has access to the testing equipment you see in the shop to take and record measurements. The shop computer links the learner to actual online reference resources and the telephone offers testing hints. When the learners are ready to interpret the data collected, they select the appropriate failure and repair action from a list. As feedback, a list of testing activities and times from an expert repair is displayed next to a list of the learner's activities and times, which were tracked during the learner's progress through the lesson.

e-Learning Architectures

Although all e-learning is delivered on a digital device, different courses reflect different assumptions of learning, which we introduce here and describe in detail in Chapter 2. During the past one hundred years, three views of learning have evolved, and you will see each view reflected in courses available today. The three architectures and the learning assumptions on which they are based, summarized in Table 1.2, are *receptive* based on an *information acquisition* view, *directive* based on a *response strengthening* view, and *guided discovery* based on a *knowledge construction* view. We describe these three views in greater detail in Chapter 2.

Table 1.2. Three e-Learning Architectures.

Architecture	View	Inter-Activity	Used For
Receptive	Information Acquisition	Low	Inform training goals such as new hire orientation
Directive	Response Strengthening	Medium	Perform procedure training goals such as software skills
Guided Discovery	Knowledge Construction	High	Perform strategic training goals such as problem solving

Interactivity in the Architectures

The interactivity of the lessons (from low to high) is one important feature that distinguishes lessons built using the various architectures. Receptive types of e-learning fall at the lower end of the behavioral interactivity continuum as they incorporate little or no opportunities for overt learner responses. Receptive lessons are used most frequently for inform training goals. For learning to occur, the lesson must include techniques that prompt high psychological engagement in the absence of behavioral activity. In other words, effective receptive lessons would fall into the upper left quadrant of the engagement matrix shown in Figure 1.5.

Directive lessons follow a sequence of "explanation-example-question-feedback." These architectures, commonly designed for perform procedure training goals, incorporate highly structured practice opportunities designed to guide learning in a step by step manner. The Excel lessons shown in Figures 1.1 and 1.2 reflect a directive architecture. The high degree of structure and guidance in directive architectures makes them suitable for learners who are new to the content and skills.

Effective guided discovery forms of e-learning, including simulations and games, engage learners both behaviorally and psychologically. For example, Figure 1.6 shows the interface for a guided discovery course in which the learner is problem solving by selecting and interpreting troubleshooting tests leading to accurate diagnosis of an automotive failure. We describe guided discovery architectures in Chapters 15 and 16. Because these types of lessons require learners to solve a problem and learn from its solution, they impose more mental load than the directive architectures. Therefore, they are generally more appropriate for more experienced learners and for building far transfer skills.

Learning is possible from any of these three architectures if learners engage in active knowledge construction. In receptive courses, you will want to use media elements and instructional methods that stimulate psychological activity in the absence of behavioral activity. We will review many proven methods of this type in Chapters 4 through 11. In directive and guided discovery architectures, knowledge construction is overtly promoted by the interactions built into the lessons. In the next chapter we dig a little deeper into the psychological processes needed for learning and how instructional methods can support or defeat those processes.

What Is Effective e-Courseware?

A central question for our book is: "What does effective courseware look like?" Throughout the book we recommend specific features to look for or to design into your e-learning. However, you will need to adapt our recommendations based on three main considerations—the goal of your training, the prior knowledge of your learners, and the environment in which you will develop and deploy your training.

Training Goals

The goals or intended outcomes of your e-learning will influence which guidelines are most appropriate for you to consider. Earlier in this chapter we made distinctions among three types of training designed to inform the student, to perform procedures, and to perform strategic tasks. For inform e-lessons, you should apply the guidelines in Chapters 4 through 11 regarding the best use of media elements, including visuals, narration, and text to present information as well as how to use examples effectively. To help learners acquire procedural skills, you should apply these guidelines and add to them relevant evidence for best design of practice sessions in Chapter 12. If, however, your goal is to develop strategic or far transfer skills, you will want to apply the guidelines from all the chapters, including Chapter 15 on teaching problem-solving skills and Chapter 16 on games and simulations.

Learner Differences

In addition to selecting or designing courseware specific to the type of outcome desired, lessons should include instructional methods appropriate to the learner's characteristics. While various individual differences such as learning styles have received the attention of the training community, research has shown that the learner's prior knowledge of the course content exerts the most influence on learning. Learners with little prior knowledge will benefit from different instructional strategies than will learners who are relatively experienced.

For the most part, the guidelines we provide in this book are based on research conducted with adult learners who were new to the course content. If your target audience has greater background knowledge in the course content, some of these guidelines may be less applicable. For example, Chapter 6 suggests that if you explain graphics with audio narration rather than text, you reduce the mental workload required of the learner and thereby increase learning. However, if your learners are experienced regarding the skills you are teaching, overload is not as likely and they will probably learn effectively from either text or audio explanations of visuals.

Environment

A third factor that affects e-learning is the environment—including such issues as technical constraints of the delivery platform, network, and software, cultural factors in institutions such as the acceptance of and routine familiarity with technology, and pragmatic constraints related to budget, time, and management expectations. In this book we focus on what works best from a psychological perspective, but we recognize that you will have to adapt our guidelines to your own unique set of environmental factors.

Learning in e-Learning

The challenge in e-learning, as in any learning program, is to build lessons in ways that are compatible with human learning processes. To be effective, instructional strategies must support these processes. That is, they must foster the psychological events necessary for learning. While the computer technology for delivery of e-learning is upgraded weekly, the human side of the equation—the neurological infrastructure underlying the learning process—is very old and designed for change only over evolutionary time spans. In fact, technology can easily deliver more sensory data than the human nervous system can process. To the extent that audio and visual elements in a lesson interfere with human cognition, learning will be depressed.

We know a lot about how learning occurs. Over the past twenty years, hundreds of research studies on cognitive learning processes and methods that support them have been published. Much of this new knowledge remains inaccessible to those who are producing or evaluating online learning because it has been distributed primarily within the research community. This book fills the gap by summarizing research-based answers to questions that multimedia producers and consumers ask about what to look for in effective e-learning.

COMING NEXT

Since instructional methods must support the psychological processes of learning, the next chapter summarizes those processes. We include an overview of our current understanding of the human learning system and the processes involved in building knowledge and skills in learners. We provide examples of how instructional methods used in e-lessons support cognitive processes.

Suggested Readings

Clark, R.C. (2010). *Evidence-based training methods.* Alexandria, VA: ASTD Press.

Clark, R.C., & Mayer, R.E. (2008). Learning by viewing versus learning by doing: Evidence-based guidelines for principled learning environments. *Performance Improvement, 47,* 5–13.

Clark, R.E. (1994). Media will never influence learning. *Educational Technology Research and Development, 42,* 21–30.

Mayer, R.E. (2004). Should there be a three-strikes rule against pure discovery learning: The case for guided methods of instruction. *American Psychologist, 59*(1), 14–19.

CHAPTER OUTLINE

How Do People Learn?

Learning with Technology

What Is Learning and Instruction?

Three Metaphors for Learning

Principles and Processes of Learning

Managing Limited Cognitive Resources During Learning

How e-Lessons Affect Human Learning

Methods for Directing Selection of Important Information

Methods for Managing Limited Capacity in Working Memory

Methods for Integration

Methods for Retrieval and Transfer

Summary of Learning Processes

2

How Do People Learn from e-Courses?

FROM LAS VEGAS–STYLE MEDIA with games and glitz at one extreme to page turners consisting of text on screens at the other, many e-learning courses ignore human cognitive processes and as a result do not optimize learning. In writing this book, we were guided by two fundamental assumptions: the design of e-learning courses should be based on (1) a cognitive theory of how people learn and (2) on scientifically valid research studies. In other words, e-learning courses should be constructed in light of how the mind learns and experimental evidence concerning e-learning features that best promote learning. In this chapter we focus on the first assumption by describing how learning works and how to help people learn. We have added a rationale for considering how learning works and a more detailed description how instruction can be designed in light of obstacles to learning. We have moved our description of what makes good research to be part of new expanded chapter on evidence-based training (Chapter 3), which focuses on the second assumption.

DESIGN DILEMMA: YOU DECIDE

Suppose you are in charge of the training department at Thrifty Savings and Loan. Your boss, the HR director, has just returned from an e-learning conference and asks you to develop a series of courses to be delivered via the corporate intranet: "With the recent merger, we need more cost-effective ways to deliver training to the local branches. We need to both create self-study lessons, virtual classroom sessions, and promote informal learning through social media. By using technology we can save money and also make learning fun. My kids really enjoy playing games online and connecting with others through Facebook and Twitter! Let's showcase our training to upper management by using the cutting edge of learning technology."

Your director of human resources is espousing what can be called a technology-centered approach to e-learning. For her, e-learning courses should take advantage of powerful, cutting-edge technologies such as mobile computing, video, games, and social media available on the web. In taking a technology-centered approach, she is basing her decisions about how to design e-learning courses on the capabilities afforded by new technologies.

Your intuition is that something is wrong with the technology-centered approach. In every era, strong claims have been made for the educational value of hot new technologies, but the reality somehow has never lived up to expectations. You wonder why there have been so many failures in the field of educational technology. Perhaps expectations have been unrealistic? Today, many of the same old claims about revolutionizing learning can be heard again, this time applied to online games, simulations, or to the Web 2.0. You decide it's time to take a learner-centered approach, in which technology is adjusted to fit in with the way that people learn. But you wonder if there is a learning theory with sufficient detail to guide tactical decisions in e-learning design.

Based on your own experience or intuition, which of the following options would you select?

A. Online applications such as games, simulations, and social media are engaging and should be a central feature of all new e-learning initiatives.

B. Online applications such as games, simulations, and social media may interfere with human learning processes and should be avoided.

C. We don't know enough about human learning to make specific recommendations about how to use new technology features.

D. Not sure which options are correct.

How Do People Learn?

Let's begin our review of what works in e-learning with a discussion of technology and learner-centered views of instruction.

Learning with Technology

Today, there is an impressive arsenal of instructional technologies that can be used, ranging from educational games played on mobile devices to virtual reality environments to online learning with animated pedagogic agents and with video and animation. Is there anything special about learning with technology? Examine the following questions about learning with technology and place a check mark next to the one you think is most important:

☐ How can we use cutting-edge technology in training?

☐ How can we leverage technologies that younger generations have grown up using?

☐ What are the best technologies for e-learning?

☐ How can we adapt technology to aid human learning?

If you checked any of the first three items, you appear to be taking a technology-centered approach to learning with technology. In a technology-centered approach, you focus on the capabilities of educational technology and seek to promote learning with technology (Mayer, 2009). For example, your goal is to incorporate cutting-edge technologies such as social media and mobile learning into your training repertoire.

What's wrong with this view of learning with technology? The problem is that when you focus too much on the role of cutting-edge technology, you may ignore the role the learner. Cuban (1986) has described the history of educational technology since the 1920s, including motion pictures in the 1920s, educational radio in the 1930s and 1940s, educational television in the 1950s, and programmed instruction in the 1960s. In each case, strong claims were made for the potential of the cutting-edge technology of the day to revolutionize education, but in each case that potential was not reached. The reason for the disappointing history of educational technology may be that instructors expected learners to adapt to the technology and therefore did not design learning environments that were consistent with how people learn.

If you checked the last item, you are taking a learner-centered approach to learning with technology. In a learner-centered approach, the focus is on how people learn and technology is adapted to the learner in order to assist the learning process (Mayer, 2009). The rationale for taking a learner-centered approach is that it has been shown to be more effective in promoting productive learning. A learner-centered approach does not rule out the use of new technological innovations. It does however require the adaptation of those innovations in ways that support human learning processes. In this book, we take a learner-centered approach, so in this chapter we begin by taking a look at how learning works.

What Is Learning and Instruction?

Consistent with the consensus among learning scientists (Mayer, 2011a), we define learning as a change in the learner's knowledge due to experience. This definition has three main elements:

- Learning involves a change.
- The change is in what the learner knows.
- The change is caused by the learner's experience.

First, if you are involved in e-training, your job is to help people change. Change is at the center of learning. Second, the change is personal in that it takes place within the learner's information processing system. A change in what the learner knows can include changes in facts, concepts, procedures, strategies, and beliefs. You can never directly see a change in someone's knowledge so you have to infer that someone's knowledge has changed by observing a change in his or her behavior. Third, the change in what someone knows is caused by an instructional episode—that is, by a person's experience. If you are involved in e-training, your task is to design environments that create experiences that will foster desired change in learners' behaviors consistent with the goals of the organization. This definition of learning is broad enough to include a wide range of e-learning, including online PowerPoint presentations, virtual classrooms, simulations, and games. The goal of the science of learning is a research-based theory of how learning works.

We define instruction as the training professional's manipulation of the learner's experiences to foster learning (Mayer, 2011a). This definition has two parts. First, instruction is something that the instructional professional does to affect the learner's experience. Second, the goal of the manipulation is to cause a change in what the learner knows. This definition of instruction is broad enough to include a wide range of instructional methods in e-learning, as described in the following chapters of this book. The goal of the science of instruction is a set of research-based principles for how to design, develop, and deliver instruction.

Three Metaphors for Learning

Place a check mark next to your favorite description of how learning works:

- ☐ Learning involves strengthening correct responses and weakening incorrect responses.

- ☐ Learning involves adding new information to your memory.

- ☐ Learning involves making sense of the presented material by attending to relevant information, mentally reorganizing it, and connecting it with what you already know.

Each of these answers reflects one of the three major metaphors of learning that learning psychologists have developed during the past one hundred years, as summarized in Table 2.1 (Mayer, 2005). Your personal view of how learning works can affect your decisions about how to design instructional programs.

Table 2.1. Three Metaphors of Learning.

Adapted from Mayer, 2005.

Metaphor of Learning	Learning Is:	Learner Is:	Instructor Is:
Response Strengthening	Strengthening or weakening of associations	Passive recipient of rewards and punishments	Dispenser of rewards and punishments
Information Acquisition	Adding information to memory	Passive recipient of information	Dispenser of information
Knowledge Construction	Building a mental representation	Active sense maker	Cognitive guide

If you checked the first answer, you opted for what can be called the response-strengthening view of learning. In its original form, response strengthening viewed the learner as a passive recipient of rewards or punishments and the teacher as a dispenser of rewards (which serve to strengthen a response) and punishments (which serve to weaken a response). In Chapter 1 we referred to training based on a response-strengthening view as a directive instructional architecture. A typical instructional method is to present simple questions to learners, and when they respond tell them whether they are right or wrong. This was the approach taken with programmed instruction in the 1960s and is prevalent in some e-learning lessons today. Our main criticism of the response-strengthening metaphor is not that it is incorrect, but rather that it is incomplete—it tells only part of the story because it does not explain meaningful learning.

If you checked the second answer, you opted for what can be called the information-acquisition view of learning, in which the learner's job is to receive information and the instructor's job is to present it. A typical instructional method is a PowerPoint presentation, in which the instructor conveys information to the learner. In Chapter 1 we refer to the information-acquisition view as the basis for a receptive instructional architecture. This approach is sometimes called the empty vessel or sponge view of learning because the learner's mind is an empty vessel into which the instructor pours information. Our main criticism of this view—which is probably the most commonly held view among most people—is that it conflicts with much of what we know about how people learn. As we saw in Chapter 1, all learning requires psychological engagement—a principle that is often ignored in receptive-learning environments.

If you opted for the third alternative, you picked a metaphor that can be called knowledge construction. According to the knowledge-construction view, people are not passive recipients of information, but rather are active sense makers. They engage in active cognitive processing during learning, including attending to relevant information, mentally organizing it into a coherent structure, and integrating it with what they already know. Although we find some merit in each of the metaphors of learning, we focus most strongly on this one. In short, the goal of effective instruction is not only to present information but also to encourage the learner to engage in appropriate cognitive processing during learning.

Principles and Processes of Learning

The knowledge construction view is based on three principles from research in cognitive science:

- *Dual channels*—people have separate channels for processing visual/pictorial material and auditory/verbal material;
- *Limited capacity*—people can actively process only a few pieces of information in each channel at one time; and
- *Active processing*—learning occurs when people engage in appropriate cognitive processing during learning, such as attending to relevant material, organizing the material into a coherent structure, and integrating it with what they already know.

Figure 2.1 presents a model of how people learn from multimedia lessons. As you can see, the dual channel principle is represented by the two rows—one for processing words (across the top) and one for processing pictures (across the bottom). The limited capacity principle is represented by the large Working Memory box in the middle of the figure, in which knowledge construction occurs. The active processing principle is represented by the five arrows in the figure—selecting words, selecting images, organizing words, organizing images, and integrating—which are the cognitive processes needed for meaningful learning.

Figure 2.1. Cognitive Theory of Multimedia Learning.

Adapted from Mayer, 2005.

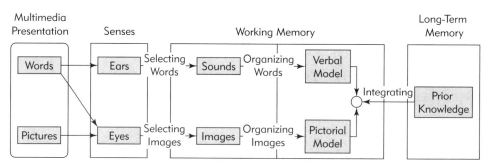

Consider what happens when you are presented with a multimedia lesson. In the left column, a lesson may contain graphics and words (in printed or spoken form). In the second column, the graphics and printed words enter the learner's cognitive processing system through the eyes, and spoken words enter through the ears. If the learner pays attention, some of the material is selected for further processing in the learner's working memory—where you can hold and manipulate just a few pieces of information at one time in each channel. In working memory, the learner can mentally organize some of the selected images into a pictorial model and some of the selected words into a verbal model. Finally, as indicated by the "integrating arrow," the learner can connect the incoming material with existing knowledge from long-term memory—the learner's storehouse of knowledge.

As you can see, there are three important cognitive processes indicated by the arrows in the figure:

- *Selecting words and images*—the first step is to pay attention to relevant words and images in the presented material;

- *Organizing words and images*—the second step is to mentally organize the selected material in coherent verbal and pictorial representations; and

- *Integrating*—the final step is to integrate incoming verbal and pictorial representations with each other and with existing knowledge.

Meaningful learning occurs when the learner appropriately engages in all of these processes.

Managing Limited Cognitive Resources During Learning

The challenge for the learner is to carry out these processes within the constraints of severe limits on how much processing can occur in each channel of working memory at one time. You may recall the expression: "Seven plus or minus two." This refers to the capacity limits of working memory—that is, people can generally think about only a few items at any one time. Let's explore three kinds of demands on cognitive processing capacity (Mayer, 2011a):

- *Extraneous processing*—is cognitive processing that does not support the instructional objective and is created by poor instructional layout (such as having a lot of extraneous text and pictures);

- *Essential processing*—is cognitive processing aimed at mentally representing the core material (consisting mainly of selecting the relevant material) and is created by the inherent complexity of the material; and

- *Generative processing*—is cognitive processing aimed at deeper understanding of the core material (consisting mainly of organizing and integrating) and is created by the motivation of the learner to make sense of the material.

The challenge for instructional professionals is that all three of these processes rely on the learner's cognitive capacity for processing information, which is quite limited.

As summarized in Table 2.2, when you take the learner's limited cognitive capacity into account, you can be faced with three possible instructional scenarios: too much extraneous processing, too much essential processing, and not enough generative processing (Mayer, 2011a). First, in extraneous overload, the amount of extraneous and essential processing exceeds the learner's cognitive capacity, that is, the learner uses so much capacity on extraneous processing (for example, reading extraneous material) that there is not enough capacity remaining for essential processing (for example, comprehending the essential material). The solution to this problem is to

Table 2.2. Approaches to Manage Challenges of Mental Load.

Challenge	Description	Solution	Examples
Too much extraneous processing	The mental load caused by extraneous and essential processes exceeds mental capacity	Use instructional methods that decrease extraneous processing	• Use audio to describe complex visuals • Write lean text and audio narration
Too much essential processing	The content is so complex that it exceeds mental capacity	Use techniques to reduce content complexity	• Segment content into small chunks • Use pretraining to teach concepts and facts separately
Insufficient generative processing	The learner does not engage in sufficient processing to result in learning	Incorporate techniques that promote psychological engagement	• Add practice activities • Add relevant visuals

reduce extraneous processing. Second, in essential overload, even though extraneous processing has been minimized, the amount of required essential processing exceeds the learner's cognitive capacity. In short, the material is so complex that the learner lacks sufficient processing capacity. The solution to this problem is to manage essential processing with a technique such as breaking complex content into smaller learning chunks. Third, in generative underutilization, the learner does not engage in generative processing, even though cognitive capacity is available, perhaps due to lack of motivation. The solution to this problem is to foster generative processing with techniques such as including relevant practice interactions. In summary, three goals for instructional designers are to create instructional environments that minimize extraneous cognitive processing (as described in Chapters 5, 6, 7, 8, 11, and 16), manage essential processing (as described in Chapter 10), and foster generative processing (as described in Chapters 4, 9, 11, 12, 15, and 16).

How e-Lessons Affect Human Learning

If you are involved in designing or selecting instructional materials, your decisions should be guided by an accurate understanding of how learning works. Throughout the book, you will see many references to cognitive learning theory, as described in the previous section. Cognitive learning theory explains how mental processes transform information received by the eyes and ears into knowledge and skills in human memory.

Instructional methods in e-lessons must guide the learner's transformation of words and pictures in the lesson through working memory so that they are incorporated into the existing knowledge in long-term memory. These events rely on the following processes:

1. Selection of the important information in the lesson.

2. Management of the limited capacity in working memory to allow the rehearsal needed for learning.

3. Integration of auditory and visual sensory information in working memory with existing knowledge in long-term memory by way of rehearsal in working memory.

4. Retrieval of new knowledge and skills from long-term memory into working memory when needed later.

In the following sections, we elaborate on these processes and provide examples of how instructional methods in e-learning can support or inhibit them.

Methods for Directing Selection of Important Information

Our cognitive systems have limited capacity. Because there are too many sources of information competing for this limited capacity, the learner must select those that best match his or her goals. We know this selection process can be guided by instructional methods that direct the learner's attention. For example, multimedia designers may use a circle or color to draw the eye to important text or visual information, as shown in Figure 2.2.

Figure 2.2. Visual Cues Help Learners Attend to Important Elements of the Lesson.

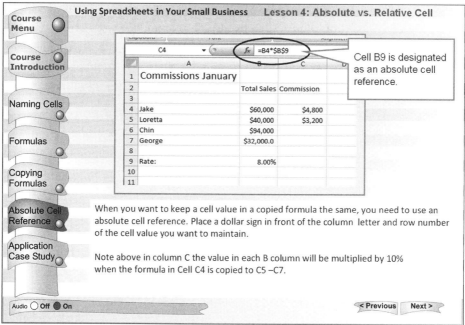

Methods for Managing Limited Capacity in Working Memory

Working memory must be free to rehearse the new information provided in the lesson. When the limited capacity of working memory becomes filled, processing becomes inefficient. Learning slows and frustration grows. For example, most of us find multiplying numbers like 968 by 89 in our heads to be a challenging task. This is because we need to hold the intermediate products of our calculations in working memory storage and continue to multiply the next set of numbers in the working memory processor. It is very difficult for working memory to hold even limited amounts of information and process effectively at the same time.

Therefore, instructional methods that overload working memory make learning more difficult. The burden imposed on working memory in the form of information that must be held plus information that must be processed is referred to as *cognitive load*. Methods that reduce cognitive load foster learning by freeing working memory capacity for learning. In the past ten years we've learned a lot about ways to reduce cognitive load in instructional materials. Many of the guidelines we present in Chapters 5 through 11 are effective because they reduce or manage load. For example, the coherence principle described in Chapter 8 states that better learning results when e-lessons minimize irrelevant or complex visuals, omit background music and environmental sounds, and use succinct text. In other words, less is more. This is because a minimalist approach that avoids overloading working memory allows greater capacity to be devoted to rehearsal processes leading to learning.

Methods for Integration

Working memory integrates the words and pictures in a lesson into a unified structure and further integrates these ideas with existing knowledge in long-term memory. The integration of words and pictures is made easier by lessons that present the verbal and visual information together rather than separated.

For example, Figure 2.3 illustrates two screens from two versions of a lesson on lightning formation in which the text is placed next to the graphic or is placed at the bottom of the screen. The integrated version resulted in better learning than the separated version. Chapter 5 summarizes the contiguity principle of instruction that recommends presenting pictures and words close together on the screen.

Figure 2.3. Screens from Lightning Lesson with Integrated Text and Graphics and Separated Text and Graphics.

Adapted from Mayer, 2001a, 2005b.

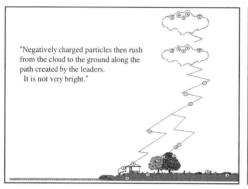

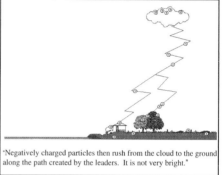

Integrated Text
and Graphics

Separated Text
and Graphics

Once the words and pictures are consolidated into a coherent structure in working memory, they must be further integrated into existing knowledge structures in long-term memory. This requires active processing in working memory. E-lessons that include practice exercises and worked examples stimulate the integration of new knowledge into prior knowledge. For example, a practice assignment asks sales representatives to review new product features and identify which of their current clients are best suited to take advantage of a product upgrade. This assignment requires active processing of the new product feature information in a way that links it with prior knowledge about their clients.

Methods for Retrieval and Transfer

It is not sufficient to simply add new knowledge to long-term memory. For success in training, those new knowledge structures must be encoded into long-term memory in a way that allows them to be easily retrieved when needed on the job. Retrieval of new skills is essential for transfer of training. Without retrieval, all the other psychological processes are meaningless since it does us little good to have knowledge stored in long-term memory that cannot be applied later.

For successful transfer, e-lessons must incorporate the context of the job in the examples and practice exercises so the new knowledge stored in long-term memory contains good retrieval hooks. For example, one multimedia exercise asks technicians to play a Jeopardy® game in which they recall facts about a new software system in response to clues. A better alternative exercise gives an equipment failure scenario and asks technicians to select a troubleshooting action based on facts about a new software system. The Jeopardy game exercise might be perceived as fun, but it risks storing facts in memory without a job context. These facts, lacking the contextual hooks needed for retrieval, often fail to transfer. In contrast, the troubleshooting exercise asks technicians to apply the new facts to a job-realistic situation. Chapters 11 and 12 on examples and practice in e-learning provide a number of guidelines with samples of ways multimedia lessons can build transferable knowledge in long-term memory.

Summary of Learning Processes

In summary, learning from e-lessons relies on four key processes.

- First, the learner must focus on key graphics and words in the lesson to select what will be processed.

- Second, the learner must rehearse this information in working memory to organize and integrate it with existing knowledge in long-term memory.

- Third, in order to do the integration work, limited working memory capacity must not be overloaded. Lessons should apply cognitive load reduction techniques, especially when learners are novices to the new knowledge and skills.

- Fourth, new knowledge stored in long-term memory must be retrieved back on the job. We call this process transfer of learning. To support transfer, e-lessons must provide a job context during learning that will create new memories containing job-relevant retrieval hooks.

All of these processes require an active learner—one who selects and processes new information effectively to achieve the learning result. The design of the e-lesson can support active processing or it can inhibit it, depending on what kinds of instructional methods are used. For example, a lesson that follows a Las Vegas approach to learning by including heavy doses of glitz may overload learners, making it difficult to process information in working memory. At the opposite extreme, lessons that use only text fail to exploit the use of relevant graphics, which are proven to increase learning (see Chapter 4).

What We Don't Know About Learning

The study of learning has a long history in psychology, but until recently most of the research involved contrived tasks in laboratory settings, such as how hungry rats learned to run a maze or how humans learned a list of words. Within the last twenty-five years, however, learning researchers have broadened their scope to include more complex and real-world kinds of learning tasks such as problem solving. What is needed is more high-quality research that is methodologically rigorous, theoretically based, and grounded in realistic e-learning situations. In short, we need research-based principles of e-learning (Mayer, 2001, 2005a). This book provides you with a progress report on research-based principles that are consistent with the current state of research in e-learning.

DESIGN DILEMMA: RESOLVED

Your HR director wanted to launch an e-learning program with popular new technological features such as games, simulations, and social media. However, you were concerned that an unbalanced focus on technology would be counterproductive. We considered the following options:

A. Online applications such as games, simulations, and social media are engaging and should be a central feature of all new e-learning initiatives.

B. Online applications such as games, simulations, and social media may interfere with human learning processes and should be avoided.

C. We don't know enough about human learning to make specific recommendations about how to use new technology features.

D. Not sure which options are correct.

We believe that the right question is NOT whether popular online features such as games or simulations are good or bad ideas. Instead, we recommend that you take a learner-centered approach and consider how all technology features from graphics to games can be used in ways that support cognitive processes of selection, rehearsal, load management, and retrieval. In this book we will address all major technology features from a learner-centered perspective.

A week later you stop by the HR director's office for a follow-up meeting. You make your case: "Using the corporate intranet for learning is not the same as using the Internet for entertainment or socializing. We really need to shape the media to our purposes, not vice versa! It's going to cost a lot to develop this training and even more for the employees to take it. Can we risk spending that money on materials that violate research-proven principles for learning? Let's use e-learning as an opportunity to improve the quality of the training we have been providing by factoring in evidence of what works!"

WHAT TO LOOK FOR IN e-LEARNING

At the end of the remaining chapters, you will find in this section a checklist of things to look for in effective e-lessons. The checklists summarize teaching methods that support cognitive processes required for learning and have been proven to be valid through controlled research studies. In Chapter 17 we present a comprehensive checklist that combines the guidelines from all of the chapters along with some sample e-learning course critiques.

COMING NEXT

We derive the instructional principles in this book not only from a theory of how people learn but also from evidence of what works best. However there are different types of evidence and some fundamental research concepts and techniques you should consider when you evaluate research claims. In the next chapter we summarize the basics of an evidence-based approach to e-learning.

Suggested Readings

Mayer, R.E. (Ed.). (2005). *The Cambridge handbook of multimedia learning.* New York: Cambridge University Press.

Mayer, R.E. (2008). *Learning and instruction* (2nd ed.). Upper Saddle River, NJ: Pearson Merrill Prentice Hall.

Mayer, R.E. (2009). *Multimedia learning* (2nd ed.). New York: Cambridge University Press.

Mayer, R.E. (2011a). *Applying the science of learning.* Upper Saddle River, NJ: Pearson.

Mayer, R.E., & Alexander, P.A. (Eds.). (2011). *Handbook of research on learning and instruction.* New York: Routledge.

Spector, J.M., Merrill, M.D., van Merrienboer, J.J.G., & Driscoll, M.P. (Eds.). (2008). *Handbook of research on educational communications and technology* (3rd ed.). New York: Routledge.

CHAPTER OUTLINE

3

Evidence-Based Practice

WHAT'S NEW IN THIS CHAPTER?

THE RECOMMENDATIONS IN THIS BOOK are based on appropriate high-quality research, or what we might simply call "good research." You might be wondering what constitutes good research, and how you can recognize and use it. We address these questions in this chapter. Some material has been adapted from what was Chapter 2 in the previous edition, and some new material has been added concerning experimental research methods.

DESIGN DILEMMA: YOU DECIDE

In your capacity as a training specialist, you have been asked by the HR director to develop a short online mini-course on sexual harassment that will be a required compliance course for all staff. The HR director hands you a two-page company document on sexual harassment and says: "We really need this lesson to go live right away, so please develop a short lesson that describes the ten main principles in this document. You can just describe each one on its own screen."

You are eager to get started, but you are a little uneasy. Isn't there some research on how to teach material like this, you wonder. What should you do to plan out your e-lesson?

A. Follow the HR director's instructions for how to design the mini-course, because her experience and approval are all you really need.

B. Go online and check your social networks to find similar courses you could use as a model.

C. Go ahead and design the course based on your own ideas. After all, you are a training specialist and your ideas should guide the design of the mini-course.

D. Explore what the research evidence has to say, so you have an idea of which instructional features would be most effective for your mini-course.

What Is Evidence-Based Practice?

When you design a course, you can base your decisions on a variety of sources, including fads (that is, do what is commonly done), opinions (that is, do what experts advise), politics (that is, do what the subject-matter experts or the legal department advises), or ideology (that is, do what seems consistent with a particular approach to instruction). Some books on e-learning may use one of these approaches—for example, they may be based on expert advice. As summarized in Figure 3.1, we advocate a different source of guidance for how to design your course—looking at what the research has to say.

e-Learning courses should incorporate instructional methods that have been shown to be effective based on high-quality research. This is the main idea we use to guide our writing of this book. In short, we favor *evidence-based practice*—the idea that instructional techniques should be based on research findings and research-based theory. Shavelson and Towne (2002, p. 1) eloquently summarize the argument for evidence-based practice in education: "No one would think of getting to the moon or of wiping out a disease

Figure 3.1. Sources for e-Learning Design Decisions.

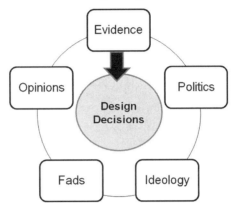

without research. Likewise, one cannot expect reform efforts in education to have significant effects without research-based knowledge to guide them."

Certainly, it is easier to base courses on the design recommendations of experts or on common practice, but it's always worthwhile to ask, "Yes, but does it work?" Until fairly recently, there was not much of a research base concerning the design of e-learning environments. However as we sit down to write the third edition of this book, we are finding a useful and growing base of research (for example, Clark, 2010, Clark & Lyons, 2011; Mayer, 2005, 2008, 2009; Mayer & Alexander, 2011; O'Neil, 2005, O'Neil & Perez, 2008; Spector, Merrill, van Merrienboer, & Driscoll, 2008). We do not want to leave the impression that all you have to do is read some research studies and they will tell you exactly what to do. Instead, we suggest that looking at what the preponderance of evidence has to say about a particular instructional feature can be useful information in helping you make decisions about how to design e-learning.

Three Approaches to Research on Instructional Effectiveness

In this book, our focus is on *instructional effectiveness*—that is, identifying instructional methods or features that have been shown to improve learning. Our goal is not to review every e-learning study, but rather to summarize some exemplary studies that represent the best established findings. In this section, we want to help you recognize high-quality research in your role as a consumer or designer of e-learning courseware. Table 3.1 summarizes three roads to research on instructional effectiveness (Mayer, 2011a):

1. *What works?* A primary question about instructional effectiveness concerns what works in helping students learn, that is, "Does an instructional method cause learning?" For example, you may want to know whether people learn more when graphics are added to a text explanation. When your goal is to determine what works, then the preferred research method is an experimental comparison. In an experimental comparison, you compare the test performance of people who learned with or without the instructional feature.

2. *When does it work?* A crucial secondary question about instructional effectiveness concerns the conditions under which an instructional method works best, that is, "Does the instructional method work better for certain kinds of learners, instructional objectives, or learning environments?" For example, you may want to know whether the effects of graphics are stronger for beginners than for more experienced learners. When your goal is to determine when an instructional method works, then the preferred research method is a

Table 3.1. Three Approaches to Research on Instructional Effectiveness.

Research Question	Example	Research Method
What works?	Does an instructional method cause learning?	Experimental comparison
When does it work?	Does an instructional method work better for certain learners?	Factorial experimental materials, or environments comparison
How does it work?	What learning processes determine the effectiveness of an instructional method?	Observation, interview, questionnaire

factorial experimental comparison. In a factorial experimental comparison, you compare the test performance of people who learned with or without the instructional feature but you also vary the type of learner, the type of learning objective, or the type of learning environment for each instructional feature.

3. *How does it work?* A fundamental secondary question about instructional effectiveness concerns the underlying mechanisms in the learning process, that is, "What learning processes underlie the effectiveness of the instructional method?" For example, you might want to know whether people learn better when relevant graphics are added because people have two exposures to the content—one through words and another through visuals. When your goal is to determine how an instructional method works, then the preferred research method is observational analysis, questionnaire, or interview. Using these research methods you carefully observe what the learner does during learning or ask the learner to tell you about the learning episode.

Which method is best? As you may suspect, there is not one best research method. In fact, multiple research methods can be helpful in addressing all of the aspects of instructional effectiveness, that is, different methods can be helpful in addressing different questions. Overall, what makes a research method useful is that it is appropriate for the research question. Shavelson and Towne (2002, p. 63) state clearly state this criterion: "The simple truth is that the method used must fit the question asked."

In this book, we focus on mainly on identifying what works, but also present complementary evidence on when and how it works. There is consensus among educational researchers that experimental comparisons are the most appropriate method when the goal is to determine whether a particular instructional method causes learning (Schneider, Carnoy, Kilpatrick, Schmidt, & Shavelson, 2007, p. 11):

"When correctly implemented, the randomized controlled experiment is the most powerful design for detecting treatment effects."

The same conclusion applies to quantitative measures (when the data are numbers) and qualitative measures (when the data are descriptions), and about behavioral measures (for example, answers on a test or ratings on a questionnaire) and physiological measures (such as eye movements or brain activity). What makes a measure useful is if it is appropriate for the question being asked, and in some cases it makes sense to use multiple measures. In this book, we focus mainly on quantitative measures of test performance, but sometimes introduce other measures such as eye-fixations. For example Figure 3.2 shows a tracing of eye fixations from a layout including text and

---

Figure 3.2. Eye-Tracking Data Shows Patterns of Attention.
With Permission from Holsanova, Holmberg, and Holmqvist, 2009.

graphics. The eye fixations provide information on where the learner directed their visual attention when viewing the page.

What to Look for in Experimental Comparisons

Your first step in selecting good research is to focus on situations that are like yours. You should select studies that focus on the instructional method you are interested in, and on learners, materials. and learning environments like yours.

Your second step in selecting good research is to focus on studies that use the appropriate research method. If you want to determine whether an instructional method works, you should be looking for research that highlights experimental comparisons.

Not all experiments are equally sound, so your third step is to focus on experimental comparisons that meet the criteria of good research methodology. Three important criteria to look for in experimental comparisons are experimental control, random assignment, and appropriate measures (Mayer, 2011a). We illustrate these criteria in Figure 3.3 and describe them on the following page.

Figure 3.3. Criteria of Good Experimental Comparisons.

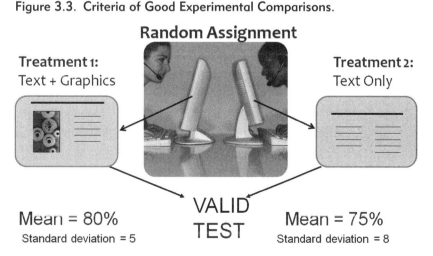

Random Assignment

Treatment 1: Text + Graphics

Treatment 2: Text Only

VALID TEST

Mean = 80%
Standard deviation = 5

Mean = 75%
Standard deviation = 8

Sample size = 25 in each version

Experimental control refers to the idea that the experimental group and the control should receive identical treatments except for one feature (that is, the instructional treatment). For example, the treatment group may view a narrated animation with background music playing, whereas the control group may view the same narrated animation without background music playing. If the researchers compare two groups that differ on many features, including the one you care about, this is not good research for you because a major criterion of experimental control is not met. For example, a research study compared learning of ecology concepts from a textbook, text with a story theme, and a virtual world version. The virtual world version resulted in best learning. At first glance, these results may seem to offer a useful argument to use virtual worlds for teaching. However, there were many differences among the three lesson versions, including the number and type of visuals, the amount of overt learner interactions with the lessons, and the novelty of learning in a virtual world. These differences make it difficult to know exactly what accounted for better learning in the virtual world version.

Random assignment refers to the idea that learners are randomly assigned to groups (or treatment conditions). For example, perhaps fifty students were selected for the treatment group and fifty students were selected for the control group, using a procedure based on chance. If the students can volunteer to be in the treatment or control groups based on their personal preference, then an important criterion is not met, so this is not good research for you. For example, many research studies have compared the differences among medical students who studied in a problem-based learning curriculum with students who studied in a traditional science-based curriculum. In most cases however, the students selected which curriculum they preferred. There could be some systematic differences between those who chose one or the other curriculum making it hard to rule out population factors that might contribute to any differences in outcomes.

Appropriate measures refers to the idea that the research report tells you the mean (M), standard deviation (SD), and sample size (n) for each group on a relevant measure of learning. If you are interested in learning effects, but the research report focuses only on student ratings of how well they liked the lessons, then an important criterion is not met, so this is not good research for you. In one research study, the discussions of medical students who viewed a text case study were compared to the discussions of students who viewed a video case study. The goal was to determine whether text or video would be a more effective way to present a case scenario. However, since learning was not directly measured, it is not possible to draw conclusions about the learning effectiveness of the text versus the video cases.

In short, as a consumer of experimental research, you need to be picky! You should rely on studies that apply the criteria of experimental control, random assignment, and appropriate measures.

How to Interpret No Effect in Experimental Comparisons

In some experiments, there may be no difference between the treatment group and the control group; for example, suppose you see a study in which a group that received a lesson with background music performed the same on a test as a group that did not receive background music with their lesson. When you see there is no difference, you should ask yourself how this happened. Here are six possible reasons for finding no instructional effect, summarized in Figure 3.4 (Mayer, 2011):

1. *Ineffective treatment:* The instructional treatment does not have an effect on learning. This is always the most obvious reason, but before you accept it you should check out the other possibilities.

Figure 3.4. Why an Experiment May Show No Instructional Effect.

❑ The instructional treatment, in fact, did not influence learning.

❑ There were insufficient learners in the experimental and control groups.

❑ The learning measure was not sensitive enough to detect differences in learning.

❑ The treatment and control groups were not different enough from each other.

❑ The learning materials were too easy for all learners so no additional treatment was helpful.

❑ Additional variables confounded the effects of the treatment.

2. *Inadequate sample size:* There are not enough learners in each group. Studies with fewer than twenty-five learners in each group may be suspect, especially if the instructional effect is not very strong.

3. *Insensitive measure:* The dependent measure was not sensitive enough to detect differences in learning outcomes. If the test does not contain enough items or the items do not adequately test what was taught, then we really can't tell whether the instruction was effective.

4. *Inadequate treatment implementation:* The treatment and control groups were not different enough from each other. For example, if the background music is played at a very low level, it might not be loud enough to be heard.

5. *Insensitivity to learners:* The learners were not sensitive enough to the treatment. For example, if the material was very easy for all learners, then adding the treatment feature is not really necessary.

6. *Confounding variables:* The treatment and control groups differ on another important variable. For example, the control group may have many more experienced learners than the treatment group.

Overall, in your search for good research, you need to be sure you can rule out all other explanations for saying the instructional method did not work.

How to Interpret Research Statistics

All of these issues relate to the applicability of the research to your learning situation, that is, to the confidence you can put in the results based on the validity of the study. Throughout this book, we report the results of statistical tests of the research we summarize. Therefore, in this section we briefly summarize how to interpret those statistical tests.

Suppose you read a study comparing two groups of students—a test group and a control group. The control group received a basic multimedia lesson that explains content with graphics and audio narration. We call this the no-music group. The test group received the same lesson with background music added to the narration. We call this the music group. Suppose the no-music group averaged 90 percent correct on a test of the material and the music group averaged 80 percent on the same test. Averages are also called means (for example, 90 percent versus 80 percent). Also suppose the scores were not very spread out, so most of the no-music students scored close to ninety and most of the music students scored close to eighty. Standard deviation tells you how spread out the scores are, or how much variation there is in the results. Powerful instructional methods should yield high averages and low standard deviations. In other words, high scores are achieved and nearly all learners score close to the average so that there is high consistency in outcomes among the learners.

As illustrated in Figure 3.5, let's suppose the standard deviation is 10 for the no-music group and 10 for the music group. Based on these means and standard deviations, can we conclude that background music hurts learning? Generally, when the difference between the score averages is high (90 percent versus 80 percent in our example) and the standard deviations are low (10 percent in our example), the difference is real. However, to accurately decide that issue requires statistical tests. Two common statistical measures associated with research studies we present in this book are probability and effect

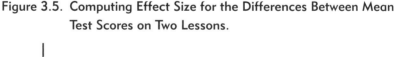

Figure 3.5. Computing Effect Size for the Differences Between Mean Test Scores on Two Lessons.

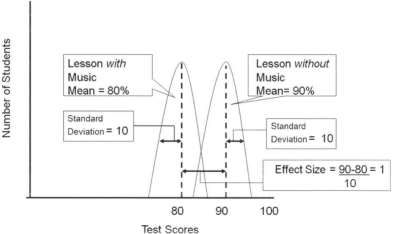

size. As you read research, look for results in which the probability is less than .05 (p < .05) and show an effect size of .5 or greater.

Statistical Significance: Probability Less Than .05

Some statistical tests yield a measure of probability such as p < .05 (which is read, "probability less than point oh five"). In the case of our background music study, this means that there is less than a 5 percent chance that the difference between 90 percent and 80 percent does NOT reflect a real difference between the two groups. In other words, if you concluded there is a difference in test performance between the groups, there is less than a 5 percent chance that you are wrong and more than a 95 percent chance that you are right. Thus we can conclude that the difference between the groups is statistically significant. In general, when the probability is less than .05, researchers conclude that the difference is real, that is, statistically significant.

Practical Significance: Effect Size Greater Than .5

Even if music has a statistically significant effect, we might want to know how strong the effect is in practical terms. We could just subtract one mean score from the other, yielding a difference of 10 in our music study. However, to tell whether 10 is a big difference, we can divide this number by the standard deviation of the control group (or of both groups pooled together). This tells us how many more standard deviations one group is compared with the other, and is called effect size (ES). In this case, the ES is 1, which is generally regarded as a strong effect. What this means is that an individual learner in the control group would see a 1 standard deviation increase (10 points in our example) if he or she were to study with a lesson that omitted music. If the ES had been .5 in our example, an individual learner in the control group would have a .5 standard deviation increase (5 points in our example). When the ES is less than .2, the practical impact of the experimental treatment is a bit too small to worry about; an effect size of .5 is moderate, and when it is .8 or above, you have a large effect (Cohen, 1988). In this book, we are especially interested in effect sizes greater than .5, that is, instructional methods that have been shown to boost learning scores by more than a half of a standard deviation.

How Can You Identify Relevant Research?

You might wonder how we selected the research we include in this book or how you could determine whether a given research study is applicable to your design decisions. The following list summarizes five questions to consider when reading research studies:

1. How similar are the learners in the research study to your learners? Research conducted on children may be limited in its applicability to adult populations. More relevant studies use subjects of college age or beyond.

2. Are the conclusions based on an experimental research design? Look for subjects randomly assigned to test and control groups.

3. Are the experimental results replicated? Look for reports of research in which conclusions are drawn from a number of studies that essentially replicate the results. The *Review of Educational Research* and *Educational Psychology Review* are good sources, as are handbooks such as *The Cambridge Handbook of Multimedia Learning* (Mayer, 2005a), the *Handbook of Research on Educational Communications and Technology* (Spector, Merrill, van Merrienboer, & Driscoll, 2008), the *Handbook of Educational Psychology* (Alexander & Winne, 2006), and the *Handbook of Research on Learning and Instruction* (Mayer & Alexander, 2011).

4. Is learning measured by tests that measure application? Research that measures outcomes with recall tests may not apply to workforce learning goals in which the learning outcomes must be application, not recall, of new knowledge and skills.

5. Does the data analysis reflect practical significance as well as statistical significance? With a large sample size, even small learning differences may have statistical significance, yet may not justify the expense of implementing the test method. Look for statistical significance of .05 or less and effect sizes of .5 or more.

What We Don't Know About Evidence-Based Practice

What is needed is a large base of research evidence concerning each of the major instructional methods. When you can find many experiments that all test the effectiveness of the same instructional method, you create a meta-analysis. In a meta-analysis you record the effect size for each study and compute an average effect size across all the studies. In Figure 1.3 we presented a bar chart of effect sizes from 318 studies that compared learning from face-to-face instruction with learning from electronic distance learning media. Most of the effect sizes were close to zero, indicating little or no differences in learning from different delivery media. As another example, Hattie (2009) has summarized the results of eight hundred meta-analyses aimed at determining what affects student achievement. The field of e-learning would benefit from continued growth in the research base so appropriate meta-analyses can be conducted. In addition, meta-analysis can help pinpoint the conditions under which strong effects are most likely to occur. For example, there are meta-analyses showing that adding graphics to text is more effective for low-knowledge learners than for high-knowledge learners.

DESIGN DILEMMA: RESOLVED

Your HR director wanted to develop an online mini-course on sexual harassment, but you were looking for guidance on how to design it. We considered the following options:

A. Follow the HR director's instructions for how to design the mini-course, because her experience and approval is all you really need.

B. Go online and check your social networks to find similar courses you could use as a model.

C. Go ahead and design the course based on your own ideas. After all, you are the training specialist and your ideas should guide the design of the mini-course.

D. Explore what the research evidence has to say, so you have an idea of which instructional features would be most effective for your mini-course.

If you chose Option D, you are displaying an interest in evidence-based practice, consistent with the theme of this book. Certainly, it is fine to respect the knowledge and seniority of your HR director (Option A), your colleagues (Option B), and even yourself (Option C), but you would be missing an important source of guidance if you ignored what the research evidence has to say.

WHAT TO LOOK FOR IN EXPERIMENTAL e-LEARNING RESEARCH

☐ Were subjects randomly assigned to treatments?

☐ Were there enough subjects to detect differences in learning?

☐ Were treatments similar except for the instructional method being tested?

☐ Was the outcome measure appropriate to measure relevant learning differences?

☐ Were the results statistically and practically significant?

☐ To what extent did the learners and lesson features (content, length, etc.) reflect your own environment?

☐ Have several experiments been conducted that supported the same conclusions?

COMING NEXT

Two fundamental tools you have for teaching are visuals and words. Is there a value to using both visuals and words? In Chapter 4 we look at evidence regarding the instructional value of graphics and consider whether some types of graphics are more effective than others as well as who benefits most from visuals.

Suggested Readings

Hattie, J. (2009). *Visible learning: A synthesis of over 800 meta-analyses relating to achievemen*t. New York: Routledge.

Mayer, R.E. (2011). *Applying the science of learning.* Upper Saddle River, NJ: Pearson.

Phye, G.D., Robinson, D.H., & Levin, J. (Eds.). (2005). *Empirical methods for evaluating educational interventions.* San Diego: Elsevier.

Schneider, B., Carnoy, M., Kilpatrick, J., Schmidt, W.H., & Shavelson, R.J. (2007). *Estimating causal effects.* Washington, DC: American Educational Research Association.

Shavelson, R.J., & Towne, L. (Eds.). (2002). *Scientific research in education.* Washington, DC: National Academy Press.

CHAPTER OUTLINE

Do Visuals Make a Difference?

Multimedia Principle: Include Both Words and Graphics

Select Graphics That Support Learning

Some Ways to Use Graphics to Promote Learning

Graphics to Teach Content Types

Graphics as Topic Organizers

Graphics to Show Relationships

Graphics as Lesson Interfaces

Psychological Reasons for the Multimedia Principle

Evidence for Using Words and Pictures

The Multimedia Principle Works Best for Novices

Should You Change Static Illustrations into Animations?

4

Applying the Multimedia Principle

USE WORDS AND GRAPHICS RATHER
THAN WORDS ALONE

WHAT'S NEW IN THIS CHAPTER?

IN THE SECOND EDITION of this book we summarized evidence for learning gains that result from combining text and relevant graphics in e-lessons. In the past few years we see growing consensus for the multimedia principle as one of the most recognized principles of learning (Halpern, Graesser, & Hackel, 2007; Pashler, Bain, Bottage, Graesser, Koedinger, McDaniel, & Metcalfe, 2007). This chapter provides updated evidence and support for the multimedia principle and explores its boundary conditions. In particular, we provide evidence concerning (1) whether the multimedia principle depends on the experience level of the learners and (2) whether the multimedia principle depends on whether the graphics are static (illustrations or photos) or dynamic (animations or video). Another addition to this chapter involves a look at whether people learn better when graphic organizers are added to text.

DESIGN DILEMMA: YOU DECIDE

The new VP of corporate learning and performance is anxious to get started with the company's new e-learning initiative. She wants to show results quickly to offset upper management's impression that e-learning development is so slow that by the time it's released, it's already out of date. She has committed to an asynchronous course on Excel for Small Business to be ready in the next month. "After all", she says to Matt, the project lead, "We already have the content from our current instructor-led course. Let's quickly put it into e-learning!"

Ben, the project programmer, works quickly converting the classroom lecture notes into HTML. He proudly shows the team his first-draft storyboards, such as the one shown in Figure 4.1.

Figure 4.1. A Screen from Ben's First Draft of the Excel Course.

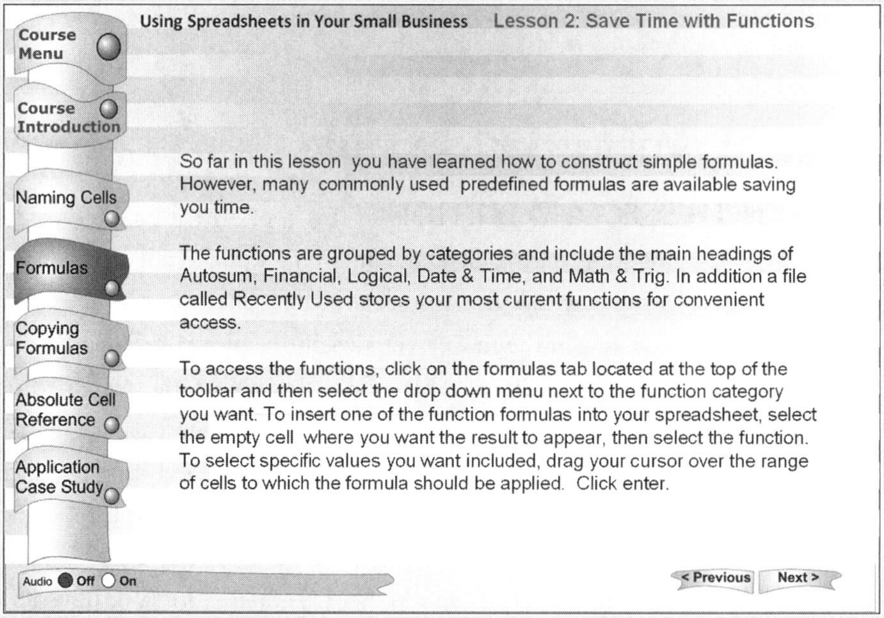

Reshmi, one of the course designers, reacts negatively: "Hey Ben, it's great that you got a draft together quickly since we don't have much development time. But this looks pretty boring to me! In e-learning the computer screen is our main connection with the students and screens filled with text will turn them off right away. We need this first project to be engaging. We need to add graphics and animations!" "Yeah," Ben replies. "Graphics are great but we don't have a graphic artist, so, other than some screen grabs, I'll have to download some clip art." "Clip art is cheesy," Reshmi replies. "Let's contract an artist to create some custom Flash animations for us so we can really show what e-learning can do". Matt, the project manager, jumps in: "It will take time to get a contract set up and get the artist up to speed—time we don't have. Let's just start simple on this first project by going with mostly text with some screen grabs and one or two pieces of clip art here and there to add interest. We can try for a graphic artist on future projects. After all, basically our goal is to explain how small businesses can use Excel, and we can do that effectively with words." Based on your own experience or intuition, which of the following options is correct:

A. Matt is right. Learning will be just as effective from good textual explanations as from text plus graphics.

B. Ben is right. Adding clip art to a few screens will make the lesson more interesting. However, to save time, providing text alone will be as effective as adding visuals.

C. Reshmi is right. Customized visuals, including animations to demonstrate how to use Excel and to show how Excel works, will add appeal and improve learning.

D. Not sure which options are correct.

Do Visuals Make a Difference?

In training, it is customary to use words—either in printed or spoken form—as the main vehicle for conveying information. Words are quick and inexpensive to produce. The question is whether there is any return on investment for supplementing words with pictures—either static graphics such as drawings or photos, or dynamic graphics such as animation or video. In particular, do people learn more deeply from words and graphics than from words alone? This is the issue we want to explore with you in this chapter.

Multimedia Principle: Include Both Words and Graphics

Based on cognitive theory and research evidence, we recommend that e-learning courses include words and graphics rather than words alone. By words, we mean printed text (that is, words printed on the screen that people read) or spoken text (that is, words presented as speech that people listen to through earphones or speakers). By graphics we mean static illustrations such as drawings, charts, graphs, maps, or photos, and dynamic graphics such as animation or video. We use the term *multimedia presentation* to refer to any presentation that contains both words and graphics. For example, if you are given an instructional message that is presented in words alone, such as shown in Figure 4.1, we recommend you convert it into a multimedia presentation consisting of words and pictures, such as shown in Figure 4.2.

Figure 4.2. A Revision of Figure 4.1 with Visuals and Words.

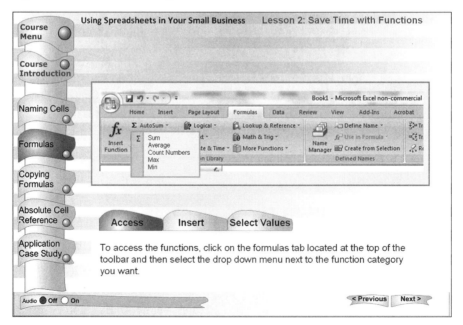

Pictures should not be an afterthought. Instead of selecting pictures after the words are written, instructional designers should consider how words and pictures work together to create meaning for the learner. Therefore, visuals as well as words should be planned together as the job analysis is conducted and the course is designed.

The rationale for our recommendation is that people are more likely to understand material when they can engage in active learning—that is, when they engage in relevant cognitive processing such as attending to the relevant material in the lesson, mentally organizing the material into a coherent cognitive representation, and mentally integrating the material with their existing knowledge. Multimedia presentations can encourage learners to engage in active learning by mentally representing the material in words and in pictures and by mentally making connections between the pictorial and verbal representations. In contrast, presenting words alone may encourage learners—especially those with less experience or expertise—to engage in shallow learning such as not connecting the words with other knowledge.

There are many examples of e-learning environments that contain window after window of text and more text. Some may even have graphics that decorate the page, but do not help you understand the text. For example, Figure 4.3

Figure 4.3. A Decorative Graphic That Does Nothing to Improve Learning.

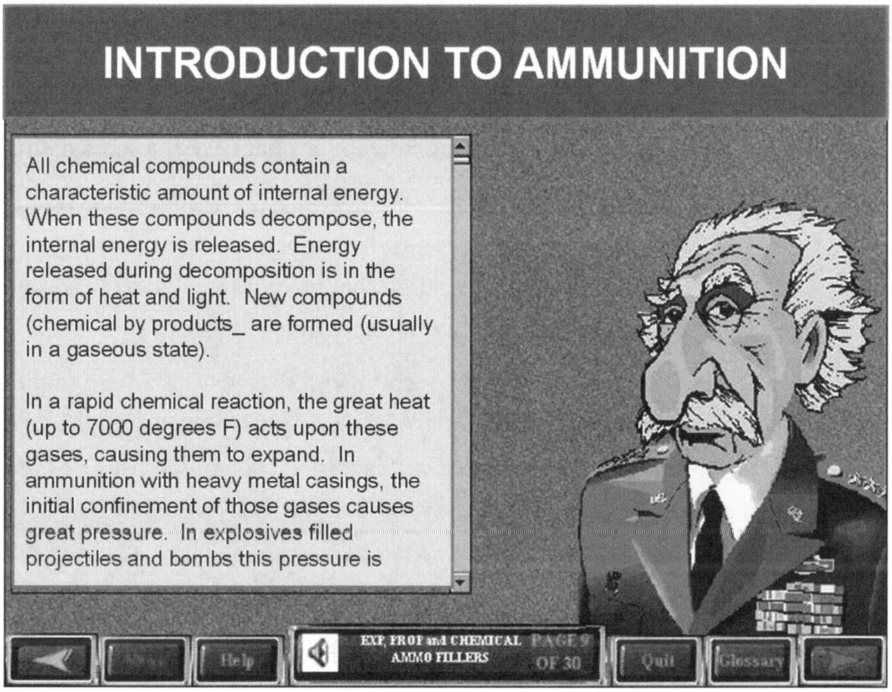

from a military course on ammunition presents scrolling text and a picture of a general as a decorative element. As you can see, the general graphic does not support the text, but rather simply serves to decorate screen space.

Select Graphics That Support Learning

Instead of presenting words alone, we recommend presenting words and graphics. However, not all kinds of graphics are equally helpful. For example, let's consider several possible functions of graphics:

1. *Decorative graphics* serve to decorate the page without enhancing the message of the lesson, such as photo or a video of person riding a bicycle in a lesson on how bicycle tire pumps work.

2. *Representational graphics* portray a single element, such as photo of the bicycle tire pump along with a caption, "Bicycle Tire Pump."

3. *Relational graphics* portray a quantitative relationship among two or more variables, such as a line graph showing the relation between years of age on the x-axis and probability of being in a bicycle accident on the y-axis.

4. *Organizational graphics* depict the relations among elements, such as a diagram of a bicycle tire pump with each part labeled or a matrix giving a definition and example of each of three different kinds of pumps.

5. *Transformational graphics* depict changes in an object over time, such as a video showing how to fix a flat tire, or a series of annotated frames showing stages of how a bicycle tire pump works.

6. *Interpretive graphics* illustrate invisible relationships such as an animation of the bicycle pump that includes small dots to show the flow of air into and out of the pump.

Based on this analysis, we recommend that you minimize graphics that decorate the page (*decorative graphics*) or simply represent a single object (*representational graphics*), and that you incorporate graphics that help the learner understand the material (*transformational* and *interpretive graphics*) or organize the material (*organizational graphics*). For example, Table 4.1 is an organizational graphic that gives the name, definition, and example of six functions of graphics in the form of a matrix. When the text describes a quantitative

Table 4.1. An Organizational Graphic of Graphic Types.

Adapted from Clark and Lyons, 2011.

Graphic Type	Description	Examples
Decorative	Visuals added for aesthetic appeal or for humor	1. The general in Figure 4.3 2. A person riding a bicycle in a lesson on how a bicycle pump works 3. Baseball-related icons as a game theme in a lesson on product knowledge
Representational	Visuals that illustrate the appearance of an object	1. The screen capture in Figure 4.2 2. A photograph of equipment in a maintenance lesson
Organizational	Visuals that show qualitative relationships among content	1. A matrix such as this table 2. A concept map 3. A tree diagram
Relational	Visuals that summarize quantitative relationships	1. A bar graph or pie chart 2. A map with circles of different sizes representing location and strength of earthquakes
Transformational	Visuals that illustrate changes in time or over space	1. An animated demonstration of a computer procedure 2. A video of how volcanoes erupt 3. A time-lapse animation of seed germination
Interpretive	Visuals that make intangible phenomena visible and concrete	1. Drawings of molecular structures 2. A series of diagrams with arrows that illustrate the flow of blood through the heart 3. Pictures that show how data is transformed and transmitted through the Internet

relationship, then a *relational graphic* is warranted; and when the text describes changes over time, then a *transformational graphic* is warranted.

In Chapter 2, we summarized the dual channels principle that learners have separate channels for processing verbal material and pictorial material. We see the job of an instructional professional as not just to present information—such as presenting text that contains everything the learner needs to know—but rather to leverage both channels in ways that enable the learner to make sense out of the material.

In Chapter 1, we introduced the engagement matrix. Relevant visuals are one powerful method to support psychological engagement in the absence of behavioral activity. In other words, visuals are one instructional method that falls into the upper left cell of the matrix shown in Figure 1.5. Providing relevant graphics with text is a proven method of fostering deeper cognitive processing in learners. In short, learning is facilitated when the graphics and text work together to communicate the instructional message.

Some Ways to Use Graphics to Promote Learning

Helping you determine how to create the best types of graphics to meet your instructional goals requires a book in itself. In fact, just such a book is *Graphics for Learning* (2nd ed.) by Ruth Colvin Clark and Chopeta Lyons. Here we offer just a few examples of the ways to use graphics that serve instructional rather than decorative roles: to teach content types, as topic organizers, and as lesson interfaces.

Graphics to Teach Content Types

Clark (2008) has identified five different kinds of content: fact, concept, process, procedure, and principle. Table 4.2 briefly describes each content type and lists graphic types commonly used to teach specific lesson content such as facts, concepts, processes, procedures, and principles.

Since 63 percent of computer-systems training is delivered by e-learning (ASTD, 2010), many e-learning graphics are screen captures. A screen capture is a graphic that is a replication of an actual software screen. For example, Figure 4.4 is a screen capture from a synchronous e-learning class on Excel. At this point in the lesson, the instructor uses the application-sharing feature of the virtual classroom to demonstrate how to use formulas in Excel. Another content type that profits from graphic support is process. A

Table 4.2. Graphics to Teach Content Types.

Adapted from Clark, 2008.

Content Type	Description	Useful Graphic Types	Example
Facts	Unique and isolated information such as specific application screens, forms, or product data	Representational, Organizational	A screen capture as in Figure 4.2 A table of parts' names and specifications
Concepts	Categories of objects, events, or symbols designated by a single name	Representational, Organizational, Interpretive	A tree diagram of biological species Three Excel formulas to illustrate formatting rules
Process	A description of how something works	Transformational, Interpretive, Relational	Animations of how the heart pumps blood Still diagrams to illustrate how a bicycle pump works An animation showing how a virus invades a cell as in Figure 4.5
Procedure	A series of steps resulting in completion of a task	Transformational	An animated illustration of how to use a spreadsheet as in Figure 4.4 A diagram with arrows showing how to install a printer cable
Principle	Guidelines that result in completion of a task; cause-and-effect relationships	Transformational, Interpretive	A video showing two effective sales approaches An animation showing genes passing from parents to offspring

Figure 4.4. A Transformation Visual of an Excel Demonstration in
Synchronous e-Learning.

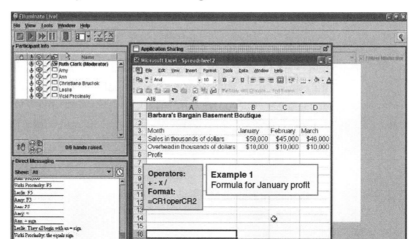

Figure 4.5. An Interpretive Graphic Illustrating the Process of AIDS
Infection.

With permission of Roche, Basel, Switzerland. Http://www.roche-hiv.com/front.cfm.

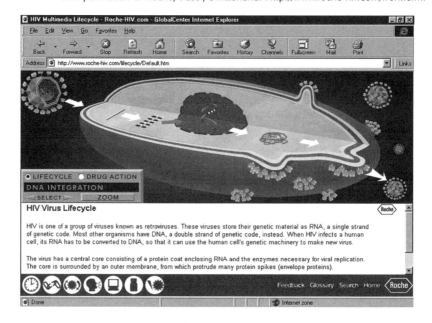

process is a step-by-step description of how a system works, including business, scientific, and mechanical systems. Process information is effectively visualized with a series of static frames or, in some cases, animations. Figure 4.5 is a screen from an animated graphic showing how the AIDS virus infects cells.

Graphics as Topic Organizers

In addition to illustrating specific content types, graphics such as topic maps can serve an organizational function by showing relationships among topics in a lesson. For example, Figure 4.6 shows a screen with a series of coaching topics mapped in the left-hand bar, including where to coach, when to coach, how long to coach, and so on. When the mouse is placed over each of the topics in the graphic organizer, a different illustration appears on the right side of the screen. In this example, the topic of formal and informal coaching sessions is explained with text and photographs.

Figure 4.6. An Organizational Graphic on Coaching Topics.

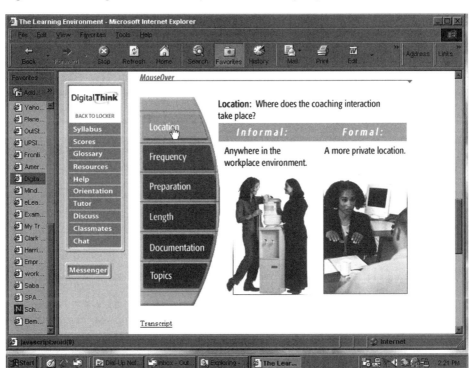

Graphics to Show Relationships

Graphics in the form of dynamic and static graphs can make invisible phenomena visible and show relationships. Imagine an e-learning lesson to teach fast-food workers safe cooking and food-handling practices. An animated line graph with numbers on the vertical axis and time on the horizontal axis illustrates changes in bacterial growth in food cooked at different temperatures or handled in safe and unsafe ways. The lesson includes an interactive simulation in which the learner adjusts the cooking temperature and sees the impact on a dynamic line graph called a "germ meter." As another example, a geographic map can illustrate population density by adding a small red dot to represent five thousand individuals. If made interactive, the map could include a slider bar that accessed different time periods allowing the viewer to see population shifts over time.

Graphics as Lesson Interfaces

Finally, courses designed using a guided discovery approach often use a graphical interface as a backdrop to present case studies. For example, in Figure 1.6 we showed an interface for a troubleshooting course for automotive technicians. The virtual shop includes most of the testing tools available in a normal shop, allowing the learner to run and interpret tests to diagnose and repair an automotive failure.

Psychological Reasons for the Multimedia Principle

Perhaps the single greatest human invention is language, and the single greatest modification of this invention is printed language. Words allow us to communicate effectively, and printed words allow us to communicate effectively across miles and years. (So does recorded speech, by the way, which is yet another modification of the great invention of language.) Therefore, it makes sense to use words when we provide training or instruction. For thousands of years, the main format for education has been words—first in spoken form and more recently in printed form (and recorded form). Words are also the most efficient and effective way of producing e-learning because words can convey a lot of information and are easier to produce than graphics.

This line of thinking is based on the information acquisition view in which teaching consists of presenting information and learning consists of acquiring information, as summarized in the middle of Table 2.1. Information can be delivered in many forms—such as printed words, spoken words, illustrations, photos, graphs, animation, video, and narration. Over the years, it has become clear that words are an efficient and effective method for presenting information, so based on this view, in most situations instruction should involve simply presenting words. According to the information acquisition view, the format of the information (for example, words versus pictures) does not matter, as long as the information is delivered to the learner.

In our opinion, the information acquisition view is based on an inadequate conception of how people learn. Instead, we favor a knowledge construction view in which learning is seen as a process of active sense-making and teaching is seen as an attempt to foster appropriate cognitive processing in the learner, as summarized in the bottom of Table 2.1. According to this learning metaphor, it is not good enough to deliver information to the learner; instructors must also guide the learner's cognitive processing during learning, thereby enabling and encouraging learners to actively process the information. An important part of active processing is to mentally construct pictorial and verbal representations of the material and to mentally connect them. This goal is more likely to be achieved with multimedia lessons containing both words and corresponding pictures that work together to explain the same to-be-learned content. Adding relevant graphics to words can be a powerful way to help learners engage in active learning. Overall, your view of the cognitive stages of how learning works (as summarized in Table 2.1) can influence your decisions about how to design instruction (Mayer, 2003).

Evidence for Using Words and Pictures

There is consistent evidence that people learn more deeply from words and pictures than from words alone, at least for some simple instructional situations. In eleven different studies, researchers compared the test performance of students who learned from animation and narration versus narration alone or from text and illustrations versus text alone (Mayer, 1989b; Mayer & Anderson, 1991, 1992; Mayer, Bove, Bryman, Mars, & Tapangco, 1996; Mayer & Gallini, 1990; Moreno & Mayer, 1999b, 2002b). The lessons taught scientific and mechanical processes, including how lightning works,

Figure 4.7. How a Bicycle Pump Works Explained with Words Alone.
From Mayer, 2009.

How a Bicycle Pump Works

"As the rod is pulled out, air passes through the piston
and fills the area between the piston and the outlet valve.
As the rod is pushed in, the inlet valve closes and the
piston forces air through the outlet valve."

how a car's braking system works, how pumps work, and how electrical generators work. For example, in one study students read an accurate verbal description of how a bicycle pump works (as shown in Figure 4.7), while others read the same verbal description and viewed a diagram depicting the same steps (as shown in Figure 4.8).

In all eleven comparisons, students who received a multimedia lesson consisting of words and pictures performed better on a subsequent transfer test than students who received the same information in words alone. Across the eleven studies, people who learned from words and graphics produced

Figure 4.8. How a Bicycle Pump Works Explained with Words and Graphics.
From Mayer, 2009.

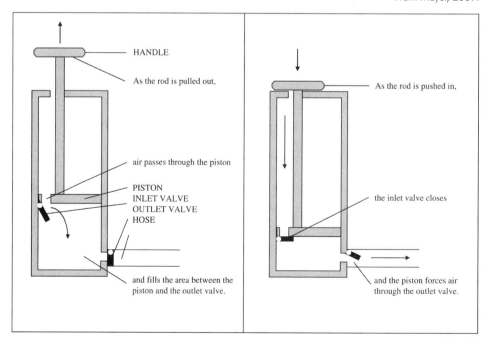

between 55 percent to 121 percent more correct solutions to transfer prob-lems than people who learned from words alone. Across all studies, a median percentage gain of 89 percent was achieved with a median effect size of 1.50. Recall from our discussion in Chapter 3 that effect sizes over .8 are consid-ered large. Figure 4.9 shows a result from one of these experiments. Similarly, Butcher (2006) found that people developed a deeper understanding of how the human heart works from text with simple illustrations than from text alone.

We call this finding the *multimedia effect*—people learn more deeply from words and graphics than from words alone. In a recent review, Fletcher and Tobias (2005, p. 128) concluded: "The multimedia principle, which suggests that learning and understanding are enhanced by adding pictures to text rather than presenting text alone, appears to be well supported by find-ings from empirical research." The multimedia effect is the starting point for our discussion of best instructional methods for e-learning because it estab-lishes the potential for multimedia lessons to improve human learning.

In recent years, the multimedia principle has been recognized as one of the most well-established principles of learning that can be applied to education. For example, in their review of twenty-five "principles of learn-ing" commissioned by the Association of Psychological Science, Halpern,

---

Figure 4.9. Learning Is Better from Words Plus Graphics Than from Words Alone.

Adapted from Mayer, 2001a.

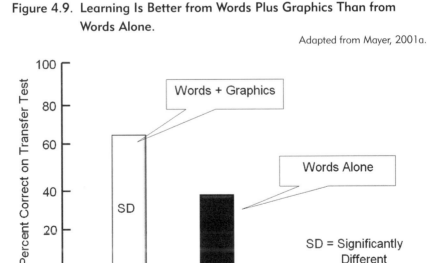

Graesser, and Hakel (2007) listed the "dual code and multimedia effects" as the third principle on their list: "Information is encoded and remembered better when it is delivered in multiple modes . . . than when delivered in only a single mode." In a practical guide on "organizing instruction and study to improve student learning" commissioned by the Institute of Education Sciences, Pashler, Bain, Bottage, Graesser, Koedinger, McDaniel, & Metcalfe (2007) offered "combine graphics with verbal descriptions" as their third of seven recommendations. In short, there is consensus among learning scientists that the multimedia principle has promise for instructional design.

The multimedia principle can apply to the design of computer-based simulations and games. In a study involving interactive multimedia, Moreno and Mayer (1999b) developed a mathematics computer game intended to teach students how to add and subtract signed numbers (such as 2–3 = _____). Some students learned from drill-and-practice problems, whereas others worked on the same problems but as feedback also saw a bunny hop along a number line to represent each problem (such as starting at two, turning to face the left, hopping backward three steps, and landing on five). Students learned better with symbols and graphics than from symbols alone.

The multimedia principle can also apply to the design of what we defined previously as organizational visuals—that is, charts that summarize the text in spatial form such as a hierarchy, matrix, or flow chart. For example, Stull and Mayer (2007) found that adding graphic organizers to the margins of a biology text resulted in improved test performance. In a related study, students learned better from a science text if it was accompanied by a causal diagram that summarized the main relationships from the text (McCrudden, Schraw, & Lehman, 2009; McCrudden, Schraw, Lehman, & Poliquin, 2007).

Finally, the multimedia principle applies to video examples, in which students learned better from reading a lesson on teaching techniques followed by viewing video examples rather than reading a lesson followed by reading text-based descriptions of examples (Moreno & Ortegano-Layne, 2008).

In the remainder of this section, we consider two additional research questions, concerning for whom the multimedia principle works (for example, novices versus experts) and where the multimedia principle works (for example, static illustrations versus animations).

The Multimedia Principle Works Best for Novices

Does the multimedia principle apply equally to all learners? There is evidence that our recommendation to use words and graphics is particularly important for learners who have low knowledge of the domain (whom we can call *novices*) rather than learners who have high knowledge of the domain (whom we can call *experts*). For example, in a series of three experiments involving lessons on brakes, pumps, and generators, Mayer and Gallini (1990) reported that novices learned better from text and illustrations (such as shown in Figure 4.8) than from words alone (such as shown in Figure 4.7), but experts learned equally well from both conditions. Apparently, the more experienced learners are able to create their own mental images as they read the text about how the pump works, whereas the less experienced learners need help in relating the text to a useful pictorial representation.

In a related study, Ollerenshaw, Aidman, and Kidd (1997) presented text lessons on how pumps work to learners who had low or high knowledge of the domain. Low-knowledge learners benefited greatly when animation was added to the text, whereas high-knowledge learners did not. These and related results (Kalyuga, Chandler, & Sweller, 1998, 2000; Mayer & Gallini, 1990; Ollerenshaw, Aidman, & Kidd, 1997) led Kalyuga and colleagues (Kalyuga, 2005; Kalyuga, Ayres, Chandler, & Sweller 2003) to propose the *expertise reversal effect*—the idea that instructional supports that help low-knowledge learners may not help (and may even hurt) high-knowledge learners. Overall, we recommend that you be sensitive to the level of prior knowledge of your learners so that you can provide needed supports—such as multimedia instruction—to low-knowledge learners. If you are working on a course for a less advanced group of learners—beginning trainees, for example—you should be especially careful to supplement text-based instruction with coordinated graphics. If you have a more advanced group of learners, such as medical residents or engineers experienced in the topic you are presenting, they may be able to learn well mainly from text or even mainly from graphics.

Should You Change Static Illustrations into Animations?

If it is important to add graphics to words, is it better to use animations or to use static illustrations? Flash animations are currently very popular additions to many e-learning lessons. At first glance, you might think that animations are best because they are an active medium, which can depict changes and movement. Similarly, you might think that static illustrations are a poorer choice because they are a passive medium, which cannot depict changes and movement in as much detail as animations can. In spite of these impressions, a number of research studies have failed to find that animations are more effective than a series of static frames depicting the same material (Betrancourt, 2005; Hegarty, Kriz, & Cate, 2003; Mayer, Hegarty, Mayer, & Campbell, 2005; Tversky, Morrison, & Betrancourt, 2002).

Let's consider two ways to use multimedia to explain how lightning storms develop—a paper-based lesson of a series of static illustrations with printed text (as shown in Figure 4.10) or a computer-based lesson of narrated animations in which the words are spoken and the transitions between frames are animated. On a transfer test, students in the paper group performed 32 percent better than students in the computer group, yielding an effect size of .55 (Mayer, Hegarty, Mayer, & Campbell, 2005). In four such comparisons—involving lessons on lightning, ocean waves, hydraulic brakes, and toilet tanks—the illustrations-and-text group always performed better than the animation-and-narration group, yielding a median effect size of .57. Presumably, the so-called passive medium of illustrations and text actually allowed for active processing because the learners had to mentally animate the changes from one frame to the next and learners were able to control the order and pace of their processing. In contrast, the so-called active medium of animations and narration may foster passive learning because the learner did not have to mentally animate and could not control the pace and order of the presentation. In addition, animation may overload the learner's working memory because the images are so rich in detail and are so transitory that they must be held in memory. In contrast, a series of static frames does not impose extra cognitive load because the learner can always review a previous frame.

Figure 4.10. A Series of Static Visuals to Teach How Lightning Forms.

From Mayer, Hegarty, Mayer, and Campbell, 2005.

1. Cool moist air moves over a warmer surface and becomes heated.

2. Warmed moist air near the earth's surface rises rapidly.

3. As the air in this updraft cools, water vapor condenses into water droplets and forms a cloud.

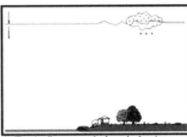

4. The cloud's top extends above the freezing level, so the upper portion of the cloud is composed of tiny ice crystals.

5. Eventually, the water droplets and ice crystals become too large to be suspended by the updrafts.

6. As raindrops and ice crystals fall through the cloud, they drag some of the air in the cloud downward, producing downdrafts.

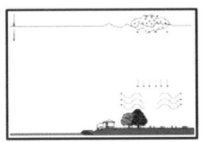

7. When downdrafts strike the ground, they spread out in all directions, producing the gusts of cool wind people feel just before the start of the rain.

8. Within the cloud, the rising and falling air currents cause electrical charges to build.

In spite of these results, there may be some content that is particularly suited to animation or video rather than static frames of illustrations or photos, such as descriptions of how to perform a motor skill. There is some evidence that animations (or video) may be particularly helpful for tasks that require complicated manual skills. For example, animation was more effective than static diagrams in helping students learn to make paper flowers and hats through paper folding (ChanLin, 1998; Wong, Marcus, Ayres, Smith, Cooper, Paas, & Sweller, 2009) and in helping students learn to tie knots and complete puzzle rings (Ayres, Marcus, Chan, & Qian, 2009). In contrast, studies in which static diagrams are better or just as effective as animations tend to involve explanations of how a complex system works, such as a braking system or how ocean waves work. In other words, it appears that static visuals might be most effective to promote understanding of processes, whereas animated visuals may be more effective to teach hands-on procedures.

Additionally, animations can serve an interpretive function when designed with special effects that reveal relationships not otherwise visible.

Hegarty (2004) suggests that "dynamic displays can distort reality in various ways such as slowing down some processes and speeding up others, showing an object or phenomenon from different or changing viewpoints, augmenting the display with cues to draw viewers' attention to the most relevant parts, or having moving objects leave a trace or wake" (p. 345). A time-lapse video of seed germination or a slow-motion video of hummingbirds in flight are two examples of how special effects can make phenomena visible.

Animations can cost more to develop than static diagrams, so it makes sense to use a series of static frames as our default graphic. Overall, our recommendation is to use static illustrations unless there is a compelling instructional rationale for animation. In particular, when you have an explanative illustration, we recommend presenting a series of static frames to depict the various states of the system rather than a lock-step animation.

What We Don't Know About Visuals

We have good evidence that relevant visuals promote learning. Now it's time to find out more about what types of visuals are most effective for different learners and instructional goals. Some of the unresolved issues around graphics include:

1. When is an animation more effective than a static graphic?

2. What are the long-term effects of graphics? Most of our research data measures learning immediately after taking the lesson. We need more information on the effectiveness of visuals for longer term learning.

3. What is the return on investment of graphics? Explanatory visuals can be time-consuming to produce and require an investment in graphic design resources. What are the cost benefits for creating customized visuals to illustrate technical content?

DESIGN DILEMMA: RESOLVED

In our chapter introduction, you considered the following options for use of graphics in the database course:

A. Matt is right. Learning will be just as effective from good textual explanations as from text plus graphics.

B. Ben is right. Adding clip art to a few screens will make the lesson more interesting. However, to save time, providing text alone will be as effective as adding visuals.

C. Reshmi is right. Customized visuals including screen shot animation demonstrations to illustrate the content will add appeal and improve learning.

D. Not sure which options are correct.

Based on the evidence we presented in this chapter, we conclude that Reshmi is on the right track. e-Learning is a visual medium and relevant graphics will add appeal and improve learning. The lesson segments that involve Excel procedures might benefit from animated demonstrations. However, lesson sections that explain Excel concepts and processes will benefit as much from static graphics. Ben's idea to add decorative graphics in the form of clip art will most likely not contribute to learning and in fact, as we will see in Chapter 8 on the coherence principle, may even detract from learning. We recommend that the team use an authoring system to capture animated screen procedures and engage a graphic designer to create a few simple but functional visuals to support the lesson concepts—including visuals that serve organizational, transformational, and interpretive functions. Even if a few extra days are required, the improvement in instructional quality and appeal is worth the investment.

WHAT TO LOOK FOR IN e-LEARNING

☐ Graphics and text are used to present instructional content.

☐ Graphics are relevant to the instructional purpose rather than decorative.

☐ Representative graphics are used to illustrate concrete facts, concepts, and their parts.

☐ Animations are used primarily to illustrate hands-on procedures.

☐ Organizational graphics are used to show relationships among ideas or lesson topics or where the parts are located within a whole structure.

☐ Relational graphics are used to show quantitative relationships among variables.

☐ Transformational graphics, such as a video showing how to operate equipment, are used to show changes over time.

☐ Interpretive graphics, such as a series of static frames, are used to explain how a system works or to make invisible phenomena visible.

☐ Graphics are used as a lesson interface for case studies.

COMING NEXT

In this chapter we have seen that learning is improved by the use of relevant graphics combined with words to present instructional content. In the next chapter, we will build upon this principle by examining the contiguity principle that addresses the best ways to position graphics and related text on the screen.

Suggested Readings

Butcher, K.R. (2006). Learning from text with diagrams: Promoting mental model development and inference generation. *Journal of Educational Psychology, 98,* 182–197.

Clark, R.C., & Lyons, C. (2011). *Graphics for learning* (2nd ed.) San Francisco: Pfeiffer.

Fletcher, J.D., & Tobias, S. (2005). The multimedia principle. In R.E. Mayer (Ed.), *The Cambridge handbook of multimedia learning* (pp. 117–134). New York: Cambridge University Press.

Mayer, R.E. (1989b). Systematic thinking fostered by illustrations in scientific text. *Journal of Educational Psychology, 81*, 240–246.

Mayer, R.E., & Anderson, R.B. (1992). The instructive animation: Helping students build connections between words and pictures in multimedia learning. *Journal of Educational Psychology, 84,* 444–452.

Mayer, R.E., & Anderson, R.B. (1991). Animations need narrations: An experimental test of a dual-processing system in working memory. *Journal of Educational Psychology, 90,* 312–320.

Mayer, R.E., & Gallini, J.K. (1990). When is an illustration worth ten thousand words? *Journal of Educational Psychology, 88,* 64–73.

Mayer, R.E., Hegarty, M., Mayer, S., & Campbell, J. (2005). When static media promote active learning: Annotated illustrations versus narrated animations in multimedia instruction. *Journal of Experimental Psychology: Applied, 11*, 256–265.

Robinson, D.H. (2002). Spatial text adjuncts and learning. *Educational Psychology Review*, 14(1).

CHAPTER OUTLINE

5

Applying the Contiguity Principle

ALIGN WORDS TO CORRESPONDING GRAPHICS

SOMETIMES IN E-LEARNING that uses on-screen text to explain graphics, a scrolling screen reveals the text, followed by the graphic further down the screen. When you scroll down to the graphic, the corresponding text has scrolled out of the window from above; when you scroll up to see the text, the corresponding graphic has scrolled out of the window from below. The result is a physical separation of the text and the graphic. Alternatively, audio narration may be presented before or after the graphics it describes. When you click on a speaker icon, you can hear a brief narration, and when you click on a movie icon, you can see a brief animation, but the narration and animation are separated in time. In this chapter we summarize the empirical evidence for learning gains resulting from presenting text and graphics in an integrated fashion (that is, placing printed words placed next to the part of the graphic they describe or presenting spoken words at the same time as a corresponding graphic), rather than presenting the same information separately. The psychological advantage of integrating text and graphics results from a reduced need to search for which parts of a graphic correspond to which words, thereby allowing the user to devote limited cognitive resources to understanding the materials.

In this third edition, we present new evidence concerning the contiguity principle. The new evidence includes research on eye-tracking and pop-up windows. In this new edition, we also clarify some of the boundary conditions under which the contiguity principle applies most strongly.

DESIGN DILEMMA: YOU DECIDE

The e-learning design team is reviewing storyboards for their course on spreadsheets for small business owners. To accommodate different learning styles, they have decided to include both text and audio options in the lessons. To apply the multimedia principle discussed in Chapter 4, Ben has added some simple but relevant visuals to illustrate the concepts. For example, to show how to use the logic functions in spreadsheets, he gives an explanation in text and includes two small examples. As shown in Figure 5.1, he asks the learner to click on the small example screens to view the examples.

In reviewing the screens, Reshmi feels that the text explanations and the visual examples should be viewed together. "I recall reading research proving that it is better to allow the learner to view both text and visuals in close alignment." "That's a good idea in many situations," Ben replies. "However, it would take too much screen real estate to include a large graphic and a coherent text explanation!" Based on your own experience or intuition, which of the following options is best:

A. Ben is right. To make sense, the visual examples must be displayed as small screens to be viewed after reading the text explanation.

B. Reshmi is right. Learning is more efficient when visuals and text are integrated. The text explanation should be integrated close to the visual examples.

C. Both ideas could be accommodated by placing text directions in a roll-over box on top of a large screen shot example.

D. Not sure which option is best.

Figure 5.1. Ben's First Draft Storyboards for the Excel Lesson.

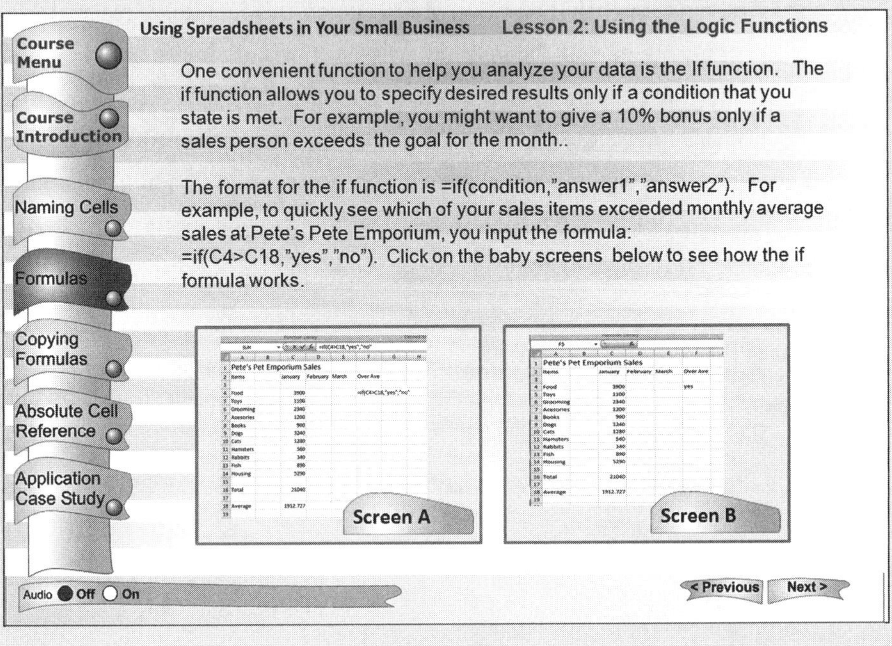

Contiguity Principle 1: Place Printed Words Near Corresponding Graphics

The principle of contiguity involves the need to coordinate printed words and graphics. In this chapter, we focus on the idea that on-screen words should be placed near the parts of the on-screen graphics to which they refer. We recommend that corresponding graphics and printed words be placed near each other on the screen (that is, contiguous in space).

In designing or selecting e-learning courseware, consider how on-screen text is integrated with on-screen graphics. In particular, when printed words refer to parts of on-screen graphics, make sure the printed words are placed next to the corresponding part of a graphic to which they refer. For example, when the graphic is a diagram showing the parts of an object, the printed names of the parts should be placed near the corresponding parts of the diagram, using a pointing line to connect the name to the part, rather than at the bottom of the graphic as a caption or legend. Similarly, when a lesson presents words that describe actions (or states) depicted in the series of still frames, make sure that text describing an action (or state) is placed near the corresponding part of the graphic, using a pointing line to connect the text with the graphic, rather than in a caption or in the main text.

When there is too much text to fit on the screen, the text describing each action or state can appear as a small pop-up message that appears when the mouse touches the corresponding portion of the graphic. This technique is called a mouse-over or rollover. For example, Figure 5.2 shows an application

Figure 5.2. A Screen Rollover Integrates Text Below Section 1 of Graphic.
From Clark and Lyons, 2011.

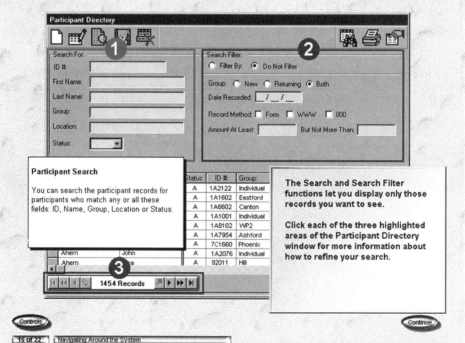

screen that uses the rollover technique. When learners place their cursors over different sections of the application screen, a text caption appears that explains that section. In Figure 5.2 the mouse has rolled over section 1 and the text window below it appears as long as the mouse remains in that area of the screen. One problem with rollovers is that they are transient. The text box disappears when the cursor moves to a different location on the screen. Thus, rollovers may not be appropriate for situations in which it's important for the learner to view more than one block of rollover text at a time or to take an action that relies on rollover text.

Violations of Contiguity Principle 1

Violations of the contiguity principle are all too common. The following list gives some of the most common violations (although there are more) of this principle that are frequently seen in e-learning courseware:

- In a scrolling window, graphics and corresponding printed text are separated, one before the other, and partially obscured because of scrolling screens.

- Feedback is displayed on a separate screen from the practice or question.

- Links leading to an on-screen reference appear in a second browser window that covers the related information on the initial screen (that is, printed text is in one window and graphics are in another).

- Directions to complete practice exercises are placed on a separate screen from the application screen in which the directions are to be followed.

- All text is placed at the bottom of the screen away from graphics.

- An animation plays on one half of the screen while text describing the animation is displayed simultaneously on the other half of the screen

- Key elements in a graphic are numbered, and a legend at the bottom of the screen includes the name for each numbered element.

Avoid Separation of Text and Graphics on Scrolling Screens

Sometimes scrolling screens are poorly designed so that text is presented first and the visual illustration appears further down the screen, as illustrated in Figure 5.3. As the user scrolls down to view the graphic, the text is no longer visible and vice versa. This is a common problem we see in many courses that use scrolling screens to present instructional content. This particular problem can be remedied by integrating text and visuals on a scrolling screen, as shown in Figure 5.4. Another remedy to the scrolling screen problem is to use text boxes that pop up over graphics when the graphic is touched by the cursor (as shown in Figure 5.2). Alternatively, fixed screen displays can be used when it is important to see the text and graphic together. On a fixed screen, the graphic can fill the screen and text can be embedded within the graphic near the element being described.

Figure 5.3. Text and Graphic Separated on Scrolling Screen.

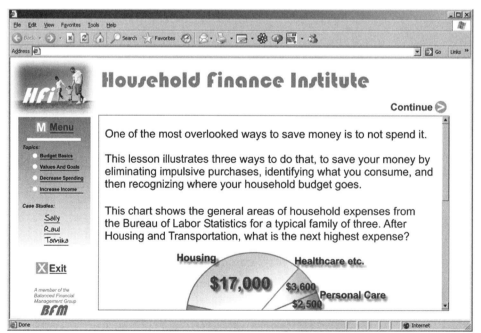

Figure 5.4. Text and Graphic Visible Together on a Scrolling Screen.

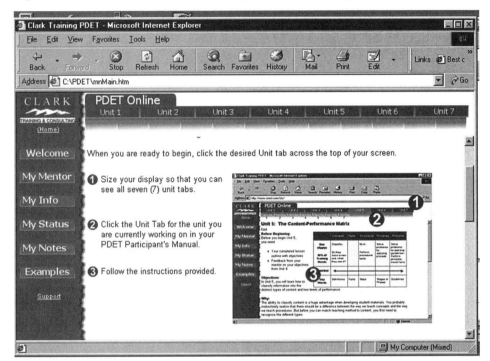

Avoid Separation of Feedback from Questions or Responses

Another common violation of the contiguity principle is when feedback is placed on a screen separate from the question or from the learner's answers. This requires the learner to page back and forth between the question and the feedback, adding cognitive load to learning. For example, in Figure 5.5 from our pharmaceutical sales example lesson, a multiple-select question (not shown) requires the learner to select physicians whose practice would benefit from a new drug. When the learner clicks "done," he or she is routed to a screen (Feedback A) that shows the correct answers. In order to compare their answers with the correct answers, the learners must page back to the question screen. A better solution is shown in the Feedback B screen. In this screen the learner's answers (checks in boxes) have been carried over from the

Figure 5.5. Ineffective and Effective Placement of Feedback.

Ineffective Feedback

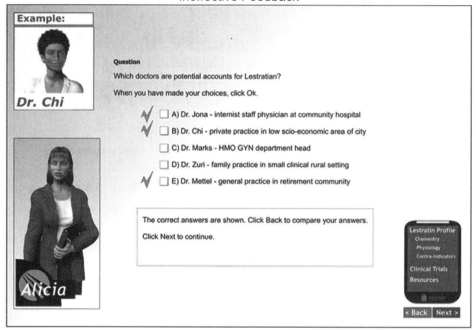

Effective Feedback

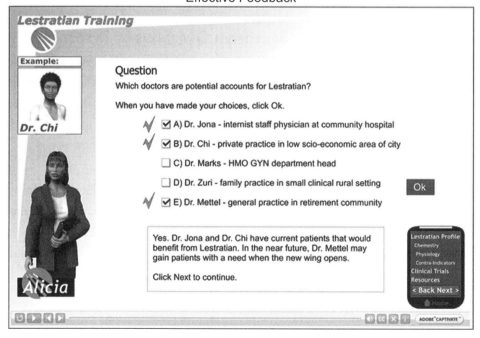

question screen and placed next to the correct answer, allowing a quick and easy comparison without paging back.

Avoid Separating Lesson Screens with Linked Windows

The use of links that lead to adjunct information is common in e-learning. However, when the linked information covers related information on the primary screen, this practice can create a problem. For example, a link on an application screen leads to a window containing a job aid. Having access to reference material is a good idea for memory support. However, if the resulting window covers the graphic example that it describes, the contiguity principle is violated. A better solution is to link to a window that is small, can be moved around on the main screen, and/or can be printed.

Avoid Presenting Exercise Directions Separate from the Exercise

Another common violation of the contiguity principle is the practice of presenting exercise directions in text separated from the screens on which the actions are to be taken. For example, in Figure 5.6 we see textual directions for a case study from an Excel e-learning lesson. When moving to the spreadsheet on the next screen, the learner no longer has access to the directions. A better alternative is to put the step-by-step directions in a box that can be minimized or moved on the application screen.

Avoid Displaying Captions at the Bottom of Screens

For consistency, many e-learning designs place all text in a box at the bottom of the screen such as the frame shown in Figure 5.7A. The problem with this layout is that the learner needs to scan back and forth between the words at the bottom of the screen and the part of the graphic they describe. A better arrangement is to relocate the text closer to the visual as well as to insert lines to connect the text and visual, as shown in Figure 5.7B. Alternatively, the text can be broken into shorter segments, with each segment placed next to the part of the graphic it describes.

Figure 5.6. Separating Exercise Directions from Application Screen Adds
Extraneous Cognitive Load.

Figure 5.7. Text Placed at Bottom of Screen Versus Next to Visual.

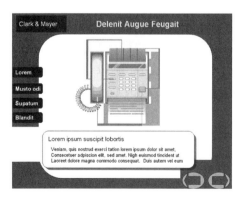 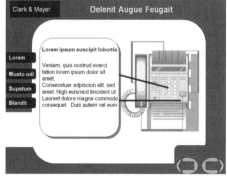

A.   Text at Bottom of Screen   B.   Text Next to Visual

Avoid Simultaneous Display of Animations and Related Text

You may want to use an animation to depict movement such as to show how to perform a computer application or to illustrate how equipment works. If the animation is playing at the same time as the text is displayed, the learners can either view the animation or read the descriptive text. If they read the text, they miss much of the animation or if they watch the animation then they will read the text after the animation has run. A better solution is to present the text for reading and instruct the learner to press a play button to view the animation after reading, as shown in Figure 5.8. The text remains on the screen for review as desired while the learner watches the animation.

Figure 5.8. Using a Play Button to Start the Animation Avoids Splitting Attention Between the Text and the Visual.

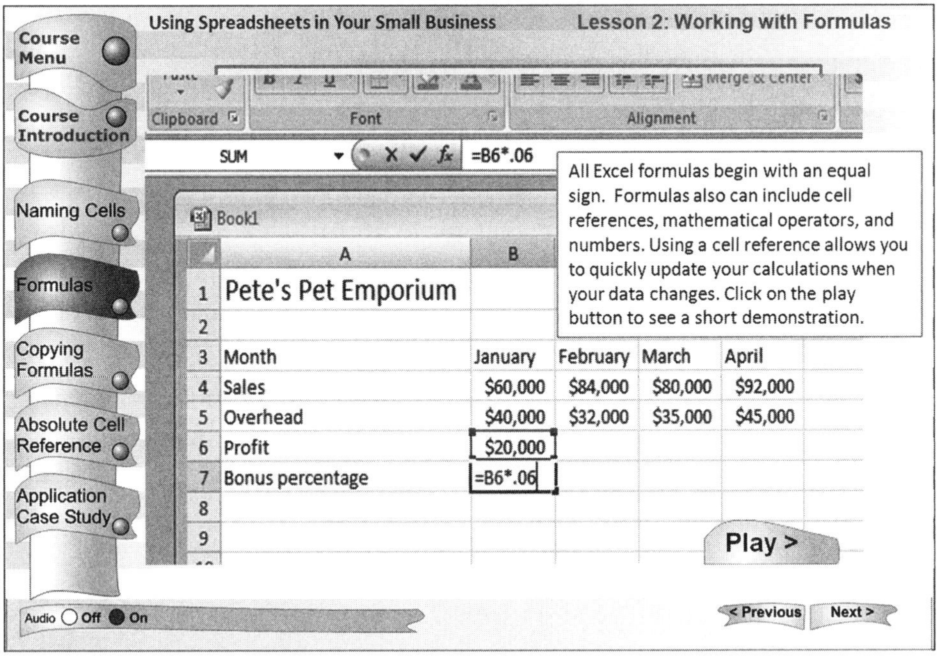

Avoid Using a Legend to Indicate the Parts of a Graphic

Suppose you wanted students to learn about the parts in a piece of equipment. You could show them an illustration in which each equipment part is numbered and a legend below the illustration describes each one. The problem with this layout is that the learner must scan between the number and the legend, which creates wasted cognitive processing. A more efficient design would place the name and part description in a separate box near the corresponding part on the visual. The text could be placed in a rollover box or in a fixed display on the screen. If the learner will benefit from seeing several parts simultaneously, leaving them on the screen in a fixed display would be better than a rollover box that disappears when the cursor is moved.

Contiguity Principle 2: Synchronize Spoken Words with Corresponding Graphics

Another version of the contiguity principle deals with the need to coordinate spoken words and graphics. In this section we focus on the idea that spoken words (narration) that describe an event should play at the same time as the graphic (animation or video) depicting the event. In short, we recommend that corresponding graphics and spoken words be presented at the same time (that is, contiguous—next to each other—in time).

When e-learning courseware contains narration and corresponding graphics (animation or video), you should consider how spoken words are integrated with on-screen graphics. In particular, when spoken words describe actions that are depicted in the on-screen graphics, make sure the corresponding spoken words and graphics are presented at the same time. For example, when the graphic is an animation showing the steps in a process, the narration describing a particular step should be presented at the same time that the step is shown on the screen. When the graphic is a video showing how to perform a task, the narration describing each step should be presented at the same time as the action shown on the screen.

Violations of Contiguity Principle 2

Violations of the contiguity principle include the following:

- A link to audio is indicated by one icon and a link to video is indicated by another icon.

- A segment provides a narrated description followed by animation or video.

Avoid Separation of Graphics and Narration Through Icons

Suppose you click on "How the Heart Works" in an online encyclopedia, and two buttons appear—a speaker button indicating that you can listen to a short narration about the four steps in heart cycle and a movie button indicating that you can watch a short animation, as illustrated in Figure 5.9. You click on the speaker button and listen to a description of the four steps in the heart cycle. Then you click on the movie button and watch a narration showing the four steps in the heart cycle. You might think this is an excellent presentation because you can select which mode of presentation you prefer. You might like the idea that you listen to the explanation first and then watch, or vice versa, thereby giving you two complementary exposures to the same material.

What's wrong with this situation? The problem is that, when a lesson separates corresponding words and graphics, learners experience a heavier load on working memory—leaving less capacity for deep learning. Consider the learner's cognitive processing during learning when a narration is followed

Figure 5.9. Narration Is Presented Separately from Animation.

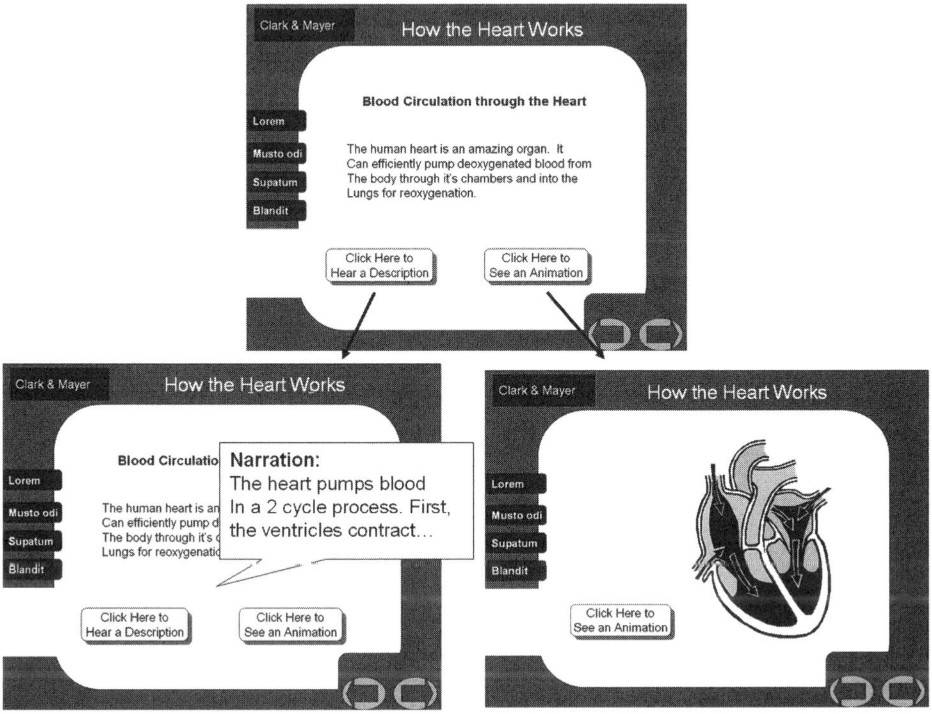

by an animation. After listening to the narration, the learner needs to hold all the relevant words in working memory and then match up each segment with the corresponding segment of the animation. However, having to hold so much information in working memory can be overwhelming, so the learner may not be able to engage in other cognitive processes needed for deep learning. This is the type of load we called extraneous processing in Chapter 2. Extraneous processing refers to mental load that does *not* contribute to learning. Therefore, we recommend that you avoid e-learning lessons that present narration and graphics separately.

Avoid Separation of Graphics and Narration in a Continuous Presentation

Even when a lesson presents graphics and narration as a continuous unit, a lesson may be designed so that an introduction is presented as a brief narration that is followed by graphics (such as an animation, video, or series of still frames depicting the same material). For example, consider a multimedia presentation on "How the Heart Works" that begins with a narrator describing the four steps in the heart cycle, followed by four still frames depicting the four steps in the heart cycle.

At first glance, you might like this arrangement because you get a general orientation in words before you inspect a graphic. Yet, like the previous scenario, this situation can create cognitive overload because the learner has to mentally hold the words in working memory until the graphic appears—thereby creating a form of extraneous cognitive processing. To overcome this problem, we recommend presenting the narration at the same time the static frames are presented. In this situation, the learner can more easily make mental connections between corresponding words and graphics.

Psychological Reasons for the Contiguity Principle

As we have reviewed in the examples shown in the previous sections, it is not unusual to see (1) corresponding printed text and graphics physically separated in e-lessons or (2) corresponding narration and graphics presented at different times in e-lessons. The physical separation may occur because of vertical placement of printed text and graphics (one on top of the other), which separates them when the screen is scrolled, or by a text window covering a graphics window or vice versa, or by placing related information on separate fixed screen displays. The temporal separation may occur because a narrated introduction precedes a graphic, or graphics and narration are accessed through clicking on different icons.

Some designers separate words and pictures because they haven't stopped to think about whether it's an effective way to present information. Others reason that presenting the same material in two different places on the page or at two different times allows learners to choose the format that best suits their needs or even to experience the same information in two different ways. We recommend against separating words and pictures, even for environments with high traffic and low bandwidth, because it is not based on an accurate understanding of how people learn. Rather than being copy machines that record incoming information, humans are sense-makers who try to see the meaningful relations between words and pictures. When words and pictures are separated from one another on the screen or in time, people must use their scarce cognitive resources just to match them up. This creates what we call *extraneous processing*—cognitive processing that is unrelated to the instructional goal. When learners use their limited cognitive capacity for extraneous processing, they have less capacity to use to mentally organize and integrate the material.

In contrast, when words and pictures are integrated, people can hold them together in their working memories and therefore make meaningful connections between them. This act of mentally connecting corresponding words and pictures is an important part of the sense-making process that leads to meaningful learning. As we saw in Chapter 2, it is in working memory that the related incoming information is organized and integrated with existing knowledge in long-term memory. When the learner has to do the added work of coordinating corresponding words and visual components that are separated on the screen or in time, the limited capacity of working memory is taxed—leading to cognitive overload. Ayres and Sweller (2005) argue that putting corresponding words and pictures far apart from each other (or presenting them at different times) creates what they call *split attention*, which forces the learner to use limited working memory capacity to coordinate the multiple sources of information. You should avoid instructional designs that cause split attention because they force the learner to waste precious cognitive processing on trying to coordinate two disparate sources of information.

Evidence for Presenting Printed Words Near Corresponding Graphics

Our first recommendation—presenting corresponding printed text and graphics near each other on the screen—is not only based on cognitive theory, but it is also based on several relevant research studies (Mayer, 1989b; Mayer, Steinhoff, Bower, & Mars, 1995; Moreno & Mayer, 1999a). In five different tests involving lessons on lightning formation and how cars' braking systems work, learners received printed text and illustrations containing several frames (or on-screen text with animation). For one group of learners (integrated group), text was placed near the part of the illustration that it described, as you can see in Figure 5.10A. For another group (separated group), the same text was placed under the illustration as a caption, as you

---

Figure 5.10. **Screens from Lightning Lesson with Integrated Text and Graphics and Separated Text and Graphics.**

Adapted from Mayer, 2001, 2005c.

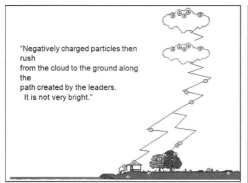

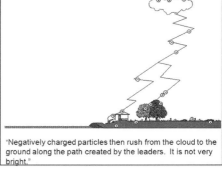

A. Integrated
Presentation

B. Separated
Presentation

can see in Figure 5.10B. In five studies, the integrated group performed better on problem-solving transfer tests than the separated group. Overall, the integrated group produced between 43 and 89 percent more solutions than the separated group. The median gain across all the studies was 68 percent for an effect size of 1.12, which, as mentioned in Chapter 3, is a large effect. Figure 5.11 summarizes the results from one of the experiments.

Figure 5.11. Learning Is Better from Integrated Text and Graphics Than from Separated Text and Graphics.
Adapted from Mayer 2001a, 2005b.

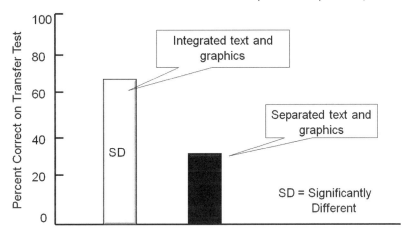

Similar results have been found with training programs for technical tasks (Chandler & Sweller, 1991; Paas & Van Merrienboer, 1994; Sweller & Chandler, 1994; Sweller, Chandler, Tierney, & Cooper, 1990), practical training in physical therapy (Pociask & Morrison, 2008), and even with a single scientific illustration and explanatory text presented on a computer screen (Florax & Ploetzner, 2010). Erhel and Jamet (2006) found that people learned better from an online lesson on the human heart when pop-up windows containing text appeared next to the part of the graphic they described, rather than having the text at the bottom of the screen. In a systematic review of thirty-seven studies, Ginns (2006) found strong support for the benefits of spatial contiguity, with an average effect size of .72.

Additional evidence comes from eye-tracking studies involving text and corresponding diagrams. Successful learners tended to read a portion of the text, then search the diagram for the object being described in the text, then read the next portion of text and search the diagram for the object being described, and so on (Hegarty, Carpenter, & Just, 1996; Schmidt-Weigand, Kohnert, & Glowalla, 2010). It seems reasonable that we can simplify this process for all learners by breaking text into chunks and by placing each chunk of text near the part of the graphic that it describes. For example, in a naturalistic eye-tracking study shown in Figure 5.12, newspaper readers were more likely to look back and forth between corresponding words and graphics (which contributes to meaningful learning) if the words were placed next to corresponding graphics on the newspaper page (Holsanova, Holmberg, & Holmqvist, 2009). Overall, there are numerous studies that support our recommendation.

Figure 5.12. Eye-Tracking Shows Better Integration of Text and Visual When Visuals Are Integrated into the Text.

From Holsannova, Holmberg, and Holmqvist, 2009.

Separated Presentation   Integrated Presentation

Some possible boundary conditions are that the spatial contiguity recommendation may most strongly apply for low-knowledge learners (Mayer, Steinhoff, Bower, & Mars, 1995) and when the graphic and words are complex (Ayres & Sweller, 2005).

Evidence for Presenting Spoken Words at the Same Time as Corresponding Graphics

Our second recommendation—presenting corresponding speech and graphics at the same time—is also based on research evidence (Mayer & Anderson, 1991, 1992; Mayer, Moreno, Boire, & Vagge, 1999; Mayer & Sims, 1994). In one experiment, some students (integrated group) viewed a thirty-second narrated animation that explained how a bicycle tire pump works, in which the spoken words described the actions taking place on the screen. For example, when the narrator's voice said, "the inlet valve opens," the animation on the screen showed the inlet valve moving from the closed to the open position. Other students (separated group) listened to the entire narration and then watched the entire animation (or vice versa). On a subsequent transfer test the integrated group generated 50 percent more solutions than did the separated group, yielding an effect size greater than 1, which is considered large.

Overall, across eight different experimental comparisons involving pumps, brakes, lightning, and lungs, students who received integrated presentations generated 60 percent more solutions on a transfer test than did students who received separated presentations. The median effect size across all eight experiments was 1.30, which is considered a large effect in practical terms. Research by Baggett (1984) and Baggett and Ehrenfeucht (1983) shows that learners experience difficulty in learning from a narrated video even when corresponding words and graphics are separated by a few seconds. In a systematic review of thirteen studies, Ginns (2006) found strong evidence for temporal contiguity with an average effect size of .87. As you can see, when you have a narrated animation, narrated video, or even a narrated series of still frames, there is consistent evidence that people learn best when the words describing an element or event are spoken at the same time that the animation (or video or illustration) depicts the element or event on the screen. A possible boundary condition is that the temporal contiguity recommendation applies most strongly when the narration and animation segments are long and when students cannot control the order and pace of presentation (Mayer, Moreno, Boire, & Vagge, 1999; Micas & Berry, 2000).

What We Don't Know About Contiguity

Overall, our goal is to reduce the need for learners to engage in extraneous processing by helping them see the connection between corresponding words and graphics. Two techniques we explored in this chapter are to present printed words near the part of the graphic they refer to and to present spoken text at the same time as the portion of graphic they refer to. Some unresolved issues concern:

1. How much detail should be in the graphics and in the words?

2. When is it better to use printed words and when is it better to use spoken words?

3. How does the conversational style of the words affect learning?

4. How do characteristics of the voice affect learning with spoken words?

DESIGN DILEMMA: RESOLVED

Ben and Reshmi are debating the best placement of text in the Excel lesson. Some alternatives raised were:

A. Ben is right. To make sense, the visual examples must be displayed as small screens to be viewed after reading the text explanation.

B. Reshmi is right. Learning is more efficient when visuals and text are integrated. The text explanation should be integrated close to the visual examples.

C. Both ideas could be accommodated by placing text directions in a rollover box on top of a large screen shot example.

D. Not sure which option is best.

We recommend Option B for most situations. We show one alternative display in Figure 5.13. Although rollovers can be a useful way to ensure contiguity between visuals and text, rollovers can be transient with the information disappearing when the cursor is moved. In the case of text that will be referred to over time, such as directions for an exercise, a more permanent display that integrates text and graphic will impose less mental load on learners.

Figure 5.13. This Alternative to Figure 5.1 Applies the Contiguity Principle.

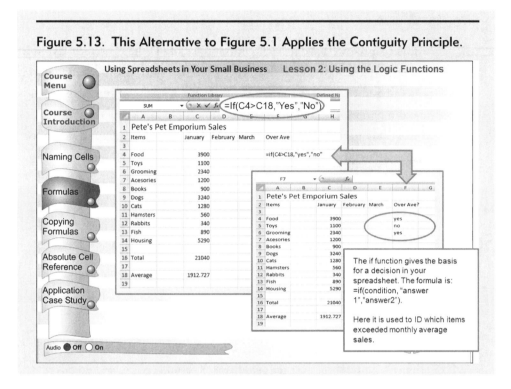

WHAT TO LOOK FOR IN e-LEARNING

☐ Screens that place printed text next to the portion of the graphic it describes

☐ Feedback that appears on the same screen as the question and responses

☐ Directions that appear on the same screen in which the steps are to be applied

☐ Linked information does not appear in windows that obscure related information on the primary screen

☐ Animations that can be played independently of text that describes the animation

☐ Text placed next to or within graphics rather than below them

☐ Legend callouts that are embedded within the graphic rather separated from it

☐ Narrated graphics in which corresponding words and graphics are presented at the same time

COMING NEXT

In this chapter, we have seen the importance of (1) the on-screen layout of printed text and graphics and (2) the coordination of corresponding narration and graphics. Next we will consider the benefits of presenting words in audio narration rather than in on-screen text. We know that audio adds considerably to file sizes and requires the use of sound cards and sometimes headsets. Does the use of audio add anything to learning? In the next chapter we examine the modality principle, which addresses this issue.

Suggested Readings

Ayres, P., & Sweller, J. (2005). The split-attention principle in multimedia learning. In R.E. Mayer (Ed.), *The Cambridge handbook of multimedia learning* (pp. 135–146). New York: Cambridge University Press.

Ginns, P. (2006). Integrating information: A meta-analysis of spatial contiguity and temporal contiguity effects. *Learning and Instruction, 16,* 511–525.

Holsanova, J., Holmberg, N., & Holmqvist, K. (2009). Reading information graphics: The role of spatial contiguity and dual attention guidance. *Applied Cognitive Psychology, 23,* 1215–1226.

Mayer, R.E. (1989b). Systematic thinking fostered by illustrations in scientific text. *Journal of Educational Psychology, 81*, 240–246.

Mayer, R.E. (2005b). Principles for reducing extraneous processing in multimedia learning: Coherence, signaling, redundancy, spatial contiguity, and temporal contiguity. In R.E. Mayer (Ed.), *The Cambridge handbook of multimedia learning* (pp. 183–200). New York: Cambridge University Press.

Mayer, R.E., & Anderson, R.B. (1991). Animations need narrations: An experimental test of a dual-coding hypothesis. *Journal of Educational Psychology, 83*, 484–490.

Mayer, R.E., & Anderson, R.B. (1992). The instructive animation: Helping students build connections between words and pictures in multimedia learning. *Journal of Educational Psychology, 84,* 444–452.

Mayer, R.E., Steinhoff, K., Bower, G., & Mars, R. (1995). A generative theory of textbook design: Using annotated illustrations to foster meaningful learning of science text. *Educational Technology Research and Development, 43,* 31–43.

Moreno, R., & Mayer, R.E. (1999a). Cognitive principles of multimedia learning: The role of modality and contiguity. *Journal of Educational Psychology, 91,* 358–368.

CHAPTER OUTLINE

6

Applying the Modality Principle

PRESENT WORDS AS AUDIO NARRATION RATHER
THAN ON-SCREEN TEXT

WHAT'S NEW IN THIS CHAPTER?

THE MODALITY PRINCIPLE has the most research support of
any of the principles described in this book. Technical constraints on
the use of audio in e-learning may lead consumers or designers of e-learning
to rely on text to present content and describe visuals. However, when it's
feasible to use audio, there is considerable evidence that presenting words
in audio rather than on-screen text can result in significant learning gains.
In this chapter, we summarize the empirical evidence for learning gains that
result from using audio rather than on-screen text to describe graphics. To
moderate this guideline, we also describe a number of situations in which
memory limitations require the use of text rather than audio. The psychological advantage of using audio presentation is a result of the incoming
information being split across two separate cognitive channels—words in the
auditory channel and pictures in the visual channel—rather than concentrating

both words and pictures in the visual channel. What is new in this chapter is an update to the evidence reported in the second edition of *e-Learning and the Science of Instruction*, including extensions of the modality principle to classroom contexts and supporting evidence from eye-tracking studies. We also have added more discussion of the boundary conditions for the modality principle—that is, the situations in which it applies most strongly. Overall, there continues to be strong and consistent support for using narration rather than on-screen text to describe graphics, especially when the presentation is complex or fast-paced and when the verbal material is familiar or short. In particular, audio narrations must be brief and clear to be effective.

DESIGN DILEMMA: YOU DECIDE

Now that they have agreed on the value of adding relevant visuals, as described in Chapter 4, the Excel design team has bogged down in discussions about how best to explain those graphics. Reshmi, the instructional designer, believes that providing words in text, as shown in Figure 6.1, allows learners to move at their own pace rather than have to wait for audio to play. "Besides that," she adds, "we must meet 508 compliance to accommodate learners with hearing loss. We must provide words in text!" Matt, the project leader, also prefers using text, as file sizes will be smaller and updates will be easier. However, Michael, a graduate student in multimedia learning who is interning from the local university, disagrees strongly: "In our class last semester, the professor went on and on about the benefits of audio. You are losing a big learning opportunity if you rely on text alone!" Based on your experience or intuition, which option(s) do you select:

A. Reshmi and Matt are right. The advantages of explaining on-screen graphics with text outweigh the disadvantages.

B. Michael is right. Learning is much better when words are presented in audio narration.

C. Everyone can be accommodated by providing words in both text and audio.

D. Not sure which options are correct.

Figure 6.1. Visual Described by On-Screen Text.

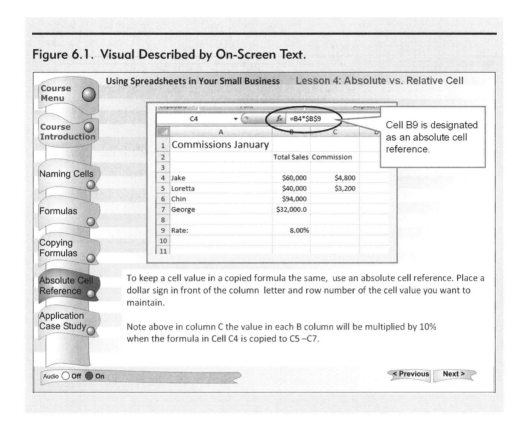

Modality Principle: Present Words as Speech Rather Than On-Screen Text

Suppose you are presenting a verbal explanation along with an animation, video, or series of still frames. Does it matter whether the words in your multimedia presentation are represented as printed text (that is, as on-screen text) or as spoken text (that is, as narration)? What do cognitive theory and research evidence have to say about the modality of words in multimedia presentations? You'll find the answer to these questions in the next few sections of this chapter.

Based on cognitive theory and research evidence, we recommend that you put words in spoken form rather than printed form whenever the graphic (animation, video, or series of static frames) is the focus of the words and both are presented simultaneously. Thus, we recommend that you avoid e-learning courses that contain crucial multimedia presentations where all words are in printed rather than spoken form, especially when the graphic is complex, the words are familiar, and the lesson is fast-paced.

The rationale for our recommendation is that learners may experience an overload of their visual/pictorial channel when they must simultaneously process graphics and the printed words that refer to them. If their eyes must attend to the printed words, they cannot fully attend to the animation or graphics—especially when the words and pictures are presented concurrently at a rapid pace, the words are familiar, and the graphic is complex. Since being able to attend to relevant words and pictures is a crucial first step in learning, e-learning courses should be designed to minimize the chances of overloading learners' visual/pictorial channel.

Figure 6.2 illustrates a multimedia course that effectively applies the modality principle. This section of the lesson is providing a demonstration of how to use a new online telephone management system. As the animation

Figure 6.2. Audio Explains the Animated Demonstration of the Telephone System.

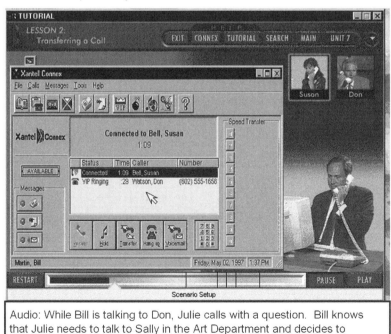

Audio: While Bill is talking to Don, Julie calls with a question. Bill knows that Julie needs to talk to Sally in the Art Department and decides to transfer her while he is talking to Don.

Figure 6.3. Visual Described by Audio Narration.

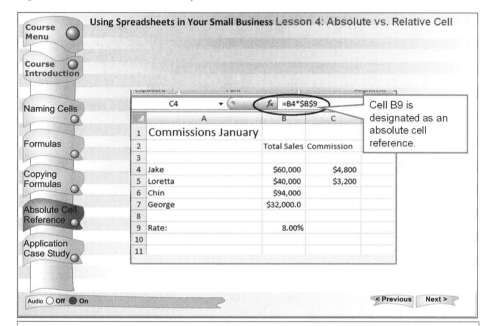

Audio: To keep a cell value in a copied formula the same, use an absolute cell reference. Place a dollar sign symbol in front of the column letter and row number of the cell value you want to maintain. Note above in column C the value in each B column cell will be multiplied by 8% when the formula in Cell C4 is copied to cells C5 –C7.

illustrates the steps on the computer screen, the audio describes the actions of the user. Another good example is seen in Figure 6.3 from our Excel sample lesson. Audio narration describes the visual illustration of formatting an absolute cell reference in Excel. In both of these examples, the visuals are relatively complex, and therefore using audio allows the learner to focus on the visual while listening to the explanation.

Limitations to the Modality Principle

When simultaneously presenting words and the graphics explained by the words, use spoken rather than printed text as a way of reducing the demands on visual processing. We recognize that in some cases it may not be practical to implement the modality principle, because the creation of sound may involve technical demands that the learning environment cannot meet (such as bandwidth, sound cards, headsets, and so on), or may create too much noise in the learning environment. Using sound also may add unreasonable expense or may make it more difficult to update rapidly changing information. We also recognize the recommendation is limited to those situations in which the words and graphics are simultaneously presented, and thus does not apply when words are presented without any concurrent picture or other visual input.

Additionally, there are times when the words should remain available to the learner for memory support—particularly when the words are technical, unfamiliar, not in the learner's native language, or needed for future reference. For example, a mathematical formula may be part of an audio explanation of an animated demonstration, but because of its complexity, it should remain visible as on-screen text. Key words that identify the steps of a procedure may be presented by on-screen text and highlighted (thus used as an organizer) as each step is illustrated in the animation and discussed in the audio. Another common example involves the directions to a practice exercise. Thus, we see in Figure 6.4 (from an Excel virtual classroom session)

Figure 6.4. Practice Directions Provided in On-Screen Text in a Virtual Classroom Session.

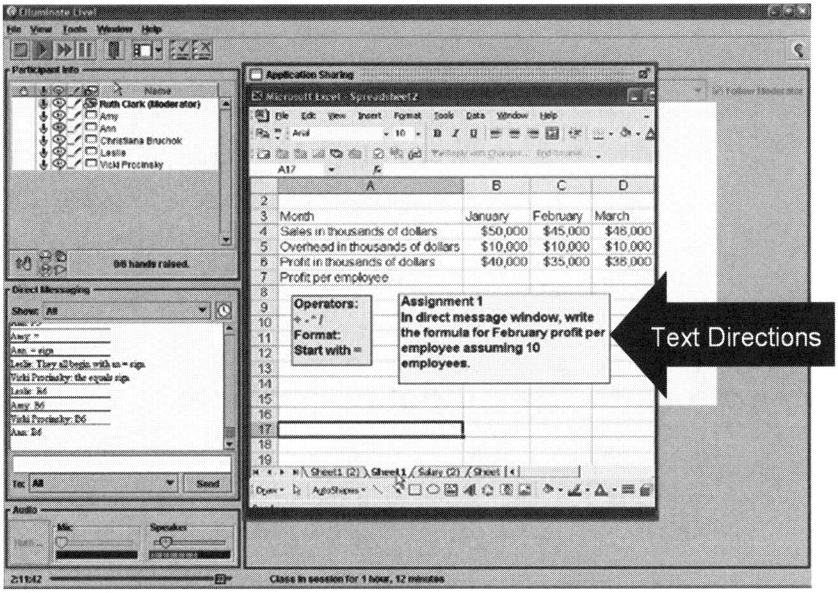

that the instructor narration throughout most of the program is suspended when the learner comes to the practice screen. Instead, the directions to the practice remain in text in the box on the spreadsheet for reference as the learners complete the exercise.

One advantage to virtual classrooms is the use of instructor speech to describe graphics projected on the whiteboard or through application sharing. In virtual classroom sessions, participants hear the instructor either through telephone conferencing or through their computers via voice-over-IP. However, virtual classroom facilitators should be careful to place text on their slides for instructional elements such as practice directions, memory support, and technical terms.

Psychological Reasons for the Modality Principle

If the purpose of the instructional program is to present information to the learner, then it does not matter whether you present graphics with printed text or graphics with spoken text. In both cases, identical pictures and words are presented, so it does not matter whether the words are presented as printed text or spoken text. This approach to multimedia design is suggested by the information acquisition view of learning—the idea that the instructor's job is to present information and the learner's job is to acquire information. Following this view, the rationale for using on-screen text is that it is generally easier to produce printed text rather than spoken text and it accomplishes the same job—that is, it presents the same information.

The trouble with the information acquisition view is that it conflicts with much of the research evidence concerning how people learn. This book is based on the idea that the instructional professional's job is not only to present information, but also to present it in a way that is consistent with how people learn. Thus, we adopt the cognitive theory of multimedia learning, in which learning depends both on the information that is presented and on the cognitive processes used by the learner during learning.

Multimedia lessons that present words as on-screen text can create a situation that conflicts with the way the human mind works. According to the cognitive theory of learning—which we use as the basis for our

Figure 6.5. Overloading of Visual Channel with Presentation of Written Text and Graphics.

Adapted from Mayer, 2001a.

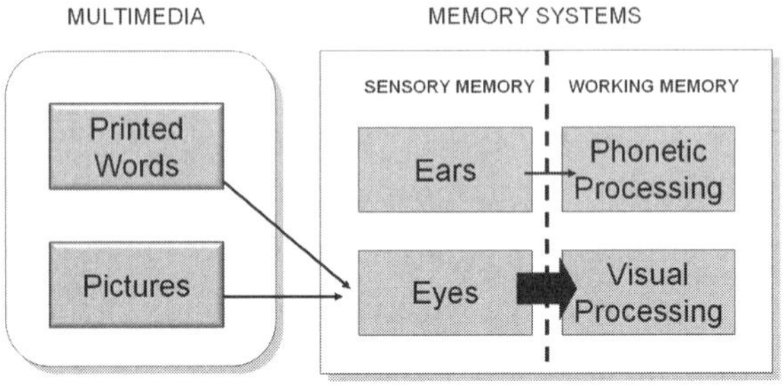

recommendations—people have separate information processing channels for visual/pictorial processing and for auditory/verbal processing. When learners are given concurrent graphics and on-screen text, both must be initially processed in the visual/pictorial channel. The capacity of each channel is limited, so the graphics and their explanatory on-screen text must compete for the same limited visual attention. When the eyes are engaged with on-screen text, they cannot simultaneously be looking at the graphics; when the eyes are engaged with the graphics, they cannot be looking at the on-screen text. Thus, even though the information is presented, learners may not be able to adequately attend to all of it because their visual channels become overloaded.

In contrast, we can reduce this load on the visual channel by presenting the verbal explanation as speech. Thus, the verbal material enters the cognitive system through the ears and is processed in the auditory/verbal channel. At the same time, the graphics enter the cognitive system through the eyes and are processed in the visual/pictorial channel. In this way neither channel is overloaded but both words and pictures are processed.

The case for presenting verbal explanations of graphics as speech is summarized in Figures 6.5 and 6.6. Figure 6.5 shows how graphics and on-screen text can overwhelm the visual channel, and Figure 6.6 shows how graphics and speech can distribute the processing between the visual and auditory channels. This analysis also explains why the case for presenting words as speech only applies to situations in which words and pictures are presented

Figure 6.6. Balancing Content Across Visual and Auditory Channels with Presentation of Narration and Graphics.

Adapted from Mayer, 2001a.

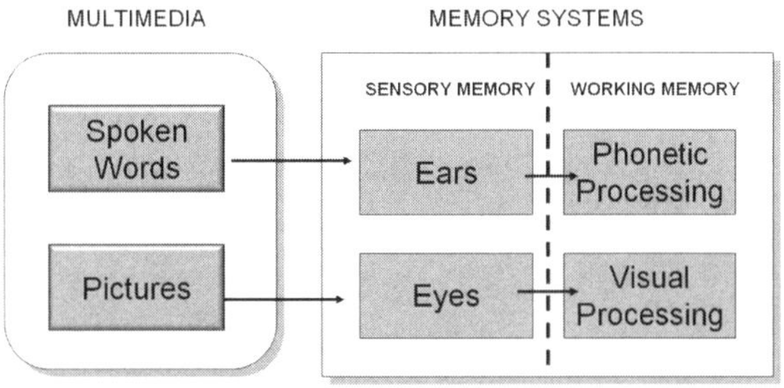

simultaneously. As you can see in Figure 6.5, there would be no overload in the visual channel if words were presented as on-screen text in the absence of concurrent graphics that required the learner's simultaneous attention.

Evidence for Using Spoken Rather Than Printed Text

Do students learn more deeply from graphics with speech (for example, narrated animation) than from graphics with on-screen text (for example, animation with on-screen text blocks), as suggested by cognitive theory? Researchers have examined this question in several different ways, and the results consistently support our recommendation. Let's consider several studies that compare multimedia lessons containing animation with concurrent narration versus animation with concurrent on-screen text, in which the words in the narration and on-screen text are identical. Some of the multimedia lessons present an explanation of how lightning forms, how a car's braking system works, or how an electric motor works (Craig, Gholson, & Driscoll, 2002; Mayer, Dow, & Mayer, 2003; Mayer & Moreno, 1998; Moreno & Mayer, 1999a). Others are embedded in an interactive game intended to teach botany (Moreno, Mayer, Spires, & Lester, 2001; Moreno & Mayer 2002b), and a final set are part of a virtual reality training episode concerning the operation of an aircraft fuel system (O'Neil, Mayer, Herl, Niemi, Olin, & Thurman, 2000).

Figure 6.7. Screens from Lightning Lesson Explained with Audio Narration.
From Moreno and Mayer, 1999a.

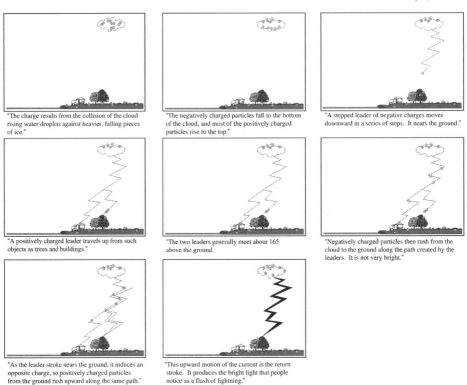

"The charge results from the collision of the cloud rising water droplets against heavier, falling pieces of ice."

"The negatively charged particles fall to the bottom of the cloud, and most of the positively charged particles rise to the top."

"A stepped leader of negative charges moves downward in a series of steps. It nears the ground."

"A positively charged leader travels up from such objects as trees and buildings."

"The two leaders generally meet about 165 above the ground.

"Negatively charged particles then rush from the cloud to the ground along the path created by the leaders. It is not very bright."

"As the leader stroke nears the ground, it induces an opposite charge, so positively charged particles from the ground rush upward along the same path."

"This upward motion of the current is the return stroke. It produces the bright light that people notice as a flash of lightning."

For example, in one study (Moreno & Mayer, 1999a) students viewed an animation depicting the steps in lightning formation along with concurrent narration (Figure 6.7) or concurrent on-screen text captions (Figure 6.8). The words in the narration and the on-screen text were identical, and they were presented at the same point in the animation. On a subsequent test in which students had to solve transfer problems about lightning, the animation-with-narration group produced more than twice as many solutions to the problems as compared to the animation-with-text group, yielding an effect size greater than 1. The results are summarized in Figure 6.9. We refer to this finding as the modality effect—people learn more deeply from multimedia lessons when words explaining concurrent graphics are presented as speech rather than as on-screen text.

Figure 6.8. Screens from Lightning Lesson Explained with On-Screen Text.

From Moreno and Mayer, 1999a.

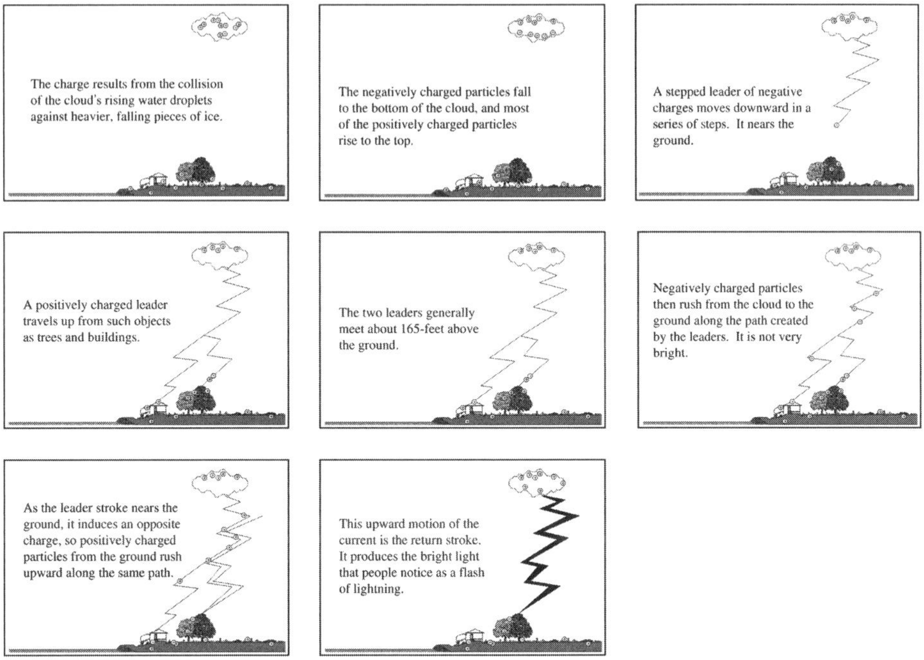
The charge results from the collision of the cloud's rising water droplets against heavier, falling pieces of ice.
The negatively charged particles fall to the bottom of the cloud, and most of the positively charged particles rise to the top.
A stepped leader of negative charges moves downward in a series of steps. It nears the ground.
A positively charged leader travels up from such objects as trees and buildings.
The two leaders generally meet about 165-feet above the ground.
Negatively charged particles then rush from the cloud to the ground along the path created by the leaders. It is not very bright.
As the leader stroke nears the ground, it induces an opposite charge, so positively charged particles from the ground rush upward along the same path.
This upward motion of the current is the return stroke. It produces the bright light that people notice as a flash of lightning.

Figure 6.9. Better Learning When Visuals Are Explained with Audio Narration.

From Marino and Mayer, 1999a.

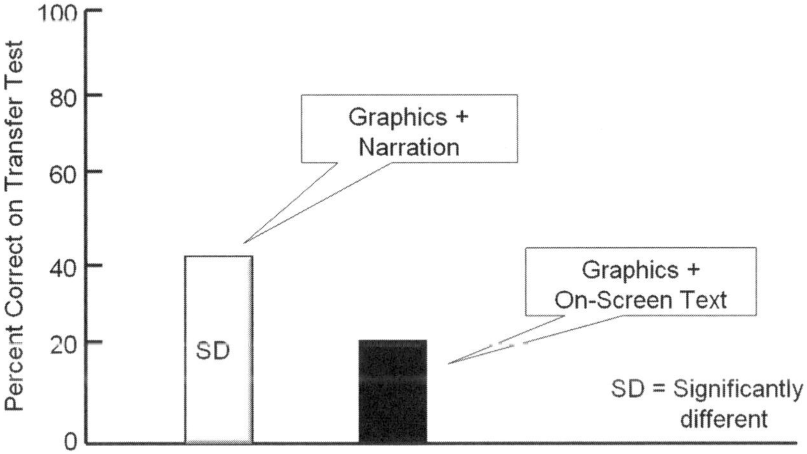
100
80
60
40
20
0
Percent Correct on Transfer Test
Graphics + Narration
SD
Graphics + On-Screen Text
SD = Significantly different

Figure 6.10. Responses to Questions in Audio Narration (A) or in On-Screen Text (B).

From Mayer, Dow, and Mayer, 2003.

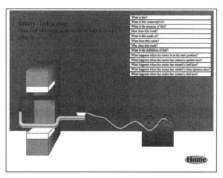

Select a Question

Response A

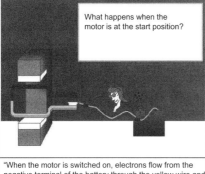

Response B

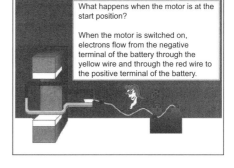

In a more interactive environment aimed at explaining how an electric motor works, students could click on various questions and for each see a short animated answer along with narration or printed text delivered by a character named Dr. Phyz (Mayer, Dow, & Mayer, 2003). In the frame on the right side of the top screen in Figure 6.10, suppose the student clicks the question, "What happens when the motor is in the start position?" As a result, the students in the animation-with-text group see an animation along with on-screen text, as exemplified in the B frame on the bottom right side of Figure 6.10. In contrast, students in the animation-with-narration group see the same animation and hear the same words in spoken form as narration as in the A frame on the bottom left side of Figure 6.10. Students who received narration generated 29 percent more solutions on a subsequent problem-solving transfer test, yielding an effect size of .85.

A more recent study found that the modality effect applies to students in a high school setting. The students learned better from web-based biology lessons that contained illustrations and narration than for lessons containing illustrations and on-screen text (Harskamp, Mayer, & Suhre, 2007). Replicating the modality effect in a more naturalistic environment such as a high school class boosts our confidence that the guidelines derived from laboratory studies apply to real-world learning environments.

Consistent with cognitive theory, recent eye-tracking studies found that students who viewed animation with narration on lightning formation spent more time looking at the graphics than did students who received animations with on-screen text (Schmidt-Weigand, Kohnert, & Glowalla, 2010a, 2010b). When graphics were described by on-screen text, students were largely guided by the text so processing of the graphics suffered.

Also consistent with cognitive theory, researchers have found that the modality effect is stronger for less-skilled learners than for more-skilled learners (Seufert, Schutze, & Brunken, 2009).

In a review of research on modality, Mayer (2005c) identified twenty-one experimental comparisons of learning from printed text and graphics versus learning from narration and graphics, based on published research articles. The lessons included topics in mathematics, electrical engineering, environmental science, and aircraft maintenance as well as explanations of how brakes work, how lightning storms develop, and how an electric motor works. In each of the twenty-one comparisons, there was a modality effect in which students who received narration and graphics performed better on solving transfer problems than did students who received on-screen text and graphics. The median effect size was .97, which is considered a large effect. Based on the growing evidence for the modality effect, we feel confident in recommending the use of spoken rather than printed words in multimedia messages containing graphics with related descriptive words.

In a somewhat more lenient review that included both published articles and unpublished sources (such as conference papers and theses) and a variety of learning measures, Ginns (2005) found forty-three experimental tests of the modality principle. Overall, there was strong evidence for the modality effect, yielding an average effect size of .72, which is considered moderate to large. Importantly, the positive effect of auditory modality was stronger for more complex material than for less complex material, and stronger for computer-controlled pacing than for learner-controlled pacing. Apparently, in situations that are more likely to require heavy amounts of essential cognitive processing to comprehend the material—that is, lessons with complex material or fast pacing—it is particularly important to use instructional designs that minimize the need for extraneous processing.

When the Modality Principle Applies

Does the modality principle mean that you should never use printed text? The simple answer to this question is: Of course not. We do not intend for you to use our recommendations as unbending rules that must be rigidly applied in all situations. Instead, we encourage you to apply our principles in ways that are consistent with the way that the human mind works—that is, consistent with the cognitive theory of multimedia learning rather than the information delivery theory. As noted earlier, the modality principle applies in situations in which you present graphics and their verbal commentary at the same time, and particularly, when the material is complex and presented at a rapid continuous pace. If the material is easy for the learner or the learner has control over the pacing of the material, the modality principle becomes less important.

As we noted previously, in some cases words should remain available to the learner over time—particularly, when the words are technical, unfamiliar, not in the learner's native language, lengthy, or needed for future reference. For example, when you present technical terms, list key steps in a procedure, or are giving directions to a practice exercise, it is important to present words in writing for reference support. When the learner is not a native speaker of the language of instruction or is extremely unfamiliar with the material, it may be appropriate to present printed text. Further, if you present only printed words on the screen (without any corresponding graphic) then the modality principle does not apply. Finally, in some situations people may learn better from multimedia lessons that have a few well-placed printed words along with spoken words, as we describe in the next chapter on the redundancy principle.

What We Don't Know About Modality

Overall, our goal in applying the modality principle is to reduce the cognitive load in the learner's visual/pictorial channel (that is, through the eyes) by off-loading some of the cognitive processing onto the auditory/verbal channel (that is, through the ears). Some unresolved issues concern:

1. When is it helpful to put printed words on the screen with a concurrent graphic?

2. Is it helpful to put concise summaries or labels for key components on the screen as printed words?

3. When it is not feasible to provide audio, how can we eliminate any negative effects of on-screen text?

4. Do the negative effects of on-screen text decline over the course of long-term training?

DESIGN DILEMMA: RESOLVED

The Excel design team was in a quandary about use of text and audio in their course. The options presented were:

A. Reshmi and Matt are right. There are many advantages to communicating words as on-screen text.

B. Michael is right. Learning is much better when words are presented in audio narration.

C. Everyone can be accommodated by providing words in both text and audio.

D. Not sure which options are correct.

We recommend that audio narration will promote better learning on screens that include important and detailed graphics as shown in Figure 6.3. Therefore we select Option B. Although Option C might seem like a good compromise, as we will see in the next chapter, using both text and audio to explain a graphic can be problematic. Some elements in the Excel lesson should be presented as text, such as unfamiliar terms and directions for practice exercises.

WHAT TO LOOK FOR IN e-LEARNING

☐ Use of audio narration to explain on-screen graphics or animations

☐ Use of text for information that learners will need as reference, such as technical terms or directions to practice exercises

---

COMING NEXT

In this chapter we have seen that learning is improved when graphics or animations presented in e-lessons are explained using audio narration rather than on-screen text. What would be the impact of including both text and narration? In other words, would learning be improved if narration were used to read on-screen text? We will address this issue in the next chapter.

Suggested Readings

Ginns, P. (2005). Meta-analysis of the modality effect. *Learning and Instruction, 15,* 313–331.

Harskamp, E.G., Mayer, R.E., & Suhre, C. (2007). Does the modality principle for multimedia learning apply to science classrooms? *Learning and Instruction, 17,* 465–477.

Low, R., & Sweller, J. (2005). The modality effect in multimedia learning. In R. E. Mayer (Ed.), *The Cambridge handbook of multimedia learning* (pp. 147–158). New York: Cambridge University Press.

Mayer, R.E. (2005c). Principles for managing essential processing in multimedia learning: Segmenting, pretraining, and modality principles. In R.E. Mayer (Ed.), *The Cambridge handbook of multimedia learning* (pp. 147–158). New York: Cambridge University Press.

Mayer, R.E., & Moreno, R. (1998). A split-attention effect in multimedia learning: Evidence for dual processing systems in working memory. *Journal of Educational Psychology, 90,* 312–320.

Moreno, R., & Mayer, R.E. (1999a). Cognitive principles of multimedia learning: The role of modality and contiguity. *Journal of Educational Psychology, 91,* 358–368.

CHAPTER OUTLINE

7

Applying the Redundancy Principle

EXPLAIN VISUALS WITH WORDS IN AUDIO
OR TEXT: NOT BOTH

WHAT'S NEW IN THIS CHAPTER

SOME e-LEARNING DESCRIBES graphics using words in both on-screen text and audio narration in which the audio repeats the text. We call this technique *redundant* on-screen text because the printed text (the on-screen text) is redundant with the spoken text (the narration or audio). In this chapter, we summarize empirical evidence that people learn better from concurrent graphics and audio than from concurrent graphics, audio, and on-screen text. In this chapter we update research and theory that has appeared since the previous edition of this book, but the overall message remains the same: In general, do not add printed text to a narrated graphic. The psychological advantage of presenting words in audio alone is that you avoid overloading the visual channel of working memory. There are also certain situations that benefit from the use of redundant on-screen text, which we call *boundary conditions*. We describe those here as well, including new boundary conditions discovered since the previous edition.

DESIGN DILEMMA: YOU DECIDE

Now that the Excel e-learning design team has decided to add relevant visuals, as described in Chapter 4, their focus is on how best to explain those visuals. Reshmi, the instructional designer, recommends explaining visuals with a combination of text and audio: "I've reviewed the latest storyboards and I'm concerned. We know some people have visual learning styles and some are auditory learners so we need to accommodate both. Also 508 compliance requires us to accommodate learners who have visual and hearing deficits. So we have to provide words in a visual format with on-screen text and also in an auditory format with narration of that text. That way we cover all our bases!" Figure 7.1 shows one of Reshmi's revised storyboards.

Figure 7.1. Visual Described by On-Screen Text and Narration.

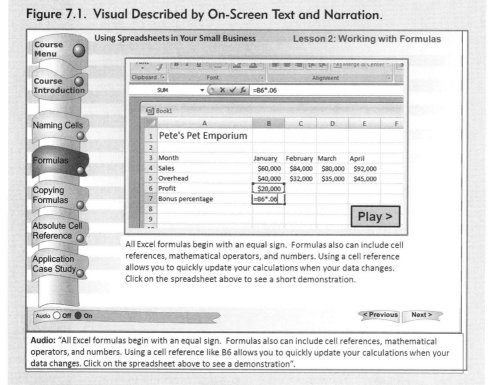

Charlene, the graphic artist who has been contracted to help with visuals, protests: "We've discussed this issue before and we decided to go with audio narration to describe the visuals. I've designed large visuals and there is no screen real estate reserved for lengthy text passages!" Based on your experience or intuition which options are best:

A. Communicate words in both on-screen text and audio narration to accommodate different learning styles and to meet 508 compliance.

B. Explain visuals with audio alone to promote best learning per the modality principle described in Chapter 6.

C. Let the learner select either audio or text as part of the course introduction.

D. Not sure which options are correct.

Redundancy Principle 1: Do Not Add On-Screen Text to Narrated Graphics

If you are planning a multimedia program consisting of graphics (such as animation, video, or even static pictures or photos) explained by narration, should you also include on-screen text that duplicates the audio? We explore this question in this section.

Based on research and theory in cognitive psychology, we recommend that you avoid e-learning courses that contain redundant on-screen text presented at the same time as on-screen graphics and narration. Our reason is that learners might pay so much attention to the printed words that they pay less attention to the accompanying graphics. When their eyes are on the printed words, learners cannot be looking at the on-screen graphics. In addition, learners may try to compare and reconcile on-screen text and the narration, which requires cognitive processing extraneous to learning the content. For example, Figure 7.2 shows a screen from a lesson on ammunition safety that uses video to illustrate an explosion. Note that the on-screen text is the same as the narration, so we call it *redundant* on-screen text. In contrast, Figure 7.3 shows a screen from an animated demonstration of how to use a new computerized telephone system. The procedural steps are narrated with audio. Note the absence of on-screen text that duplicates the narration.

Figure 7.2. Graphics Explained Using Identical Text and Audio
Narration.

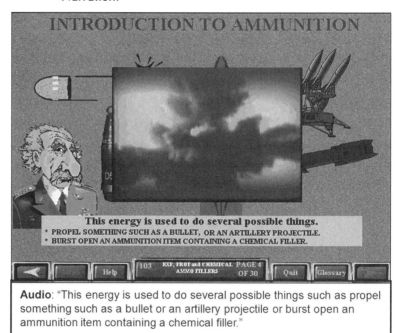

Audio: "This energy is used to do several possible things such as propel something such as a bullet or an artillery projectile or burst open an ammunition item containing a chemical filler."

Figure 7.3. Graphics Explained Using Audio Alone.

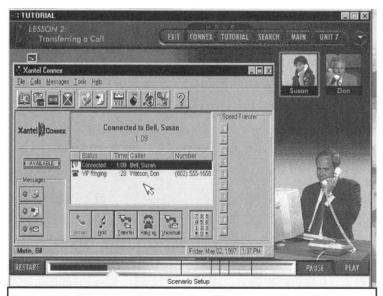

Audio: While Bill is talking to Don, Julie calls with a question. Bill knows that Julie needs to talk to Sally in the Art Department and decides to transfer her while he is talking to Don.

Psychological Reasons for the Redundancy Principle

There is a common belief that some people have visual learning styles, while others have auditory learning styles. Therefore, it seems that words should always be presented in both spoken and printed form so learners can choose the presentation format that best matches their learning preferences. We call this idea the *learning styles hypothesis* because it plays on the common sense argument that instruction should be flexible enough to support different learning styles. Accommodating different learning styles may seem appealing to e-learning designers who are fed up with the "one-size-fits-all" approach and to clients who intuitively believe there are visual and auditory learners.

The learning styles hypothesis is based on the information acquisition theory of multimedia learning, which holds that learning consists of receiving information. In our Design Dilemma section, the multimedia lesson illustrated in Figure 7.1 provides three delivery routes for information—by pictures (in the illustrations), by spoken words (in the narration), and by written words (in the on-screen text). In contrast, you could drop the third route and describe graphics with words in audio—but not with words both in audio and on-screen text. According to the information acquisition theory, three ways of delivering the same information is better than two, especially if one or two of the routes do not work well for some learners. Therefore, the information acquisition theory predicts that students will learn more deeply from multimedia presentations when redundant on-screen text is included rather than excluded.

The learning styles view—and the information acquisition theory upon which it is built—seems to make sense, but let's look a little deeper. What's wrong with the information acquisition theory? Our major criticism is that it makes unwarranted assumptions about how people learn. For example, it assumes that people learn by adding information to memory, as if the mind were an empty vessel that needs to be filled with incoming information.

Another major problem with the learning styles view is that it is not supported by the available research evidence. In a recent review of the scientific research evidence on adapting instruction to learning styles, Pashler, McDaniel, Rohrer, and Bjork (2008) were unable to find evidence that visualizers learn better with visual forms of instruction and verbalizers learn better with verbal modes of instruction. The lack of empirical support for the learning styles view led them to conclude: "The contrast between the enormous popularity of the learning-styles approach within education and the lack of credible evidence for its utility is, in our opinion, striking and disturbing" (p. 117).

In contrast to the information acquisition view, the cognitive theory of multimedia learning is based on the assumptions that (1) all people have separate channels for processing verbal and pictorial material, (2) each channel is limited in the amount of processing that can take place at one time, and (3) learners actively attempt to build pictorial and verbal models from the presented material and build connections between them. These assumptions are consistent with theory and research in cognitive science and represent a consensus view of how people learn.

According to the cognitive theory of multimedia, adding redundant on-screen text to a multimedia presentation could overload the visual channel. For example, Figure 7.4 summarizes the cognitive activities that occur for a presentation containing animation, narration, and concurrent on-screen text. As you can see, the animation enters the learner's cognitive system through the eyes and is processed in the visual/pictorial channel, whereas the narration enters the learner's cognitive system through the ears and is processed in the auditory/verbal channel. However, the on-screen text also enters through the eyes and must be processed (at least initially) in the visual/pictorial channel. Thus, the limited cognitive resources in the visual channel must be shared in processing both the animation and the printed text. If the pace of presentation is fast and learners are unfamiliar with the material, learners may experience cognitive overload in

Figure 7.4. Overloading of Visual Channel with Graphics Explained by Words in Audio and Written Text.

Adapted from Mayer, 2001a.

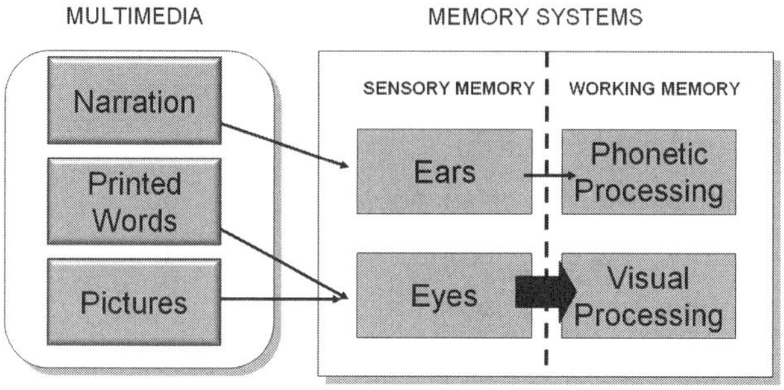

the visual/pictorial channel. As a result, some important aspects of the animation may not be selected and organized into a mental representation.

Now, consider what happens when only narration and animation are presented. The animation enters through the eyes and is processed in the visual/pictorial channel, whereas the narration enters through the ears and is processed in the auditory/verbal channel. The chances for overload are minimized, so the learner is more able to engage in appropriate cognitive processing. Thus, the cognitive theory of multimedia learning predicts that learners will learn more deeply from multimedia presentations in which redundant on-screen text is excluded rather than included.

Mayer and Moreno (2003) and Mayer (2005b) describe another potential problem with adding redundant on-screen text. Learners may waste precious cognitive resources in trying to compare the printed words with the spoken words as they are presented. We refer to this wasted cognitive processing as *extraneous cognitive processing*. According to the cognitive theory of multimedia learning, learners have limited cognitive capacity, so if they use their cognitive capacity to reconcile printed and spoken text, they can't use it to make sense of the presentation.

Evidence for Omitting Redundant On-Screen Text

Several researchers have put these two competing predictions to a test. In a set of studies (Craig, Gholson, & Driscoll, 2002; Mayer, Heiser, & Lonn, 2001; Moreno & Mayer, 2002a), some students (non-redundant group) viewed an animation and listened to a concurrent narration explaining the formation of lightning. Other students (redundant group) received the same multimedia presentation, but with concurrent, redundant on-screen text. In this series of four comparisons, students in the non-redundant group produced more solutions (ranging between 43 to 69 percent more) on a problem-solving transfer test than did students in the redundant group. The median effect size was greater than 1, which is considered to be large. Figure 7.5 shows the results from one of these studies.

Kalyuga, Chandler, and Sweller (1999, 2000) provide complementary evidence. One group (non-redundant) received training in soldering (that is, techniques for joining metals) through the use of static diagrams presented on

Figure 7.5. Better Learning When Visuals Are Explained by Audio Alone.

From Moreno and Mayer, 1999a.

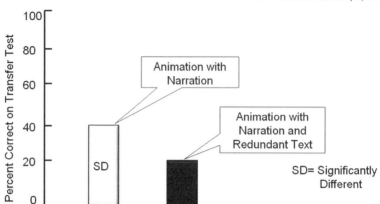

a computer screen along with accompanying speech, whereas another group (redundant group) received the same training along with on-screen printed text duplicating the same words as the audio. On a problem-solving transfer test involving troubleshooting, the non-redundant group outperformed the redundant group—producing an effect size of .8 in one study and greater than 1 in another. Kalyuga, Chandler, and Sweller (2004) found similar results in three additional experiments involving technical trainees learning how to set controls on power machinery for cutting. In this case, simply presenting the text after presenting the narration resulted in better test performance than presenting them at the same time, yielding a median effect size of .8.

More recently, Jamet and Le Bohec (2007) presented an eleven-minute online slide presentation on human memory that consisted of illustrations with auditory explanation (non-redundant group) or the same lesson with onscreen text that was presented either sentence-by-sentence sequentially along with the narration (sequential redundant text group) or all at once on each slide (full text redundant group). The lesson was fast-paced and under system control. On a subsequent transfer test, the non-redundant group performed much better than the redundant groups, with effect sizes in the medium to large range (.72 for sequential text and .63 for full text).

Finally, Moreno and Mayer (2002b) also found a redundancy effect within the context of an educational computer game both when played on a desktop computer and within a virtual reality version using a head-mounted display. An on-screen agent explained the mechanics of plant growth using speech or speech and on-screen text while an animation was presented. Although students who received animation and narration performed better on subsequent tests than did students who learned with animation, narration, and on-screen text, the effect sizes were much smaller—approximately .2, which is considered a small effect. Perhaps students were better able to ignore some of the on-screen text in the game environment, although it was still a mild detriment to learning.

Mayer (2005b) refers to this result as a *redundancy effect* to reflect the idea that adding redundant on-screen text to narrated graphics tends to hurt learning. Overall, these kinds of results support the conclusion that, in some cases, less is more. Because of the limited capacity of the human information processing system, it can be better to present less material (graphics with corresponding narration) than more material (graphics with corresponding narration and printed text). Some important boundary conditions for obtaining the redundancy effect are that the multimedia lesson is fast-paced, the words are familiar, and a lot of words are presented on the screen. In other words, the negative effects of redundancy will be most evident when the multimedia program is system-controlled, includes words familiar to the target audience, and incorporates a lot of on-screen text, as shown in Figure 7.1.

Redundancy Principle 2: Consider Adding On-Screen Text to Narration in Special Situations

Are there any situations in which e-learning courses would be improved by adding redundant on-screen text? Although we recommend omitting redundant on-screen text in most e-learning programs, consider using it in special situations that will not overload the learner's visual information processing system, such as when:

- There is no pictorial presentation (for example, when the screen contains no animation, video, photos, graphics, illustrations, and so on),

- There is ample opportunity to process the pictorial presentation (for example, when the on-screen text and corresponding graphics are presented sequentially or when the pace of presentation is sufficiently slow), or

- The learner must exert much greater cognitive effort to comprehend spoken text than printed text (for example, for learners who are not native speakers or who have specific learning disabilities, or when the verbal material is long and complex or contains unfamiliar key words).

- Only a few selected key words are presented next to the element in the graphic they describe.

REDUNDANT ON-SCREEN TEXT: WHEN TO LOSE IT AND WHEN TO USE IT

Avoid narrating on-screen text when:

Words and pictures are presented simultaneously at a fast pace

Consider narrating on-screen text when:

There are no pictures
The learner has ample time to process the pictures and words
The learner is likely to have difficulty processing spoken words
A few key words are presented next to the corresponding part of the picture

For example, Figure 7.6 is an introductory screen that presents the learning objectives of a multimedia lesson. Since there are no graphic illustrations, narration of the objectives presented in text on the screen should not depress learning. As described in Chapter 6, situations in which learners need to refer to information over time (such as directions to exercises) are best presented as text alone.

Psychological Reasons for Exceptions to the Redundancy Principle

The major exceptions to the redundancy principle occur in special situations in which on-screen text either does not add to the learner's processing demands or actually diminishes them. For example, consider the situation

Figure 7.6. When No Visuals Are Present, Content Can Be Presented with Text and Redundant Narration.

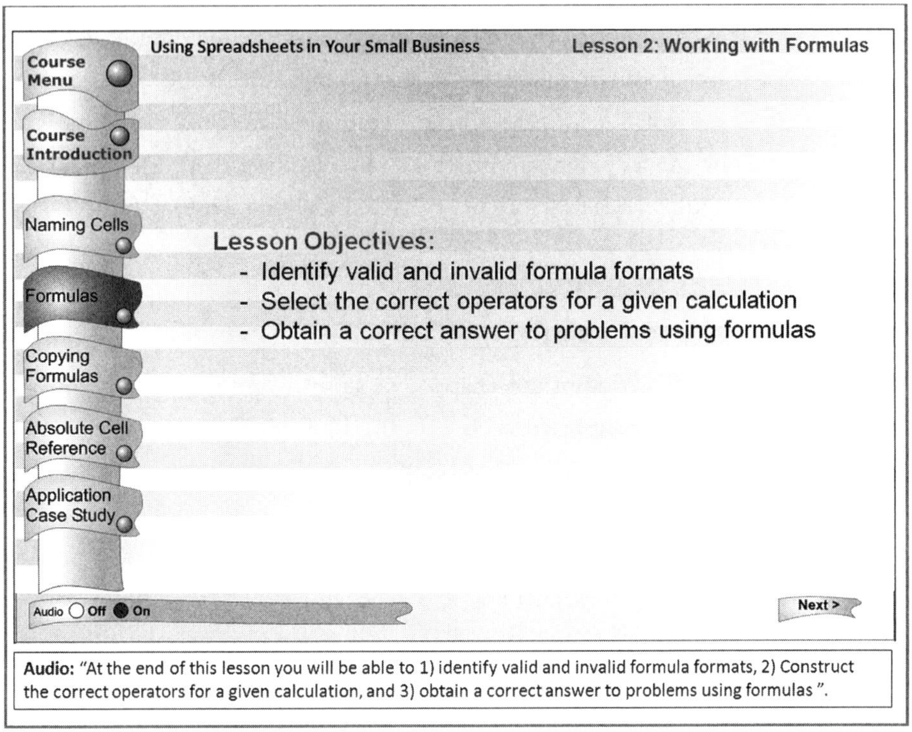

| Using Spreadsheets in Your Small Business | Lesson 2: Working with Formulas |

Course Menu

Course Introduction

Naming Cells

Formulas

Copying Formulas

Absolute Cell Reference

Application Case Study

Lesson Objectives:
- Identify valid and invalid formula formats
- Select the correct operators for a given calculation
- Obtain a correct answer to problems using formulas

Audio ○ Off ● On   Next >

Audio: "At the end of this lesson you will be able to 1) identify valid and invalid formula formats, 2) Construct the correct operators for a given calculation, and 3) obtain a correct answer to problems using formulas ".

in which an instructional presentation consists solely of spoken words with no graphics—such as in a podcast. In this case, information enters through the ears so the verbal channel is active, but the visual channel is not active. Now, consider what happens in the learner's cognitive system when you use redundant on-screen text, for example, presented as text on a computer screen using the same words as the narration. In this case, spoken words enter through the ears and text words enter through the eyes, so neither channel is overloaded. Using dual modes of presentation can be helpful when the spoken material may be hard to process, or if seeing and hearing the words provides a benefit (such as learning a technical subject or a foreign language).

Similarly, consider a situation in which the lesson is presented at a slow pace or is under learner control. For example, presenting concurrent narration, on-screen text, and static graphics under learner control is less likely to cause cognitive overload in the visual channel, because the learner has time to process all of the incoming material. Similarly, printing unfamiliar technical terms on the screen may actually reduce cognitive processing because the learner does not need to grapple with decoding the spoken words. Finally. printing a few key words next to the corresponding part of graphic can aid cognitive processing by directing the learner's attention—a technique than is called *signaling* (Mayer, 2005b, 2009).

Evidence for Including Redundant On-Screen Text

In the first section of this chapter, we summarized research in which people learned less about the process of lightning formation when the presentation included animation with redundant on-screen text than when the presentation included animation with concurrent narration alone. In this section, we explore special situations in which adding redundant on-screen text has been shown to help learning.

Research shows that in certain situations learners generate approximately three times as many correct answers on a problem-solving transfer test from presentations containing concurrent spoken and printed text than from spoken text alone (Moreno & Mayer, 2002a). In these studies there were no graphics on the screen and thus the visual system was not overloaded. In another study, the animation presentation was broken into a series of sixteen short animation clips, with each clip preceded by a corresponding sentence. Thus, the learner sees and hears a sentence, then views ten seconds of animation corresponding to it, then sees and hears the next sentence, then views ten seconds of corresponding animation, and so on. In this way, the learner can view the animation without any interference from printed text. In this situation, learners who received redundant on-screen text and spoken text generated an average of 79 percent more correct answers on a problem-solving test than learners who received only spoken text (Moreno & Mayer, 2002a). Of course, this choppy sequential presentation is somewhat unusual and therefore is not likely to be applicable to most e-learning situations.

More recently, Mayer and Johnson (2008) compared the learning outcomes of students who learned about lightning formation or brakes from an online slide presentation with illustrations and narration (non-redundant) or the same lesson with each slide containing a few printed words placed next to the corresponding part of the illustration (redundant group). For example, in the first slide of the lightning passage, the voice says "Cool moist air moves over a warmer surface and becomes heated" and the redundant group also saw the text "Air becomes heated" on the slide next to wavy lines that represent moving air. In two experiments, the redundant group significantly outperformed the non-redundant group on retention and performed no worse on transfer. Based on this finding, Mayer and Johnson (2008, p. 380) called for "revising the redundancy principle" to allow for short amounts of printed text to be placed next to the corresponding part of the graphic. As an example, in Figure 7.7 a technical lesson on engine maintenance uses brief text callouts along with descriptive audio.

Figure 7.7. Use of Audio and Text Callouts Can Benefit Learning.

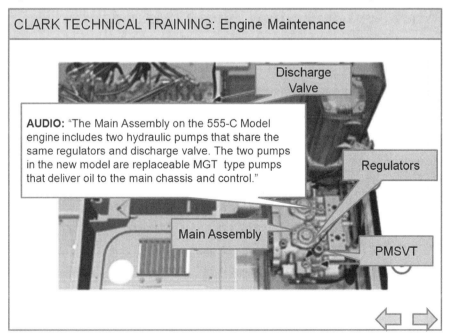

Based on the research and theory presented in this chapter, we offer the redundancy principle: When the instructional message includes graphics, explain the graphics with narration alone. Do not add redundant on-screen text. However, there are important boundary conditions: When there is limited graphic information on the screen or when the words are technical or the audience has language difficulties or the printed words are unobtrusive, consider the use of redundant on-screen text. As described in Chapter 6, use on-screen text without narration to present information that needs to be referenced over time, such as directions to complete a practice exercise.

Overall, the theme of this chapter is that e-learning should not add redundant on-screen text (that is, the same words that are being spoken) when attending to the text could distract the learner from viewing important graphics that are being presented at the same time. However, redundant printed and spoken words may be appropriate when there are no concurrent graphics, the text is unfamiliar to the learner, the printed words are unobtrusive, or you can use the printed words to signal where to look on the screen.

What We Don't Know About Redundancy

Research is needed to determine the situations in which the redundancy principle does not hold—including the kinds of learners, materials, and presentation methods that do not create a redundancy effect.

1. *Kinds of learners*—Does adding redundant on-screen text to a narrated graphic not hurt (or even help) non-native speakers or learners with very low prior knowledge?

2. *Kinds of material*—Does adding redundant on-screen text to a narrated graphic not hurt (or even help) when the on-screen material is technical terms, equations, or brief headings?

3. *Kinds of presentation methods*—Does adding redundant on-screen text to a narrated graphic not hurt (or even help) when the presentation pace is slow, when the presentation pace is under learner

control, when the narration precedes the on-screen text, or when the learner is given pre-training in names and characteristics of the key concepts?

It would be particularly helpful to pinpoint situations in which some form of redundancy helps learning.

DESIGN DILEMMA: RESOLVED

The Excel team members disagreed about how best to describe the visuals they decided to add. To accommodate the modality principle described in Chapter 6, they decided to use audio. But some team members wanted to also add on-screen text to accommodate different learning styles and to meet 508 compliance. The options were:

A. Communicate words in both on-screen text and audio narration to accommodate different learning styles and to give multiple learning opportunities.

B. Explain visuals with audio alone to promote best learning per the modality principle described in Chapter 6.

C. Let the learner select either audio or text as part of the course introduction.

D. Not sure which options are correct.

It's a common misconception that learning is better from adding redundant on-screen text to audio that describes visuals. However, we have reviewed evidence in this chapter that learning is generally improved by using audio alone to describe graphics. Therefore, we select Option B. However, what about 508 compliance? We recommend that your e-learning program default to audio describing visuals. However, to accommodate learners who for various reasons may not be able to access audio, offer an "audio off" button. When the "audio off" button is activated, narration is replaced by on-screen text, as shown in Figure 7.8. In this arrangement the learner receives words in audio narration as the default but can also access words via text when audio is turned off. However they do not have the option for *both* audio narration and text of that narration.

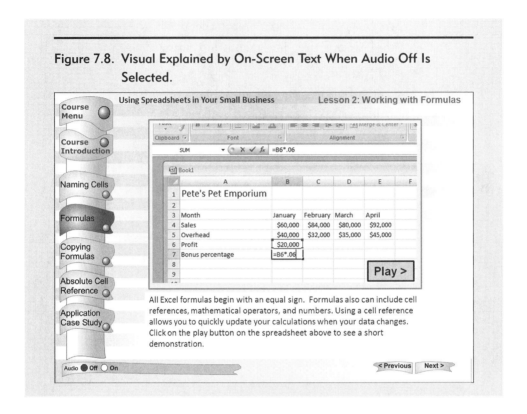

Figure 7.8. Visual Explained by On-Screen Text When Audio Off Is Selected.

WHAT TO LOOK FOR IN e-LEARNING

☐ Graphics are described by words presented in the form of audio narration, not by concurrent narration and redundant text.

☐ On-screen text can be narrated when the screens do not include graphics.

☐ When language is challenging, words are presented as text.

☐ Short text labels are expanded with audio narration.

COMING NEXT

In the previous four chapters we have described a number of principles for best use of text, audio, and graphics in e-learning. We have seen that the appropriate use of these media elements can improve learning. However, there are circumstances when too much of these elements can actually depress learning. In the next chapter we review how to apply the *coherence* principle to your e-learning decisions.

Suggested Readings

Jamet, E., & Bohec, O. (2007). The effect of redundant text in multimedia instruction. *Contemporary Educational Psychology, 32*, 588–598.

Mayer, R.E. (2005c). Principles for reducing extraneous processing in multimedia learning: Coherence, signaling, redundancy, spatial contiguity, and temporal contiguity. In R.E. Mayer (Ed.), *The Cambridge handbook of multimedia learning* (pp. 183–200). New York: Cambridge University Press.

Mayer, R.E., Heiser, J., & Lonn, S. (2001). Cognitive constraints on multimedia learning: When presenting more material results in less understanding. *Journal of Educational Psychology, 93*, 187–198.

Mayer, R.E., & Johnson, C.I. (2008). Revising the redundancy principle in multimedia learning. *Journal of Educational Psychology, 100*, 380–386.

Moreno, R., & Mayer, R.E. (2002a). Verbal redundancy in multimedia learning: When reading helps listening. *Journal of Educational Psychology, 94*, 151–163.

CHAPTER OUTLINE

8

Applying the Coherence Principle

ADDING MATERIAL CAN HURT LEARNING

PERHAPS OUR SINGLE MOST IMPORTANT recommendation is to keep the lesson uncluttered. In short, according to the coherence principle, you should avoid adding any material that does not support the instructional goal. The *coherence principle* is important because it is commonly violated, is straightforward to apply, and can have a strong impact on learning. Mayer and Moreno (2003) use the term *weeding* to refer to the need to uproot any words, graphics, or sounds that are not central to the instructional goal of the lesson. In spite of our calls for conciseness, you might be tempted to embellish lessons in an effort to motivate learners. For example, in order to counter high e-learning dropout rates, some designers attempt to spice up their materials by adding entertaining or motivational elements such as dramatic stories, pictures, or background music. Our advice is: *Don't do it!* In this chapter we summarize the empirical evidence for *excluding* rather than including extraneous information in the form of background sound, added text, and added graphics. What is new in this chapter is some updating of the growing research base, but the main conclusion remains the same: Adding interesting but unnecessary material to e-learning can harm the learning process.

DESIGN DILEMMA: YOU DECIDE

"This spreadsheet lesson is pretty boring. We are dealing with the YouTube and videogame generation here. They are used to high-intensity multimedia. But don't worry! I've added some really important information that everyone should know about spreadsheets and I've energized the information with some visual effects. Take a look at this example. On this screen (Figure 8.1), I'm giving them some key historical information about the evolution of electronic spreadsheets."

Ben, the team programmer, has challenged the idea of a simple e-learning program—especially for younger learners. Reshmi, the instructional designer agrees:

Figure 8.1. A Screen to Add Interest to the Excel Lesson.

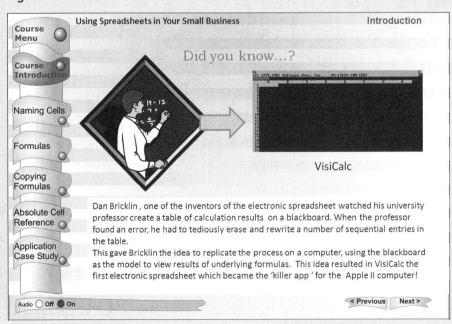

"Ben is right. We know that dropout rates from asynchronous e-learning are high. By adding some interesting information about spreadsheets throughout the lesson, we can hold everyone's interest. In fact, I learned in an accelerated learning class that soft background classical music helps people retain information better. Could we add a soft instrumental to the narration?"

Matt, the project manager, interjects: "How much will the extra visual and audio effects add to the budget and delay our timeline?" Shouldn't we just stick to the basics?" Based on your intuition or experience, which of the following options do you choose:

A. Ben is correct. Adding some interesting words and visuals will improve interest and learning—especially among younger learners.

B. Reshmi is correct. Learning is better in the presence of soft music—especially classical music.

C. Matt is right. Less is more for most learners.

D. Everyone is correct. Different learners benefit from different instructional methods.

The added sounds, graphics, and words such as those in Figure 8.1 are examples of *seductive details*, interesting but irrelevant material added to a multimedia presentation in an effort to spice it up (Garner, Gillingham, & White, 1989). The following three sections explore the merits of adding extra sounds, pictures, and words that are intended to make multimedia environments more interesting to the learner.

Coherence Principle 1: Avoid e-Lessons with Extraneous Audio

First, consider the addition of background music and sounds to a narrated animation. Is there any theoretical rationale for adding or not adding music and sounds, and is there any research evidence? These questions are addressed in this section.

Based on the psychology of learning and the research evidence summarized in the following paragraphs, we recommend that you avoid e-learning courseware that includes extraneous sounds in the form of background music or environmental sounds. Like all recommendations in this book, this one is limited. Recommendations should be applied based on an understanding of how people learn from words and pictures rather than a blind application of rules in all situations.

Background music and sounds may overload working memory, so they are most dangerous in situations in which the learner may experience heavy cognitive load, for example, when the material is unfamiliar, when the material is presented at a rapid rate, or when the rate of presentation is not under learner control. More research is needed to determine whether there are some situations in which the advantages of extraneous sounds outweigh the disadvantages. For example, in a review of twelve award-winning instructional

Figure 8.2. Sounds of Explosion and Bullets Added to Narration of On-Screen Text.

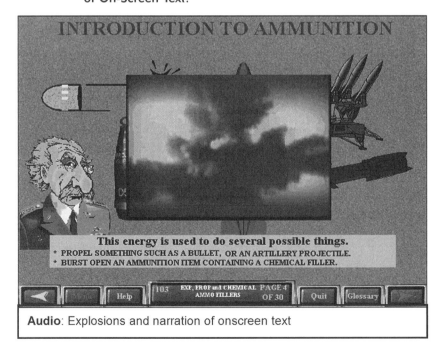

software products, Bishop, Amankwaita, and Cates (2008) found that sound was sometimes used to direct, focus, and hold the learner's attention and music was used to promote deeper processing—but there was no evidence of their effectiveness. Additionally, sound effects have been used to provide feedback in educational games (Mayer & Johnson, 2010)—but again there is not convincing evidence of their effectiveness. At this point, our recommendation is to avoid adding extraneous sounds or music to instructional presentations, especially in situations in which the learner is likely to experience heavy cognitive processing demands.

For example, Figure 8.2 shows a screen from a military multimedia lesson on ammunition. As the lesson illustrates the different types of ammunition that workers may encounter, background sounds such as bullets flying, bombs exploding, and tanks firing are included. These sounds are extraneous to the points being presented and are likely to prove distracting. Figure 8.3 shows

Figure 8.3. Learners Can Select Music During Course Introduction.

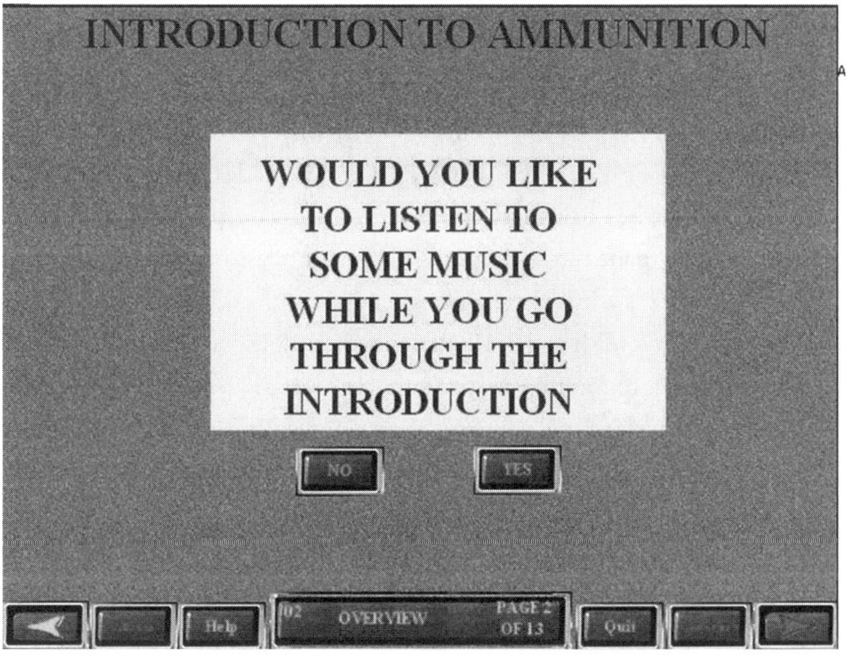

a screen from the same program that invites the learners to select the type of background music they want to hear during the course introduction. Again, the addition of extra sounds in the form of music is likely to depress learning.

Psychological Reasons to Avoid Extraneous Audio in e-Learning

For some learners e-learning can seem boring, and you might be concerned with reports that claim high dropout rates in e-learning (Svetcov, 2000). Therefore, developers may feel compelled to spice up their materials to arouse the learner's interest. Similarly, consumers may feel that a "jazzier" product is especially important for the new generation of learners raised on high intensity multimedia such as YouTube and videogames. This is the premise underlying arousal theory, the idea that entertaining and interesting embedded effects cause learners to become more emotionally aroused and therefore they work harder to learn the material. In short, the premise is that emotion (for example, arousal caused by emotion-grabbing elements) affects cognition (for example, higher cognitive engagement). Arousal theory predicts that students will learn more from multimedia presentations that contain interesting sounds and music than from multimedia presentations without interesting sounds and music.

Arousal theory seems to make sense, so is there anything wrong with it? As early as 1913, Dewey argued that adding interesting adjuncts to an otherwise boring lesson will not promote deep learning: "When things have to be made interesting, it is because interest itself is wanting. Moreover, the phrase is a misnomer. The thing, the object, is no more interesting than it was before" (pp. 11–12). The theoretical rationale against adding music and sounds to multimedia presentations is based on the cognitive theory of multimedia learning, which assumes that working memory capacity is highly limited. Background sounds can overload and disrupt the cognitive system, so the narration and the extraneous sounds must compete for limited cognitive resources in the auditory channel. When learners pay attention to sounds and music, they are less able to pay attention to the narration describing the relevant steps in the explanation. The cognitive theory of multimedia learning predicts that students will learn more deeply from multimedia presentations *that do not* contain interesting but extraneous sounds and music than from multimedia presentations that do.

Evidence for Omitting Extraneous Audio

Can we point to any research that examines extraneous sounds in a multimedia presentation? Moreno and Mayer (2000a) began with a three-minute narrated animation explaining the process of lightning formation and a forty-five-second narrated animation explaining how hydraulic braking systems work. They created a music version of each by adding a musical loop to the background. The music was an unobtrusive instrumental piece, played at low volume that did not mask the narration nor make it less perceptually discernable. Students who received the narrated animation remembered more of the presented material and scored higher on solving transfer problems than students who received the same narrated animation along with background music. The differences were substantial—ranging from 20 to 67 percent better scores without music—and consistent for both the lightning and brakes presentations. Clearly, adding background music did not improve learning, and in fact, substantially hurt learning.

Moreno and Mayer (2000a) also created a background sound version of the lightning and brakes presentations by adding environmental sounds. In the lightning presentation, the environmental sounds included the sound of a gentle wind (presented when the animation depicted air moving from the ocean to the land), a clinking sound (when the animation depicted the top portion of cloud forming ice crystals), and a crackling sound (when the animation depicted charges traveling between ground and cloud). In the brakes presentation, the environmental sounds included mechanical noises (when the animation depicted the piston moving forward in the master cylinder) and grinding sounds (when the animation depicted the brake shoe pressing against the brake drum). On the lightning presentation, students who received the narrated animation without environmental sounds performed as well on retention and transfer as students who received the narrated animation with environmental sounds; on the brakes presentation, students who received narrated animation performed better on retention and transfer than students who received the narrated animation with environmental sounds.

For both lightning and brakes presentations, when students received both background music and environmental sounds, their retention and transfer performance was much worse than when students received neither—ranging between 61 to 149 percent better performance without the extraneous sounds and music. The average percentage gain from all the studies was 105 percent, with a very high effect size of 1.66. Figure 8.4 shows a result from one of these studies.

Figure 8.4. Learning Is Better When Sounds and Music Are Excluded.

Adapted from Mayer, 2001a.

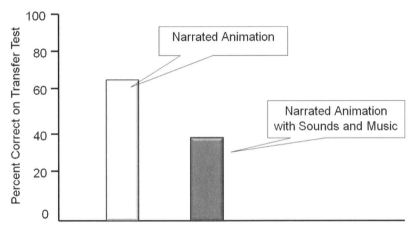

Related evidence points to the mental toll that can be levied by extraneous sounds. Knez and Hygge (2002) compared learning from a seven-page text read in a quiet environment with learning from reading the same text in the presence of irrelevant conversational background speech. Recall of text ideas was significantly better among those reading in a silent environment. Ransdell and Gilroy (2001) compared the quality and efficiency of essay writing in the presence of music (vocal and instrumental) with writing in a quiet environment. They found that the quality of the essays was similar in all conditions but that those working in the presence of music required significantly more time. To maintain quality, writers slow down their production in the presence of background music. The research team recommends that: "For all those college students who listen to music while they write on a computer, the advice from this study is clear. One's writing fluency is likely to be disrupted by both vocal and instrumental music" (p. 147).

Coherence Principle 2: Avoid e-Lessons with Extraneous Graphics

The previous section shows that learning is depressed when we add extraneous sounds to a multimedia presentation, so perhaps we should try another way to spice up our lessons, namely interspersing interesting video clips. For example, in a database lesson we could insert some news video discussing recent database thefts from government agency computers. What is the learning impact of adding related but not directly relevant pictures and video clips to e-learning lessons?

Based on what we know about human learning and the evidence we summarize next, we offer a second version of the coherence principle: Avoid adding extraneous pictures. This recommendation does not mean that interesting graphics are harmful in all situations. Rather, they are harmful to the extent that they can interfere with the learner's attempts to make sense of the presented material. Extraneous graphics can be distracting and disruptive of the learning process. In reviews of science and mathematics books, most illustrations were found to be irrelevant to the main theme of the accompanying lesson (Mayer, 1993; Mayer, Sims, & Tajika, 1995). In short, when pictures are used only to decorate the page or screen, they are not likely to improve learning. As an example, Figure 8.5 shows a screen from our sample pharmaceutical sales lesson that includes graphics and words about obesity—content related to the topic but distracting and irrelevant to the learning objective. Some of the information is quite interesting but not related to the knowledge and skills needed to effectively explain the product. We recommend excluding this type of information.

Figure 8.5. Interesting But Irrelevant-to-Learning Information
              Should Be Excluded.

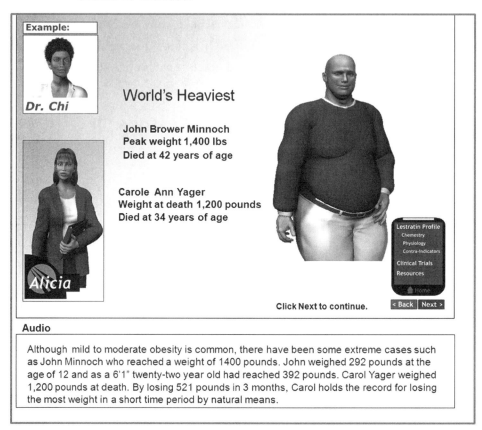

Although mild to moderate obesity is common, there have been some extreme cases such as John Minnoch who reached a weight of 1400 pounds. John weighed 292 pounds at the age of 12 and as a 6'1" twenty-two year old had reached 392 pounds. Carol Yager weighed 1,200 pounds at death. By losing 521 pounds in 3 months, Carol holds the record for losing the most weight in a short time period by natural means.

Psychological Reasons to Avoid Extraneous Graphics in e-Learning

Pictures—including color photos and action video clips—can make a multimedia experience more interesting. This assertion flows from arousal theory—the idea that students learn better when they are emotionally aroused. In this case, photos or video segments are intended to evoke emotional responses in learners, which in turn are intended to increase their level of cognitive engagement in the learning task. Thus, pictures and video are emotion-grabbing devices that make the learner more emotionally aroused, and therefore more actively involved in learning the presented material. Arousal theory predicts that adding interesting but extraneous pictures will promote better learning.

What's wrong with this justification? The problem—outlined in the previous section—is that interest cannot be added to an otherwise boring lesson like some kind of seasoning (Dewey, 1913). According to the cognitive theory of multimedia learning, the learner is actively seeking to make sense of the presented material. If the learner is successful in building a coherent mental representation of the presented material, the learner experiences enjoyment. However, adding extraneous pictures can interfere with the process of sense-making because learners have a limited cognitive capacity for processing incoming material. According to Harp and Mayer (1998), extraneous pictures (and their text captions) can interfere with learning in three ways:

- *Distraction*—by guiding the learner's limited attention away from the relevant material and toward the irrelevant material,

- *Disruption*—by preventing the learner from building appropriate links among pieces of relevant material because pieces of irrelevant material are in the way, and

- *Seduction*—by priming inappropriate existing knowledge (suggested by the added pictures), which is then used to organize the incoming content.

Thus, adding interesting but unnecessary material—including sounds, pictures, or words—to e-learning can harm the learning process by preventing the learner from processing the essential material. The cognitive theory of multimedia learning, therefore, predicts that students will learn more deeply from multimedia presentations that do not contain interesting but extraneous photos, illustrations, or video.

Evidence for Omitting Extraneous Graphics Added for Interest

What happens when entertaining but irrelevant video clips are placed within a narrated animation? Mayer, Heiser, and Lonn (2001) asked students to view a three-minute narrated animation on lightning formation, like the one described in the previous section. For some students, the narrated animation contained six ten-second video clips intended to make the presentation more entertaining, yielding a total presentation lasting four minutes. For example, one video clip showed trees bending against strong winds, lightning striking into the trees, an ambulance arriving along a path near the trees, and a victim being carried in a stretcher to the ambulance near a crowd of onlookers. At the same time, the narrator said: "Statistics show that more people are injured by lightning each year than by tornadoes and hurricanes combined." This video clip and corresponding narration were inserted right after the narrated animation describing a stepped leader of negative charges moving toward the ground. Thus, the narrated video was related to the general topic of lightning strikes but was not intended to help explain the cause-and-effect chain in lightning formation.

Students who received the lightning presentation without the inserted video clips performed better on solving transfer problems than students who received the lightning presentation with inserted video clips—producing about 30 percent more solutions, which translated into an effect size of .86. Mayer, Heiser, and Lonn (2001, p. 187) note that this result is an example of "when presenting more material results in less understanding."

Harp and Mayer (1997) found a similar pattern of results using a paper-based medium. Some students were asked to read a 550-word, six-paragraph passage containing six captioned illustrations. The passage described the cause-and-effect sequence leading to lightning formation, and the captioned illustrations depicted the main steps (with captions that repeated the key events from the passage). Each illustration was placed to the left of the paragraph it depicted. Other students read the same illustrated passage, along with six color pictures intended to spice up the presentation. Each picture was captioned and was placed to the right of a paragraph to which it was related. For example, next to the paragraph about warm moist air rising, there was a color photo of an airplane being hit by lightning accompanied by the following text: "Metal airplanes conduct lightning very well, but they sustain little damage because the bolt, meeting no resistance, passes right through." In another section of the lesson, a photo of a burned uniform from a football player stuck by lightening was included. Figure 8.6 shows an example of one of these visuals.

Figure 8.6. Interesting But Unrelated Graphics Added to Lightning Lesson.
Adapted from Harp and Mayer, 1998.

When flying through updrafts, an airplane ride can become bumpy. Metal airplanes conduct lightning very well, but they sustain little damage because the bolt passes right through.

Students who received the lightning passage without added color photos performed better on retention and transfer tests than students who received the lightning passage with color photos, generating about 52 percent more solutions on the transfer test, which translates into an effect size greater than 1. This is another example of how adding interesting but irrelevant graphics can result in less learning from a multimedia presentation. In each of four follow-up experiments, Harp and Mayer (1998) found that adding interesting but irrelevant captioned illustrations to the lightning lesson tended to hurt student performance on subsequent transfer tests, yielding effect sizes greater than 1.

For those who argue that these guidelines won't apply to the new generation raised on high-intensity media, we should mention that all of the above research was conducted with young adults. The subjects in these experiments were college-aged students ranging in age from eighteen to twenty-two years. Therefore, we cannot agree that members of the younger generation are less susceptive to mental overload as a result of intensive multimedia exposure.

Sanchez and Wiley (2006) identified a possible boundary condition for the coherence principle: Adding irrelevant illustrations to scientific text hurt learning particularly for students who have lower capacity for processing information. (For example, if we read a short list of words to these low-ability learners, they would make mistakes reciting the words back to us.) Apparently, the low-ability students were more easily overloaded by the extraneous material. In a follow-up study involving eye-tracking, low-ability students spent more time looking at irrelevant illustrations than did high-working-memory students, indicating that extraneous graphics can be particularly distracting for learners with low ability. Overall, it appears that good design principles—such as the coherence principle—are particularly important for the most at-risk learners.

Evidence for Using Simpler Visuals

In the previous section we focused on visuals that were extraneous to the learning goal. As we saw, adding extraneous visuals depressed learning. In this section, we recommend using simpler visuals, especially when understanding of a process or principles is the goal. By "simple" we mean visuals with fewer details presented at one time. For example, among static graphics, a two-dimensional line drawing is simpler than a three-dimensional drawing or a photograph. A series of static line drawings that can be viewed one at a time is simpler than an animation that presents a great deal of visual information in a transitory manner. Among animations, a computer-generated visual that omits extraneous elements in the background is simpler than a video that records all visual elements in the scene.

We have several research studies in which a simpler graphic led to better learning than a more realistic or complex visual. For example, Butcher (2006) asked college students to study a lesson on the human heart that contained text and simple illustrations or text and detailed illustrations, as shown in Figure 8.7. On subsequent tests of understanding of how the heart works, the students who had learned with text and simple drawings performed better than those who had learned with text and detailed drawings.

Figure 8.7. A Simple Visual (a) Led to Better Understanding Than a
          Detailed Visual (b).

From Butcher, 2006.

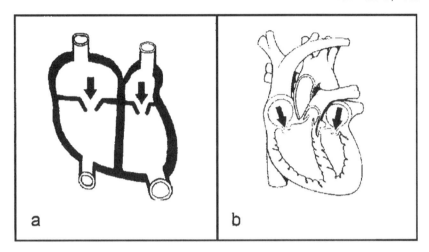

During learning, students who studied text and simple illustrations made
more integration inferences—indicating an attempt to understand how the
heart works—than did students who studied text and complex illustrations.

Compare the visuals in Figure 8.8. Scheiter, Gerjets, Huk, Imhof, and
Kammerer (2009) found that schematic animations were more effective
than video recorded animations in a multimedia lesson on cell replication.

Figure 8.8. Schematic Animations Led to Better Learning Than Video-Recording.

From Scheiter, Gerjets, Huk, Imhof, and Kammerer, 2008.

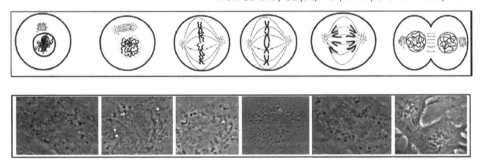

Multiple-choice tests and visual identification tests were used to measure learning. The simpler schematic animation led to better scores on the multiple-choice test and supported accurate visual identification of realistic images, even though the learners in the schematic group never saw realistic images. The research team concludes: "It seems that learners [in the video group] were overwhelmed with the amount of realistic detail and failed to come to a proper understanding of the process of mitosis" (p. 9).

In Chapter 4, we reviewed research reported by Mayer, Hegarty, Mayer, and Campbell (2005) that compared a series of static visuals with an animation of processes such as how a toilet flushes and how brakes work. The static visuals led to learning that was better than or equal to the animated versions.

Taken together this research sounds a cautionary note to those considering highly realistic learning or simulation interfaces. Of course, there are likely some learning goals that may benefit from more realistic visuals, and we look forward to additional research for clarification on this issue.

Coherence Principle 3: Avoid e-Lessons with Extraneous Words

Our third version of the coherence principle recommends that you should avoid adding extraneous words to lessons. When the goal is to promote learning of the target material—such as the workings of a cause-and-effect system—adding interesting but extraneous words may result in poorer learning.

This guideline is helpful when limited screen real estate and bandwidth suggest shorter rather than longer narrations. Rather than fully embellished textual or narrative descriptions, as in Figure 8.9, stick to basic and concise descriptions of the content, as in Figure 8.10. It also helps implement the modality principle effectively. By keeping the narration on each screen concise, learners won't become as frustrated waiting for lengthy audio segments to play.

Figure 8.9. Extensive Text Overly Details Spreadsheet Concepts.

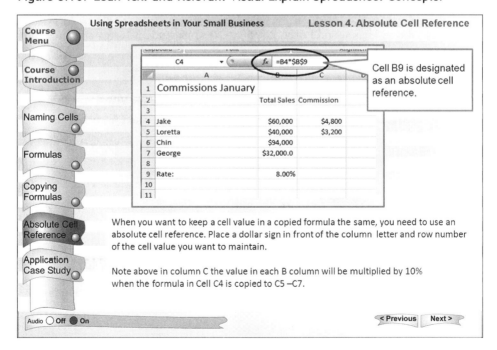

Using Spreadsheets in Your Small Business   Lesson 4. Absolute Cell Reference

Course Menu
Course Introduction
Naming Cells
Formulas
Copying Formulas
Absolute Cell Reference
Application Case Study

Absolute VS Relative Cell References

When you copy a formula containing cell references into a new cell, all of the cell references will update to reflect the new location. For example, if you copy the formula = B1+B3 from cell B4 to cell C4, the formula will automatically update to: = C1+C3. This is called relative cell references.

However, sometimes you may want the value in one or more of the cells in your source formula to remain constant. For example if you applied a commission of 10% given to all sales staff in January to February sales, you would not want the 10% value to change. Holding a cell value constant when it is copied is called an absolute cell reference and is designated by placing a dollar sign in front of the column and row number you want to copy unchanged. For example: = B4*B10.

Audio ○ Off ● On   < Previous   Next >

Figure 8.10. Lean Text and Relevant Visual Explain Spreadsheet Concepts.

Using Spreadsheets in Your Small Business   Lesson 4. Absolute Cell Reference

Course Menu
Course Introduction
Naming Cells
Formulas
Copying Formulas
Absolute Cell Reference
Application Case Study

C4   fx =B4*B9

Cell B9 is designated as an absolute cell reference.

	A	Total Sales	Commission
1	Commissions January		
2		Total Sales	Commission
3			
4	Jake	$60,000	$4,800
5	Loretta	$40,000	$3,200
6	Chin	$94,000	
7	George	$32,000.0	
8			
9	Rate:		8.00%
10			
11			

When you want to keep a cell value in a copied formula the same, you need to use an absolute cell reference. Place a dollar sign in front of the column letter and row number of the cell value you want to maintain.

Note above in column C the value in each B column will be multiplied by 10% when the formula in Cell C4 is copied to C5 –C7.

Audio ○ Off ● On   < Previous   Next >

Psychological Reasons to Avoid Extraneous Words in e-Learning

For the same reasons that extraneous sounds and graphics can be distracting, adding extra words can interfere with the learning process. We address three types of extraneous wording. First, additional words may be added for interest. The extra words are related to the topic but are not relevant to the primary instructional goal. Second, extra words may be added to expand upon the key ideas of the lesson. A third purpose for extra words is to add technical details that go beyond the key ideas of the lesson. Subject-matter experts like to incorporate considerable amounts of technical information that expands on the basics. We recommend against extraneous words added for interest, for elaboration, or for technical depth.

Evidence for Omitting Extraneous Words Added for Interest

Do students learn more deeply from a narrated animation when interesting verbal information is added to the narration? To address this question, Mayer, Heiser, and Lonn (2001) asked some students to view a three-minute narrated animation about lightning formation, like the one described in the previous section. Other students viewed the same three-minute presentation, but with six additional narration segments inserted at various points. The narration segments were short and fit within the three-minute presentation at points that otherwise were silent. For example, after saying that water vapor forms a cloud, the narrator added: "On a warm, cloudy day, swimmers are sitting ducks for lightning." Similarly, after saying that electrical charges build in a cloud, the narrator added: "Golfers are vulnerable targets because they hold metal clubs, which are excellent conductors of electrical charges." Students who received the lightning presentation without additional narration segments performed better on transfer tests than students who received the lightning presentation with added narration segments—generating about

34 percent more solutions on the transfer test, which translated into an effect size of .66.

In a related study, Lehman, Schraw, McCrudden, and Hartley (2007) found that college students who read the lightning lesson with seductive details spent less time reading the relevant text, recalled less of the relevant text, and showed shallower processing on an essay task as compared to students who read the lightning passage without seductive details. These results show that adding seductive details harms learning by distracting learners from the important information and by disrupting the coherence of the lesson.

Finally, consider what happened when college students received a PowerPoint multimedia lesson explaining how a virus causes a cold or how the human digestive system words. The lesson consisted of series of slides with text and an illustration on each one, but some students also received interesting sentences mainly about sex or death embedded in the text. We show the two versions in Figure 8.11. Won't the interesting material help students pay

---

Figure 8.11. High and Low Interest Statements Added to a Lesson.
From Mayer, Griffith, Jurkowitz, and Rothman, 2008.

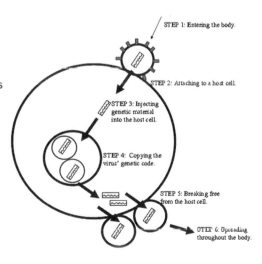

A. High Interest Statement:
A study conducted by researchers at Wilkes University in Wilkes-Barre, Pennsylvania, reveals that people who make love once or twice a week are more immune to colds than folks who abstain from sex. Researchers believe that bedroom activity somehow stimulates an immune-boosting antibody called IgA. .

B. Low-Interest Statement :
A virus is about 10 times smaller than a bacterium, which is approximately 10 times smaller than a typical human cell. A typical human cell is 10 times smaller than a human hair. Therefore, it can be concluded that a virus is about 1000 times smaller than a human hair.

Figure 8.12. High Interest Statements Added to a Lesson Depress Learning.
Based on data from Experiment 1, PowerPoint Version, Mayer, Griffith, Jurkowitz, and Rothman, 2008.

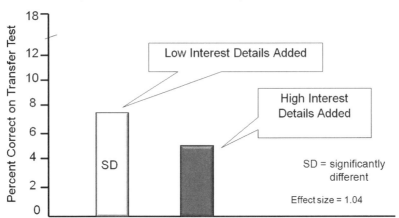

better attention and therefore learn better? As you can see in Figure 8.12, the answer is clearly "no." Mayer, Griffith, Jurkowitz, and Rothman (2008) found that college students actually learned less from lessons containing highly interesting seductive details than from lessons containing less interesting seductive details. It appears that increasing the interestingness of the seductive details created greater distraction away from the important material in the lessons.

Again, these results show that adding interesting but irrelevant material does not help learning, and in this case even hurts learning.

Evidence for Omitting Extraneous Words Added to Expand on Key Ideas

In a more extreme version of this research (Mayer, Bove, Bryman, Mars, & Tapangco, 1996), students read the standard lightning passage like the one described above (that is, with six hundred words and five captioned illustrations) or a summary consisting of five captioned illustrations. The captions described the main steps in the lightning formation and the corresponding illustrations depicted the main steps. Approximately eighty words—taken from the standard passage—were used in the captioned illustrations. In three separate experiments, students who read the summary performed better on tests of retention and transfer than students who received the whole passage—in some cases, producing twice as many steps in the causal chain on the retention test and twice as many solutions on the transfer test. Figure 8.13 shows results from one of the experiments in this study. Mayer, Bove, Bryman, Mars, and Tapangco (1996, p. 64) conclude that this research helps show "when less is more."

Figure 8.13. Learning Is Better When Non-Essential Text Is Excluded.
Adapted from Mayer, 2001a.

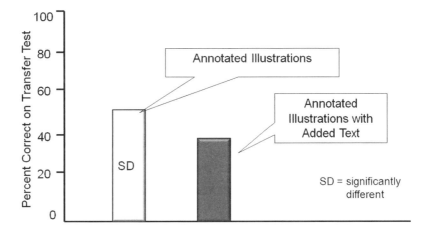

More recently, Mayer, Deleeuw, and Ayres (2007) extended the coherence principle by examining what happens when you add material to a multimedia lesson on how hydraulic brakes work. The added material consisted of companion multimedia lessons on how caliper brakes work and on how air brakes work. College students performed better on retention and transfer tests concerning hydraulic brakes if they received a multimedia lesson only about hydraulic brakes rather than the same hydraulic brake lesson along with lessons on two other kinds of braking systems.

Overall, providing a concise summary of what you want students to learn results in better learning than providing the same material along with additional complementary material.

Evidence for Omitting Extraneous Words Added for Technical Depth

Mayer and Jackson (2005) compared learning from a multimedia lesson on how ocean waves work in concise form with one that included additional technical information. The embellished version contained additional words and graphics about computational details, such as how to apply formulas related to ocean waves. The versions with additional quantitative details depressed performance on a subsequent problem-solving transfer test focusing on conceptual understanding—yielding effect sizes of .69 for a computer-based lesson and .97 for a paper-based lesson. Mayer and Jackson (2005, p. 13) conclude that "the added quantitative details may have distracted the learner from constructing a qualitative model of the process of ocean waves." In an important follow-up study, Verkoeijen and Tabbers (2009) replicated this finding with Dutch students.

In short, when tempted to add more words, ask yourself whether additional verbiage is really needed to achieve the instructional objectives. If not, weed out extra words!

What We Don't Know About Coherence

As you can see in this chapter, there is strong and consistent support for the coherence effect. In the latest review, Mayer (2008) listed positive results for eliminating extraneous materials in thirteen out of fourteen experiments, with a median effect size near 1. In spite of this initial body of useful research evidence, there is still much we do not know about the coherence principle. Much of the research reported in this chapter deals with short lessons delivered in a controlled lab environment. Does the coherence effect also apply to longer term instruction presented in an authentic learning environment, such as a training program? It would be useful to determine whether students can learn to ignore irrelevant material or whether lessons can be redesigned to highlight relevant material—a technique that can be called *signaling* (Mautone & Mayer, 2001; Mayer,

2005b; Mayer & Moreno, 2003). Signaling includes using headings, bold, italics, underlining, capital letters, larger font, color, white space, arrows, and related techniques to draw the learner's attention to specific parts of the display or page. Preliminary research (de Koning, Tabbers, Rikers, & Paas, 2010; Harp & Mayer, 1997; Mautone & Mayer, 2001) shows that signaling can improve learning from multimedia lessons, but additional research is needed.

When it comes to educational games and simulations, sound effects and music may play a useful role under some circumstances, but currently there is insufficient evidence to guide instructional game designers.

In addition, we do not know much about how individual characteristics of learners are related to the effectiveness of the coherence principle. Most of the research reported in this chapter is based on learners who are novices—that is, who lack prior knowledge in the domain of the lesson. Does the coherence effect also apply to high-knowledge learners? Research on the expertise reversal effect (Kalyuga, 2005) suggests that instructional design techniques that are effective for beginners may not be effective for more experienced learners. For example, Mayer and Jackson (2005) found that adding computational details hurt learning for beginners, but it is possible that students who had extensive physics backgrounds might have benefited from the added material. Similarly, research by Sanchez and Wiley (2006) provides preliminary evidence that adding irrelevant material can be particularly damaging for lower-ability learners. In short, research is needed to determine for whom the coherence principle applies.

Finally, you should not interpret the coherence principle to mean that lessons should be boring. There is ample evidence that students learn better when they are interested in the material (Hidi & Renninger, 2006). However, the challenge for instructional professionals is to stimulate interest without adding extraneous material that distracts from the cognitive objective of the lesson. Is there a way to add interesting words or graphics that serve to support the instructional goal while at the same time promote interest? Research is needed on how to interest learners and at the same time be sensitive to limits on their cognitive processing capacity.

DESIGN DILEMMA: RESOLVED

In an effort to accommodate younger learners used to high-intensity media, the spreadsheet team considered adding interesting visuals, audio, and words to the basic lesson. The options we considered were:

A. Ben is correct. Adding some interesting words and visuals about spreadsheets will improve interest and learning—especially among younger learners.

B. Reshmi is correct. Learning is better in the presence of soft music, especially classical music.

C. Matt is right. Less is more for most learners.

D. Not sure who is correct.

Based on the evidence presented in this chapter, we vote for Option C. The project manager will be happy because resources needed to create interesting visuals and narrations will not be needed, since evidence suggests their effects are deleterious to learning. Since the evidence for the coherence principle is based on performance of college-aged subjects, we reject the generational argument. We suggest that the team consider other ways to make the lesson engaging, such as using examples and practice exercises that are relevant to the work tasks that learners will face on the job and making the benefits of spreadsheets explicit in the process.

We recommend that you make a distinction between *emotional interest* and *cognitive interest*. Emotional interest occurs when a multimedia experience evokes an emotional response in a learner, such as reading a story about a life-threatening event or seeing a graphic video. There is little evidence that emotion-grabbing adjuncts—which have been called seductive details—promote deep learning (Garner, Gillingham, & White, 1989; Renninger, Hidi, & Krapp, 1992). In short, attempts to force excitement do not guarantee that students will work hard to understand the presentation. In contrast, cognitive interest occurs when a learner is able to mentally construct a model that makes sense. As a result of attaining understanding, the learner feels a sense of enjoyment. In summary, understanding leads to enjoyment. The achievement of cognitive interest depends on active reflection by the learner rather than exposure to entertaining but irrelevant sights and sounds.

Overall, the research and theory summarized in this chapter show that designers should always consider the cognitive consequences of adding extraneous sounds, pictures, or words. In particular, designers should consider whether the proposed additions could distract, disrupt, or seduce the learner's process of knowledge construction.

WHAT TO LOOK FOR IN e-LEARNING

☐ Lessons that *do not* contain extraneous sounds in the form of background music or sounds

☐ Lessons that *do not* use illustrations, photos, and video clips that may be interesting but are not essential to the knowledge and skills to be learned

☐ Lessons that *do not* contain interesting stories or details that are not essential to the instructional goal

☐ Lessons that use simpler visual illustrations such as line drawings when the goal is to help learners build understanding

☐ Lessons that present the core content with the minimal amount of words and graphics needed to help the learner understand the main points

---

COMING NEXT

We have seen in this chapter that extraneous sounds, graphics, and textual details can depress learning compared to more concise lessons. In the next chapter on the personalization principle, we ask about the learning effects of formal versus informal language in e-lessons and preview an area of emerging research on the benefits of different voices in narration and on the use of virtual coaches.

Suggested Readings

Avoid Adding Extraneous Sounds

Moreno, R., & Mayer, R.E. (2000). A coherence effect in multimedia learning: The case for minimizing irrelevant sounds in the design of multimedia instructional messages. *Journal of Educational Psychology, 92,* 117–125.

Avoid Adding Extraneous Pictures

Butcher, K.R. (2006). Learning from text with diagrams: Promoting mental model development and inference generation. *Journal of Educational Psychology, 98,* 182–197.

Mayer, R.E., Heiser, J., & Lonn, S. (2001). Cognitive constraints on multimedia learning: When presenting more material results in less understanding. *Journal of Educational Psychology, 93,* 187–198.

Avoid Adding Extraneous Words

Harp, S.F., & Mayer, R.E. (1998). How seductive details do their damage: A theory of cognitive interest in science learning. *Journal of Educational Psychology, 90,* 414–434.

Lehman, S., Schraw, G., McCrudden, M.T., & Hartley, K. (2007). Processing and recall of seductive details in scientific text. *Contemporary Educational Psychology, 32,* 569–587.

Mayer, R.E., Griffith, E., Jurkowitz, I.T., & Rothman, D. (2008). Increased interestingness of extraneous details in a multimedia science presentation leads to decreased learning. *Journal of Experimental Psychology: Applied, 14,* 329–339.

Mayer, R.E., Heiser, J., & Lonn, S. (2001). Cognitive constraints on multimedia learning: When presenting more material results in less understanding. *Journal of Educational Psychology, 93,* 187–198.

CHAPTER OUTLINE

Personalization Principle 1: Use Conversational Rather Than Formal Style

Psychological Reasons for the Personalization Principle

Evidence for Using Conversational Style

Promote Personalization Through Voice Quality

Promote Personalization Through Polite Speech

Personalization Principle 2: Use Effective On-Screen Coaches to Promote Learning

What Are Pedagogical Agents?

Do Agents Improve Student Learning?

Do Agents Need to Look Real?

Do Agents Need to Sound Real?

Should Agents Match the Gender or Ethnicity of the Learners?

Personalization Principle 3: Make the Author Visible to Promote Learning

What Is a Visible Author?

Psychological Reasons for Using a Visible Author

Evidence for the Visible Author

9

Applying the Personalization Principle

USE CONVERSATIONAL STYLE AND VIRTUAL COACHES

WHAT'S NEW IN THIS CHAPTER?

SOME e-LEARNING LESSONS rely on a formal style of writing to present information. In this chapter we summarize the empirical evidence that supports using a conversational style of writing (including using first- and second-person language) and a friendly human voice. We also explore preliminary evidence for how to use on-screen pedagogical agents and for how to make the author more visible by using self-revealing comments and video transcripts. Since the second edition of this book, the research base for using conversational style has grown, and new evidence has emerged concerning the role of politeness in on-screen agents' feedback and hints. The most important advance has been the establishment of boundary conditions that specify when the personalization principle is most likely to be effective—such as the finding that in some cases personalization works best for less experienced learners and when the amount of personalization is modest enough to not detract from the lesson.

The personalization principle is particularly important for the design of pedagogical agents—on-screen characters who help guide the learning processes during an instructional episode. While research on agents is somewhat new, we present evidence—including new evidence since the previous edition—for the learning gains achieved in the presence of an agent as well as for the most effective ways to design and use agents. The psychological advantage of conversational style, pedagogical agents, and visible authors is to induce the learner to engage with the computer as a social conversational partner.

DESIGN DILEMMA: YOU DECIDE

Reshmi has been working on the script for a new product lesson for pharmaceutical sales representatives. As a former classroom instructor, she is convinced that a more relaxed instructional environment leads to better learning. Therefore she is writing in a conversational rather than a formal style. She also has designed an on-screen coach to guide learners through the lesson. "The agent adds a personal touch that leads to a more friendly learning environment," she claims as she shows her draft storyboard (Figure 9.1).

Figure 9.1. An Informal Approach Uses an Agent and Conversational Language.

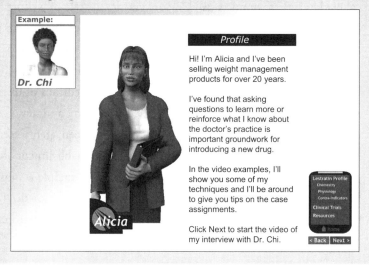

Matt, the project manager, has his doubts. "I don't think Legal is going to approve of this approach. And neither will the communications department. They are going to require us to use the official corporate communication standards. No contractions—no slang! That new VP is pretty traditional. He will think the character—what did you call it? An agent? Well anyway, he will think it's a cartoon. I suggest for our first e-learning we follow the corporate tradition with something more like this" (Figure 9.2).

Figure 9.2. An Formal Approach Omits the Agent and Uses More Formal Language.

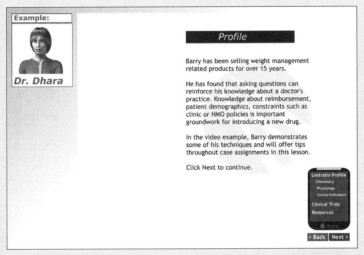

The pharma sales e-learning team is divided over the tone of the lesson, including the use of an agent. Based on your own experience or intuition, which of the following options would you select?

A. Reshmi is correct. A more informal approach plus an agent will lead to better learning.

B. Matt is correct. A more formal tone will fit the corporate image better, leading to a more credible instructional message.

C. The tone of the lesson should be adjusted for the learners. Women will benefit from more informality and men will find a formal approach more credible.

D. Not sure which option is correct.

Personalization Principle 1: Use Conversational Rather Than Formal Style

Does it help or hurt to change printed or spoken text from formal style to conversational style? Would the addition of a friendly on-screen coach distract from or promote learning? In this chapter, we explore research and theory that directly addresses these issues.

Consider the lesson introduction shown in Figure 9.1. As you can see, an on-screen agent uses an informal conversational style to introduce the lesson. This approach resembles human-to-human conversation. Of course, learners know that the character is not really in a conversation with them, but they may be more likely to act as if the character is a conversational partner. Now, compare this with the introduction shown in Figure 9.2. Here the overall feeling is quite impersonal. The agent is gone and the tone is more formal. Based on cognitive theory and research evidence, we recommend that you create or select e-learning courses that include some spoken or printed text that is conversational rather than formal.

Let's look at a couple of e-learning examples. The screen in Figure 9.3 summarizes the rules for calculating compound interest. Note that the on-screen

---

Figure 9.3. Passive Voice Leads to a Formal Tone in the Lesson.

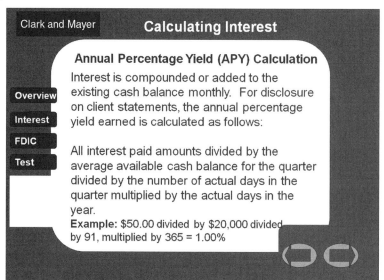

Figure 9.4. Use of Second-Person and Informal Language Lead to a Conversational Tone in the Lesson.

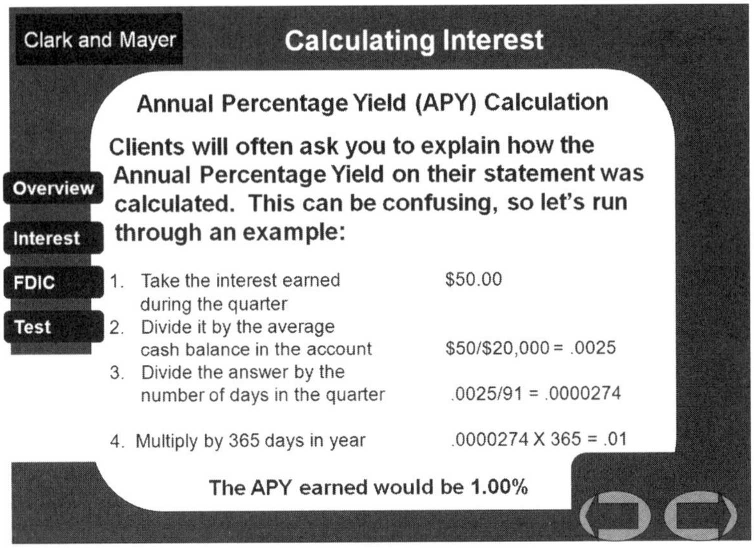

text is quite formal. How could this concept be made more conversational? Figure 9.4 shows a revised version. Rather than passive voice, it uses second-person active voice and includes a comment about how this concept relates to the learner's job. It rephrases and segments the calculation procedure into four directive steps. The overall result is a more user-friendly tone.

Psychological Reasons for the Personalization Principle

Let's begin with a common-sense view that we do not agree with, even though it may sound reasonable. The rationale for putting words in formal style is that conversational style can detract from the seriousness of the message. After all, learners know that the computer cannot speak to them. The goal of a training program is not to build a relationship but rather to convey important information. By emphasizing the personal aspects of the training—by using words like "you" and "I"—you convey a message that training is not serious. Accordingly, the guiding principle is to keep things simple by presenting the basic information.

This argument is based on an *information delivery* view of learning in which the instructor's job is to present information and the learner's job is to acquire the information. According to the information delivery view, the training program should deliver information as efficiently as possible. A formal style meets this criterion better than a conversational style.

Why do we disagree with the call to keep things formal and the information delivery view of learning on which it is based? Although the information delivery view seems like common sense, it is inconsistent with how the human mind works. According to cognitive theories of learning, humans strive to make sense of presented material by applying appropriate cognitive processes. Thus, instruction should not only present information but also prime the appropriate cognitive processing in the learner. Research on discourse processing shows that people work harder to understand material when they feel they are in a conversation with a partner, rather than simply receiving information (Beck, McKeown, Sandora, Kucan, & Worthy, 1996). Therefore, using conversational style in a multimedia presentation conveys to the learners the idea that they should work hard to understand what their conversational partner (in this case, the course narrator) is saying to them. In short, expressing information in conversational style can be a way to prime appropriate cognitive processing in the learner.

According to cognitive theories of multimedia communication (Mayer, 2005d), Figure 9.5 shows what happens within the learner when a lesson contains conversational style and when it does not contain conversational style. On the top row, you can see that instruction containing social cues (such as conversational style) activates a sense of social presence in the learner (a feeling of being a conversation with the author). The feeling of social presence, in turn, causes the learner to engage in deeper cognitive processing during learning (by working harder to understand what the author is saying), which results in a better learning outcome. In contrast, when an instructional lesson does not contain social cues, the learner does not feel engaged with the author and therefore will not work as hard to make sense of the material. In Chapter 1 we introduced the Engagement Matrix (see Figure 1.5). Making your materials more personable is another instructional technique that falls into the upper left quadrant in which behavioral activity is low (that is, the

Figure 9.5. How the Presence or Absence of Social Cues Affects Learning.

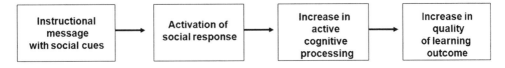

How Social Cues Prime Deeper Learning

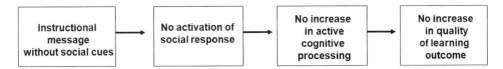

How Lack of Social Cues Does Not Prime Deeper Learning

learner reads the materials) but psychological activity is enhanced (that is, the learner processes the materials more deeply). The challenge for instructional processionals is to avoid over-using conversational style to the point that it becomes distracting to the learner.

Evidence for Using Conversational Style

Although this technique as it applies to e-learning is just beginning to be studied, there is already preliminary evidence concerning the use of conversational style in e-learning lessons. In a set of five experimental studies involving a computer-based educational game on botany, Moreno and Mayer (2000b, 2004) compared versions in which the words were in formal style with versions in which the words were in conversational style. For example, Figure 9.6 gives the introductory script spoken in the computer-based botany game; the top portion shows the formal version and the bottom shows the personalized version. As you can see, both versions present the same basic information, but in the personalized version the computer is talking directly to the learner. In five out of five studies, students who learned with personalized text performed better on subsequent transfer tests than students who learned with formal text. Overall, participants in the personalized group

Figure 9.6. Formal vs. Informal Lesson Introductions Compared
in Research Study.

From Moreno and Mayer, 2000b.

Formal Version:

"This program is about what type of plants survive on different planets.
For each planet, a plant will be designed. The goal is to learn what type
of roots, stems, and leaves allow the plant to survive in each environment.
Some hints are provided throughout the program."

Personalized Version:

"You are about to start a journey where you will be visiting different
planets. For each planet, you will need to design a plant. Your mission
is to learn what type of roots, stems, and leaves will allow your plant to
survive in each environment. I will be guiding you through by giving out
some hints."

produced between 20 to 46 percent more solutions to transfer problems than the formal group, with effect sizes all above 1. Figure 9.7 shows results from one study where improvement was 46 percent and the effect size was 1.55, which is considered to be large.

People can also learn better from a narrated animation on lightning formation when the speech is in conversational style rather than formal style (Moreno & Mayer, 2000b). For example, consider the last sentence in the lightning lesson: "It produces the bright light that people notice as a flash of lightning." To personalize, we can simply change "people" to "you." In addition to changes such as this one, Moreno and Mayer (2000b) added direct comments to the learner, such as, "Now that your cloud is charged up, let me tell you the rest of the story." Students who received the personalized version of the lightning lesson performed substantially better on a transfer test than those who did not, yielding effect sizes greater than 1 across two different experiments.

These results also apply to learning from narrated animations involving how the human lungs work (Mayer, Fennell, Farmer, & Campbell, 2004). For example, consider the final sentence in the lungs lesson: "During exhaling, the diaphragm moves up, creating less room for the lungs, air travels through the bronchial tubes and throat to the nose and mouth where it

Figure 9.7. Better Learning from Personalized Narration.
From Moreno and Mayer, 2000b.

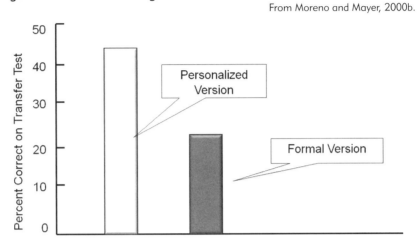

leaves the body." Mayer, Fennell, Farmer and Campbell (2004) personalized this sentence by changing "the" to "your" in five places, turning it into: "During exhaling, your diaphragm moves up, creating less room for your lungs; air travels through your bronchial tubes and throat to your nose and mouth where it leaves your body." Overall, they created a personalized script for the lungs lesson by changing "the" to "your" in eleven places. Across three experiments, this fairly minor change resulted in improvements on a transfer test yielding a median effect size of .79.

More recently, Kartel (2010) gave students multimedia lessons on stellar evolution and death that included illustrations and animation along with printed and spoken words. The words were either in formal style (for example, "The white dwarf cools down slowly in time") or enhanced with additional personalized comments (for example, "The white dwarf cools down slowly in time. Now we know what will happen to our smallest star in the end."). On a subsequent problem-solving test, students performed better if they had received personalized rather than formal wording, with a medium-to-large effect size of .71.

Overall, there is evidence that personalization can result in improvements in student learning. However, there may be some important boundary conditions, so these results should not be taken to mean that personalization is always a useful idea. There are cases in which personalization can be overdone.

For example, consider what happens when you add too much personal material, such as, "Wow, hi dude, I'm here to teach you all about . . ., so hang onto your hat and here we go!" The result can be that the advantages of personalization are offset by the disadvantages of distracting the learner and setting an inappropriate tone for learning. Thus, in applying the personalization principle it is always useful to consider the audience and the cognitive consequences of your script—you want to write with sufficient informality so that the learners feel they are interacting with a conversational partner but not so informally that the learner is distracted or the material is undermined. In fact, implementing the personalization principle should create only a subtle change in the lesson; a lot can be accomplished by using a few first- and second-person pronouns or a friendly comment.

Promote Personalization Through Voice Quality

Research summarized by Reeves and Nass (1996) shows that, under the right circumstances, people "treat computers like real people." Part of treating computers like real people is to try harder to understand their communications. Consistent with this view, Mayer, Sobko, and Mautone (2003) found that people learned better from a narrated animation on lightning formation when the speaker's voice was human rather than machine-simulated, with an effect size of .79. In another study, Atkinson, Mayer, and Merrill (2005) presented online mathematics lessons in which an on-screen agent named Peedy the parakeet explained the steps in solving various problems. Across two experiments, students performed better on a subsequent transfer test when Peedy spoke in a human voice rather than a machine voice, yielding effect sizes of .69 and .78. We can refer to these findings as the *voice principle*: People learn better from narration with a human voice than a machine voice. Nass and Brave (2005) have provided additional research showing that characteristics of the speaker's voice can have a strong impact on how people respond to computer-based communications.

There is also some preliminary evidence that people learn better from a human voice with a standard accent rather than a foreign accent (Mayer, Sobko, & Mautone, 2003), but this work is limited by focusing only on a Russian accent used over a short presentation. There is also some preliminary evidence that both men and women prefer to learn from female voices for female-stereotyped subjects such as human relationships and to learn from male voices for male-stereotyped subjects such as technology (Nass & Brave, 2005).

However, in contrast to these findings, recent research has found better learning from female narration of math lessons, which are male-stereotypic subjects. Linek, Gerjets, and Scheiter (2010) tested the learning effects of a male and female narrator on male and female German university students in a multimedia lesson on probability. In their first experiment, they found that learners rated the female narrators more positively and showed better problem-solving performance from female-narrated lessons. In a second experiment, male and female university students stated their preferences for a male or female narrator after listening to brief audio samples and then completed the probability lesson narrated by the speaker of their choice. A female speaker was chosen by about 70 percent of the learners. Regardless of preference, as in Experiment 1, learning was better from a female voice. The research team suggests that the speaker-gender effect they obtained provides strong support for the impact of social factors in learning, and they recommend the use of female narrators at least in mathematical subjects.

More work is needed to determine how the gender and ethnicity of the narrator affect learning outcomes for different learning domains and different learner populations such as higher or lower background knowledge.

Promote Personalization Through Polite Speech

A related implication of the personalization principle is that on-screen agents should be polite. For example, consider an instructional game in which an on-screen agent gives you feedback. A direct way to put the feedback is to for the agent to say, "Click the ENTER key," and a more polite wording is, "You may want to click the ENTER key" or "Do you want to click on the ENTER key?" or "Let's click the ENTER key." A direct statement is, "Now use the quadratic formula to solve this equation," and a more polite version is "What about using the quadratic formula to solve this equation?" or "You could use the quadratic formula to solve this equation," or "We should use the quadratic formula to solve this equation." According to Brown and Levinson's (1987) politeness theory, these alternative wordings help to save face—by allowing the learner to have some freedom of action or by allowing the learner to work cooperatively with the agent. Mayer, Johnson, Shaw, and Sandhu (2006) found that students rated the reworded statements as more polite than the direct statement, indicating that people are sensitive to the politeness tone of feedback statements. Students who had less experience in working with computers were most sensitive to the politeness tone of the on-screen agent's feedback statements, so they were more offended by direct statements (such as "Click the ENTER key") and more impressed with polite statements (such as "Do you want to click the ENTER key?").

Do polite on-screen agents foster deeper learning than direct agents? A study by Wang, Johnson, Mayer, Rizzo, Shaw, and Collins (2008) indicates that the answer is yes—especially for less experienced learners. Students interacted with an on-screen agent while learning about industrial engineering by playing an educational game called Virtual Factory. On a subsequent problem-solving transfer test, students who had learned with a polite agent performed better than those who learned with a direct agent, yielding an effect size of .73. Importantly, the effect was strong and significant for students without a background in engineering but not for students with a background in engineering.

In a related study by McLaren, DeLeeuw, and Mayer (2011), students learned to solve chemistry stoichiometry problems with a web-based intelligent tutor that provided hints and feedback using either polite language ("Shall we calculate the result now?") or direct language ("The tutor wants you to calculate the result now"). The results showed a pattern in which students with low knowledge of chemistry performed better on a subsequent problem-solving test if they had learned with a polite rather than a direct tutor, whereas high knowledge learners showed the reverse trend.

Overall, there is evidence that student learning is not only influenced by what on-screen agents say but also by how they say it. An important boundary condition is that the positive effects of politeness are strongest for learners who do not have much knowledge of the domain. These results have important implications for virtual classroom facilitators. In many virtual classrooms, only the instructor's voice is transmitted. The virtual classroom instructor can apply these guidelines by using polite conversational language as one tool to maximize the benefits of social presence on learning.

Personalization Principle 2: Use Effective On-Screen Coaches to Promote Learning

In the previous section, we provided evidence for writing with first- and second-person language, speaking with a friendly human voice, and using polite wording to establish a conversational tone in your training. In some of the research described in the previous section, the instructor was an on-screen character who interacted with the learner. A related new area of research focuses specifically on the role of on-screen coaches, called pedagogical agents, on learning.

What Are Pedagogical Agents?

Personalized speech is an important component in animated pedagogical agents developed as on-screen tutors in educational programs (Cassell, Sullivan, Prevost, & Churchill, 2000; Graesser, Jeon, & Duffy, 2008; Moreno, 2005; Moreno, Mayer, Spires, & Lester, 2001). Pedagogical agents are on-screen characters who help guide the learning process during an e-learning episode. Agents can be represented visually as cartoon-like characters, as talking-head video, or as virtual reality avatars; they can be represented verbally through machine-simulated voice, human recorded voice, or printed text. Agents can be representations of real people using video and human voice or artificial characters using animation and computer-generated voice. Our major interest in agents concerns their ability to employ sound instructional techniques that foster learning.

On-screen agents are appearing frequently in e-learning. For example, Figure 9.8 introduces Jim in a lesson on reading comprehension. Throughout the lesson, Jim demonstrates techniques he uses to understand stories followed by exercises that ask learners to apply Jim's guidelines to comprehension of stories.

Figure 9.8. On-Screen Coach Used to Give Reading Comprehension Demonstrations.

With permission from Plato Learning Systems.

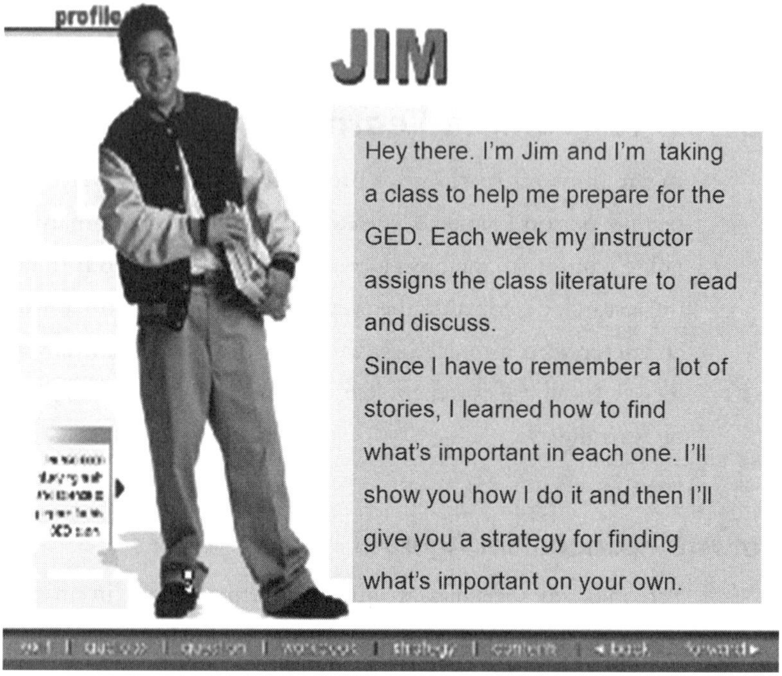

Figure 9.9 shows a screen from a guided discovery e-learning game called Design-A-Plant in which the learner travels to a planet with certain environmental features (such as low rainfall and heavy winds) and must choose the roots, stem, and leaves of a plant that could survive there. An animated pedagogical agent named Herman-the-Bug (in lower left corner of Figure 9.9) poses the problems, offers feedback, and generally guides the learner through the game. As you can see in the figure, Herman is a friendly little guy and research shows that most learners report liking him (Moreno & Mayer, 2000b; Moreno, Mayer, Spires, & Lester, 2001).

In another program, an animated pedagogical agent is used to teach students how to solve proportionality word problems (Atkinson, 2002; Atkinson, Mayer, & Merrill, 2005). In this program, an animated pedagogical bird agent named Peedy provides a step-by-step explanation of how to

Figure 9.9. Herman-the-Bug Used in Design-A-Plant Instructional Game.
From Moreno, Mayer, Spires, and Lester, 2001.

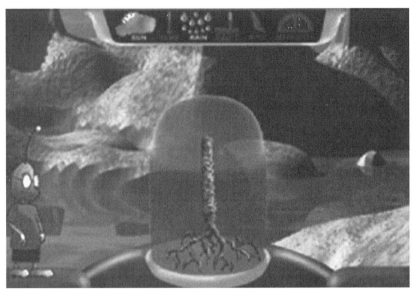

solve each problem. Although Peedy doesn't move much, he can point to relevant parts of the solution and make some simple gestures as he guides the students. Peedy and Herman are among a small collection of agents who have been examined in controlled research studies.

Computer scientists are doing a fine job of producing lifelike agents who interact well with humans (Cassell, Sullivan, Prevost, & Churchill, 2000). For example, an on-screen agent named Steve shows students how to operate and maintain the gas turbine engines aboard naval ships (Rickel & Johnson, 2000); an on-screen agent named Cosmo guides students through the architecture and operation of the Internet (Lester, Towns, Callaway, Voerman, & Fitzgerald, 2000); and an on-screen agent named Rea interacts with potential home buyers, takes them on virtual tours of listed properties, and tries to sell them a house (Cassell, Sullivan, Prevost, & Churchill, 2000).

In spite of the continuing advances in the development of on-screen agents, research on their effectiveness is just beginning (Atkinson, 2002; Graesser, Jeon, & Duffy, 2008; Moreno, 2005; Moreno & Mayer, 2000b; Moreno, Mayer, Spires, & Lester, 2001; Wouters, Paas, & van Merrienboer,

2008). Let's look at some important questions about agents in e-learning courses and see how the preliminary research answers them.

Do Agents Improve Student Learning?

An important primary question is whether adding on-screen agents can have any positive effects on learning. Even if computer scientists can develop extremely lifelike agents that are entertaining, is it worth the time and expense to incorporate them into e-learning courses? In order to answer this question, researchers began with an agent-based educational game called Design-A-Plant, described previously (Moreno, Mayer, Spires, & Lester, 2001). Some students learned by interacting with an on-screen agent named Herman-the-Bug (agent group), whereas other students learned by reading the identical words and viewing the identical graphics presented on the computer screen without the Herman agent (no-agent group). Across two separate experiments, the agent group generated 24 to 48 percent more solutions in transfer tests than did the no-agent group.

In a related study (Atkinson, 2002), students learned to solve proportionality word problems by seeing worked-out examples presented via a computer screen. For some students, an on-screen agent spoke to them, giving a step-by-step explanation for the solution (agent group). For other students, the same explanation was printed as on-screen text without any image or voice of an agent (no-agent group). On a subsequent transfer test involving different word problems, the agent group generated 30 percent more correct solutions than the no-agent group. Although these results are preliminary, they suggest that it might be worthwhile to consider the role of animated pedagogical agents as aids to learning.

Do Agents Need to Look Real?

As you may have noticed in the previously described research, there were many differences between the agent and no-agent groups, so it is reasonable to ask which of those differences has an effect on student learning. In short, we want to know what makes an effective agent. Let's begin by asking about the looks of the agent, such as whether people learn better from human-looking agents or cartoon-like agents. To help answer this question, students learned about botany principles by playing the Design-A-Plant game with one of two agents—a cartoon-like animated character named Herman-the-Bug or a talking-head video of a young male who said exactly the same words as Herman-the-Bug (Moreno, Mayer, Spires, & Lester, 2001). Overall, the groups did not differ much in their test performance, suggesting that a real character did not work any better than a cartoon character. In addition, students learned just as well when the image of the character was present or absent, as long as the students could hear the agent's voice. These preliminary results (including similar findings by Craig, Gholson, & Driscoll, 2002) suggest that a lifelike image is not always an essential component in an effective agent.

Although onscreen agents may not have to look real, there is some evidence that they should behave in a human-like way in terms of their gestures, movements, and eye-gaze. For example, Lusk and Atkinson (2007) found that students learned better from an on-screen agent who demonstrated how to solve mathematics problems when the on-screen agent was fully embodied (that is, used human-like locomotion, gestures, and eye-gazes) rather than minimally embodied (that is, was physically present but did not move, gesture, or gaze at the learner). In an eye-tracking study, Louwerse, Graesser, McNamara, and Lu (2009) found that learners looked at gesturing on-screen agents as they spoke, indicating that the learners were treating the on-screen agents as conversational partners.

Overall, the research shows that on-screen pedagogical agents do not need realistic human-like appearance but do need realistic human-like behavior.

Do Agents Need to Sound Real?

Even if the agent may not look real, there is compelling evidence that the agent has to sound conversational. First, across four comparisons (Moreno, Mayer, Spires, & Lester, 2001; Moreno & Mayer, 2004), students learned better in the Design-A-Plant game if Herman's words were spoken rather than presented as on-screen text. This finding is an indication that the modality effect (as described in Chapter 6) applies to on-screen agents. Second, across three comparisons (Moreno and Mayer, 2000b), as reported in the previous section, students learned better in the Design-A-Plant game if Herman's words were spoken in a conversational style rather than a formal style. This finding is an indication that the personalization effect applies to on-screen agents. Finally, as reported in the previous section, Atkinson and colleagues (Atkinson, 2002; Atkinson, Mayer, and Merrill, 2005) found some preliminary evidence that students learn to solve word problems better from an on-screen agent when the words are spoken in a human voice rather than a machine-simulated voice. Overall, these preliminary results show that the agent's voice is an important determinant of instructional effectiveness.

Should Agents Match the Gender or Ethnicity of the Learners?

Moreno and Flowerday (2006) found that students who were allowed to select an on-screen pedagogical agent that was the same ethnicity or gender for a multimedia science lesson performed more poorly on subsequent transfer tests than students who were not given a choice.

Although it is premature to make firm recommendations concerning on-screen pedagogical agents, we are able to offer some suggestions based on the current state of the field. We suggest that you consider using on-screen agents, and that the agent's words be presented as speech rather than text, in conversational style rather than formal style, and with human-like rather than machine-like articulation. Although intense work is underway to create entertaining agents who display human-like gestures and facial expressions, their educational value is just beginning to be demonstrated.

We further suggest that you use agents to provide instruction rather than for entertainment purposes. For example, an agent can explain a step in a demonstration or provide feedback to a learner's response to a lesson question. In contrast, the cartoon puppy in Figure 9.10 is not an agent, as he is never used for any instructional purpose. Likewise, there is a common unproductive tendency to insert theme characters from popular games and movies who are added only for entertainment value and serve no instructional role. These embellishments are likely to depress learning, as discussed in Chapter 8.

Based on the cognitive theory and research we have highlighted in this chapter, we can propose the personalization principles. First, present words in conversational style rather than formal style. In creating the script for a narration or the text for an on-screen passage, you should use some first- and

Figure 9.10. The Puppy Character Plays No Instructional Role So Is Not an Agent.

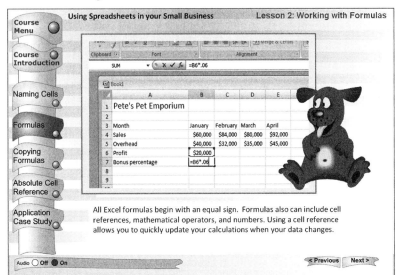

second-person constructions (that is, involving "I," "we," "me," "my," "you," and/or "your") to create the feeling of conversation between the course and the learner. However, you should be careful not to overdo the personalization style because it is important not to distract the learner. Second, use on-screen agents to provide coaching in the form of hints, worked examples, demonstrations, and explanations.

Personalization Principle 3: Make the Author Visible to Promote Learning
What Is a Visible Author?

Instructional text is often written in a formal and impersonal style, in which the author seems invisible. Invisible authors do not tell you anything about themselves, whereas visible authors reveal information about themselves and highlight their personal perspective (Nolen, 1995; Paxton, 2002). Converting an invisible author to a visible one can be called giving a voice to the text

(Beck, McKeown, Sandora, Kucan, and Worthy, 1996). Take a minute to review the two descriptions of Mayer's multimedia research shown in Figure 9.11. Sample A is a factual summary of Mayer's multimedia research. Sample B discusses similar material but uses an interview format. In Sample B, Mayer speaks directly to the reader in a personal style. In Sample B, the author is visible, whereas in Sample A the author is invisible.

In a statistics lesson on correlation, visible authors might include themselves in an example (Nolen, 1995, p. 61): "Yet, least anyone become too hopeful that correlation represents a magic method for unambiguous identification of cause, consider the relationship between my age and the price of gasoline during the past ten years. The correlation is nearly perfect, but no one would suggest any assignment of cause." As another example from a

---

Figure 9.11. Invisible (A) vs. Visible (B) Author in Summaries of Mayer's Research.

A. Review of Richard Mayer's Research by Kiewra and Creswell, 2000

"Another example of Mayer's systematic approach to writing review articles is seen in his article "Multimedia Learning: Are We Asking the Right Questions? "(Mayer, 1997). Here Mayer reviews research showing that (a) multimedia delivery systems are better than verbal explanations alone, (b) instructional methods involving coordinated verbal and visual explanations are better than explanations separated by time or space (c) effects are strongest for students with low prior knowledge and high spatial ability (p. 144).

B. Interview of Richard Mayer by Suomala and Shaughnessy, 2000

Q: What are you currently researching?
A: For the past decade, my colleagues and I at Santa Barbara have been studying multimedia learning. Multimedia learning occurs when material is presented in more than one format, such as in words and in pictures. In particular we have been tracking down the conditions under which multimedia presentations concerning scientific explanations lead to meaningful, constructivist learning. We have found, for example, that adding animation to narration improves learner's understanding and we have identified six principles for how to combine visual and verbal materials (p. 478).

history lesson on the fall of Rome, visible authors might reveal personal beliefs (Paxton, 2002, p. 244): "To those of us looking back at the ancient past, Julius Caesar remains one of the most controversial figures. I, for one, still have a hard time determining if he was a great leader, or a terrible dictator. Other historians have the same problem. Let's see what you think." One final example involves providing transcripts (or video clips) of interviews with famous scholars, so they can describe their ideas in their own words (Inglese, Mayer, & Rigotti, 2007).

The visible author principle can be applied in both synchronous and asynchronous forms of e-learning. For example, review the narration shown in Figure 9.12. The lesson topic is branding. The instructor applies the visible author principle by revealing his favorite brand typed into the chat window.

Figure 9.12. A Visible Instructor in a Virtual Classroom.

Psychological Reasons for Using a Visible Author

The main rationale for using a visible author style is to promote learner motivation. For example, Nolen (1995, p. 47) suggests that when authors are visible, students might see the author as "a personal guide through an otherwise difficult domain." Paxton (2002, p. 202) proposes that "a human-to-human relationship between author and reader is encouraged by the presence of a visible author." Consistent with Mayer's (2005d) extension of the cognitive theory of multimedia learning shown in Figure 9.5, the visible author technique can help prime a sense of social presence in the learner—a feeling of being in a conversation with the author. The activation of social presence, in turn, encourages the learner to engage in deeper cognitive processing during learning, leading to a better learning outcome. The underlying rationale for the visible author approach is that people work harder to understand a lesson when they feel they are in a conversation with the author. However, the danger of over-emphasis on the author's self-revealing remarks is that they can become seductive details, which distract the learner (and violate the coherence principle described in the previous chapter). Good instructional design involves adding just the right amount of social cues to prime a sense of social presence in the learner, without adding so much that the learner is distracted.

Evidence for the Visible Author

There is some preliminary evidence that using the visible author style can promote deeper engagement in some learners. Paxton (2002) asked high school students to read a history lesson that featured an anonymous author (one who writes in the third person, revealing little about personal beliefs or self) or a visible author. On a subsequent essay writing task, students in the visible author group worked harder—as is indicated by writing longer essays that showed greater sensitivity to the audience. Inglese, Mayer, and Rigotti (2007) asked students at an Italian-speaking university to view online video clips and read online transcripts of various scholars in a course on political theory. On subsequent tests, non-native speakers wrote more and provided richer answers concerning visible authors than for scholars whose theories had been described without any interviews, whereas the effects of author visibility were not as strong for native speakers. An important boundary condition is that the positive effects of visible authors may be strongest for students who might otherwise be losing interest in the course. At this time, there is not a strong database to support the widespread use of the visible author technique, but we anticipate more research on this potentially useful technique in the future.

What We Don't Know About Personalization

Although personalization can be effective in some situations, additional research is needed to determine when it becomes counterproductive by being distracting or condescending. Further work also is needed to determine conditions—if any—under which the visible author technique can be effective. Perhaps the most exciting application of the personalization principle involves the design of pedagogical agents, so research is needed to determine which features of an agent promote learning, such as the role of gesturing, eye fixations, and locomotion. In addition, we do not know whether specific types of learners benefit more than others from the personalization principle. For example, would there be any differences between novice and experienced learners, learners who are committed to the content versus learners who are taking required content, male versus female learners? When it comes to the gender of the narrator, does the content make a difference? For example, in mathematics, which is considered a male-dominant domain, a female narrator was more effective than a male narrator. Finally, research is needed to determine the long-term effects of personalization, that is, does the effect of conversational style (or politeness) diminish as students spend more time with the course?

DESIGN DILEMMA: RESOLVED

The pharmaceutical sales team was debating the tone of their lesson defined by the language used and by adding a learning agent. The options considered were:

A. Reshmi is correct. A more informal approach plus an agent will lead to better learning.

B. Matt is correct. A more formal tone will fit the corporate image better, leading to a more credible instructional message.

C. The tone of the lesson should be adjusted for the learners. Women will benefit from more informality and men will find a formal approach more credible.

D. Not sure which option is correct.

Based on the evidence reviewed in this chapter, we would select Option A. Until we have more research on individual differences in response to the personalization principle, we cannot make any comment about Option C. We recommend that Matt make a case to the legal department as well as to communications showing the evidence for learning benefits from an e-learning environment in which social presence is heightened through the use of second-person constructions and an on-screen agent who guides the learning process.

WHAT TO LOOK FOR IN e-LEARNING

☐ Instructional content is presented in conversational language using "you," "your," "I," "our," and "we."

☐ Coaching is provided via conversational narration from on-screen characters (that is, pedagogical agents).

☐ Agents do not need to look realistic but should exhibit human behaviors.

☐ Agent dialog is presented via audio narration.

☐ Voice quality and script are natural and conversational.

☐ Agents serve a valid instructional purpose.

☐ The course author expresses his or her own point of view or experience in ways that are relevant to the instructional goals.

COMING NEXT

The next chapter on segmenting and pretraining completes the basic set of multimedia principles in e-learning. These principles apply to training produced to inform as well as to increase performance; in other words, they apply to all forms of e-learning. After reading the next chapter, you will have topped off your arsenal of basic multimedia instructional design principles described in Chapters 4 through 10.

Suggested Readings

Mayer, R.E. (2005). Principles based on social cues: Personalization, voice, and image principles. In R.E. Mayer (Ed.), *The Cambridge handbook of multimedia learning* (pp. 201–212). New York: Cambridge University Press.

Mayer, R.E., Sobko, K., & Mautone, P.D. (2003). Social cues in multimedia learning: Role of speaker's voice. *Journal of Educational Psychology, 95*, 419–425.

Moreno, R., & Mayer, R.E. (2000). Engaging students in active learning: The case for personalized multimedia messages. *Journal of Educational Psychology, 93,* 724–733.

Moreno, R., & Mayer, R.E. (2004). Personalized messages that promote science learning in virtual environments. *Journal of Educational Psychology, 96,* 165–173.

Moreno, R., Mayer, R.E., Spires, H., & Lester, J. (2001). The case for social agency in computer-based teaching: Do students learn more deeply when they interact with animated pedagogical agents? *Cognition and Instruction, 19*, 177–214.

Nass, C., & Brave, S. (2005). *Wired for speech: How voice activates and advances the human-computer relationship.* Cambridge, MA: MIT Press.

Reeves, B., & Nass, C. (1996). *The media equation: How people treat computers, television, and new media like real people and places.* New York: Cambridge University Press.

Wang, N., Johnson, W.L., Mayer, R.E., Rizzo, P., Shaw, E., & Collins, H. (2008). The politeness effect: Pedagogical agents and learning outcomes. *International Journal of Human Computer Studies, 66,* 98–112.

Wouters, P., Paas, F.G.W.C., & van Merrienboer, J.J.G., (2008). How to optimize learning from animated models: A review of guidelines based on cognitive load. *Review of Educational Research, 78,* 645–675.

CHAPTER OUTLINE

Segmenting Principle: Break a Continuous Lesson into Bite-Size Segments

Psychological Reasons for the Segmenting Principle

Evidence for Breaking a Continuous Lesson into Bite-Size Segments

Pretraining Principle: Ensure That Learners Know the Names and Characteristics of Key Concepts

Psychological Reasons for the Pretraining Principle

Evidence for Providing Pretraining in Key Concepts

10

Applying the Segmenting and Pretraining Principles

MANAGING COMPLEXITY BY BREAKING
A LESSON INTO PARTS

WHAT'S NEW IN THIS CHAPTER?

IN SOME OF THE PREVIOUS CHAPTERS you learned how to reduce extraneous processing (that is, processing caused by poor instructional design), by eliminating extraneous words and pictures (Chapter 8), by placing corresponding words and illustrations near each other on the screen (Chapter 5), or by refraining from adding redundant on-screen text to a narrated animation (Chapter 7). In Chapter 2, we introduced the concept of *essential cognitive processing* that results from the complexity of the material. In this chapter we focus on situations in which learners must engage in so much essential processing that their cognitive systems are overwhelmed. In particular, in this chapter we focus on techniques for managing essential processing, including segmenting (breaking a lesson into manageable segments) and pretraining (providing pretraining in the names and characteristics of key concepts). This chapter represents an update on the growing research base on techniques for managing the learning of complex material.

DESIGN DILEMMA: YOU DECIDE

The Excel lesson team is working on their lesson design. They have completed their job analysis and identified five key steps involved in setting up a spreadsheet. Sergio, the subject-matter expert, offers the team an outline. "Here", he says, "let me save you some time. This is the outline I use when I teach in the classroom. (See Sergio's outline in Figure 10.1) It works really well because I teach one step at a time." "Thanks, Serg. It really helps to have the content broken out," Reshmi replies, "but after I reviewed our job analysis, I came up with a slightly different sequence. Take a look." (See Reshmi's outline in Figure 10.1). After reading Reshmi's outline, Sergio reacts: "Wow, Reshmi! I think your outline is confusing. My plan places all of the key concepts with each step. That way they learn each concept in the context in which they will use it! We can use that new screen capture tool to run my slides continuously while the narration plays." Reshmi is not convinced by Sergio's argument: "Yes, but your plan lumps a lot of content together. I think it will overwhelm people new to Excel—and many of our learners will be new users."

Figure 10.1. Two Organizational Sequences for the Excel Lesson.

Sergio's Outline	Reshmi's Outline
I. Introduction	I. Introduction
II. Step 1 – Enter data in cells	II. What are cells
A. What are cells	III. What are cell references
B. What are cell references	IV. About formulas
III. Step 2 – Enter formula	V. Demonstration: Calculate Jan sales
A. What are formulas	VI. Practice: Calculate Feb sales
B. How are formulas formatted	VI. Absolute & relative cell references
IV. Step 3 – Click on enter key	VII. Demonstration: Calculate taxes owed
V. Step 4 – Identify unchanging variables	VIII. Practice: Calculate taxes owed
A. What are relative and absolute formulas	
VI. Step 5 – Enter a relative and absolute formula	

Sergio and Reshmi disagree about the sequencing of content as well as how to display the content. Based on your own experience or intuition, which of the following options would you select?

A. Sergio's plan is better because it teaches all content in context of the procedure.

B. Reshmi's plan is better because she has separated the key concepts from the procedure.

C. It is better to let the lesson "play" like a video so learners have a continuous picture of the entire procedure.

D. It is better to let the learners control the sequence by selecting screens in small bites so they can work at their own rate.

E. Not sure which options are correct.

Segmenting Principle: Break a Continuous Lesson into Bite-Size Segments

How can you tell that material is so complex that it will overload the learner's cognitive system? A good way to gauge the complexity of a lesson is to tally the number of elements (or concepts) and the number of interactions among them. For example, consider a narrated animation on how a bicycle tire pump works that has the script: "When the handle is pulled up, the piston moves up, the inlet valve opens, the outlet valve closes, and air enters the cylinder. When the handle is pushed down, the piston moves down, the piston moves down, the inlet valve closes, the outlet valve opens, and air exits from the cylinder through the hose." In this case there are five main elements—handle, piston, cylinder, inlet valve, and outlet valve. The relations among them constitute a simple chain in which a change in one element causes a change in the next element and so on. Overall, this is a fairly simple lesson that probably requires just two segments—one showing what happens when the handle is pulled up and one showing what happens when the handle is pushed down.

Next, consider a lesson on lightning formation, such as shown in Figure 10.2. This is a much more complex lesson because it has many more elements—warm and cold air, updrafts and downdrafts, positive and negative particles in the cloud, positive and negative particles on the ground, leaders and return strokes, and so on. This lesson can be broken into sixteen segments, each describing one or two major steps in the causal chain, such

Figure 10.2. Screens from Lightning Lesson.

From Moreno and Mayer, 1999a.

"The charge results from the collision of the cloud's rising water droplets against heavier, falling pieces of ice."

"The negatively charged particles fall to the bottom of the cloud, and most of the positively charged particles rise to the top."

"A stepped leader of negative charges moves downward in a series of steps. It nears the ground."

"A positively charged leader travels up from such objects as trees and buildings."

"The two leaders generally meet about 165-feet above the ground."

"Negatively charged particles then rush from the cloud to the ground along the path created by the leaders. It is not very bright."

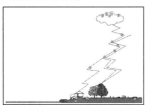

"As the leader stroke nears the ground, it induces an opposite charge, so positively charged particles from the ground rush upward along the same path."

"This upward motion of the current is the return stroke. It produces the bright light that people notice as a flash of lightning."

as, "Cool moist air moves over a warmer surface and becomes heated." Each of the frames shown in Figure 10.2 constitutes a segment—involving just a few elements and relations between them.

As training professionals, you have probably worked with content that was relatively simple as well as with content that was more complex. For example, if you are teaching a class on editing text in Microsoft Word, you need to teach a four-step procedure. First, learners must use the mouse to select the text they want to edit. Second, they click on the scissors icon to cut the text from its present location. Next, learners place their cursors at the insertion point and click on the paste icon. This software procedure is quite linear and relatively simple. It is made easier by having only a few steps and by using onscreen icons that call up familiar metaphors such as scissors

Figure 10.3. Constructing a Formula in Excel Is a Complex Task.

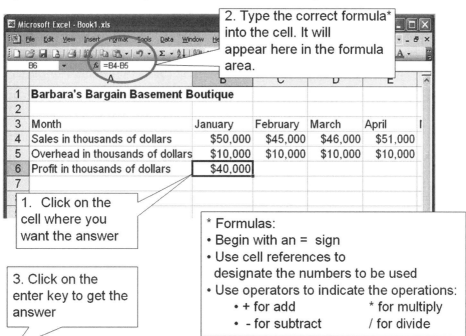

for cutting. However, in many cases, your content is more complex than this example. Even an introductory Excel class offers greater degrees of complexity. As you can see in Figure 10.3, constructing a formula in Excel can be quite complex for someone new to spreadsheets and to Excel. One of the key concepts involves the construction of a formula that uses the correct formatting conventions to achieve the desired calculation. For someone new to Excel, we would rate this as a more complex task than the word processing editing task.

When the material is complex, you can't make it simpler by leaving out some of the elements or steps in the explanation—because that would destroy the accuracy of the lesson. However, you can help the learner manage the complexity by breaking the lesson into manageable segments—parts that convey just one or two or three steps in the process or procedure or describe just one or two or three major relations among the elements. We recommend that you break a complex lesson into smaller parts, which are presented one at a time. We call this recommendation the *segmenting principle.*

Psychological Reasons for the Segmenting Principle

Suppose that, as part of an e-course, the learner clicked on an entry for "lightning" from a multimedia encyclopedia and then watched a 2.5-minute narrated animation explaining lightning formation—as shown in Figure 10.2. The figure shows some of the frames in the animation along with the complete spoken script indicted in quotation marks at the bottom of each frame. As you can see, the lesson is complex—with many interacting elements—and is presented at a fairly rapid pace. If a learner misses one point, such as the idea that a cloud rises to the point that the top is above the freezing level and the bottom is below, the entire causal chain will no longer make sense. If a learner is unfamiliar with the material, he or she may need time to consolidate what was just presented. In short, when an unfamiliar learner receives a continuous presentation containing a lot of interrelated concepts, the likely result is that the cognitive system becomes overloaded—too much essential processing is required. In short, the learner does not have sufficient cognitive capacity to engage in the essential processing required to understand the material.

One solution to this dilemma that we recommend is to break the lesson into manageable parts, such as sixteen segments with a "Continue" button in the bottom right corner of each. Figure 10.4 shows an example of a frame from one of the segments. As you can see, the learner receives a short clip approximately ten seconds in length, along with one sentence describing the actions that are depicted. The learner can completely digest this link in the causal chain before clicking on the "Continue" button to go on to the next segment. This technique—which can be called *segmenting*—allows the learner to manage essential processing. Thus, the rationale for using segmenting is that it allows the learner to engage essential processing without overloading the learner's cognitive system.

We saw that a lesson on Excel offers greater complexity than one on text editing. In a procedural lesson you can let an animated sequence play continuously, demonstrating how to complete a task such as construct or enter a formula. Alternatively, you can divide the procedure into two or three segments, presenting each one independently with a continue button. In the segmented version, the learner receives only a small amount of content and then clicks on the lower right hand "Continue" button when he or she is ready to move to the next small bite. For someone new to Excel, the segmented version will impose less mental load.

Figure 10.4. Adding a Continue Button Allows Learners to Progress at Their Own Rate.

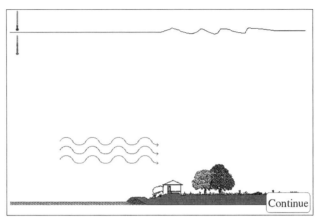

"Cool moist air moves over a warmer surface and becomes heated."

Evidence for Breaking a Continuous Lesson into Bite-Size Segments

The previous section tells a nice story, but is there any evidence that segmenting helps people learn better? The answer is yes. Mayer and Chandler (2001) carried out the study using the lightning lesson as described in the previous section. They found that learners who received the segmented presentation performed better on transfer tests than the learners who received a continuous presentation, even though identical material was presented in both conditions. In a similar study, prospective teachers who viewed a continuous twenty-minute video that demonstrated various exemplary teaching techniques performed worse on a transfer test than did students who received the identical video broken into seven segments, each focusing on one technique (Moreno, 2007).

In another set of studies (Mayer, Dow, & Mayer, 2003), students learned how an electric motor works by watching a continuous narrated animation or by watching a segmented version. In the segmented version, the learner could click on a question and then see part of the narrated animation, click on another question and see the next part, and so on. The material was identical for both the continuous and segmented versions, but learners performed much better on transfer tests if they had received the segmented lesson. Overall, in three out of three studies the results provided strong positive effects for segmenting, yielding a median effect size of about 1. We conclude that there is tantalizing preliminary evidence in favor of segmenting, but additional research is needed.

Schar and Zimmermann (2007) compared learning from an animation lesson that played continuously without controls for pausing with an animation that included a pause button. Having a pause button would allow learners to stop and start the animation when they desired. They found no differences in learning in the two versions, primarily because most learners did not use the pause button, instead allowing the animation to play as a continuous presentation. Therefore, both experimental groups ended up with more or less the same treatments. The research team suggests that you design animated sequences to stop at a logical segment with a continue button for the learner to resume play, as shown in Figure 10.4. As we will see in Chapter 14, learners—especially novice learners—may not make good instructional decisions and instead benefit from greater instructional control. In other words, the lesson designer can best determine optimal segments and insert pauses at those points rather than relying on the learner to make that determination.

Pretraining Principle: Ensure That Learners Know the Names and Characteristics of Key Concepts

Segmenting appears to be a promising way to address the situation in which the learner is overloaded by the need to engage in essential processing—that is, the learner is overwhelmed by the amount of essential processing required to understand a complex lesson. In this section, we examine a related technique, which can be called the *pretraining principle*: Provide pretraining in the names and characteristics of the key concepts in the lesson. For example, before viewing a narrated animation on how the digestive system works, learners could receive pretraining in which they learn the names and locations of key body parts such as the esophagus, epiglottis, trachea, pharynx, upper esophageal sphincter, lower esophageal sphincter, and stomach.

We mentioned previously that for a new student or instructor, using the various facilities in the virtual classroom can be overwhelming. Therefore, we recommend a quick orientation session at the start of a virtual classroom session that applies the pretraining principle. During the orientation, the instructor can show the different parts of the virtual classroom, as in Figure 10.5, followed by some introductory exercises during which each student uses those facilities. We also categorized learning how to use Excel formulas as another complex task. To apply the pretraining principle, the lesson shown in Figure 10.6 begins by teaching formula formatting conventions. Following this portion of the lesson, the instructor demonstrates the procedure of how to enter a formula into a spreadsheet.

Figure 10.5. Pretraining Illustrates the Parts and Functions of the Virtual Classroom Interface.

From Clark and Kwinn, 2007.

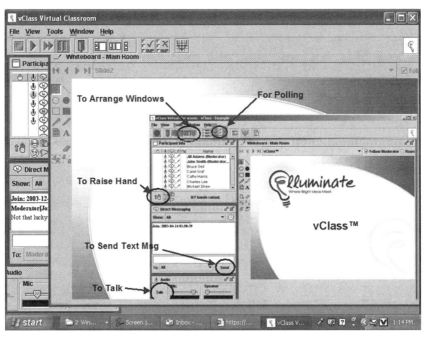

Figure 10.6. Pretraining Teaches Formula Format Before Procedure.
From Clark and Kwinn (2007).

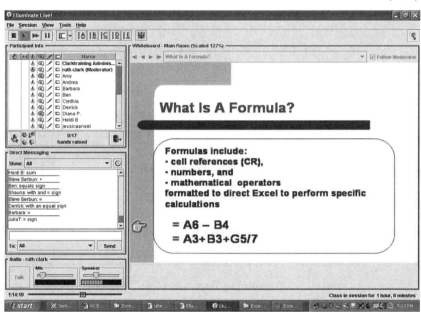

Psychological Reasons for the Pretraining Principle

The pretraining principle is relevant in situations when trying to process the essential material in the lesson would overwhelm the learner's cognitive system. In these situations involving complex material, it is helpful if some of the processing can be done in advance. When you see a narrated animation on how the digestive system works, for example, you need to build a cause-and-effect model of how a change in one part of the system causes a change in the next part and so on, and you need to understand what each part does. We can help the learner understand the cause-and-effect chain by making sure the learner already knows the name and characteristics of each part. When you hear a term like "upper esophageal sphincter" in a narrated animation, you need to try to figure out what this term refers to and how it works. Learners who are more familiar with the content area may not need pretraining because they already know the names and characteristics of key concepts. In short, pretraining can help beginners to manage their processing of complex material by reducing the amount of essential processing they do at the time of the presentation. If they already know what terms like "upper esophageal sphincter" mean, they can devote their cognitive processing to building a mental model of how that component relates to others in the causal chain. Thus, the rationale for the pretraining principle is that it helps manage the learner's essential processing by redistributing some of it to a pretraining portion of the lesson.

To implement the pretraining principle, evaluate the material you need to teach—such as a procedure or how a process works. If it is complex for your audience, then identify key concepts that could be presented prior to teaching the main lesson. For example, you could begin with a short section on the key concepts, even including a practice exercise on them. For example, in Figure 10.7 we show an example that applies both segmenting and

Figure 10.7. This Lesson Applies Both Segmenting and Pretraining Principles.
With permission from Raytheon Professional Services.

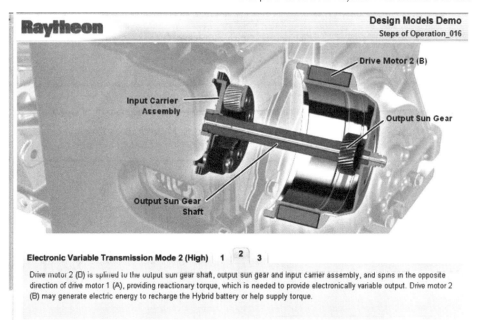

Electronic Variable Transmission Mode 2 (High)   1   **2**   3

Drive motor 2 (D) is splined to the output sun shaft, output sun gear and input carrier assembly, and spins in the opposite direction of drive motor 1 (A), providing reactionary torque, which is needed to provide electronically variable output. Drive motor 2 (B) may generate electric energy to recharge the Hybrid battery or help supply torque.

pretraining to a technical lesson on how transmissions work. Tabs are used to segment content into small chunks and the names of the parts of the transmission are labeled in the first tab. Note, however, in this example as well as in Figure 10.5, the parts are shown in the context of the entire screen interface or equipment sketch. In this way, the individual parts shown during pretraining maintain the context to the whole environment. After the pretraining, you can move into the main lesson—such as describing how to carry out a procedure or how a process works.

Evidence for Providing Pretraining in Key Concepts

Suppose we asked some learners to watch a sixty-second narrated animation on how a car's braking system works (that is, no pretraining condition), containing the script: "When the driver steps on a car's brake pedal, a piston moves forward in the master cylinder. The piston forces brake fluid out of the master cylinder and through the tubes to the wheel cylinders. In the wheel cylinders, the increase in fluid pressure makes a smaller set of pistons move. Those smaller pistons activate the brake shoes. When the brake shoes press against the drum, both the drum and the wheel stop or slow down." Figure 10.8 shows part of the animation that goes with this script. As you can see, this lesson is somewhat complex, partly because it contains some unfamiliar terms. It describes interactions

Figure 10.8. Part of a Multimedia Presentation on How Brakes Work.
From Mayer, Mathias, and Wetzell, 2002.

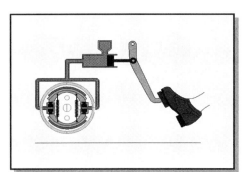 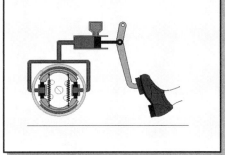

among many parts such as brake pedal, piston in master cylinder, brake fluid in tube, pistons in wheel cylinders, brake shoes, drum, and wheel. The learner must learn the relations among the parts as well as the characteristics of the parts themselves.

What can be done to provide some pretraining so the learner can be relieved of some of the essential processing during the narrated animation? Mayer, Mathias, and Wetzell (2002) constructed a short pretraining episode in which learners saw a labeled diagram of the braking system on the screen and could click on any part, as shown in Figure 10.9. When they

---

Figure 10.9. Pretraining on How Brakes Work.

From Mayer, Mathias, and Wetzell, 2002.

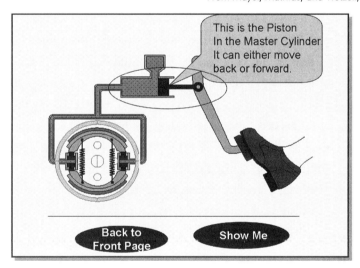

clicked on a part, they were told the name of the part and its main characteristics. In three separate studies, learners who received this kind of pretraining before the narrated animation performed better on transfer tests than did learners who did not receive pretraining, yielding a median effect size of .9. The results from one of these studies is shown in Figure 10.10.

In an e-learning environment, students learned to solve electronics troubleshooting problems better if they received factual information before training, rather than within the context of training (Kester, Kirshner, & van

Figure 10.10. Pretraining Version Resulted in Better Learning.
Based on data from Mayer, Mathias, and Wetzell, 2002.

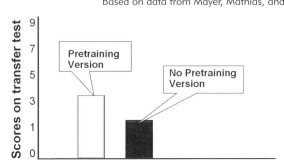

Merrienboer, 2006). In another set of studies (Pollock, Chandler, & Sweller, 2002), electrical engineering trainees took a course that included a multimedia lesson on conducting safety tests for electrical appliances. The no-pretraining group was shown how all the electrical components worked together within an electrical system. The pretraining group first was shown how each component worked individually. Across two separate experiments, the pretraining group outperformed the no-pretraining group on transfer tests, yielding effect sizes greater than 1. Overall, there is encouraging preliminary evidence for the pretraining principle, but an important possible boundary condition is that the effect may be strongest for low-knowledge learners (Pollock, Chandler, & Sweller, 2002).

What We Don't Know About Segmenting and Pretraining

Research on segmenting and pretraining is not as well developed as research supporting other principles in this book, so we need a larger research base that examines whether the effects replicate with different materials, learners, and learning contexts. We do not yet know how big a segment should be, that is, we need to determine how much information should be in a bite-sized chunk. Should a segment last for ten seconds, thirty seconds, sixty seconds, or more? How do you determine where to break a continuous lesson into meaningful segments? The issue of how much learner control is optimal is examined in Chapter 14, but also is not a resolved issue. We also do not yet know how best to identify key concepts that should be included in pretraining or how extensive the pretraining needs to be. Is it enough for learners to simply know the names and locations of the key components in a to-be-learned system? Also, there may be situations in which learning will be better when key concepts are presented in the context of an authentic task such as in whole-task learning designs. We will discuss these designs in more detail in Chapter 15. Answering these questions depends, in part, on the characteristics of the learner, especially the learner's prior knowledge.

DESIGN DILEMMA: RESOLVED

The Excel e-learning team was debating the best way to sequence and to display their content. The options considered were:

A. Sergio's plan is better because it teaches all content in context of the procedure.

B. Reshmi's plan is better because she has separated the key concepts from the procedure.

C. It is better to let the lesson "play" like a video so learners have a continuous picture of the entire procedure.

D. It is better to let the learners see the lesson in small bites so they can work at their own rate.

E. Not sure which options are correct.

Our first question is whether setting up a spreadsheet is a complex task. The answer is "yes" for learners who are new to electronic spreadsheets. There are a number of concepts to consider and to weigh when setting up a spreadsheet. Given a complex instructional goal, we recommend applying the segmenting and pre-training principles suggested in Options B and D. We do agree that it's a good idea to teach the supporting concepts in job context and recommend that these concepts be shown in the context of setting up a simple spreadsheet. If you plan to use an animated sequence, we recommend that you pause the animation at logical intervals, giving the learner the option to replay or continue the animation when he or she is ready.

WHAT TO LOOK FOR IN e-LEARNING

☐ Material is presented in manageable segments (such as short clips of narrated animation) controlled by the learner, rather than as a continuous unit (such as a long clip of narrated animation).

☐ Animation sequences pause at logical segments with provision of a replay or continue button.

☐ Key concepts are named and their characteristics are described before presenting the processes or procedures to which the concepts are linked.

☐ Concepts or terms included in pretraining are introduced in the context of the whole process or procedure.

COMING NEXT

One of the most popular and powerful instructional techniques is the example. Just about all effective lessons incorporate examples. What is the best way to use examples in your e-lessons? How can examples actually accelerate learning? How can you make examples engaging? In the next chapter you will learn important guidelines and the evidence behind the guidelines for the best design, placement, and layout of examples in your e-learning.

Suggested Readings

Mayer, R.E., (2005). Principles for managing essential processing in multimedia learning: Segmenting, pretraining, and modality principles. In R.E. Mayer (Ed.), *The Cambridge handbook of multimedia learning* (pp. 169–182). New York: Cambridge University Press.

Mayer, R.E., & Chandler, P. (2001). When learning is just a click away: Does simple user interaction foster deeper understanding of multimedia messages? *Journal of Educational Psychology, 93,* 390–397.

Mayer, R.E., Mathias, A., & Wetzell, K. (2002). Fostering understanding of multimedia messages through pretraining: Evidence for a two-stage theory of mental model construction. *Journal of Experimental Psychology: Applied, 8,* 147–154.

CHAPTER OUTLINE

What Are Worked Examples?

Worked Examples for Strategic Tasks

Modeling Examples

The Psychology of Worked Examples

Evidence for the Benefits of Worked Examples

Worked Example Principle 1: Fade from Worked Examples to Problems

Worked Example Principle 2: Promote Self-Explanations

Add Self-Explanation Questions to Your Worked Examples

Encourage Self-Explanations Through Active Observation

Worked Example Principle 3: Include Instructional Explanations of Worked Examples in Some Situations

Worked Example Principle 4: Apply Multimedia Principles to Your Examples

Illustrate Worked Examples with Relevant Visuals: Multimedia Principle

Present Steps with Audio—NOT Audio and Text: Modality and Redundancy Principles

Present Steps with Integrated Text: Contiguity Principle

Present Steps in Conceptually Meaningful Chunks: Segmenting Principle

Present Steps with Learner Control of Pacing: Segmenting Principle

Familiarize Learners with Example Context: Pretraining Principle

Worked Example Principle 5: Support Learning Transfer

Design Guidelines for Far Transfer Worked Examples

Far Transfer Guideline 1: Use Varied Context Worked Examples

Far Transfer Guideline 2: Include Self-Explanation Questions

Far Transfer Guideline 3: Require Active Comparison of Varied Context Examples

11

Leveraging Examples in e-Learning

SINCE OUR SECOND EDITION of *e-Learning and the Science of Instruction*, there continues to be a wealth of research focused on worked examples. The most recent research has extended guidelines on worked examples used to illustrate well-structured math solutions to worked examples for tasks that involve problem solving and multiple appropriate solutions. This research leaves us with important new guidelines for development of worked examples to build critical thinking skills that require flexible and creative approaches.

We have also added important new research on modeling examples—worked examples that incorporate people as they are solving problems or as they demonstrate interpersonal tasks such as teaching or selling. As in our first editions, we discuss the application of the multimedia principles to worked examples as well as design techniques to promote far transfer.

DESIGN DILEMMA: YOU DECIDE

In the pharmaceutical sales course, Reshmi wants to add some interactivity to the video examples. "These video models are great, but our new sales recruits are not getting half the value from them that they could. We need to add some questions about the examples. Or we could insert scenarios in which we demonstrate the first few steps and ask learners to finish them." Matthew disagrees: "We could save time by asking learners to review the examples with partners and collaboratively diagram the sales techniques. That way we would not need to add anything or change the video examples we've planned." Based on your own experience or intuition, which of the following options would you select?

A. Reshmi is correct. Video examples should be accompanied by questions that engage learners in the examples.

B. Asking learners to complete a partial example would be better than asking questions about the examples

C. Matthew is correct. It would be more effective to ask learners to review examples in pairs

What Are Worked Examples?

Examples are one of the most powerful methods you can use to build new cognitive skills, and they are popular with learners. Learners often bypass verbal descriptions in favor of examples. For example, LeFevre and Dixon (1986) evaluated learners who were free to study either textual descriptions or examples to help them complete problem assignments. The information in the text was deliberately written to contradict the examples. By evaluating the learners' solutions, it was clear that the learners used the examples, *not the text*, as their preferred resource.

In this chapter we write about a specific type of example called a *worked example*. A worked example is a step-by-step demonstration of how to perform a task or solve a problem. Worked examples can be designed to help learners build *procedural* skills such as how to use a spreadsheet or *strategic* skills such as how to conduct a negotiation. In Figure 11.1 we show a three-step worked example used in a statistics lesson to illustrate calculation of probability. In Figure 11.2 we show a screen capture from part of a worked

Figure 11.1. A Worked Example of a Probability Problem.

From Atkinson, Renkl, and Merrill, 2003.

Problem: From a ballot box containing three red balls and two white balls, two balls are randomly drawn. The chosen balls are not put back into the ballot box. What is the probability that the red ball is drawn first and a white ball is second?

First Solution Step	Total number of balls: 5 Number of red balls: 3 Probability of red ball first 3/5 = .6

Second Solution Step	Total number of balls after first draw: 4 (2 red and 2 white balls) Probability of a white ball second: 2/4 = .5

Third Solution Step	Probability that a red ball is drawn first and a white ball is second: 3/5 x ½ = 3/10 = .3 <u>Answer:</u> The probability that a red ball is drawn first and white ball is second is 3/10 or .3.

[Next]

Figure 11.2. A Modeled Worked Example from a Sales Lesson.

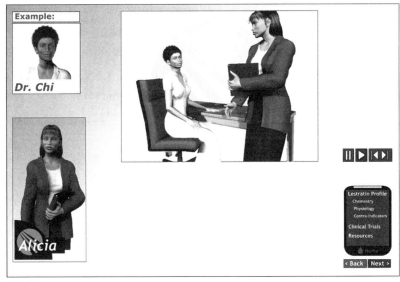

Dr. Chi: I have a lot of overweight patients in my practice, can you just highlight the contra-indications?
Alicia: The key ones are pregnant or nursing mothers, any liver disease, and patients with a history of depression although your Lestratin drug sheet lists others. Are many of your overweight and obese patients already taking weight-reducing drugs?

example from our pharmaceutical sales lesson. While worked examples are not new, we have new evidence on worked examples to support learning of strategic skills including video or animated examples that model thinking or interpersonal skills.

Worked Examples for Strategic Tasks

Most of the early research on worked examples focused on relatively straightforward tasks that illustrated the steps to solve a well structured mathematical problem such as the probability problem we show in Figure 11.1.

However, research reported since our second edition has demonstrated the benefits of worked examples for strategic tasks such as how to construct an effective argument, how to devise a mathematical proof, or how to troubleshoot equipment. These research studies are especially relevant to workforce learning goals that involve higher level cognitive tasks and problem solving such as consultative selling, financial analysis, troubleshooting, diagnosis, report writing, and many managerial tasks.

Modeling Examples

A modeling example is a worked example in which a human provides a demonstration of how to complete a task, usually accompanied by commentary. The early worked examples primarily illustrating mathematic content were generally displayed with words (in text or in audio) and perhaps simple diagrams similar to the example we show in Figure 11.1. People were typically not included. In contrast, a modeling example involves a demonstration from a person that may be mediated in a face-to-face classroom by an instructor or by a video-recorded or animated demonstration.

We review two types of modeled examples: (1) cognitive models, which focus on skills such as how to set up an Excel spreadsheet and (2) interpersonal skills models, which focus on social skills such as how to sell a new product. A cognitive model uses an individual, usually an instructor or a tutor, to demonstrate how he or she resolves a problem. For example, a video may show a dialog between a student trying to solve a physics problem and the tutor guiding the student through the solution. In contrast, an interpersonal skills model typically shows expert performance of a task involving social skills such as a teacher managing a classroom or a salesperson discussing product features with the client, as shown in Figure 11.2.

The Psychology of Worked Examples

Sweller (2004) proposed a "Borrowing and Reorganizing Principle" of human learning. He suggests that the main path to building new knowledge in long-term memory is through imitating others—in other words to borrow knowledge that others have acquired and to reorganize it into workable knowledge in long-term memory. Worked examples offer an especially efficient opportunity to borrow knowledge from others.

Traditional training plans present some guidelines or steps along with one or two examples followed by many practice exercises. However, research shows that learning is more efficient with a greater initial reliance on worked examples in place of some practice exercises. While studying an example (in contrast to solving a problem), working memory is relatively free to borrow and reorganize new knowledge. Once basic knowledge structures have formed, practice helps learners automate the new knowledge. In other words, you can reduce extraneous cognitive load by initially relying on worked examples that promote borrowing and then transition into practice exercises that help more learners consolidate and automate new knowledge and skills.

Evidence for the Benefits of Worked Examples

The early research on worked examples compared the learning outcomes of studying algebra examples to working multiple algebra practice problems (Sweller & Cooper, 1985). One lesson version (all practice) assigned learners eight practice problems. The second lesson version (examples–practice pairs) assigned learners a worked example followed by a practice exercise four times. In this version the learner would study an example followed by a similar practice problem, then study a second example followed by another similar practice problem, continuing this pattern two more times. Both groups were exposed to eight problems, with the worked example group only solving four of the eight. Following the lesson, learners took a test with six new

Table 11.1. Worked Example Problem Pairs Result in Faster Learning and
          Performance.

From: Sweller and Cooper (1985).

Outcome	Worked Examples–Practice Pairs	All Practice
Training Time (Sec)	32.0	185.5
Training Errors	0	2.73
Test Time	43.6	78.1
Test Errors	.18	.36

problems similar to those used in the lessons. The results are shown in
Table 11.1. It's not surprising that those who worked all eight problems took
a lot longer to complete the lesson—almost six times longer! Notice, however, that the number of errors during training and in the test was higher for
the all-practice groups (that is, the groups that were given problems to solve
without any worked examples). This was the first of many experiments demonstrating the benefits of replacing some practice with worked examples.

Since those initial studies, worked examples have proven beneficial
for learning not only in structured domains such as algebra and statistics,
but also for more strategic skills such as identifying design styles (Rourke
& Sweller, 2009), learning argumentation techniques (Schworm & Renkl,
2007), electrical troubleshooting (van Gog, Paas, & van Merrienboer, 2008),
geometry proving skills (Hilbert, Renkl, Kessler, & Reiss, 2008) and application of teaching principles (Moreno & Ortegano-Layne, 2008; Moreno &
Valdez, 2007).

Research since our second edition has focused on instructional methods
you can use to maximize the benefits of worked examples. We organize the
evidence into the following principles:

Principle 1: Fade from worked examples to problems
Principle 2: Promote self-explanations

Principle 3: Include instructional explanations of worked examples in
some situations

Principle 4: Apply the multimedia principles to examples

Principle 5: Support learning transfer

Worked Example Principle 1: Fade from Worked Examples to Problems

In fading, you first provide a fully worked example similar to the examples in
Figures 11.1 and 11.2. You follow the initial example with a second example,
in which most of the steps are worked out and the learner completes the
final steps. As examples progress, the learner gradually completes more of
the steps. You end with a practice problem the learner must solve entirely on
his or her own. Figure 11.3 illustrates the concept of fading. The grey area
represents steps demonstrated by the instruction and the white area represents steps completed by the learner. Suppose, for example, you were teaching probability calculations in a statistics class. You start with a fully worked
example, as represented by the all grey circle on the left in Figure 11.3.
Next you fade out the last steps in a second worked example, as shown in

Figure 11.3. Fading from a Full Worked Example to a Practice Problem.
From Clark, Nguyen, and Swoller, 2006.

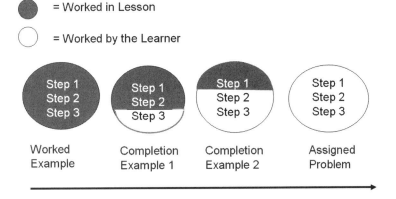

Figure 11.4. A Faded Worked Probability Problem.
From Atkinson, Renkl, and Merrill, 2003.

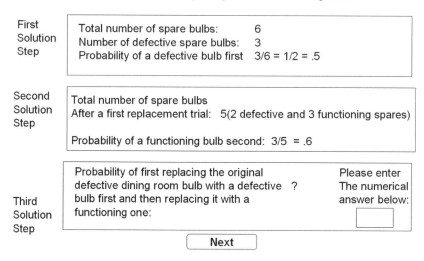

Problem: The bulb of Mrs. Dark's dining room table is defective. Mrs. Dark had six spare bulbs on hand. However, three of them are also defective. What is the probability that Mrs. Dark first replaces the original defective bulb with another defective bulb before then replacing it with a functioning one?

First Solution Step

Total number of spare bulbs:	6
Number of defective spare bulbs:	3
Probability of a defective bulb first	3/6 = 1/2 = .5

Second Solution Step

Total number of spare bulbs
After a first replacement trial: 5(2 defective and 3 functioning spares)

Probability of a functioning bulb second: 3/5 = .6

Third Solution Step

Probability of first replacing the original defective dining room bulb with a defective ? bulb first and then replacing it with a functioning one:

Please enter The numerical answer below:

Next

Figure 11.4. In this problem, the first two steps are worked by the instruction and the learner is required to complete the final step. This example matches the second circle in Figure 11.3. At the end of the series, a probability problem is assigned to the learner as a practice problem to work on his or her own. In progressing through a series of faded worked examples, the learner gradually assumes more and more of the mental work until at the end of the sequence he or she is completing full practice problems.

Although worked examples are proven to be the most effective path during the initial stages of learning, as learners gain more expertise, worked examples can actually impede learning. This phenomenon is an example of the *expertise reversal effect* that we discussed in Chapter 4. In expertise reversal, an instructional method that benefits novice learners does not help and sometimes even hinders learning of high knowledge learners (Kalyuga, 2007). For example, novices benefit from the cognitive load relief of studying an example rather than solving a problem as the basis for initial learning.

However, once the new knowledge is stored in memory, studying a worked example adds no value. In fact, the worked example may conflict with the learner's unique approach to completing the task. At that point, learners need to practice in order to automate their new skills.

Worked Example Principle 2: Promote Self-Explanations

A potential problem with worked examples is that many learners either ignore them altogether or review them in a very shallow manner. Chi and others (1989) found that better learners reviewed worked examples by explaining to themselves the principles reflected in the examples. For example, when studying the worked example shown in Figure 11.1, a shallow processor might be thinking: "To get the answer they multiplied 3/5 by 1/2." In contrast, a deeper processor might be thinking: "To determine the probability of two events, you have to multiply the probability of the first event by the probability of the second event assuming the first event happened." The shallow processor more or less repeats the content of the example, in contrast to the deeper processor, who focuses on the principles being illustrated. Thus, successful learning from worked examples requires psychological engagement.

To overcome this potential limitation of worked examples, you can encourage deeper learning through techniques that promote deeper processing of worked examples. Two proven techniques are adding self-explanation questions and promoting collaborative explanations of worked examples.

Add Self-Explanation Questions to Your Worked Examples

A self-explanation question is an interaction—often multiple choice in e-learning—that requires the learner to review the worked out step(s) and identify the underlying principles or rationale behind them. Note that the worked example we show in Figure 11.5 includes a multiple-choice question next to the first worked step. The learner is required to identify the principle that supports each step demonstrated in the worked example. In Figure 11.6, we add a self-explanation question to our pharmaceutical sales modeling example. The goal of any self-explanation question is two-fold.

Figure 11.5. A Self-Explanation Question Focused on First Solution Step of Probability Problem.

From Atkinson, Renkl, and Merrill, 2003.

Problem: From a ballot box containing three red balls and two white balls, two balls are randomly drawn. The chosen balls are not put back into the ballot box. What is the probability that a red ball is drawn first and a white ball is second?

First
Solution
Step

Total number of balls:	5
Number of red balls:	3
Probability of a defective bulb first	3/5= .6

Please enter the letter of the rule/principle
Used in this step:

Next

Probability Rules/
Principles:

a) Probability of an event
b) Principle of complementarity
c) Multiplication principle
d) Addition principle

Figure 11.6. A Self-Explanation Question Encourages Deeper Processing of the Sales Modeled Example.

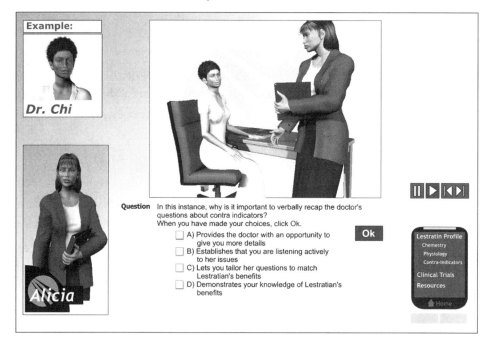

Figure 11.7. Worked Examples with Self-Explanation Questions Result in Better Learning Than Worked Examples Without Questions.

From Experiment 2, Near Transfer Learning, Atkinson, Renkl, and Merrill, 2003.

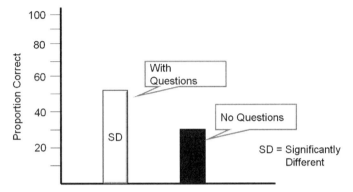

First, it discourages bypassing the worked example because an overt response is required. Second, by asking learners to identify the rationale that underlies each step, they are encouraged to process that step in a meaningful way.

Self-explanation questions will require additional time for the developer to construct and for the learner to respond. Do we have evidence that this time investment will pay off? Atkinson, Renkl, and Merrill (2003) compared the learning of high school students from faded worked examples that included self-explanation questions like the one in Figure 11.5 with the same faded worked examples without questions. As you can see in Figure 11.7, adding the questions resulted in greater learning from the worked examples.

Encourage Self-Explanations Through Active Observation

In this section, we review new research showing the benefits of collaboration during observational learning of modeled examples. Observational learning refers to watching a human tutor explain problems to a student. Chi, Roy, and Hausmann (2008) found that pairs of learners solving physics problems while viewing a video recording of a tutor helping a student solve the same problem, learned as much as the students who were directly tutored. The video recording provided a modeled worked example, and the assigned problem ensured that learners actively processed the worked example.

The research team calls this technique *active observing,* defined as "observing that facilitates engagement with the materials so as to encourage deeper processing" (Craig, Chi, & VanLehn, 2009, p. 781). The research team derived three conditions to maximize the benefits of active observing. First, learners should solve problems as they observe the video; second, they should do so in pairs rather than working alone; and third, best learning stems from video models using high ability tutees who ask the tutor deeper level questions than lower ability tutees do.

Research on active observing is in its early stages. Because of the potential efficiencies of distributing a recorded model of a tutoring session to many learners, this technique has high potential for applications in workforce learning. We need to determine the extent to which active observing will apply to problem-solving domains other than physics and can be adapted to online collaboration.

Worked Example Principle 3: Include Instructional Explanations of Worked Examples in Some Situations

In our second edition, we recommended adding instructional explanations to worked examples. For example in e-learning, a "help" button might offer more specific details or rationale for the guidelines illustrated in the worked example. A number of studies showed positive learning benefits of adding help, provided either on demand or simply included as part of the worked example.

However, evidence accumulated in the last few years suggests that instructional explanations can be problematic—sometimes even depressing learning (Renkl, Hilbert, & Schworm, 2009). Under what conditions are instructional explanations of a worked example helpful?

Renkl (2011) describes three situations (what instructional psychologists call *boundary conditions*) in which adding explanations has proven helpful. First, adding explanations can be effective when conceptual understanding is the goal rather than problem solving performance. Second, explanations are most helpful when there are no self-explanation questions requiring a learner response. Learners may invest less effort in a self-explanation question if an instructional explanation is available. Finally, explanations seem especially effective with mathematical content, perhaps because many learners are intimidated by mathematics. The worked example we show in Figure 11.1 meets all three of these criteria. This worked example may benefit by adding an explanation.

We look forward to additional research suggesting the kinds of explanations to provide learners and when a self-explanation question is more effective than providing an instructional explanation.

Worked Example Principle 4: Apply Multimedia Principles to Examples

In Chapters 4 through 10 we presented Mayer's multimedia principles pertaining to the use of graphics, text, audio, and content sequencing. Some of the earliest research on worked examples found that they failed to have a positive effect when the multimedia principles were violated. For example, if the contiguity principle was violated by separating text steps from a relevant visual in a worked example, split attention negated the benefits of the worked example. To maximize the cognitive load benefits of worked examples, it is important that you apply the multimedia principles to their design. In this section we show you how.

Illustrate Worked Examples with Relevant Visuals: Multimedia Principle

We saw in Chapter 4 that relevant visuals benefit learning, in contrast to lessons that use text alone to present content. The same guideline applies to design of worked examples. Where possible, include relevant visuals to illustrate the steps. For example, when demonstrating how to enter a formula into an Excel spreadsheet, a screen shot of a spreadsheet with data provides a relevant visual.

Moreno and Valdez (2007) and Moreno and Ortegano-Layne (2008) compared learning of teaching principles from lessons with no examples with lessons that added classroom modeled examples presented in narrative text, in video, and in animation.

Figure 11.8. Better Learning from Case Examples in Video or Animation Than Text or No Example.

Based on data from Moreno and Ortegano-Layne, 2008.

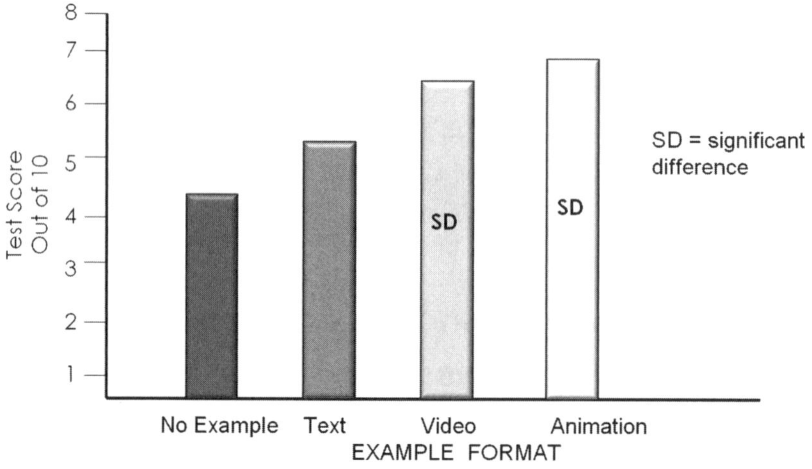

As you can see in Figure 11.8, the visualized case examples—either video or animation—resulted in better learning than text or no-example groups, which did not significantly differ from each other.

Present Steps with Audio—NOT Audio and Text: Modality and Redundancy Principles

In Chapters 6 and 7 we summarized research showing that learning is better when a relevant visual is explained with words presented in audio rather than text or audio and text. The same guideline applies to worked examples. Leahy, Chandler, and Sweller (2003) compared learning from a worked example of how to calculate temperature changes from the graph shown in Figure 11.9. Three different modality combinations were used to present the steps: text, audio, and text plus audio. The text version looked similar to Figure 11.9, with the three numbered steps explained with callouts near the relevant part of the graph. In the audio version, the text you see in Figure 11.9 was presented with audio narration only and the callouts did not appear. The audio and text version used the text callouts similar to

Figure 11.9. A Worked Example with Steps Presented in Text, Audio, or Text and Audio.

Adapted from Leahy, Chandler, and Sweller, 2003.

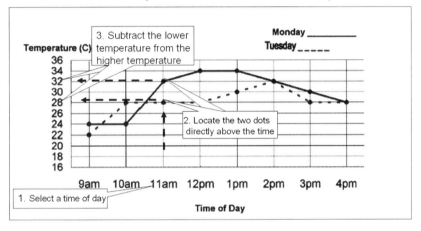

Figure 11.9 and added audio that repeated the text. The research team found that, for complex problems for which cognitive load would be the highest, learning was better when the graph was explained with audio alone.

Keep in mind, however, that applying the modality principle sometimes creates more cognitive load than it saves. For example, you should avoid audio in situations in which learners need to refer to words at their own pace. For example, when including self-explanation questions, present the steps and the question in text, permitting flexible review of those steps in order to correctly identify the appropriate principle. In addition, we saw in Chapter 7 that learning is not hurt and can even be helped when a few important words are placed in text on the screen and elaborated with audio.

Present Steps with Integrated Text: Contiguity Principle

We recommend that you make audio the default modality option in multimedia lessons when presenting steps related to a visual. However, examples should be presented in text when you need to accommodate learners who may have hearing impairments, who are not native speakers of the language used in the instruction, or who may not have access to technology that can deliver sound, as well as to help learners review steps in faded worked examples or steps accompanied by self-explanation questions. When using text to present steps accompanied by a visual, implement the contiguity principle by placing the text close to the relevant visual.

Present Steps in Conceptually Meaningful Chunks: Segmenting Principle

Often worked examples may include eleven or more steps. Learners may follow each step individually, failing to see the conceptual rationale for the steps or for combinations of steps. For example, in the probability problems shown in Figures 11.1 and 11.4, the steps are grouped into three segments, each segment illustrating the application of a probability principle. Atkinson and Derry (2000) showed that, in multimedia, better learning results from worked examples in which each step is presented on a new screen in a building fashion rather than when the steps are presented all together. Your challenge is to group your steps into meaningful chunks and draw learner attention to those chunks by visually isolating them, by building them through a series of overlays, or by surrounding related steps with boxes to signal the underlying principles.

Present Steps with Learner Control of Pacing: Segmenting Principle

In Chapter 10 we showed that, for complex content, learning was better when students could move through screens at their own pace by clicking on the "continue" button rather than viewing the content in a non-stop video manner. This guideline also applies to worked examples that are complex. After a few steps, an animated demonstration should pause, allowing the learner to click "continue" when they are ready to move forward.

Familiarize Learners with Example Context: Pretraining Principle

Have you ever found that you could not really understand an example because the content used as context for the example was unfamiliar? If learners are viewing an example and lack knowledge of both the learning goal and the context for the example, the value of the worked example may be at risk. Imagine that your instructional goal is to teach how to write an effective learning objective. If you were to use unfamiliar technical content, say geometry or electronics, in your examples of effective learning objectives, learners can become bogged down in the technical content and fail to learn the guidelines of objective construction.

Hilbert, Renkl, Kessler, and Reiss (2008) pre-tested learners on the content knowledge of the worked examples used in their research and found a significant correlation between knowledge of the example content and acquiring the intended skills. Renkl, Hilbert, and Schworm (2009) recommend pretraining when the example content will be difficult to understand. Alternatively, as you design worked examples, select illustrative content that is likely to be familiar to your learners. Rather than using geometry or electronics, use a more familiar context such as basic Internet searching or everyday skills such as brushing teeth or cooking.

Worked Example Principle 5: Support Learning Transfer

Since the publication of the second edition, much research on worked examples has focused on use and design of worked examples for what we call far transfer learning of strategic tasks.

In some training situations, the main goal is to teach learners procedures—tasks that are performed pretty much the same way each time they are completed. Accessing your e-mail or filling out a customer order form are two typical examples. When teaching procedures, your goal is to help learners achieve *near transfer*. In other words, your goal is to help learners apply steps learned in the training to similar situations in the work environment.

However, in other situations your goal is to build job skills that will require the worker to use judgment in order to adapt strategies to new work situations. In a sales setting, for example, the product, the client, and the situation will vary each time. It is not productive to teach sales skills as an invariant set of steps because each situation will require adaptation. Rather, you need to teach a set of strategies. Your goal is to help learners adapt strategies learned in the training to the work environment, where each situation will vary. When teaching strategies, your goal is to help learners achieve *far transfer*. Management training, customer service training, consultative selling, and non-routine troubleshooting are all examples of tasks that require far transfer skills.

Design Guidelines for Far Transfer Worked Examples

The key to success in design of worked examples for far transfer learning is to illustrate guidelines with differing contexts and to promote learner processing of those examples. In this section we will offer guidelines for creating varied context worked examples and for encouraging learners to engage with those worked examples in ways that promote deeper, more flexible knowledge.

Far Transfer Guideline 1: Use Varied Context Worked Examples

Let's begin our discussion of varied context examples with a short demonstration. Take a minute to review the following tumor problem.

THE TUMOR PROBLEM

Suppose you are a doctor faced with a patient who has a malignant tumor in his stomach. It is impossible to operate on the patient, but unless the tumor is destroyed, the patient will die. There is a kind of ray that at a sufficiently high intensity can destroy the tumor. Unfortunately, at this intensity, the healthy tissue that the rays pass through on the way to the tumor will also be destroyed. At lower intensities, the rays are harmless to healthy tissue but will not affect the tumor either. How can the rays be used to destroy the tumor without injuring the healthy tissue? (Duncker, 1945).

What are some possible solutions to the tumor problem? The preferred solution is to aim several weak rays from different directions so they converge on the tumor. This problem was used in a classic experiment in which different groups had different pre-work assignments (Gick & Holyoak, 1980). One group read a story about a general who captured a mined fortress by splitting up his troops and attacking from different directions. Another group read the fortress story, plus a story about putting out a fire on an oil rig. A single hose was not able to disperse sufficient foam, so the fire was put out by directing many small hoses toward the middle of the fire. In these three stories, the contexts are quite different. One is about a medical problem, another is about a fire, and a third is about a fortress. However, the underlying principle—a convergence principle—is the same.

Gick and Holyoak (1980) found that most individuals who tried to solve the tumor problem without first reading any other stories did not arrive at the convergence solution. Even those who read the fortress problem prior to the tumor problem did not have much better luck solving the tumor problem. But the group that read both the fire and the fortress stories had much better success. By studying two examples from different contexts that reflect the same principle, learners were able to abstract the underlying principle that connected them. An important implication is that people are better able to abstract a general principle or procedure when they learn about it in many different contexts.

When teaching far transfer skills, build several (at least two) worked examples in which you vary the context but illustrate the same guidelines in each. For example, the pharmaceutical sales lesson shown in Figure 11.10 uses three physicians, each with different practice and patient profiles. In this lesson the learner will observe a worked example involving Dr. Chi. Next they will practice sales skills with Dr. Jones and Dr. Valdez, who have different practice parameters.

Creating several examples of different contexts will increase your development time. Do we have any evidence that varied context examples promote learning? The answer is yes. Quilici and Mayer (1996) created examples to illustrate three statistical tests of t-test, correlation, and chi-square. Each of these test types require a different mathematical procedure and are most appropriately applied to different types of data. For each test type, they created three examples. Some example sets used the same context. For example, the three t-test problems used data regarding experience and typing speed,

Figure 11.10. Different Physician Profiles Vary the Sales Context.

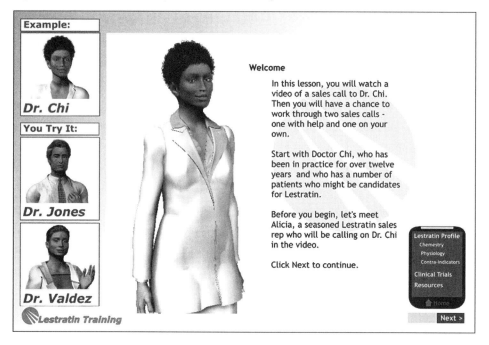

the three correlation examples used data regarding temperature and precipitation, and the three chi-square examples included data related to fatigue and performance. An alternative set of examples varied the context. For example, the t-test was illustrated by one example that used experience and typing speed, a second example about temperature and precipitation, and a third example about fatigue and performance.

After reviewing the examples, participants were tested for their understanding of the different statistical categories. As shown in Figure 11.11, the varied context examples led to significantly greater discrimination among the test types.

Far Transfer Guideline 2: Include Self-Explanation Questions

Schworm and Renkl (2007) reported that worked examples helped learners build argumentation skills only when learners were required to respond to self-explanation questions that focused on the argumentation principles. In

Figure 11.11. Varied Context Worked Examples Resulted in More Correct Discrimination of Statistical Test Type.

From Experiment 3, Quilici and Mayer, 1996.

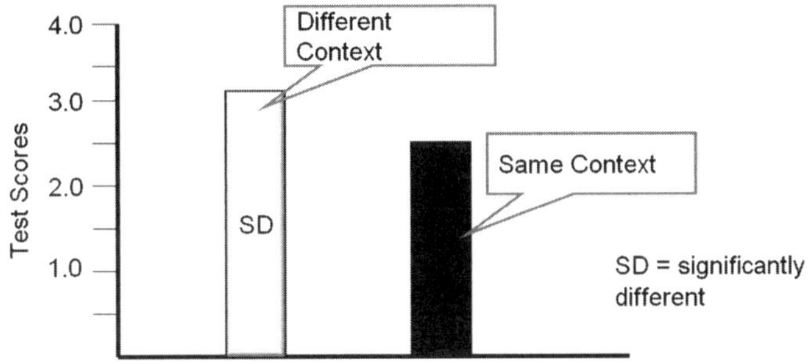

their research student teachers were assigned to lesson versions that did or did not accompany video examples of argumentation with self-explanation questions. Learning to apply argumentation skills was better when self-explanation questions were included.

Far Transfer Guideline 3. Require Active Comparison of Varied Context Examples

Gentner, Loewenstein, and Thompson (2003) designed a lesson on negotiation skills that focused on the benefits of a negotiated strategy based on a safeguard solution rather than a less effective tradeoff solution. They presented one worked example of negotiation that involved a conflict between a Chinese and American company over the best way to ship parts. They illustrated both the tradeoff (less effective) and the safeguard (more effective) negotiation strategies using the shipping context. In the next part of the lesson, they illustrated the safeguard and tradeoff solutions using a different context involving a conflict between two travelers over where to stay on a planned trip.

The placement of and engagement with the different examples was varied in three lesson versions, as illustrated in Figure 11.12. In one version (separate examples lesson) participants reviewed the shipping and traveling examples, each on a separate page. After reading each example, participants

Figure 11.12. Alternative Placement of Negotiation Strategy Worked Examples in Three Lesson Versions.

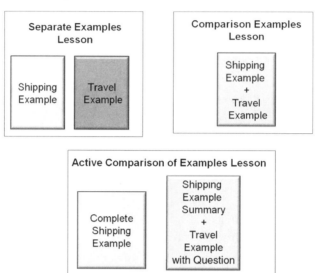

were asked questions about each individual example such as, "What is going on in this negotiation?" In this lesson version, learners reviewed each example separately, rather than make a comparison between them. In a second version (comparison examples lesson), participants saw both examples displayed on the same page and were directed to think about the similarities between the two situations. A third group (active comparison of examples lesson) was presented the full shipping example on one page. A summary of the shipping example was placed on the second page that also presented the full traveler example. In this version, learners were required to respond to questions about the similarities between the two examples. A fourth group received no training.

Following the training, all participants were tested in a role-played face-to-face negotiation over salary. As you can see in Figure 11.13, the third version lesson that required an active comparison of the two examples resulted in best learning. This experiment is especially relevant to workforce learning practitioners, as the task involved negotiations—a common soft skill taught

Figure 11.13. Best Learning from Active Comparisons of Examples.
Adapted from Gentner, Loewenstein, and Thompson, 2003.

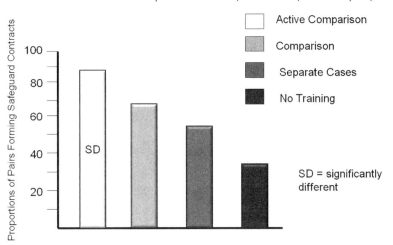

in workforce learning—and the learning was measured by a role-play performance test. What we learn from this experiment is when presenting varied context examples, it is better (1) to display them in a contiguous fashion such as on the same page and (2) to ask questions that promote active comparisons of the examples.

What We Don't Know About Worked Examples

We have learned a great deal in the past few years about the most effective way to design worked examples to maximize learning. Still there are a number of issues that remain to be resolved.

1. *When to use fading versus self-explanation questions.* A few recent studies that used both fading and self-explanation questions to promote deeper processing of worked examples found that self-explanation questions alone led to best learning (Hilbert, Renkl, Kessler, & Reiss, 2008). Perhaps a combination of fading and self-explanation questions added too much cognitive load for more complex skill domains. Future research should help us define how and when to use fading and self-explanation questions.

2. *How to design and use modeling examples.* In this edition, we added new research on both cognitive and interpersonal skill modeling examples. It will be helpful to see whether guidelines we have presented that apply to traditional worked examples also apply to modeling examples. For example, will a modeling example benefit from fading, from self-explanation questions, or from comparisons? Also since modeling examples often use video, how can extraneous load from the visuals be minimized?

3. *How active observation can be applied to workforce learning.* We reviewed some promising research showing the learning value of pairs of learners observing a tutor-tutee dialog on a physics problem while solving the same problem. To what extent will these results apply to less structured domains? Can active observation techniques be effectively implemented in asynchronous e-learning?

DESIGN DILEMMA: RESOLVED

In the pharmaceutical sales course, Reshmi wants to add some interactivity to the video examples with self-explanation questions or with faded examples that learners must complete. Matt agrees with the benefits of interactivity but feels it would be less expensive to incorporate some collaborative learning activity around the videos.

A. Reshmi is correct. Video examples should be accompanied by questions that engage learners in the examples.

B. Asking learners to complete a partial example would be better than asking questions about the examples.

C. Matthew is correct. It would be more effective to ask learners to review examples in pairs.

We have evidence in this chapter that potentially could support any of the above engagement strategies. We know that worked examples have potential to accelerate learning, but techniques such as fading, self-explanation questions and active observations are needed to maximize their value. We will need further research to determine when and for whom each of the engagement strategies described above would be most effective.

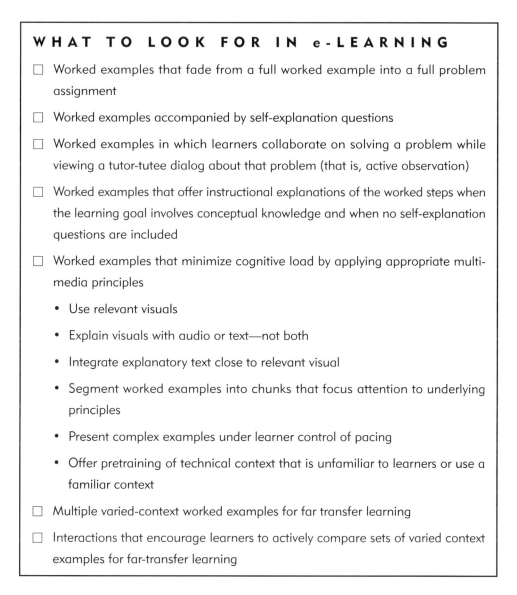

WHAT TO LOOK FOR IN e-LEARNING

☐ Worked examples that fade from a full worked example into a full problem assignment

☐ Worked examples accompanied by self-explanation questions

☐ Worked examples in which learners collaborate on solving a problem while viewing a tutor-tutee dialog about that problem (that is, active observation)

☐ Worked examples that offer instructional explanations of the worked steps when the learning goal involves conceptual knowledge and when no self-explanation questions are included

☐ Worked examples that minimize cognitive load by applying appropriate multimedia principles

  • Use relevant visuals

  • Explain visuals with audio or text—not both

  • Integrate explanatory text close to relevant visual

  • Segment worked examples into chunks that focus attention to underlying principles

  • Present complex examples under learner control of pacing

  • Offer pretraining of technical context that is unfamiliar to learners or use a familiar context

☐ Multiple varied-context worked examples for far transfer learning

☐ Interactions that encourage learners to actively compare sets of varied context examples for far-transfer learning

COMING NEXT

Although we recommend that you replace some practice with worked examples, you will still need to include effective practice in your training. In the next chapter we offer evidence for the number, type, design, and placement of practice, along with new guidelines on design of practice feedback that will optimize learning.

Suggested Readings

Gentner, D., Loewenstein, J., & Thompson, L (2003). Learning and transfer: A general role for analogical encoding. *Journal of Educational Psychology*, *95*(2), 393–408.

Moreno, R., & Valdez, A. (2007). Immediate and delayed effects of using a classroom case exemplar in teacher education: The role of presentation format. *Journal of Educational Psychology, 99,* 194–206.

Renkl, A. (2011). Instruction based on examples. In R.E. Mayer & P.A. Alexander (Eds.) *Handbook of research on learning and instruction.* New York: Routledge.

Renkl, A., Hilbert, T., & Schworm, S. (2009). Example-based learning in heuristic domains: A cognitive load theory account. *Educational Psychology Review, 21,* 67–78.

CHAPTER OUTLINE

What Is Practice in e-Learning?

The Paradox of Practice

Practice Principle 1: Add Sufficient Practice Interactions to e-Learning to Achieve the Objective

The Benefits of Practice

Practice Benefits Diminish Rapidly

Adjust the Amount of Practice Based on Task Criticality

Limited Benefits of Over-Learning in Mathematics

Practice Principle 2: Mirror the Job

Practice Principle 3: Provide Effective Feedback

Provide Explanatory Feedback

Evidence for Benefits of Explanatory Feedback

Focus Learner Attention to the Task, Not the Learner

Provide Step-by-Step Feedback When Steps Are Interdependent

Practice Principle 4: Distribute and Mix Practice Among Learning Events

Distribute Practice Throughout the Learning Environment

Mix Practice Types in Lessons

Tips for Determining the Number and Placement of Practice Events

Practice Principle 5: Apply Multimedia Principles

Modality and Redundancy Principles

Contiguity Principle

Coherence Principle

Practice Principle 6: Transition from Examples to Practice Gradually

12

Does Practice Make Perfect?

IN THE SECOND EDITION of *e-Learning and the Science of Instruction*, we recommended that you design practice accompanied by feedback to build job-relevant skills and adjust the amount and placement of practice to match job proficiency requirements. These guidelines are still valid today. There has been a moderate amount of new research on practice since our second edition. In this chapter we update the research on practice guidelines and add a new guideline regarding mixing categories of practice in a lesson when it's important to help learners discriminate among different problem types.

As described in our second edition, you should distribute interactions throughout the instructional environment and apply Mayer's multimedia principles to the design and layout of e-learning interactions.

DESIGN DILEMMA: YOU DECIDE

Reshmi, Sergio, and Ben have very different ideas about how to design practice for the pharmaceutical sales lesson. Sergio and Ben want to add a Jeopardy-type game like the one shown in Figure 12.1. They feel that sales staff are competitive and adding some fun games will increase engagement and motivation. Reshmi does not like the Jeopardy idea. She would prefer to include short interactive scenarios about different physician practice settings.

Figure 12.1. A Jeopardy Game Design for the Pharmaceutical Sales Lesson.

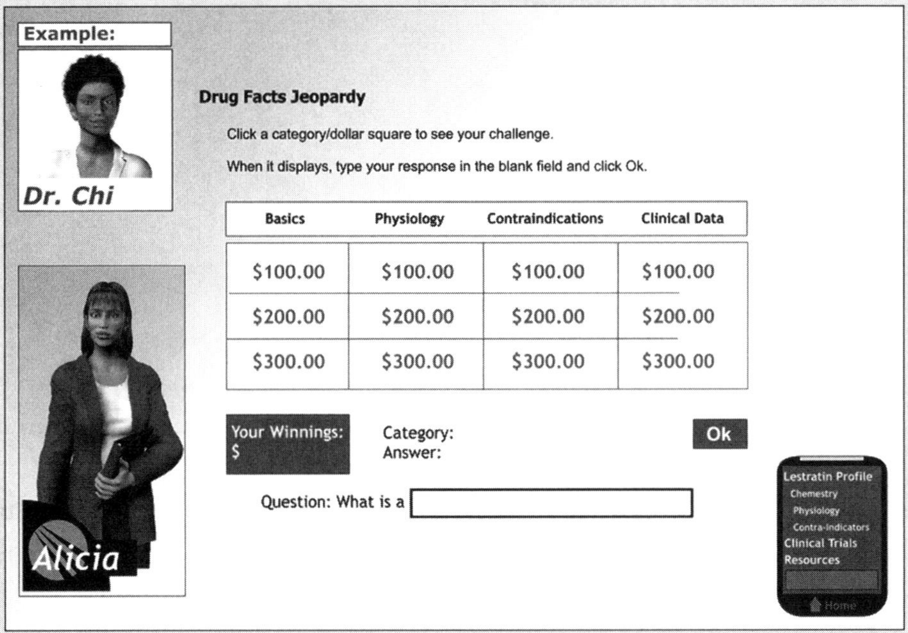

Regarding feedback, Reshmi and Ben disagree about what kind of feedback to include. Reshmi wants to tell participants whether they answered correctly or incorrectly and explain why. Ben feels they can save a lot of development time by simply using the automatic program feature of their authoring tool that tells learners whether they are correct or incorrect. Otherwise, the team will have to devote a large block of time to writing tailored explanations for all correct and incorrect response options. Based on your own experience or intuition, which of the following options would you select:

A. Adding some familiar and fun games like Jeopardy will make the lesson more engaging for learners and lead to better learning.

B. It would be better to use physician scenarios as the basis for interactions.

C. The extra time invested in writing tailored feedback explanations will pay off in increased learning.

What Is Practice in e-Learning?

Effective e-learning engages learners with the instructional content in ways that foster the selection, organization, integration, and retrieval of new knowledge. First, attention must be drawn to the important information in the training. Then the instructional words and visuals must be integrated with each other and with prior knowledge. Finally, the new knowledge and skills that are built in long-term memory must be retrieved from long-term memory after the training when needed on the job. Effective practice exercises support all of these psychological processes. In this chapter we will review research and guidelines for optimizing learning from online practice.

Practice events in e-learning are often referred to as *interactions*. However, there are many types of interactions. For example, Moreno and Mayer (2007) identify interactive categories for navigating, for searching, for controlling the pacing of the presentation, and for dialoging. In this chapter we primarily focus on interactions in the form of questions inserted by the program designer or instructor requiring the learner to respond in ways that promote learning of lesson content.

e-Learning practice interactions may use formats similar to those used in the classroom, such as selecting the correct answer in a multiple-choice list, checking a box to indicate whether a statement is true or false, or even typing in short answers. Other interactions use formats that are unique to computers such as drag-and-drop and simulations.

However, the psychological effectiveness of a practice exercise is more important than its format. In Chapter 1, we introduced the Engagement Matrix shown in Figure 12.2. Practice exercises will fall into one of the right-hand quadrants of the matrix since they require a behavioral response. However, if the behavior falls into the lower right quadrant, the result is mindless activity that does not support processing associated with the learning goal. Instead it is important to design practice that will fall into the upper right quadrant in which learners are both behaviorally and psychologically active.

Figure 12.2. Practice Exercises Should Fall into the Upper Right Quadrant of the Engagement Matrix.

Adapted from Stull and Mayer, 2007.

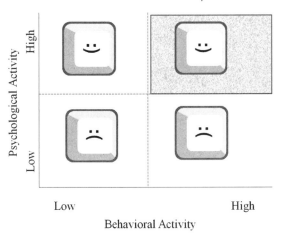

For example, you could ask a multiple-choice question about a new drug requiring learners to recognize drug facts such as contraindications, dosages, and so forth. To respond to this type of question, the learner need only recognize the facts provided in the lesson. We call these kinds of interactions *"regurgitative."* Regurgitative questions promote shallow processing and we place them in the lower right quadrant of the Engagement Matrix. Regurgitative questions are common in training because they are quick and easy to develop. In contrast, to respond to the question in Figure 12.3, the learner needs to apply his or her understanding of the drug features to physician profiles. This question involves not only behavioral activity but also productive psychological

Figure 12.3. This Multiple-Select Question Requires the Learner to Match Drug Features to the Appropriate Physician.

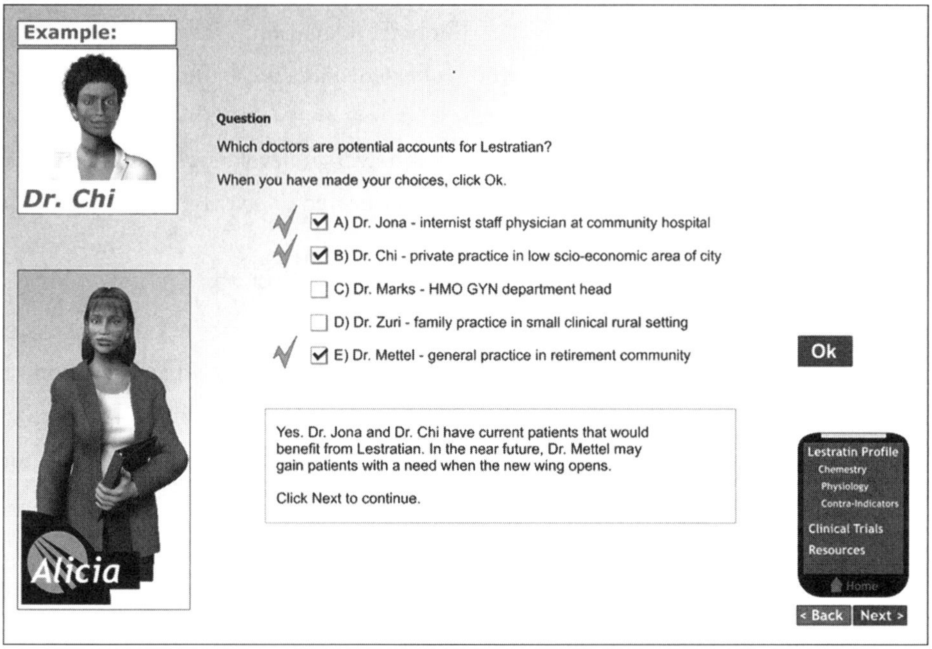

engagement. This question requires a deeper level of processing than a multiple-choice fact recognition question and falls into the upper right cell of the Engagement Matrix.

The Paradox of Practice

We've all heard the expression that "practice makes perfect," but how important is practice to skill acquisition? Studies of top performers in music, games such as chess and Scrabble, and sports point to the criticality of practice in the development of expertise. Sloboda, Davidson, Howe, and Moore (1996) compared the practice schedules of higher and lower performing teenage music students of equal early musical ability and exposure to music lessons. All of the students began to study music around age six. However, the higher performers had devoted much more time to practice. By age twelve, higher performers were practicing about two hours a day, compared to fifteen minutes a day for the lower performers. The researchers concluded that "there was a very strong relationship between musical achievement and the amount of formal practice undertaken" (Sloboda, Davidson, Howe, & Moore, 1996, p. 287). In fact, musicians who had reached an elite status at a music conservatory had devoted over ten thousand hours to practice by the age of twenty! More recent comparisons of elite and average level Scrabble players found that in a ten-year period, elite players devoted an average of 3,541 hours to serious study, compared to 886 hours for average players (Tuffiash, Roring, & Ericsson, 2007).

However, time devoted to practice activity does not tell the whole story. Most likely you know individuals of average proficiency in an avocation such as golf or music who spend a considerable amount of time practicing with little improvement. Based on studies of expert performers in music, sports, typing, and games such as Scrabble, Ericsson (2006) concludes that practice is a *necessary but not sufficient condition* to reach high levels of competence. What factors differentiate practice that leads to growth of expertise from practice that does not?

Ericsson (2006) refers to practice that builds expertise as *deliberate practice.* He describes deliberate practice as tasks presented to performers that "are initially outside their current realm of reliable performance, yet can be mastered within hours of practice by concentrating on critical aspects and by gradually refining performance through repetitions after feedback" (p. 692). Deliberate practice involves five basic elements: (1) effortful exertion to improve performance, (2) intrinsic motivation to engage in the task, (3) carefully tailored practice tasks that focus on areas of weakness, (4) feedback that provides knowledge of results, and (5) continued repetition over a number of years (Kellogg & Whiteford, 2009).

For example, elite Scrabble players devoted time to skill-practice exercises directly related to Scrabble scores such as analysis of their own previous Scrabble games, anagramming, and studying word lists. They focused on Scrabble-specific payoff skills such as seven-letter words that earn bonus points and words that use high-scoring letters such as Q and Z. However, elite players did not differ from average players regarding time devoted to activities not directly related to Scrabble such as playing other word games and puzzles (Tuffiash, Roring, & Ericsson, 2007).

In our second edition, we showed evidence that practice should be job-relevant, distributed throughout the learning environment, and that more practice leads to improved performance. We update and extend these recommendations with the following guidelines:

Principle 1: Add sufficient practice interactions to e-learning to achieve the learning goal

Principle 2: Mirror the job

Principle 3: Provide effective feedback

Principle 4: Distribute and mix practice among learning events

Principle 5: Apply the multimedia principles

Principle 6: Transition from examples to practice gradually

Practice Principle 1: Add Sufficient Practice Interactions to e-Learning to Achieve the Objective

Practice exercises are expensive. First, they take time to design and to program. Even more costly will be the time learners invest in completing the practice. Does practice lead to more learning? How much practice is necessary? In this section we describe evidence that will help you determine the optimal amount of practice to include in your e-learning environments.

The Benefits of Practice

Some e-learning courses in both synchronous and asynchronous formats include little or no opportunities for overt practice. In Chapters 1 and 2 we classified these types of courses as receptive. Can learning occur without practice? How much practice is needed?

Moreno and Mayer (2005, 2007) compared learning from a Design-A-Plant game described in Chapter 9. In the game participants construct plants from a choice of roots, leaves, and stems in order to build a plant best suited to an imaginary environment. The object of the game is to teach the adaptive benefits of plant features for specific environments, such as heavy rainfall, sandy soil, and others. They compared learning from interactive versions in which the learner selected the best plant parts to survive in a given environment with the same lesson in which the on-screen agent selected the best parts. As you can see in Figure 12.4, interactivity improved learning with an effect size of .63, which is considered moderate.

In the same research report, a second form of interactivity asked learners to explain why an answer was correct or not correct to promote reflection on responses. This treatment is similar to self-explanations of a worked example that we discussed in Chapter 11. Asking learners to provide an explanation proved beneficial when the on-screen agent rather than the learners selected the plant parts. In fact, learner explanations promoted learning only when learners explained correct answers from the agent rather than their own answers, which may have been incorrect. From these results we conclude that interactions are beneficial to learning but that one form of interaction (either selecting the plant parts OR giving an explanation for correct selections made by the agent) is probably sufficient. In other words, strike a balance with practice assignments that require enough processing for learning but do not overload learners.

Figure 12.4. Better Learning from e-Learning with Interactions.
Based on data from Experiment 2, Moreno and Mayer, 2005.

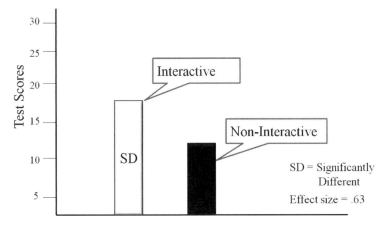

Practice Benefits Diminish Rapidly

Practice can improve performance indefinitely, although at diminishing levels. Timed measurements of workers using a machine to roll cigars found that, after thousands of practice trials conducted over a four-year period, proficiency continued to improve (Crossman, 1959). Proficiency leveled off only after the speed of the operator exceeded the physical limitations of the equipment. In plotting time versus practice for a variety of motor and intellectual tasks, a logarithmic relationship has been observed between amount of practice and time to complete tasks (Rosenbaum, Carlson, & Gilmore, 2001). Thus the logarithm of the time to complete a task decreases with the logarithm of the amount of practice. This relationship, illustrated in Figure 12.5, is called the *power law of practice*. As you can see, while the greatest proficiency gains occur on early trials, even after thousands of practice sessions, incremental improvements continue to accrue. Practice likely leads to improved performance in early sessions as learners find better ways to complete the tasks and in later practice sessions as automaticity increases efficiency.

Figure 12.5. The Power Law of Practice: Speed Increases with Practice But at a Diminishing Rate.

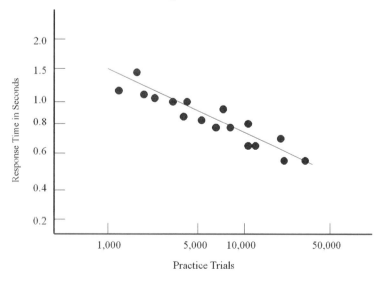

Elite performers in athletics, music and games such as chess and Scrabble have devoted more than ten thousand hours to deliberate practice. However, proficient performance in most jobs will not require elite levels of performance. You will need to consider the return on investment on your practice interactions. How much practice will you need to provide to ensure your learners have an acceptable level of job proficiency? We turn to this question next.

Adjust the Amount of Practice Based on Task Criticality

Schnackenberg and others compared learning from two versions of computer-based training, one offering more practice than the other (Schnackenberg, Sullivan, Leader, & Jones, 1998; Schnackenberg & Sullivan, 2000). In their experiment, two groups were assigned to study from a full practice version lesson with 174 information screens and sixty-six practice questions or from a lean practice version with the same 174 information screens and twenty-two practice questions. Participants were divided into high- and low-ability groups based on their grade point averages and randomly assigned to complete either the full- or lean-practice versions. Outcomes included scores on a fifty-two-question test and average time to complete each version. Table 12.1 shows the results.

Table 12.1. Better Learning with More Practice.

From Schnackenberg, Sullivan, Leader, and Jones, 1998.

Ability Level	Lesson with 66 Questions		Lesson with 22 Questions	
	Low	High	Low	High
Test Scores	32.25	41.82	28.26	36.30
Time to Complete Lesson (minutes)	146	107	83	85

As expected, higher-ability learners scored higher and the full version took longer to complete. The full version resulted in higher average scores, with an effect size of .45, which is considered moderate. The full-practice version resulted in increased learning for both higher- and lower-ability learners. The authors conclude: "When instructional designers are faced with uncertainty about the amount of practice to include in an instructional program, they should favor a greater amount of practice over a relatively small amount if higher student achievement is an important goal" (Schnackenberg, Sullivan, Leader, & Jones, 1998, p. 14).

Notice, however, that lower-ability learners required 75 percent longer to complete the full-practice version than the lean-practice version for a gain of about four points on the test. Does the additional time spent in practice warrant the learning improvement? The answer in this research, as in your own training, will depend on the consequences of error on task performance.

Limited Benefits of Over-Learning in Mathematics

During a lesson, learners may practice until they correctly solve one or two problems or they may continue to practice after obtaining a correct answer. Over-learning refers to situations in which learners continue to practice after they have correctly solved one or two practice problems. A number of studies have shown benefits of over-learning. However, most experiments have measured learning quite soon after the practice sessions—usually less than one hour. What benefits might over-learning have over a longer retention period?

Rohrer and Taylor (2006) assigned college students a letter permutation problem in which they determined how many different combinations could be made out of a letter sequence such as abbbcc. The tutorial taught a mathematical procedure for calculating permutations and then assigned practice problems. One group completed three practice problems. A second group completed nine practice problems. Three practice problems proved sufficient for most subjects to learn the permutation procedure. Therefore, the nine-problem group served as an "over-learning" group.

Figure 12.6. No Learning Benefits Gained from Over-Learning.
Based on data from Experiment 2, Rohrer and Taylor, 2006.

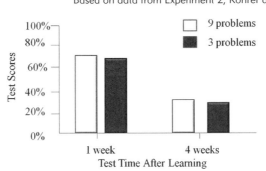

As you can see in Figure 12.6, there were no differences between low- and high-practice groups either on a one-week or on a four-week test. The research team recommends that "assignments should err slightly in the direction of too much practice, perhaps by including three or four problems relating to each new concept in the most recent lesson. However, beyond these first three or four problems, the present data suggest that the completion of additional problems of same type is a terribly inefficient use of study time" (p. 1218).

If your goal is to build knowledge and skills, you need to add practice interactions. To decide how much practice your e-learning courses should include, consider the nature of the job task and the criticality of job performance and include more practice for highly critical skills.

Practice Principle 2: Mirror the Job

Skill building requires practice on the component skills that make up the infrastructure of a specific work domain. Therefore, your interactions must require learners to respond in a job-realistic context. Questions that ask the learner to merely recognize or recall information presented in the training will not promote learning that transfers to the job.

Begin with a job and task analysis in order to define the specific cognitive and physical processing required in the work environment. Then create *transfer appropriate interactions*—activities that require learners to respond in similar ways during the training as in the work environment. The more the features of the job environment are integrated into the interactions, the more likely the right cues will be encoded into long-term memory for later transfer. The Jeopardy game shown in Figure 12.1 requires only recall of information. Neither the psychological nor the physical context of the work environment is reflected in the game. In contrast, the question shown in Figure 12.3 requires learners to process new content in a job-realistic context and therefore is more likely to support transfer of learning.

For the most part, avoid interactions that require simple regurgitation of information provided in the training program. These questions do not support the psychological processes needed to integrate new information with existing knowledge. They can be answered without any real understanding of the content, and they don't implant the cues needed for retrieval on the job. Instead, as you design your course, keep in mind the ways that your workers will apply new knowledge to their job tasks.

Practice Principle 3: Provide Effective Feedback

In a comparison of meta-analyses of 138 different factors that affect learning, Hattie (2009) ranked feedback as number ten in influence. In spite of the known benefits and extensive use of feedback, hundreds of research experiments on feedback reveal both positive and negative effects and few consistent patterns (Kluger & DeNisi, 1996; Shute, 2008). As with many instructional methods, some factors that influence the effectiveness of feedback include the learning objectives and associated tasks, features of the learner, including prior knowledge and self-confidence, as well as how and when feedback is formulated and presented to learners. Here we provide a brief summary of some guidelines to consider when designing feedback.

Provide Explanatory Feedback

Take a look at the two feedback responses to the incorrect question response shown in Figures 12.7 and 12.8. The feedback in Figure 12.7 tells you that your answer is wrong. However, it does not help you understand why your answer is wrong. The feedback in 12.8 provides a much better opportunity for learning because it incorporates an explanation. A missed question is a teachable moment. The learner is open to a brief instructional explanation that will help build the right mental model. Although the benefits of explanatory feedback seem obvious, crafting explanatory feedback is much more

Figure 12.7. This Feedback Tells the Learner That the Response Is Incorrect.

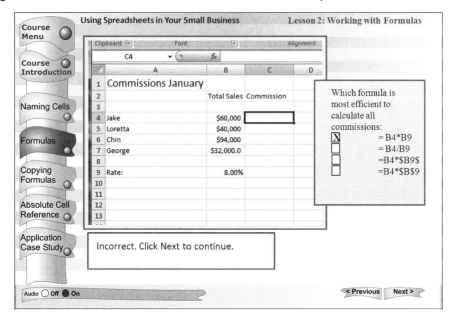

Figure 12.8. This Feedback Tells the Learner That the Response Is Incorrect and Provides an Explanation.

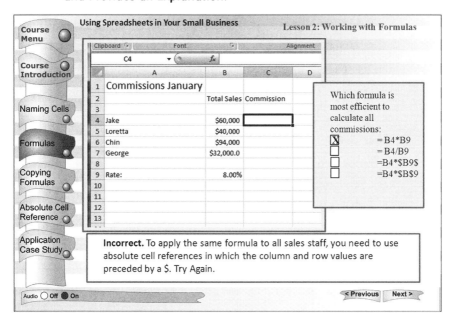

labor-intensive than corrective feedback, which can be automated in many authoring tools with only a few key strokes. What evidence do we have that explanatory feedback will give a return sufficient to warrant the investment?

Evidence for Benefits of Explanatory Feedback

Moreno (2004) compared learning from two versions of a computer botany game called Design-A-Plant, described previously in this chapter. Either *corrective* or *explanatory feedback* was offered by a pedagogical agent in response to a plant design. For explanatory feedback, the agent made comments such as: "Yes, in a low sunlight environment, a large leaf has more room to make food by photosynthesis" (for a correct answer) or "Hmmm, your deep roots will not help your plant collect the scarce rain that is on the surface of the soil" (for an incorrect answer). Corrective answer feedback told the learners whether they were correct or incorrect but did not offer any explanation. As you can see in Figure 12.9, better learning resulted from explanatory feedback, with a large effect size of 1.16. Students rated the version with explanatory feedback as more helpful than the versions with corrective feedback. Moreno and Mayer (2005) reported similar results using the same botany game environment in a follow-up study. They found that explanatory feedback resulted in much better learning than corrective feedback, with a very high effect size of 1.87.

Figure 12.9. Better Learning from Explanatory Feedback.

From data in Experiment 1, Moreno, 2004.

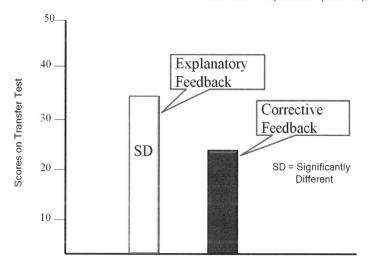

Focus Learner Attention to the Task—Not the Learner

In a review of feedback drawing on multiple research studies, Hattie and Gan (2011), Shute (1998), and Kluger and DeNisi (1996) recommend that feedback should focus learner attention to the task or task process but minimize responses that the learners will perceive as feedback on themselves. For example, the feedback in Figure 12.8 tells the learner he or she is wrong and includes an explanation. This feedback, as well as the Design-A-Plant feedback described in the previous paragraphs, are examples of task-focused feedback. In contrast, feedback that involves some kind of normative information such as a grade or even feedback that involves praise can direct attention to the ego and result in diminished effects. Hattie and Gan (2011) comment that "Praise usually contains little task-related information and is rarely converted into more engagement, commitment to the learning goals, enhanced self-efficacy, or understanding about the task" (p. 261).

If the learner is solving a problem, process feedback would focus on the strategies the learner used. For example, feedback in a search strategies lesson might say: "You could likely get more relevant search hits by using the 'BUT NOT' instead of the 'AND' operator."

Provide Step-by-Step Feedback When Steps Are Interdependent

In many problem-solving tasks, a wrong step early in problem solving can derail the remaining attempted steps. Corbalan, Paas, and Cuypers (2010) compared the effects of feedback given on the final solution with feedback given on all solution steps on learning and motivation in linear algebra problems. The research team found that participants were more motivated and had better learning outcomes when feedback was provided on all solution steps rather than just the final step. The research suggests that electronic environments should incorporate step-wise guidance in highly structured subjects such as linear algebra.

In contrast to highly structured domains such as mathematics, there is some evidence that delayed feedback may be more effective for conceptual or strategic skills as well as for simpler tasks (Shute, 2008). However, we will need more research for firm recommendations on the timing of feedback for different tasks and learners.

Tips for Feedback

- After the learner responds to a question, provide feedback that tells the learner whether the answer is correct or incorrect and provide a succinct explanation.

- Focus the explanation in the feedback on either the task itself or on the process involved in completing the task.

- Avoid feedback such as "Well Done!" that draws attention to the ego and away from the learning.

- Likewise, avoid normative feedback such as grades that encourage learners to compare themselves with others.

- Emphasize progress feedback in which attention is focused on improvement over time.

- Position the feedback so that the learner can see the question, his or her response to the question, and the feedback in close physical approximation to minimize split attention.

- For multi-step problems for which steps are interdependent, provide step-by-step feedback.

- For a question with multiple answers, such as the example in Figure 12.4, show the correct answers next to the learner's answers and include an explanation for the correct answers.

Practice Principle 4: Distribute and Mix Practice Among Learning Events

We've seen that the benefits of practice have a diminishing effect as the number of exercises increases. However, there are some ways to extend the long-term benefits of practice just by where you place and how you sequence even a few interactions.

Distribute Practice Throughout the Learning Environment

The earliest research on human learning conducted by Ebbinghaus in 1913 showed that distributed practice yields better long-term retention. According to Druckman and Bjork (1991), "The so-called spacing effect—that practice sessions spaced in time are superior to massed practices in terms of long-term retention—is one of the most reliable phenomena in human experimental psychology. The effect is robust and appears to hold for verbal materials of all types as well as for motor skills" (p. 30). As long as eight years after an original training, learners whose practice was spaced showed better retention than those who practiced in a more concentrated time period (Bahrick, 1987).

The spacing effect, however, does not result in better immediate learning. Only after a period of time are the benefits of spaced practice realized. Since most training programs do not measure delayed learning, the benefits of spaced practice often go unnoticed. Only in long-term evaluation would this advantage be seen. Naturally, practical constraints will dictate the amount of spacing that is feasible.

At least three recent studies show the benefits of distributed practice. Two studies focused on reading skills and a third on mathematics. Seabrook, Brown, and Solity (2005) showed that recall of words among various age groups was best for words in a list that were repeated after several intervening words than words that were repeated in sequence. To demonstrate the application of this principle to instructional settings, they found that phonics skills taught in reading classes scheduled in three two-minute daily sessions showed an improvement six times greater than those practicing in one six-minute daily session.

Rawson and Kintsch (2005) compared learning among groups of college students who read a text once, twice in a row, or twice with a week separating the readings. They found that reading the same text twice in a row (massed practice) improved performance on an immediate test, whereas reading the same text twice with a week in between readings (distributed practice) improved performance on a delayed test.

Rohrer and Taylor (2006) used mathematical permutation problems described previously in this chapter and compared the effects of spaced and massed practice on learning one week and four weeks after practice. After completing a tutorial in Session 1, students were assigned ten practice problems. The massed group worked all ten practice problems in the second session, whereas the spaced practice group worked the first five problems in

Session 1 and the second five problems in Session 2. As you can see in Figure 12.10, learning in the two groups was equivalent after one week, but spaced learners had much better four-week retention of skills.

Figure 12.10. Best Learning on the Delayed Test Among Students Practicing Math Problems in a Spaced Format.

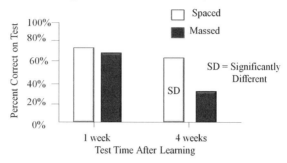

Taken together, evidence continues to recommend practice that is scheduled throughout a learning event rather than concentrated in one time or place. To apply this guideline, incorporate review practice exercises among the various lessons in your course and within a lesson distribute practice throughout the lesson rather than all in one place. Also consider ways to leverage media in ways that will extend learning over time. For example, schedule an asynchronous class a week or so prior to an instructor-led synchronous session. Follow these two sessions by a third learning event in which participants complete a workplace assignment to be reviewed by a supervisor. The use of diverse delivery media to spread practice over time will improve long-term learning.

Mix Practice Types in Lessons

Imagine you have three or more categories of skills or problems to teach, such as how to calculate the area of a rectangle, a circle, and a triangle. A traditional approach is to show an example followed by practice of each area calculation separately. For example, first demonstrate how to calculate the area of a rectangle followed by five or six problems on rectangles. Next show how to calculate the area of a circle followed by several problems on circles.

This traditional approach is what instructional psychologists called "*blocked practice*." Practice exercises are blocked into learning segments based on their common solutions.

Recent research, however, suggests that a mixed practice format will lead to poorer practice scores but, counter-intuitively, pay off in better learning on a test given a day later. Taylor and Rohrer (2010) asked learners to calculate the number of faces, edges, corners, or angles in four unique geometric shapes. Following a tutorial that included examples, learners were assigned thirty-two practice problems—eight of each of the four types. The blocked group worked eight faces problems, eight edges problems, eight corners problems, and eight angles problems, for a total of thirty-two problems. The mixed group worked a practice problem from each of the four types eight times, also for a total of thirty-two problems. For example, in the mixed group the learner would work one problem dealing with faces followed by a problem dealing with edges, then a problem dealing with corners, and finally a problem dealing with angles. This pattern was repeated eight times. One day after practice, each student completed a test. As you can see in Figure 12.11, the practice scores in the blocked practice group were higher than those in the mixed group. However, the mixed practice group scored much better on the test.

Figure 12.11. Mixed Practice Leads to Poorer Practice Scores But Better Learning.

Based on data from Taylor and Rohrer, 2010.

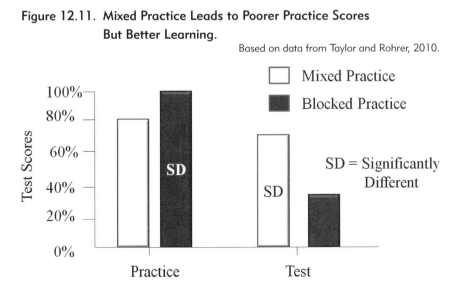

Recall from Chapter 11 that varied context examples led to better learning than examples that used a similar cover story. The benefits of mixed practice may be based on a similar mechanism. By mixing together problems that must be discriminated in order to identify the most appropriate solution, learners receive much more discrimination practice. In situations where problem types are easy to discriminate, mixed practice may have less benefit.

Tips for Determining the Number and Placement of Practice Events

We have consistent evidence that practice interactions promote learning. However, the greatest amount of learning accrues on the initial practice events. Over-learning, at least in a structured domain such as mathematics, has not proven beneficial. We also know that greater long-term learning occurs when practice is distributed throughout the learning environment rather than all at once. In addition, when it's important to discriminate among different problem types, it's better to mix types during practice than to group them by the same type. To summarize our guidelines for practice we recommend that you:

- Analyze the task performance requirements:
  - Is automatic task performance needed? If so, is automaticity required immediately or can it develop during job performance?
  - Does the task require an understanding of concepts and processes along with concomitant reflection?
- For less critical tasks or for tasks that do not require automaticity, avoid over-learning that wastes time.
- Assign larger numbers of exercises when automaticity is needed.
- For tasks that require automatic responses, use the computer to measure response accuracy and response time. Once automated, responses will be both accurate and fast.
- Distribute practice among lessons in the course, within any given lesson, and among multiple learning events.
- In synchronous e-learning courses, extend learning by designing several short sessions of one to two hours with asynchronous practice assigned between sessions.

- When your goal is to teach discrimination among problem types, mix types together during practice rather than segregating them by type.

Practice Principle 5: Apply Multimedia Principles

In Chapters 4 through 9, we presented six principles for design of multimedia pertaining specifically to the use of graphics, text, and audio in e-learning. Here are some suggestions for ways to apply those principles to the design of practice interactions.

Modality and Redundancy Principles

According to the modality principle described in Chapter 6, audio should be used to explain visuals in your lesson. However, audio is too transient for practice exercises. Learners need to refer to the directions while responding to questions. Any instructions or information learners need in order to answer a question should remain in text on the screen while the learner formulates a response.

Previously in this chapter, we focused on the importance of explanatory feedback. Feedback should also be presented in text so that learners can review the explanations at their own pace. Based on the redundancy principle described in Chapter 7, use text alone for most situations. Do not narrate on-screen text directions, practice questions, or feedback.

Contiguity Principle

According to the contiguity principle, text should be closely aligned to the graphics it is explaining to minimize extraneous cognitive load. Since you will be using text for your questions and feedback, the contiguity principle is especially applicable to design of practice questions. Clearly distinguish response areas by placement, color, or font and place them adjacent to the question. In addition, when laying out practice that will include feedback to a response, leave an open screen area for feedback near the question and as close to the response area as possible so learners can easily align the feedback to their response and to the question. In multiple-choice or multiple-select items, use color or bolding to show the correct options as part of the feedback.

Recent research shows that contiguity applies also to the type of behavioral interaction required. Rey (2011) found greater transfer learning from a simulation in which learners adjusted parameters via either scroll bars or drag and drop than by text input. Having to split attention between the keyboard and the screen when inputting text depressed learning. We will need more research indicating the tradeoffs to different forms of physical engagement during e-learning.

Coherence Principle

In Chapter 8 we reviewed evidence suggesting that violation of the coherence principle imposes extraneous cognitive load and may interfere with learning. Specifically, we recommended you exclude stories and graphics added for entertainment value, complex graphics, background music and sounds, and detailed textual descriptions. Our bottom line is *less is usually more.*

We recommend that practice opportunities be free of extraneous visual or audio elements such as gratuitous animations or sounds (applause, bells, or whistles) associated with correct or incorrect responses. Research has shown that, while there is no correlation between the amount of study and grade point average in universities, there is a correlation between the amount of *deliberate practice* and grades. Specifically, research recommends study in distraction-free environments, that is, alone in a quiet room rather than with a radio or in a team leads to better learning (Knez & Hugge, 2002; Plant, Ericsson, Hill, & Asberg, 2005). During virtual classroom synchronous sessions, the instructor should maintain a period of silence during practice events.

Tips for Applying the Multimedia Principles to Your Interactions

- Include relevant visuals as part of your interaction design.
- Align directions, practice questions, and feedback in on-screen text so that learners can easily see all the important elements in one location.

- Minimize split attention in behavioral response required by using on-screen rather than keyboard input modes.

- Minimize extraneous text, sounds, or visuals during interactions.

Practice Principle 6: Transition from Examples to Practice Gradually

Completing practice exercises imposes a great deal of mental load. In Chapter 11, we showed evidence that using healthy doses of worked examples along with practice will result in more efficient learning. In fact, faded worked examples are a proven strategy to impose load gradually as learners gain expertise. Start with a full worked example and gradually increase the amount of work the learner must perform, ending with a full practice assignment, as described in Chapter 11.

What We Don't Know About Practice

We conclude that, while practice does not necessarily lead to perfect, deliberate practice that includes effective feedback does. We still need to know more about the best types of feedback to give. For example, should feedback be detailed or brief? Is feedback provided immediately after a response always most effective? Finally, we need to know more about the source of feedback. In some situations, guided peer feedback has proven effective. Under what conditions can peer feedback supplement instructor feedback?

DESIGN DILEMMA: RESOLVED

The pharmacological sales design team had disagreements about the type of practice and practice feedback to include in the new product lesson leading to the following alternatives:

A. Adding some familiar and fun games like Jeopardy will make the lesson more engaging for learners and lead to better learning.

B. It would be better to use physician scenarios as the basis for interactions.

C. The extra time invested in writing tailored feedback explanations for practice responses will pay off in increased learning.

Based on the research we have summarized in this chapter, we recommend Options B and C. Games like Jeopardy reinforce factual level learning. Instead, questions that require learners to apply factual information to a work-realistic scenario would mirror the job and promote transfer of learning. Regarding Option C, we have evidence that explanatory feedback does pay off in additional learning.

WHAT TO LOOK FOR IN e-LEARNING

- ☐ Job-relevant overt practice questions that require participants to apply new content in authentic ways

- ☐ Feedback that not only tells the respondent whether an answer is correct or incorrect but gives an explanation as well

- ☐ Explanatory feedback that focuses on the task or on the task process

- ☐ The number of practice opportunities reflects the criticality of the job skills and the need for automaticity

- ☐ Practice exercises distributed throughout the learning event

- ☐ For less critical tasks that do not require over-learning, fewer practice exercises

- ☐ For learning to respond to categories of problems, practice interactions mix categories

- ☐ Practice exercises that minimize extraneous cognitive load by applying appropriate multimedia principles

  - Use relevant visuals

  - Use text to provide directions and feedback close to related visuals or response areas

  - Avoid split attention with response formats

  - Avoid gratuitous sounds or other distractions

- ☐ Faded worked examples that end in a practice assignment

COMING NEXT

From discussion boards to blogs to breakout rooms and social media, there are numerous computer facilities for synchronous and asynchronous forms of collaboration among learners and instructors during e-learning events. There has been a great deal of research on how to best structure and leverage online collaboration to maximize learning. Unfortunately, we still have few solid guidelines from that research. In the next chapter we look at what we know about online collaboration and learning.

Suggested Readings

Hattie, J., & Gan, M. (2011). Instruction based on feedback. In R.E. Mayer & P.A. Alexander (Eds.), *Handbook of research on learning and instruction.* New York: Routledge.

Moreno, R., & Mayer, R.E. (2007). Interactive multimodal learning environments. *Educational Psychology Review, 19,* 309–326.

Plant, E.A., Ericsson, K.A., Hill, L., & Asberg, K. (2005). Why study time does not predict grade point average across college students: Implications of deliberate practice for academic performance. *Contemporary Educational Psychology, 30,* 96–116.

Rohrer, D., & Taylor, K. (2006). The effects of over-learning and distributed practice on the retention of mathematics knowledge. *Applied Cognitive Psychology, 20,* 1209–1224.

Shute, V.J. (2008). Focus on formative feedback. *Review of Educational Research, 78*(1), 153–189.

CHAPTER OUTLINE

What Is Collaborative Learning?

Criteria 1: Social Interdependence

Criteria 2: Outcome Goals

Criteria 3: Quality of Collaborative Dialog

What Is Computer-Supported Collaborative Learning (CSCL)?

Diversity of CSCL Research

Some Generalizations About Collaboration

CSCL Research Summaries

Study 1: Is Problem-Solving Learning Better with CSCL or Solo?

Study 2: Are Collaborative Team Products and Individual Learning Better in Face-to-Face or Synchronous Chat Collaboration?

Study 3: Are Team Decisions Better in Virtual or Face-to-Face Environments?

Study 4: How Do Software Representations Effect Collaborative Work?

Study 5: How Do Group Roles Affect CSCL Outcomes?

Structured Controversy

Workflow for Structured Controversy

Adapting Structured Controversy to CSCL

CSCL: The Bottom Line

13

Learning Together Virtually

IN THE FIRST TWO EDITIONS of *e-Learning and the Science of Instruction,* we concluded that the research evidence was insufficient to offer firm guidelines regarding optimal use of computer-mediated collaborative learning. Therefore, we summarized main lessons learned from research on collaborative learning in face-to-face environments and reviewed a sampling of experiments on computer-supported collaborative learning (CSCL). In the five years since our second edition, we have new technology collectively called "social media," including applications such as Facebook and Twitter. However, in terms of experimental evidence of what works best in CSCL, we know little more than we did five years ago. In this chapter, we update the evidence on collaborative learning in face-to-face environments as well as via computer-supported collaboration.

DESIGN DILEMMA: YOU DECIDE

The HR director has just returned from an e-learning conference and is very keen on social media that leverage Web 2.0 to capture organizational expertise. She wants all project teams to integrate collaborative activities into both formal and informal learning programs. The sales training project manager has directed the design team to integrate some effective collaboration techniques into the new web-based pharmaceutical asynchronous course. Samya wants to incorporate collaborative projects. Specifically she would like to assign teams of five or six participants to work together in a shared online workspace to plan a marketing and sales campaign for the upcoming new product launch. Mark thinks this type of team activity will require too much instructional time. And he is skeptical about the learning outcomes of group work for the resources invested. Mark suggests that, instead of a group project, they set up a company-wide wiki to exchange field experience with the new product. Both Mark and Samya wonder about the best collaborative approach to use. Would they get better results from synchronous activities or from asynchronous discussions? Is there any advantage to digital collaboration compared to face-to-face collaboration? Based on your own experience or intuition, which of the following options are correct:

A. Individual learning will benefit from a group project more than if each class participant completed a project individually.

B. A better project will result from a team effort than if each class participant develops his or her own project individually.

C. A wiki would yield greater long-term benefits than a team project developed during the class.

D. A team project would be of better quality if accomplished through asynchronous collaboration than through synchronous collaboration.

What Is Collaborative Learning?

Is learning better when a student studies alone or with others? Are class or workplace projects of better quality when completed by an individual or a group? Does the type of technology (that is, synchronous or asynchronous communication) affect learning or product outcomes?

These are some fundamental questions about collaborative learning—also called *cooperative learning*. Research on collaborative learning in a face-to-face environment has a history of over sixty years and offers some lessons learned that can be applied to computer collaboration. The general consensus is that collaborative learning has excellent potential to improve individual learning. Slavin (2011) states that "Cooperative learning methods are extensively researched and under certain well-specified conditions they are known to substantially improve student achievement in most subjects and grade levels" (p. 344). A recent review by Johnson, Johnson, and Smith (2007) concludes that "Cooperation, compared with competitive and individualistic efforts, tends to result in higher achievement, greater long-term retention of what is learned, more frequent use of higher-level reasoning and meta-cognitive thought, more accurate and creative problem solving, more willingness to take on difficult tasks and persist in working toward goal accomplishment. . . ." (p. 19). Among 138 influences on learning, Hattie (2009) ranked the benefits of cooperative versus individual learning twenty-fourth, with an overall effect size of .59.

Yet not all research comparisons of learning together show advantages over learning alone. For example, Kirschner, Paas, and Kirschner (2009) state, "There is no clear and unequivocal picture of how, when, and why the effectiveness of individual learning and collaborative learning environments differ." So before you convert all of your learning events into group projects and team events or rush to leverage social media, keep in mind several important criteria for success summarized in Table 13.1. Applying these criteria will maximize the potential benefits of collaborative learning.

Table 13.1. Criteria for Successful Collaboration.

Success Criteria	Description
Social Interdependence	The goal of each team member depends on the achievement of all other members
Outcome Goals	The desired results of the collaboration, such as individual learning or quality of a team project
Dialog Quality	Substantive contributions made by all parties with no one ignored

Criteria 1: Social Interdependence

Have you ever been part of a team and felt that you did more than your share of the work? One of the most important criteria for collaborative learning success is what instructional psychologists call *"social interdependence."* Social interdependence means that each team member acts on the premise that achieving his or her own goals is positively affected by the achievements of team members. In other words, the learning and grade outcome of any given class member is dependent in part on the learning and accomplishment of his or her teammates.

Slavin (2011) emphasizes the importance of group rewards, which are only effective when each team member's grade is based on a sum of the learning of all group members. For example, suppose a learning team of four studies together to complete a math worksheet and then each individual takes a test. If each individual receives a grade based solely on his or her own test score, there is little incentive to help others during the group learning process. If, however, a part of each individual's grade reflects the scores or score improvement of each member of the team, there is a much greater incentive for team members to help one another. Grades that reflect not only the learning of the individual but also the learning outcomes of the entire team is what Slavin means by group rewards. Slavin reports that, of sixty-four studies of cooperative learning with group rewards, 78 percent found significantly positive effects on achievement, with a median effect size of .32, which is moderate. However, when rewards were based on a single group product that did not reflect individual learning, there were few positive results, with a median effect size of .07, which is negligible.

As you consider collaborative learning or team projects, keep in mind the incentives for each individual to participate and support the learning of the rest of the team. For example, to receive credit for a project, you might require each member of the team to attain a minimum criterion on a related individual assignment or on a test.

Criteria 2: Outcome Goals

Collaborative work typically is designed to promote one or both of the following outcomes: individual learning and/or project quality. In some situations your main focus may be the quality of a class project or problem solution. Would the quality be better if a case study is resolved by a team or by individuals working independently? Alternatively, your goal may focus on individual learning achievement as measured by an end-of-class test or job productivity measures. We might assume that if a team project product is high quality, the individuals who make up that team likewise benefited. This, however, may not always be the case. A meta-analysis of computer-supported collaborative learning studies by Lou, Abrami, and d'Apollonia (2001) separated research that measured individual achievement outcomes from studies that measured group products. They found that group performance is not necessarily predictive of individual performance. Recent research by Tutty and Klein (2008) and by Krause, Stark, and Mandl (2009) reported no relationship between the quality of a team project and individual learning after the project. It will be important for you to determine your main expectations from collaboration so you can structure the learning environment appropriately.

Criteria 3: Quality of Collaborative Dialog

Fonseca and Chi (2011) propose that effective collaborative learning activities must involve dialog during learning that includes substantive contributions from all parties with no participant ignored. For example, in a productive peer-to-peer dialog, each partner builds upon the contribution of the others, clarifies or challenges assertions, or asks and answers mutual questions. Several experiments that compared individual with collaborative learning activities reported that the collaborative conditions were more effective in most cases. In situations when the collaborative condition was less effective, an analysis of the communications showed that 72 percent of the verbal interactions consisted of knowledge-telling in which one partner repeated what he or she knew to the other. These learners were basically regurgitating what they already knew rather than engaging in dialog that would extend their knowledge.

Merely asking pairs or small teams to "work together" or to "discuss the project" may not generate the rich collaborative exchanges that lead to deeper learning. Shallow or non-participation is common in collaborative assignments when, for example, one or two members of a team complete most of the project or when the assignment does not engage productive collaboration because it is too easy or too unstructured. Your challenge is to create instructional conditions most likely to promote effective dialog. In this chapter we review some proven methods to leverage collaboration in learning.

What Is Computer-Supported Collaborative Learning (CSCL)?

By computer-supported collaborative learning (CSCL) we refer to engagements among teams of two to approximately five members using synchronous and/or asynchronous tools in ways that support an instructional goal, such as to produce a product, resolve a case study, discuss a video example of a sales engagement, solve assigned problems, or complete an instructional worksheet.

The first generations of e-learning were designed for solo learning. There were few practical ways to integrate multiple learners or instructors into asynchronous self-study e-learning. However, the emergence of the Web 2.0 in general and social software in particular have made both synchronous and asynchronous connections practical and easy. Table 13.2 summarizes common social software and some of their applications to e-learning.

Table 13.2. Some Online Facilities for Social Learning.

Facility	Description	Some e-Learning Applications
Blogs and Mini-Blogs such as Twitter	A website where individuals write commentaries on an ongoing basis. Visitors can comment or link to a blog. Some writers use blogs to organize individual thoughts while others command influential, worldwide audiences of thousands	Learning journals Pre-class intros Post-class reflections Short post-class updates (tweets) with links Informal updates on course skills and related topics Evaluation of course effectiveness, Update course content
Breakout Rooms	A conferencing facility that usually supports audio, whiteboard, polling, and chat, used for small groups in conjunction with a virtual classroom event or online conference (See Figure 13.1)	Synchronous team work during a virtual classroom session Small group meetings

(Continued)

Facility	Description	Some e-Learning Applications
Chats	Two or more participants communicating at the same time by text	Role-play practice Group decision making Group project work Pair collaborative study Questions or comments during a virtual presentation
E-mail	Two or more participants communicating at different times. Messages received and managed at the individual's mail site	Group project work Instructor-student exchanges Pair collaborative activities
Message Boards	A number of participants communicate at different times by typing comments that remain on the board for others to read and respond to. (See Figure 13.3)	Topic-specific discussions Case-study work Post-class commentaries
Online Conferencing	A number of participants online at once with access to audio, whiteboard, polling, media displays, and chat	Guest speakers Virtual classes Group project work
Social Networks	Individuals post pages with various media elements and link their pages to selected others	Finding expertise Display class agendas, objectives Icebreakers Intersession multimedia work and discussions
Wikis	A website that allows visitors to edit its contents. Can be controlled for editing/viewing by a small group or by all. (See Figure 13.2)	Collaborative work on a project document Ongoing updated repository of course information Collaborative course material construction

Chats, breakout rooms for team assignments in virtual classrooms (shown in Figure 13.1), wikis (shown in Figure 13.2), blogs, discussion boards (shown in Figure 13.3), networking, and media sharing tools offer a variety of channels for online collaboration. Since our second edition of this book, learning conferences and trade journals have spotlighted new social media such as Facebook and Twitter. However, as we write this chapter, these new forms of social media have not yet been widely embraced in the workplace (ASTD, 2010). As we have learned from a long history of media comparison research, the benefits of social media, just like the benefits of any technology, will depend on how instructional professionals exploit technology features in ways that accommodate human cognitive learning needs. Therefore, we recommend you consider how to adapt lessons learned from both in-person collaboration as well as from online collaboration as you consider the what, when, and why of new social media.

Figure 13.1. Small Teams Work on an Assignment in Virtual Classroom Breakout Rooms.

From Clark and Kwinn, 2007.

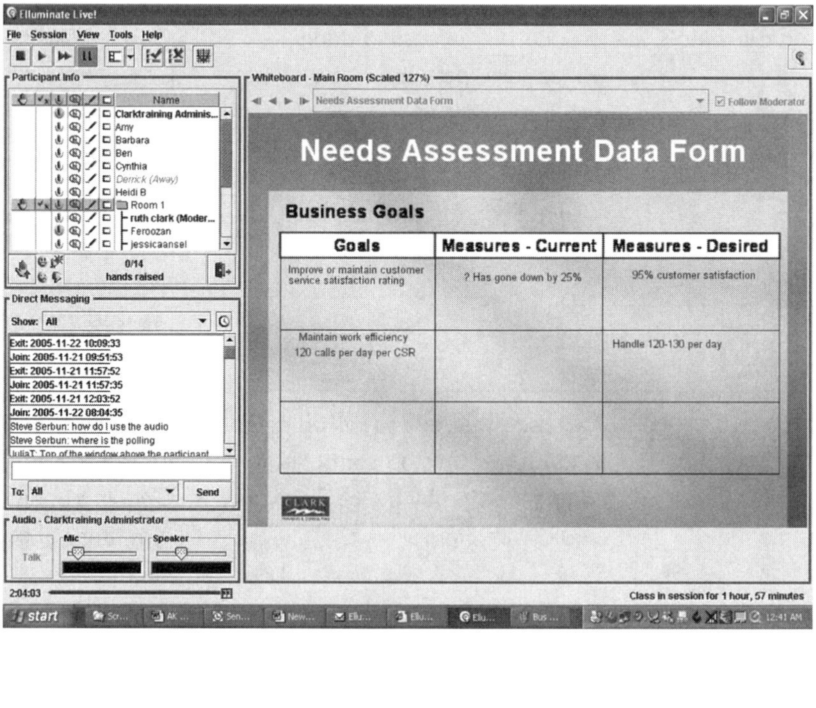

Figure 13.2. Asynchronous Collaborative Learning Using a Wiki.

Accessed from http://en.wikipedia.org August 15, 2006.

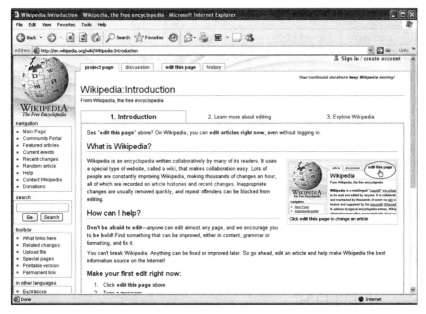

Figure 13.3. Asynchronous Collaborative Learning Using a Discussion Board.

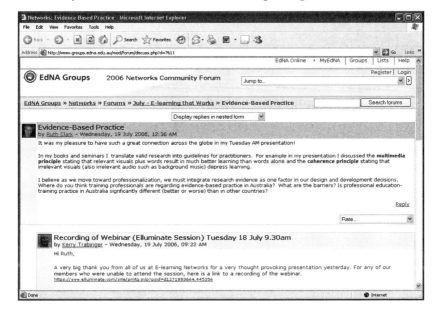

Diversity of CSCL Research

While collaboration tends to be a popular instructional method and there is currently high interest in social media, what do we actually know about the benefits of computer-mediated collaboration for learning? Quite a bit of research has focused on computer-mediated collaboration. However the research varies broadly. Some studies measure individual learning, while others evaluate the quality of a group project. These outcomes may be compared between individuals working alone versus individuals working in a face-to-face team or may be compared between individuals working as a team in a face-to-face environment versus working as a virtual team. Alternatively, the research might focus on teams working in a virtual environment under different conditions, such as size of team, background knowledge of team members, type of learning goal, or technology used, such as synchronous or asynchronous chat, to name a few. In addition to outcomes such as test scores or project quality, many studies also evaluate the communication process by analyzing the dialogs that occur during collaborative exchanges.

In Table 13.3 we summarize the main factors that can affect CSCL outcomes. Any unique combination of these factors may result in different results. For example, the individual learning of a team of two working on a procedural task in a synchronous chat mode would likely be quite different from a team of four working on a decision task in an asynchronous discussion environment. In our summary of research studies to follow, we offer a snapshot of evidence to give you an idea of the diversity of the questions addressed. Unfortunately, the heterogeneity of the research we have right now leaves us with few universal guidelines. Resta and Laferriere (2007) conclude: "It is challenging to compare and analyze CSCL studies because of the divergent views of what should be studied and how it should be studied" (p. 68).

Some Generalizations About Collaboration

Because of the diversity among computer-collaboration research studies, we have few definitive guidelines. However, based on a great deal of research on face-to-face collaboration and limited research on CSCL, we offer the following preliminary suggestions:

1. In a face-to-face environment, working together can yield greater individual learning than studying alone when (a) there is an incentive for mutual support and goal achievement and (b) a structured collaborative assignment ensures mutual on-task dialog that promotes deeper mental processing.

2. When your goal is to produce a creative product or solve an ill-defined problem (either in the workplace or as part of a class exercise), a team can produce a better quality product than an individual working alone. Lou, Abrami, and D'Apollonia (2001) found that group products are better than individual products, with an effect size of 2 or more, indicating a very high practical significance! The research team concludes: "When working together, the group is capable of doing more than any single member by comparing alternative interpretations and solutions, correcting each other's misconceptions, and forming a more holistic picture of the problem" (p. 479).

3. When your goal is to produce a creative product or solve an ill-defined problem, a virtual collaboration environment has the potential to result in a better quality outcome than a face-to-face collaboration. This is because virtual collaboration can lead to more reflection and sharing of ideas than a face-to-face environment.

4. Avoid creating teams of homogeneous low prior knowledge learners. Heterogeneous teams that include high and low prior knowledge learners or homogeneous high prior knowledge teams are best.

5. Regarding team size, consider pairs when your main goal is individual learning. However, when your goal is creative problem solving, a larger team of three to five members may be needed to contribute sufficient expertise.

6. Social presence leads to higher class satisfaction. You will receive higher class ratings from most participants if they feel they have had an opportunity to connect with the instructor and with other participants (Sitzmann, Brown, Casper, Ely, & Zimmerman, 2008). Collaborative learning is one technique to increase social presence.

Table 13.3. CSCL Factors That Can Affect Results.

Factor	Description	Guidelines	Citation
Outcome of Collaboration	individual vs. group metrics Discourse analysis	Group metrics may be independent of individual outcomes Assumes that deeper discourse equals better learning	Lou, Abrami, & d'Apollonia (2001); meta-analysis; Jonassen, Lee, Yang, & Laffey (2005)
Group Composition	Size: from two to five Makeup: heterogeneous vs. homogeneous	Best size may depend on desired outcomes; heterogeneous compositions generally favored	Lou, Abrami, & d'Apollonia (2001); meta-analysis
Technology	Synchronous vs. asynchronous Tools to support collaboration	Tool features should match outcome goals. Asynchronous better for reflection and longer time periods; Synchronous better for higher social presence. Many common tools lack capability to capture and display group thinking. Need better groupware	Kirschner, Strijbos, Kreijns, & Beers (2004); Suthers, Vatrapu, Medina, Joseph, & Dwyer (2008); McGill, Nicol, Littlejohn, Gierson, Juster, & Ion (2005); Jonassen, Lee, Yang, & Laffey (2005)
Task Assignment	Near transfer Far transfer—well structured Far transfer—ill structured	CSCL lends itself well to far transfer ill-structured problem solving with groups of three to five. Mixed results with near and well-structured far transfer assignments	Jonassen, Lee, Yang, & Laffey (2005); Kirschner, Strijbos, Kreijns, & Beers (2004); Uribe, Klein, & Sullivan (2003); Yetter, Gutkin, Saunders, Galloway, Sobansky, & Song (2006)

Factor	Levels	Findings	References
Group Roles, Processes, and Instructions	Instructor or student moderator; Assigned roles; High or low process structure; Frequency of interaction	Student moderators may be better for groups of advanced learners when argumentation structures are used; Greater structure in assignments generally leads to better outcomes than low structure; Specific instructions lead to better outcomes than general instructions	Campbell & Stasser (2006); De Wever, Van Winckel, & Valcke (2006); Nussbaum (2005); Nussbaum & Kardash (2005)
Time	Limited vs. constrained	CSCL outcomes take longer than individual outcomes; CSCL outcomes can exceed individual outcomes if there is ample processing time	Campbell & Stasser (2006)
Team Skills Training	Yes or No	Teamwork training leads to better outcomes as long as the trained group remains intact	Prichard, Bizo, & Stratford (2006)
Learner Prior Knowledge	High vs. Low	Factors that mediate CSCL among high PK learners likely different than those most appropriate for low PK learners	Uribe, Klein, & Sullivan (2003)
Incentives	The basis for awarding of points or grades	Assign points or grades on a synthesis of individual outcomes rather than a group product or individual products alone	Mayer (2007); Slavin, Hurley, & Chamberlain (2003)

CSCL Research Summaries

In the following paragraphs, we offer some snapshots of research on computer-supported collaborative learning. Our goal is not a comprehensive review of research. Rather, we want to give you a flavor for the diversity of collaboration research published. In each section we give a thumbnail summary of the study followed by a brief description of it.

Study 1: Is Problem-Solving Learning Better with CSCL or Solo?

Jonassen, Lee, Yang, and Laffey (2005) recommend that CSCL is best suited to complex ill-defined tasks for which there is no single correct solution. These types of tasks benefit from the collaboration of a group. Some examples include developing a patient treatment plan, designing a small business website, or troubleshooting a unique equipment failure. The study reviewed in this section evaluates individual learning of a process to solve ill-defined problems as a result of practice via CSCL compared to solo practice.

RESEARCH THUMBNAIL

Problem Solving: Pairs Using Chat During Practice Learn More Than Individuals Practicing Alone

Authors: Uribe, Klein, and Sullivan (2003)

Type of Study: Experimental

Task: Applying a structured problem-solving process to solve ill-structured problems

Outcome Measures: Individual scores on an essay test describing a solution to an ill-defined problem

Teams: Heterogeneous pairs of college students

Technology: Synchronous chat

Comparison: Individual learning of subjects who solved a practice problem in pairs via synchronous chat versus individuals who solved the practice problem alone

Result: Individuals who solved problems in pairs via synchronous chat during practice learned more than individuals who practiced alone.

Uribe, Klein, and Sullivan (2003) compared individual learning of a problem-solving process from pairs solving a practice problem collaboratively using synchronous chat to individuals solving the practice problem on their own. The study included three phases: First, each participant individually completed web-based self-study training on a four-step problem solving process. After the instructional period, participants were tested individually with a knowledge quiz to ensure learning of the process. In the second phase, participants were assigned an ill-structured practice problem to solve, either alone or with a virtual partner using synchronous chat. In the third phase, each participant individually completed an essay test that asked questions about the assessment problem they solved in Phase 2. Individuals who practiced with a partner scored higher on the essay questions (60 percent average) than individuals who had worked independently (50 percent average). Although the difference was statistically significant, the small effect size of .11 is in the negligible range.

Study 2: Are Collaborative Team Products *and* Individual Learning Better in Face-to-Face or Synchronous Chat Collaboration?

In this study there were two outcome measures: quality of group projects *and* end of training individual learning. These outcomes were compared among teams of two that either worked together face-to- face or in synchronous chat sessions to learn and apply spreadsheet procedures.

RESEARCH THUMBNAIL

Team Excel Product Quality and Individual Excel Learning: Virtual vs. Face-to-Face Collaboration

Authors: Tutty and Klein (2008)

Type of Study: Experimental

Task: How to construct spreadsheets

Outcome Measures: Quality of team spreadsheet project solution, individual post-test scores

Teams: Heterogeneous and homogenous pairs of college students (based on background computer knowledge)

Technology: Synchronous chat

Comparisons: Pairs working face-to-face at a computer versus pairs working via synchronous chat; homogeneous versus heterogeneous background knowledge teams

Result: Virtual collaboration resulted in *better projects* than those collaborating face-to face. Face-to face collaboration resulted in better *post-test learning* than virtual collaboration.

Tutty and Klein (2008) looked at two variables that affect the quality of synchronous team collaboration: 1) face-to- face collaboration versus collaboration via synchronous chat and 2) homogeneous versus heterogeneous background knowledge mix of the teams. A pre-test on computer literacy was used to classify college students as high or low knowledge, and teams of two were made of higher knowledge pairs, lower knowledge pairs, and mixed pairs. The teams were then randomly assigned to instruction in which they either collaborated face-to-face in front of a computer terminal or via synchronous chat. The training consisted of a computer-based instructional module on Microsoft Excel. Each student received a grade based on the team project and on the individual post-test.

Teams first participated in a grade book Excel learning activity and then were assigned a different spreadsheet task as a team project. Following the team project, individuals completed a twenty-five-item multiple-choice post-test. The research team concluded that "participants in the face-to-face collaborative condition performed significantly better on the individual post-test than those in the virtual online condition. Face-to-face students found it easier to share information throughout the lesson than virtual students. . . . In contrast, pairs that collaborated virtually performed significantly better on the group project than those who collaborated face-to-face. Observations conducted during the study revealed that pairs in the virtual condition exhibited significantly more questioning behaviors than pairs in the face-to-face condition. Several students assigned to collaborate face-to-face were observed working independently on the group project" (pp. 118–119).

Teams consisting of one or two higher prior knowledge individuals did better on the project and post-test than teams of two lower knowledge students.

Study 3: Are Team Decisions Better in Virtual or Face-to-Face Environments?

Can group decision making benefit from collaborative technology? In this research, the decisions of teams working face-to-face were compared with decisions made in a collaborative virtual environment.

RESEARCH THUMBNAIL

Team Decision Quality: Virtual vs. Face-to-Face Collaboration

Authors: Campbell and Stasser (2006)

Type of Study: Experimental

Task: Identify the guilty suspect in a crime case for which there was a correct answer that could be derived only by sharing of information given to different team members

Outcome Measures: Accuracy of group solutions to a crime decision task

Teams: Trios of college students in which each member was provided different relevant case knowledge

Technology: Synchronous chat

Comparison: Synchronous chat versus face-to-face decision accuracy; ample versus constrained time during synchronous chat

Result: Synchronous collaborators with plenty of time produced more accurate decisions than face-to-face teams or synchronous collaborators with restricted time.

Campbell and Stasser (2006) compared the accuracy of a decision task that had a correct answer from three-person groups collaborating in a face-to-face setting with the accuracy of trios collaborating via synchronous chat. The decision task involved a fictional homicide investigation with three suspects.

Each participant in the trio received a different packet of information about the crime and the suspects. A correct solution required that all three team members disclose and discuss the unique information that each had reviewed in his or her packet.

Overall, the computer-mediated groups arrived at more correct solutions (63 percent) than face to-face groups (less than 20 percent), provided the computer team was allotted sufficient discussion time. Some computer teams were given only twenty minutes to solve the problem, whereas others were instructed to take as long as they needed. The time-restricted computer-mediated groups were much less accurate when compared to computer groups given ample discussion time. The computer-mediated groups required more time to arrive at their solutions than the face-to-face groups, resulting in higher solution accuracy. The research team concluded that computer-mediated discussions are more effective for decision making than face-to-face groups, provided virtual groups have sufficient working time. They suggest that synchronous chat leads to more accurate decisions than face-to-face discussions due to parallel communications in chat, the ability to reference the group's discussion maintained in the text of the chat, as well as the anonymity of the communications. Similar to the Tutty and Klein 2008 study summarized previously, synchronous chat led to a better product than working as a face-to-face team.

Study 4: How Do Software Representations Affect Collaborative Work?

How can computer interfaces more effectively represent and support collaborative work? For example, the comments in a traditional discussion board are displayed chronologically. In a lengthy team discussion it is challenging to infer shared agreement or to make knowledge gained explicit. If you join an ongoing discussion, it can be difficult to find relevant contributions, enter your own ideas into a relevant context, or to make a determination of the outcomes. In the study summarized below, the research team evaluated the problem-solving support of an online graphic knowledge map compared with a threaded text discussion or with a combination of the map and text discussion.

RESEARCH THUMBNAIL

The Effects of Tool Interfaces on Online Collaborative Learning

Authors: Suthers, Vatrapu, Medina, Joseph, and Dwyer (2008)

Type of Study: Experimental

Task: Solving a science problem

Outcome Measures: Quality of problem solutions, convergence of reasoning in individual essays, individual post-test scores, and reasoning process of teams during problem solving

Technology: Asynchronous discussions using knowledge maps and discussion boards

Teams: Pairs of college students

Comparison: Asynchronous discussions using threaded discussions, online knowledge maps, or both threaded discussion and knowledge maps shown in Figure 13.4

Result: No differences in quality of solutions or overall post-test results; greater idea convergence in essays among those using knowledge maps

---

Figure 13.4. A Graphics Interface to Capture Group Problem-Solving Process.
From Suthers, Vatrapu, Medina, Joseph, and Dwyer, 2008.

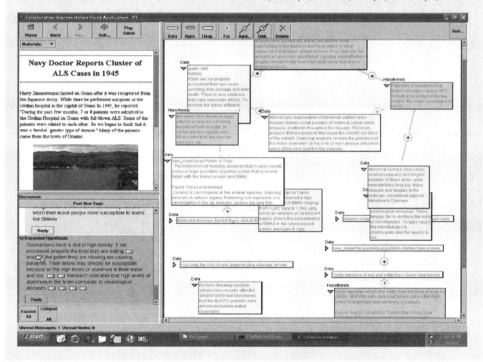

Suthers, Vatrapu, Medina, Joseph, and Dwyer (2008) evaluated the effectiveness of different interfaces to help collaborative pairs share and summarize findings while solving a science problem in an asynchronous format. The research team compared three different interfaces, including a threaded discussion board, a knowledge map, and a mix of the discussion board and knowledge map, as shown in Figure 13.4. The knowledge map representation used symbols and lines to encode facts, state hypotheses, and link facts to hypotheses. The goal of the graphic interface was to capture and summarize a group discussion around scientific topics.

Pairs were given science problems to solve, along with a number of short resource articles. Each individual received different information, thus requiring sharing of data to reach an optimal conclusion. The problem-solving collaboration was conducted with three different asynchronous collaborative interfaces: threaded discussions, online knowledge maps, or a combination of the discussion and knowledge map. Following the collaborative work period, each participant wrote an individual essay that stated the hypotheses considered, the evidence for or against the hypotheses, and the conclusion reached. A week later each individual completed a twenty-item multiple-choice post-test. The research team compared the team problem solutions as well as the convergence of ideas in essay conclusions among teams working with the different interfaces. In addition, they compared overall post-test scores. They found best convergence of ideas among teams that used the graphic representation. There were no differences in quality of the essays or overall post-test scores. However, the essays written by teams using the knowledge map interface reflected more overlap of ideas.

Study 5: How Do Group Roles and Assignments Affect CSCL Outcomes?

As we mentioned previously, the nature of the team assignment as well as assigned team roles will influence the effectiveness of the collaboration. In the research report we summarize below, team roles among medical students in CSCL discussion groups were compared.

RESEARCH THUMBNAIL

Assigned Roles in Problem-Based Learning (PBL) Online Discussions

Authors: De Wever, Van Winckel, and Valcke (2006)

Type of Study: Quasi experimental

Task: Development of treatment plans for clinical pediatric cases

Outcome Measures: Depth of group discussions

Teams: Groups of four or five medical interns

Technology: Asynchronous discussions

Comparison: Student versus instructor discussion moderation and student assigned to suggest alternative case solutions

Results: Deeper case discussions with student moderators only when another student generated alternative solutions

De Wever, Van Winckel, and Valcke (2006) adapted a face-to-face problem-based learning program to asynchronous case discussions. Pediatric interns met weekly for face-to-face case reviews. More frequent case discussions were desired, but additional face-to-face meetings were not practical due to staff schedules and ward activities. To supplement the in-person meetings, the research team tested asynchronous discussions of authentic cases, each extending over a two-week period. A complete case with diagnosis was included, along with access to electronic information resources. For the first three days, each participant worked independently to develop a patient treatment plan. Starting on day four, individual posts were opened to all and each participant was required to post at least four messages in which he or she supported the treatment plans with rationale, data, and references.

Two different team roles were studied: moderator and solutions alternatives generator. In some teams one of the interns served as a moderator, while in other teams the instructor moderated the discussions. A second variable was an assigned student role to review posted treatment suggestions and develop alternative treatments. Rather than measuring learning, the quality of discussions within the different teams was assessed with a 1 to 5 scale.

The research team found that students who were assigned the moderator role were more likely to write higher-level contributions. Further, they found that higher knowledge construction was evident in groups moderated by a student but *only when one of the participants was assigned to generate different patient treatment plans.* In the absence of this specialized role, there were no differences in the discussions of student- or instructor-moderated discussions. The research team suggests that when a student develops alternatives and the discussion is moderated by another student, there is greater freedom to critique and respond to one another than when an instructor is moderating.

In this study there were no direct measures of learning. The outcome measure was ratings of the quality of the discussions among the different teams. It is assumed that deeper-level discussions lead to better learning. In addition, as medical interns, the background knowledge level of the participants was relatively high compared to other studies in which participants had little or no entry-level knowledge of the content or skills of the class. Different results might be seen among learners more novice to the content. This study suggests that discussions will differ depending on assigned roles within a team.

Structured Controversy

The type of task assignment given to collaborative teams is a major factor influencing either group product quality *or* individual learning. Assignments that are too simple won't motivate meaningful dialog. Assignments that are too general or too vague such as "work together to discuss the case study" won't offer enough structure to encourage effective collaboration. While there are a number of collaborative learning environments that may be effective, in this section we review *structured controversy*—a type of argumentation that has been successfully used in both face-to- face and computer-supported collaborative classes. Structured controversy is a methodology for argumentation developed by Johnson and Johnson (1992). Argumentation involves developing alternative positions on an issue supported by facts and includes several phases such as making a claim or stating a theory along with evidence, statement of alternative theories, rebuttal of alternative theories, and counterarguments against the original theory and its rebuttal.

Workflow for Structured Controversy

In Figure 13.5, we summarize one way to set up a structured controversy collaborative process. Learners are assigned to heterogeneous teams of four. In Phase 1, teams of four are presented with an issue or problem that lends itself to a pro or con position. In Phase 2, teams divide into pairs, each taking either the pro or con, and develop a strong position for their perspective to include relevant facts and evidence. After developing their positions, the team of four reconvenes and one pair presents their argument to the other. After the presentation, the receiving pair must state back the argument adequately to the presenting pair to demonstrate their understanding of the presentation team's position. Then the pairs reverse roles. As a result, all team members develop an understanding of both perspectives. In Phase 3, the full team moves into a synthesis phase wherein the opposing perspectives are merged into a unified reasoned position.

Comparisons of the structured controversy method with several alternative structures, including traditional debates, individual learning, or groups that stressed concurrence, found the structured controversy method more effective, with effect sizes ranging from .42 to .77 (Johnson & Johnson, 1992).

Figure 13.5. Structured Argumentation Collaborative Learning Process.

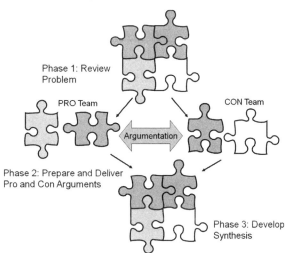

The authors recommend the following elements for successful constructive controversy:

- Ensure a cooperative context where the goal is understanding the opposing views, followed by a synthesis of perspectives.

- Structure groups to include learners of mixed background knowledge and ability.

- Provide access to rich and relevant information about the issues.

- Ensure adequate social skills to manage conflict.

- Focus group interactions on rational arguments.

Adapting Structured Controversy to CSCL

Structured controversy can use a combination of asynchronous and synchronous facilities in a CSCL adaptation. For example, present an application problem or case that lends itself to two or more alternative positions. Provide links to relevant resources. Assign pairs to research and advocate for one of the positions. Each pair can work asynchronously through newer or traditional social media to research their position and to develop their argument. They may want to schedule a synchronous meeting in breakout rooms to discuss their findings and diagram their argument on the whiteboard. Next, each pair posts their argument to an accessible online location and reviews opposing arguments. Then pairs post their summary of the opposing arguments to verify understanding. To complete the exercise, the teams could develop a wiki or shared media page (such as Facebook or Google Docs) that integrates the various perspectives articulated during the process with a multimedia presentation. Structured argumentation ported to CSCL could benefit from combination of asynchronous reflection coupled with synchronous discussions.

Don't assume that your learners will automatically be able to engage in effective argumentation. Quality argumentation is a skill that must be trained and guided in learners. Schworm and Renkl (2007) found that video-modeled worked examples of argumentation discussions coupled with questions that required learners to identify the various stages illustrated in the video facilitated the acquisition of argumentation skills. Yeh and She (2010) reported that online synchronous argumentation templates produced better arguments and learning compared to a group learning the same science concepts without argumentation support.

CSCL: The Bottom Line

In 2005 Jonassen, Lee, Yang, and Laffey concluded their review of CSCL research as follows: "More is unknown about the practice than is known. CSCL will constitute one of the pivotal research issues of the next decade" (p. 264). As we update this chapter six years later, we believe their conclusion remains essentially unchanged. At this stage you may want to apply lessons learned from face-to-face collaboration as well as limited evidence on CSCL as you leverage the opportunities afforded by social media. However, remember that what might work well for one set of learners, desired outcomes, and technology features is likely different from what is appropriate for a different set. We can point to the following enablers for you to consider as you plan online collaborative learning events:

1. Ensure social interdependence through assignments that are of sufficient complexity to engage a group, team sizes that are not too small or too large, and incentives that reward people not just for their own learning but for the learning of all team members.

2. Assign ill-structured case problems to small heterogeneous groups composed of three to five members.

3. Use guided collaborative assignments such as structured controversy.

4. Provide clear guidance, roles, and objectives for team processes.

What We Don't Know About CSCL

There is more we don't know about CSCL than what we do know. Here are some of many unresolved questions or issues:

1. What is the relationship between individual learning and group outcomes? What kinds of instructional support might optimize individual learning from a collaborative group assignment?

2. What is the best combination of synchronous and asynchronous collaborative processes to achieve different outcomes?

3. What kinds of computer representations (visual maps, online templates, etc.) can aid various group tasks, including decision making, problem solving, argumentation, and design tasks?

4. What are the tradeoffs to synchronous collaborative work using audio compared to synchronous collaborative work using chat?

5. Do deeper discussions during CSCL necessarily translate into more learning? If so, how can CSCL interfaces and support prompt deeper discussions?

6. What kinds of group roles, assignments, and structures such as argumentation are optimal for different kinds of desired outcomes?

7. What types of team skill training are most effective, and how can such training be transferred from one team to another?

8. What are the best techniques to use and roles to be assumed by discussion moderators and other team members? When is a student moderator more effective than an instructor moderator?

9. How can the features of new social media be best deployed to optimize group problem solving and/or individual learning?

DESIGN DILEMMA: RESOLVED

In our chapter introduction, you considered the following options for collaborative work associated with a web-based sales course:

A. Individual learning will benefit from a group project more than if each class participant completed a project individually.

B. A better project will result from a team effort than if each class participant develops his or her own project individually.

C. A wiki would yield greater long-term benefits than a team project developed during the class.

D. A team project would be of better quality if accomplished through asynchronous collaboration than through synchronous collaboration.

Developing a marketing and sales campaign as a class project is a far transfer task which can have multiple solutions and approaches. Evidence suggests that a better project can emerge from a team than from individuals working alone. However, better team projects will not necessarily translate into better individual learning. In addition, limited evidence suggests that an online collaboration leads to a better product than a face-to-face discussion, as online learners take more time to reflect and engage one another in the planning.

As a knowledge-management strategy, a wiki could also be a useful tool to extend learning beyond the formal training event. However, the training development team will need to consider the incentives and resources for contributing to and maintaining the wiki after the class.

Of the options above, B and D have some limited experimental support. A wiki may also be a valuable collaborative strategy, but we will need more research to warrant an evidence-based conclusion.

We believe there is rich potential for learning in collaborative environments—both in face-to-face and online settings. However, we will need more evidence in order to formulate detailed recommendations.

WHAT TO LOOK FOR IN e-LEARNING

☐ In classes that focus on far transfer outcomes, group projects or case assignments that incorporate some asynchronous work to allow time for reflection and individual research

☐ Small teams with participants of diverse prior knowledge and background

☐ Structured collaborative team processes that support individual participation and accountability to the team outcome

☐ Use of CSCL when there is adequate learning time to support team discussions and product generation

☐ Evaluations of student work that reflect the accomplishments of each member of the team to encourage interdependence

COMING NEXT

One of the unique features of asynchronous e-learning is the ability to let learners make choices. Navigational devices such as menus and links grant learners options over pacing, lesson topics, and instructional methods such as practice. How do these levels of freedom affect learning? Who benefits most from learner control? What kinds of interfaces are most effective for learner control? These are some of the issues we review in Chapter 14.

Suggested Readings

Fonseca, B.A., & Chi, M.T.H. (2011). Instruction based on self-explanation. In R.E. Mayer & P.A. Alexander (Eds.), *Handbook of research on learning and instruction.* New York: Routledge.

Johnson, D.W., Johnson, R.T., & Smith, K. (2007). The state of cooperative learning in postsecondary and professional settings. *Educational Psychology Review, 19,* 15–29.

Jonassen, D.H., Lee, C.B., Yang, C-C., Laffey, J. (2005). The collaboration principle in multimedia learning. In R.E. Mayer (Ed.), *The Cambridge handbook of multimedia learning.* New York: Cambridge University Press.

Kirschner, F., Paas, F.G.W.C., & Kirschner, P.A. (2009). A cognitive load approach to collaborative learning: United brains for complex tasks. *Educational Psychology Review, 21,* 31–42.

Lou, Y., Abrami, P.C., & d'Apollonia, S. (2001). Small group and individual learning with technology: A meta-analysis. *Review of Educational Research, 71*(3), 449–521.

Slavin, R.E. (2011). Instruction based on cooperative learning. In R.E. Mayer & P.A. Alexander (Eds.), *Handbook of research on learning and instruction.* New York: Routledge.

Resta, P., & Laferriere, T. (2007). Technology in support of collaborative learning. *Educational Psychology Review, 19,* 65–83.

CHAPTER OUTLINE

Learner Control Versus Program Control

    Three Types of Learner Control

Do Learners Make Good Instructional Decisions?

    Calibration Accuracy: Do you Know What You Think You Know?

    Do Learners Like Instructional Methods That Lead to Learning?

    Psychological Reasons for Poor Learner Choices

Learner Control Principle 1: Give Experienced Learners Control

    Evidence for Benefits of Program Control

    Evidence for Learner Control Later in Learning

Learner Control Principle 2: Make Important Instructional Events the Default

Learner Control Principle 3: Consider Adaptive Control

    Evidence for Dynamic Adaptive Control vs. Program Control

    Rapid Verification Method for Dynamic Adaptive Control

    Accuracy of Self-Explanations for Dynamic Adaptive Control

    When to Consider Adaptive e-Learning

Learner Control Principle 4: Give Pacing Control

Learner Control Principle 5: Offer Navigational Support in Hypermedia Environments

    Use Headings and Introductory Statements

    Use Links Sparingly in Lessons Intended for Novice Learners

    Use Course and Site Maps

    Provide Basic Navigation Options

14

Who's in Control?

GUIDELINES FOR E-LEARNING NAVIGATION

LEARNER CONTROL is implemented by navigational features such as menus, site maps, and links that allow learners to select the topics and instructional elements they prefer. In the second edition of *e-Learning and the Science of Instruction,* we recommended that you adjust the amount of learner control in asynchronous e-learning based primarily on the prior knowledge of your learners. Learners with higher prior knowledge can typically make good choices under conditions of high learner control. However, most novice learners often don't know enough about the content domain to benefit from learner control. Research data continue to support this recommendation. In our update we summarize new research on adaptive control in which instructional elements are dynamically personalized based on learner performance during the lesson.

Based on the segmentation principle summarized in Chapter 10, we recommend that in asynchronous e-learning, you always allow learners to control pacing so they can proceed at their own rate.

DESIGN DILEMMA: YOU DECIDE

The e-learning design team is discussing the navigation controls for the spreadsheet course currently under development:

Ben: "Here's my first cut at the navigation controls. (See Figure 14.1.) We'll set up the left navigation so they can jump to any topic they want and can skip lesson topics they don't find relevant. And to see some examples, the learner can click on the baby screens. Also I'm adding a lot of links so the learners can jump to the practice exercises or skip them if they feel that they understand the concepts. Links are also good for definitions and as a route to other relevant websites. That's what people expect on the Internet. The Millennial generation has grown up with complete control in all their digital environments."

Figure 14.1. Navigational Elements Designed for High Learner Control.

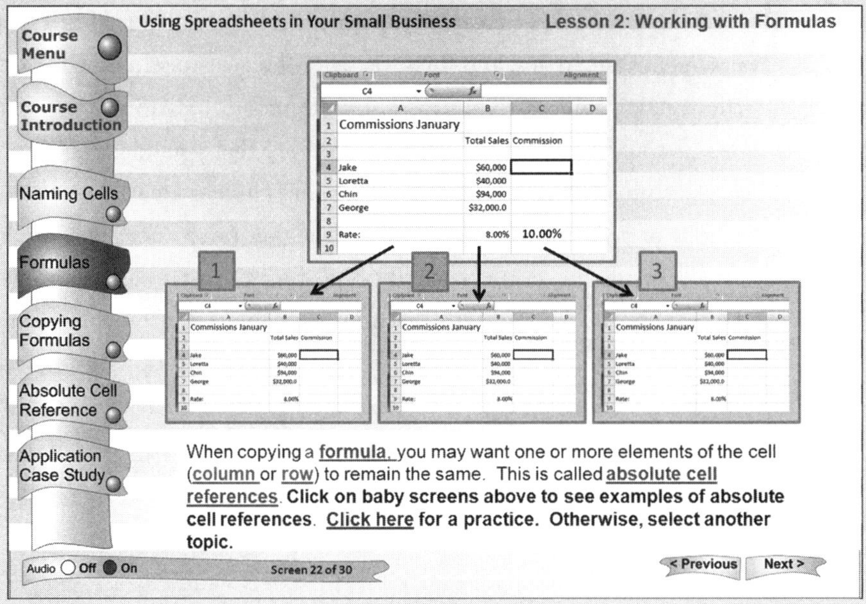

Reshmi: "But Ben, learning a new skill is not the same as surfing for informa-
           tion. We are building the lessons and topics in a logical sequence and
           including worked examples and practice exercises that should not
           be skipped. I think all those navigational features you've designed
           jeopardize the integrity of our training design. Most learners will sim-
           ply click the continue button and miss most of what you've made
           available."

Based on your own experience or intuition, which of the following options would
you select:

A. Ben is correct. The "Millenials" are used to high levels of learner control and
    will be turned off by excessive guidance.

B. Reshmi is correct. Learners do not make good decisions about what to study
    and what to skip. Program control will result in better learning.

C. Reshmi and Ben can evaluate the background knowledge of their audience and
    determine whether adaptive control would be a cost-effective option.

Control over the content and pace of a lesson is a common feature of asynchronous e-learning. Certainly the underlying scheme of the Internet is freedom of choice. How effective is learner control in training? What are the tradeoffs between learner control and program control? Fortunately, we have evidence from research and from cognitive theory to guide our decisions.

Learner Control Versus Program Control

In contrast to classroom and synchronous e-learning, asynchronous e-learning can be designed to allow learners to select the topics they want, control the pace at which they progress, and decide whether to bypass some lesson elements such as examples or practice exercises. e-Learning programs that offer these choices are considered high in *learner control*. In contrast, when the course and lesson offer few learner options, the instruction is under *program control*. Most synchronous forms of e-learning operate in program control mode—also called *instructional control.* Instructor-led virtual and face-to-face classrooms typically progress at a single pace, follow a linear sequence, and use one set of teaching techniques. The instructor facilitates a single learning path. On the other hand, asynchronous e-learning can offer many or few options and thus can be designed to be learner controlled or program controlled.

Three Types of Learner Control

Although the term "learner control" is often used generically, the actual type of control varies. Thus, two courses that are depicted as "learner-controlled" may in fact offer quite different options. In general, control options fall into three domains:

1. *Content Sequencing.* Learners can control the order of the lessons, topics, and screens within a lesson. Many e-courses such as the design in Figure 14.1 allow content control through a course menu from which learners select topics in any sequence they wish. Likewise, links placed in lessons can lead to additional pages in the course or to alternative websites with related information.

2. *Pacing.* Learners can control the time spent on each lesson page. With the exception of short video or audio sequences, a standard adopted in virtually all asynchronous e-learning allows learners to progress through the training at their own rate, spending as much or as little time as they wish on any given screen. Likewise, options to move backward or to exit are made available on every screen. A more extensive form of pacing control allows learners to use slider bars or rollers to move through the content or includes fast forward, rewind, pause, and play buttons.

3. *Access to Learning Support.* Learners can control instructional components of lessons such as examples or practice exercises. Within a given lesson, navigation buttons, links, or tabs lead to course objectives, definitions, additional references, coaches, examples, help systems, or practice exercises. In contrast, a program-controlled lesson

provides most of these instructional components by default as the learners click the forward button.

Figure 14.2 shows a screen from an asynchronous course that allows control over all three of these domains. At the bottom right of the screen the directional arrows provide for movement forward or backward at the learner's own pace. The course uses Microsoft standard control buttons in the upper right-hand corner of the screen as well as an on-screen button to exit. In the left-hand frame, the course map allows learners to select lessons in any sequence. Within the central lesson frame, the learner can decide to study the examples by clicking on the thumbnail sample screens to enlarge them. Learners can also select a practice exercise by either clicking on the link above the examples or on the navigational tab on the right-hand side. In addition, embedded links lead to definitions of terms. Table 14.1 summarizes the most common techniques used to implement various forms of learner control in asynchronous e-learning.

Figure 14.2. A Lesson with Multiple Navigational Control Elements.

With permission from Element K.

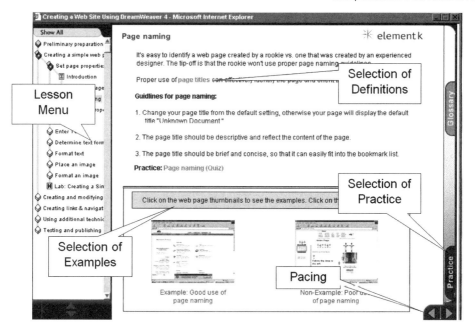

Table 14.1. Common Navigational Techniques Used in Asynchronous e-Learning.

Technique	Description	Examples
Course and lesson menus in left-hand frame, pull-down window, or section tabs	Allow learners to select specific lessons and topics within a lesson or a course	Figures 14.1 and 14.2 both use left window menu lists
Links placed within teaching frame	Allow learners to access content from other sites on the Internet or from other sections within the course	Figures 14.1 and 14.2 include links leading to definitions or practice exercises
Pop-ups or mouse-overs	Provide additional information without the learning having to leave the screen	Figure 5.2 includes roll-over functionality. When the learner clicks on a screen icon, a small window explains its functions
Buttons to activate forward, backward, pause, replay, and quit options	Permit control of pacing among pages within a lesson and of media elements such as video incorporated into a lesson page	The lesson shown in Figure 14.2 includes buttons for movement forward, backward, and exit
Guided tours	Overviews of course resources accessible from the main menu screen	Typically used in courses that offer very high learner control such as game-type interfaces with multiple paths and interface options
Active objects	Graphics on the screen serve as links leading to information or locations relevant to the object	Figure 1.6. shows an automotive shop graphic interface. All major objects are linked to either troubleshooting tests or reference guides

Learners like learner control! To the extent that student appeal is a major goal of your instructional projects, learner control is a definite satisfier. Given the high levels of control inherent on the Internet, it is likely that learners will expect the same kind of freedom in e-learning courses.

Rather than advocate for or against learner control, we provide guidelines and illustrations for when and how learner control is best used. Additionally, we describe the option of adaptive control that tailors learning environments based on an automated assessment of learner progress and needs.

Do Learners Make Good Instructional Decisions?

How accurately do you think most learners determine what they already know and what they need to learn? If learners can accurately assess themselves, they can make good decisions about topics to study and how much time and effort to put into studying those topics. In short, they are capable of good achievement when given learner control. We have two lines of evidence indicating that, in fact, most learners are not good at self-assessment: calibration accuracy and student lesson ratings.

Calibration Accuracy: Do You Know What You Think You Know?

Suppose you have to take a test on basic statistics. Prior to taking the test, you are asked to estimate your level of confidence in your knowledge. You know that even though you took statistics in college, you are a little rusty on some of the formulas, but you figure that you can score around 70 percent. After taking the test, you find your actual score is 55 percent. The correlation between your confidence estimate and your actual performance is called calibration. Had you guessed 55 percent, your calibration would have been perfect.

The focus of calibration measurement is not on what we actually know, but on the accuracy of what we think we know. If you don't think you know much and in fact your test score is low, you have good calibration. Test your own calibration now by answering this question: What is the capital of Australia? As you state your answer, also estimate your confidence in your answer as high, medium, or low. You can check your calibration on the following page.

Although most of us may feel we have a general sense of what we do and do not know, our specific calibration accuracy tends to be poor (Stone, 2000). Glenberg, Sanocki, Epstein, and Morris (1987) found calibration correlations close to zero, concluding that "contrary to intuition, poor calibration of comprehension is the rule, rather than the exception" (p. 119). Eva, Cunnington, Reiter, Keane, and Norman (2004) report poor correlations between medical students' estimates of their knowledge and their actual test scores. When comparing knowledge estimates among Year 1, Year 2, and Year 3 medical students, there was no evidence that self-assessments improved with increasing seniority. The team concludes that "Self-assessment of performance remains a poor predictor of actual performance" (p. 222).

Even experienced physicians have been shown to lack accurate self-assessment of their own performance. Violato and Lockyer (2006) compared self-assessments of physicians in several specialty areas with assessment data from their peers. Similar to 360-degree feedback management programs used in many companies, The Physician Achievement Review program provides doctors with feedback from patients, colleagues, and non-physician co-workers such as nurses. The physician also completes a self-assessment form on a five-point scale with questions such as "Compared to other physicians I know, I rate my communication skills as 1, 2, 3, 4, or 5" with 1 equal to *among the worst* and 5 equating to *among the best.* The research team compared 305 medical specialists' self-assessments with medical colleague assessments. They found that physicians with poor peer ratings rated their own performance as above average—approximately 30 to 40 percentage points higher than their peers rated them. Conversely, high-performing physicians tended to underestimate their performance. The research team concludes that "Overall results provide strong evidence to support the notion that many physicians are not very good at accurate self-assessment" (p. 239).

Now let's check on your calibration. Review your response to our question on the previous page about the capital of Australia. The capital of Australia is not Sydney, as many people guess with high confidence. It is Canberra. If you guessed Sydney with low confidence *or* if you guessed Canberra with high confidence, your calibration is high!

In comparing calibration of individuals before and after taking a test, accuracy is generally better after responding to test questions than before. Therefore, providing questions in training should lead to more accurate self-assessments. Walczyk and Hall (1989) confirmed this relationship by comparing the calibration of learners who studied using four resources: text alone, text plus examples, text plus questions, and text plus examples and questions. Calibration was best among those who studied from the version with examples and questions.

Do Learners Like Instructional Methods That Lead to Learning?

Most courses ask learners to evaluate the quality of the course with an end-of-course rating sheet. Do you think there is a high relationship between these end-of-course learner ratings and actual learning? Sitzmann, Brown, Casper, Ely, and Zimmerman (2008) correlated approximately eleven thousand student course ratings with after-training knowledge measures as well as 4,688 course ratings with after-training procedural skills. The correlations were very small: .12 and .15, respectively. Remember that correlations range from −1 to +1 with values around zero indicating no correspondence whatsoever between the values. The research team concludes: "Reactions have a predictive relationship with cognitive learning outcomes, but the relationship is not strong enough to suggest reactions should be used as an indicator of learning" (p. 289).

Do students learn more when matched to their preferred instructional methods? Schnackenberg, Sullivan, Leader, and Jones (1998) surveyed participants before taking a course regarding their preferences for amount of practice—high or low. Participants were assigned to two e-learning courses—one with many practice exercises and a second identical course with half the amount of practice. Half the learners were matched to their preference and half mismatched. Regardless of their preference, those assigned to the version with more practice achieved significantly higher scores on the post-test than those taking the version with fewer practice exercises.

The bottom line: there is little correspondence between learner perceptions of lesson effectiveness and actual instructional value. In short, liking is not the same as learning.

Psychological Reasons for Poor Learner Choices

We've seen that calibration research as well as correlations between student ratings and student learning point to a general inability to accurately assess learning needs. Metacognition refers to a learners' awareness and control of their own learning processes, such as assessing how well they understand a lesson or knowing how best to study to achieve a learning goal. Metacognition is the mind's operating system. In short, metacognition supports mental self-awareness and self-regulation. Individuals with high metacognitive skills set realistic learning goals and use effective study strategies. They have high levels of learning management skills. For example, when faced with a certification test, they plan a study schedule. Based on accurate self-assessments of their current strengths and weaknesses, they focus their time and efforts on the topics most needed for success. They use appropriate study techniques based on an accurate assessment of the certification requirements. In contrast, learners with poor metacognitive skills lack understanding of what they know and how they learn, which will lead to flawed decisions under high learner control.

Moos and Azevedo (2008) compared metacognitive activities among high and low prior knowledge learners as they researched a hypermedia resource on the circulatory system. After a pre-test to evaluate knowledge levels, college students were allowed forty minutes to study the circulatory system from an online encyclopedia that included articles, video, figures, and other information. Students were asked to talk aloud while they studied, and their self-regulatory patterns were compared. The research team found that learners with high prior knowledge used more planning and monitoring processes as they reviewed the materials. In contrast, lower prior knowledge learners did little planning or monitoring but instead took notes. Because planning and monitoring require working memory capacity, it is likely that low prior knowledge learners did not have sufficient mental resource for self-regulatory activities. The research team recommends adding guidance to hypermedia environments that will be accessed by novice learners. For example, adding frequent questions with detailed feedback may alleviate the learners' need to devote working memory resources to monitor their own progress.

How can you best apply the evidence and the psychology behind learner control to your design of effective e-courses? In the rest of this chapter, we discuss the following five proven guidelines for the best use of learner control to optimize learning:

Principle 1: Give experienced learners control.

Principle 2: Make important instructional events the default.

Principle 3: Design adaptive control.

Principle 4: Give pacing control.

Principle 5: Offer navigational support in hypermedia environments.

Learner Control Principle 1: Give Experienced Learners Control

As we have seen, most learners prefer full control over their instructional options but often don't make good judgments about their instructional needs—especially those who are novice to the content and/or who lack good metacognitive skills. Hence the instructional professional must consider the multiple tradeoffs of learner control, including learner satisfaction, the profile of the target learners, the cost of designing learner-controlled instruction, and the criticality of skills being taught.

A review of research on learner versus program control concludes that learners with little prior knowledge of the subject as well as poor metacognitive skills are likely to do better with program control—especially in high-complexity courses (Steinberg, 1989). Learner control is more likely to be successful when:

- Learners have prior knowledge of the content and skills involved in the training
- The subject is a more advanced lesson in a course or a more advanced course in a curriculum
- Learners have good metacognitive skills
- The course is of low complexity

Evidence for Benefits of Program Control

Gay (1986) found that low prior knowledge students learned more under program control than under learner control. Figure 14.3 shows learning outcomes from high and low prior knowledge students under learner and program control. In this experiment, individuals in the learner control version could control topic sequencing, presentation mode (video, audio, graphics, or text), number of examples, amount of practice, and depth of study. Those in program control could control only pacing. As you can see, while low prior knowledge learners had low scores under learner control, high prior knowledge learners did well under either condition. Gay (1986) concludes: "The results demonstrate that not all subjects were capable of making appropriate decisions. The low knowledge students practiced too little and emphasized areas with which they already had familiarity. In summary, low prior knowledge subjects did not use good learning strategies and made poor sequencing decisions under learner controlled treatment" (p. 227).

Figure 14.3. Low Prior Knowledge Students Learn Least Under Learner Control.

Based on data from Gay, 1986.

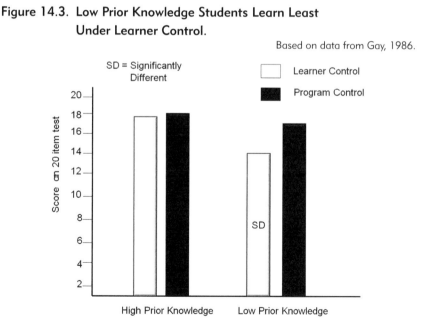

Young (1996) compared outcomes of learners with high and low self-regulatory (metacognitive) skills who took four e-lessons in either a learner-control or program-control mode. Under learner control, participants could select or bypass definitions, examples, and practice exercises, whereas those in the program-controlled version were presented with all the above options. Those in the learner-controlled version looked at less than 50 percent of the total number of screens available. As summarized in Table 14.2, Young found that learners with low metacognitive skills learned less in the learner-controlled mode than any of the other three groups did.

Table 14.2. **Test Scores of High and Low Metacognitive Learners Studying Under Learner or Program Control.**

From Young, 1996.

	Learner-Controlled	Program-Controlled
Low Metacognitive Skill	20 percent	79 percent
High Metacognitive Skill	60 percent	82 percent

Overall, there is a consistent pattern in which too much learner control can be detrimental to learners with either low prior knowledge or metacognitive skill. In contrast, high prior knowledge learners are more likely to have sufficient domain knowledge to make appropriate instructional choices.

Evidence for Learner Control Later in Learning

Lee and Lee (1991) compared learning from program control and learner control over the sequence of tasks and number of practice exercises completed in a computer-based chemistry lesson. Learning was compared during early stages of learning versus later stages of learning, when learners would have acquired a knowledge base. Program control gave better results during initial learning, whereas learner control was more effective at later stages. This outcome supports the idea that learners with greater prior knowledge are able to make more appropriate decisions under conditions of learner control. Based on evidence to date, we recommend that when selecting or designing courseware for novice learners, look for greater program control—at least in the beginning lessons in a course.

Learner Control Principle 2: Make Important Instructional Events the Default

We saw in Chapter 12 that practice is an important instructional method that leads to expertise. We also know that learners prefer learner control, and in many e-learning environments, they can easily drop out if not satisfied. Therefore, if you opt for high learner control, set the default navigation option (usually the continue button) to lead to important instructional elements such as practice exercises. In other words, require the learner to make a deliberate choice to bypass practice.

Research by Schnackenberg and Sullivan (2000) supports this guideline. Two navigational versions of the same lesson were designed. As illustrated in Figure 14.4, in one version, pressing "continue" bypassed practice while in the other version pressing "continue" led to practice. In the "more practice" default (Version 2), participants viewed nearly twice as many of the screens as those in Version 1 and scored higher on the final test.

Figure 14.4. Default Navigation Options That Bypass Practice (Version 1) Led to Poorer Learning Than Default Options That Lead to Practice (Version 2).

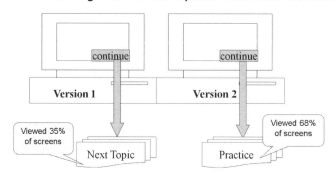

Programs that make a high amount of practice available as the default route are more likely to result in higher achievement than those that make less practice available as the default route. Schnackenberg and Sullivan (2000) suggest that program control should be a preferred mode because learner-controlled programs (1) have no instructional advantages, (2) have been shown in other studies to be disadvantageous for low-ability learners, and (3) cost more than program control.

However, their learner population consisted of students taking a required university course. In your environment, where learners have greater freedom about whether to take or complete e-learning, you may not be able to downplay user preferences to the extent recommended in this study. When designing programs with high learner control, set the continue or next button so that critical aspects of the program (such as examples or practice exercises) are the default options.

Learner Control Principle 3: Consider Adaptive Control

One of the unique features of asynchronous e-learning is the opportunity to dynamically tailor instruction to the changing needs of learners as they are learning. In *adaptive control* (also called *personalized instruction* or *user modeling*), the program dynamically adjusts lesson difficulty and support based on the program's evaluation of learner responses. As a simple example, if a learner completes six exercise questions and has them all correct, she is branched to a more difficult lesson topic. In contrast, if she has three of six correct, additional worked examples are provided followed by more practice exercises. In other words, the instruction monitors learning and adjusts the difficulty level and the amount of guidance accordingly.

As we have seen in prior chapters, many instructional methods that benefit novice learners often have no effect or even sometimes depress the learning of individuals with more background knowledge. For example, in Chapter 11 we saw evidence that worked examples that were helpful for novice learners gradually lose their effectiveness as learners gain expertise. In fact, eventually higher prior knowledge learners will do better with problem assignments than with worked examples. The different effects of instructional methods on novices compared to higher prior knowledge learners is called *expertise reversal* (Kalyuga, 2005). As a generality, expertise reversal recommends increasing the difficulty of the instructional assignments and decreasing the amount of instructional support as learning progresses. We know that learning occurs at different rates for different individuals. Therefore, one design challenge is determining at what point in the lesson to make a transition in difficulty or guidance for an individual learner. A solution to this challenge is dynamic adaptive control.

Evidence for Dynamic Adaptive Control vs. Program Control

Salden, Paas, Broers, and Van Merrienboer (2004) confirmed the advantages of dynamic adaptive e-learning. They compared the effectiveness of program control with dynamic adaptive control on learning of simulated air traffic control scenarios. Program control assigned each learner twenty practice tasks from simple to more complex. Dynamic adaptive control adjusted the number and complexity of practice tasks based on the learner's performance on practice tasks. There were no differences in learning between program and adaptive groups. However, the program-controlled version required the greatest time to complete. In the program-controlled version, all learners received twenty tasks, whereas learners in adaptive lessons completed an average of ten tasks.

Corbalan, Kester, and van Merrienboer (2008) compared learning, time spent in training, and student ratings of mental load between lessons that used adaptive control and lessons that were not adapted. Fifty-five vocational education students completed a course that involved a series of dietetics problems. For each skill area five problems were constructed ranging from simple to complex. In addition, for each problem five levels of support were constructed, ranging from full worked examples to full problem assignments. After learners completed a problem, they took a short multiple-choice test to measure competence and they rated the amount of effort they invested. Using an algorithm that included the competence score and student effort ratings, the program then selected a follow-up task. For example, the follow-up task may be of a greater difficulty level with more support or may be of the same difficulty level with less support. Participants in the non-adaptive version received the same sequence of problems regardless of how they scored on the test.

The adaptive condition led to better learning, with mean competence scores of 73, compared to 48 in the non-adaptive condition. Participants in the adaptive condition rated their lessons lower in mental load and spent more time in training than those in the non-adaptive condition.

Determining the competency of a learner as a lesson progresses requires a dynamic method of assessment. However, frequent testing is cumbersome and time-consuming. In the next sections we discuss two recent research reports that evaluated rapid diagnostic methods used to dynamically assess learner competency: rapid verification and accuracy of self-explanations.

Rapid Verification Method for Dynamic Adaptive Control

Kalyuga (2008) has validated a fast and practical method for dynamic assessment of learning. He designed tests for algebra tasks. He selected thirty-three university students with a range of mathematical background. Each participant completed a rapid computer-based diagnostic test as well as a traditional paper-based test. His goal was to determine how closely the results from the rapid test corresponded with those from the traditional test.

The rapid diagnostic test shows a problem to be solved followed by five suggested solution steps (one correct and four incorrect). For each solution step shown, the learner indicates whether it is right or wrong. Following the rapid diagnostic test, each individual completed a traditional paper-based test using problems similar to those used in the rapid test. Time to complete each test version was recorded and the scores on the rapid and traditional test were correlated to determine the extent to which the rapid test would give as accurate a diagnosis as a traditional test.

The correlations between the traditional and rapid tests were .71 and .75, suggesting the rapid tests gave a good estimate of student knowledge. Not surprising, test time for the rapid method was reduced by a factor of over three. Kalyuga concludes that the rapid verification procedure is a valid diagnostic method capable of identifying different levels of competency and is fast enough for real-time application.

In Figure 14.5, you can see an example of a rapid verification test item from the algebra lesson. To implement this method, first establish a sequence

Figure 14.5. A Sample Rapid Verification Test Item.

From Kalyuga, 2008.

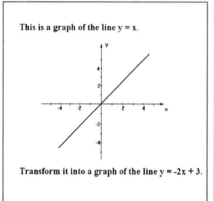

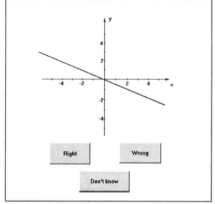

Problem Assignment	An (Incorrect) Intermediate Solution Step

of main intermediate stages in a solution procedure for a problem. Next for each stage construct one correct and two or three incorrect solution steps. Then present the original problem to the learner for a limited time, followed by a series of the selected intermediate solution steps one at a time, asking the learner to quickly verify whether the step is correct or incorrect. Use the score from the rapid assessment procedure as the basis for adjusting the problem difficulty and/or amount of guidance provided in the lesson.

Accuracy of Self-Explanations for Dynamic Adaptive Control

In this section we review a procedure that assesses competency based on correct selection of self-explanation principles associated with worked examples. Recall from Chapter 11 that a proven method to ensure deep processing of worked examples is to attach a self-explanation multiple-choice question next to a worked step. You can review examples in Figures 11.5 and 11.6. Salden, Aleven, Schwonke, and Renkl (2010) used the accuracy of self-explanations to determine when learners should transition from examples to practice. An advantage of this approach is its unobtrusiveness and efficiency, as the learner does not need to complete additional test items.

To evaluate the effectiveness, the research team compared geometry learning of ninth and tenth graders from three versions of an online geometry tutorial. The first version used the standard tutor. The second version added worked examples that faded steps out in a fixed manner. The third—adaptive version—added worked examples that were faded based on accuracy of learner selection of self-explanation options. The fading decisions were based on the programs assessment of each individual student's ability to identify valid explanations of worked-out steps. They found the adaptive fading condition led to better immediate and delayed post-test scores.

When to Consider Adaptive e-Learning

As you can see, creating e-learning that dynamically adjusts instruction based on the learner's demonstrated competence during learning does show promise for better and more efficient learning. At the same time, any form of adaptive learning will require additional development by the instructional team. Extra time and resources will have to be devoted to designing the assessment devices, programming decision logic, and preparing alternative paths of instruction for different learners. Will this investment pay off?

We suggest that you consider adaptation when you have a large group of heterogeneous learners for which you would anticipate quite different levels of instructional support needed to achieve the learning objective. Assuming the group is large enough and/or highly paid, the time savings of adaptive learning may outweigh development costs. Likewise, if you have a heterogeneous audience and it is critical that all participants reach a minimum level of competence, adaptive learning can adjust the difficulty and level of support needed to ensure universal goal achievement.

Learner Control Principle 4: Give Pacing Control

Most asynchronous e-learning programs allow learners to proceed at their own pace by pressing the "forward" button. Video or animated demonstrations typically have slider bar controls indicating progress as well as "replay" and "quit" options. Research by Mayer and Chandler (2001), Mayer, Dow, and Mayer (2003), and Mayer and Jackson (2005) summarized in Chapter 10 recommends that asynchronous e-learning be divided into small chunks that learners access at their own pace. In Chapter 10 we refer to this guideline as the segmenting principle.

Tabbers and de Koeijer (2010) revisited pacing control by comparing learning between two versions of the lightning lesson we illustrated in Figure 10.2. In the program-control version, sixteen narrated slides were shown for thirteen seconds each, after which the next slide was automatically displayed. The learner-controlled version shown in Figure 14.6 included the same slides but allowed the following interruptions: (1) stop and replay, (2) replay of the audio narration, or (3) selection of specific slides from a left menu. Similar to the Mayer and Chandler (2001) study, they found that transfer learning was better from the learner-controlled version. The participants in the learner-controlled version spent an average of almost three times longer than those using the program-controlled versions. This additional time was primarily used to re-inspect slides previously seen by using the left navigation menu and repeating the audio narration. The research team concluded that adding learner control to an animated instruction can increase understanding, but the tradeoff is additional time taken with the learning materials. Recall from Chapter 10 that Schar and Zimmermann's 2007 research recommends that you automatically stop an animation at logical points and allow the learners to replay or continue from that point, rather than relying on the learners to use the pause and replay buttons on their own.

Figure 14.6. A Screen from a Learner-Controlled Version of the Lightning Lesson.

From Tabbers and de Koeijer, 2010.

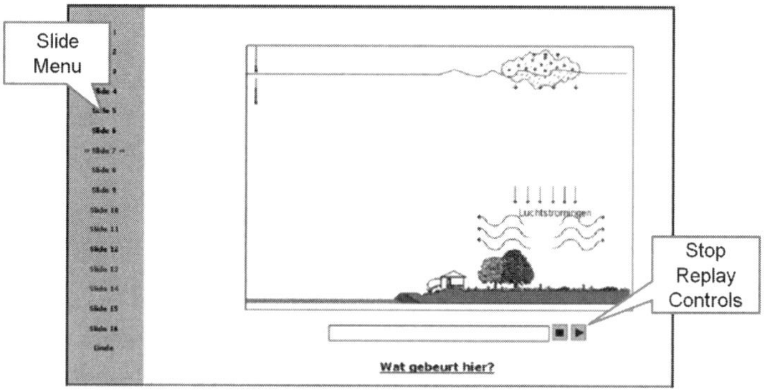

Learner Control Principle 5: Offer Navigational Support in Hypermedia Environments

Screen titles, embedded topic headers, topic menus, course maps, links, and movement buttons (forward, backward, and exit) are common navigational elements that influence comprehension. What evidence do we have for the benefits of various navigational elements commonly used in e-learning and hypermedia reference materials?

Use Headings and Introductory Statements

Content representations such as headings and introductory sentences improve memory and comprehension in traditional text documents. For example, Lorch, Lorch, Ritchey, McGovern, and Coleman (2001) asked readers to generate summaries of texts that included headings for half of the paragraphs. They found that the summaries included more content from paragraphs with headers and less from paragraphs lacking headers. Mayer (2005b) refers to headings as a form of signaling—providing cues concerning the important information in a lesson. We recommend that similar devices be used in e-learning programs. Screen headings, for example, might include the lesson title followed by the topic. On-screen text segments and visuals should likewise be signaled with brief descriptive labels similar to paper documents.

Use Links Sparingly in Lessons Intended for Novice Learners

Use links that take the learner off the teaching screen as well as links leading to important instructional events sparingly. By definition, links signal to the user that the information is adjunct or peripheral to the main content of the site. Learners will bypass many links. Based on the research described previously, we discourage using links for access to essential skill-building elements such as worked examples or practice, especially with novice audiences.

Neiderhauser, Reynolds, Salmen, and Skolmoski (2000) presented two related concepts in two separate lessons. In each lesson, links led learners to correlated information about the concept in the other lesson. For example, if reading about the benefits of concept A in Lesson 1, a link would bring up benefits of Concept B in Lesson 2 for purposes of contrast. They found that nearly half the learners frequently made use of these links. The other half either never used the links or used them briefly before abandoning them in favor of a more linear progression whereby they moved through one lesson from start to finish before moving to the other. Contrary to the authors' expectations, they found that extensive use of the links was negatively related to learning. They attribute their findings to adverse impact of hypertext navigation on cognitive load.

If, however, your materials do include links, Shapiro (2008) suggests adding annotations to the links that will give novice learners a short preview of what is behind the link or to judiciously highlight links that are especially relevant to a specific learning goal.

Use Course and Site Maps

A course or site map is a type of menu or concept map that graphically represents the topics included in a course or reference resource. Nilsson and Mayer (2002) define a concept map as "a graphic representation of a hypertext document, in which the pages of the document are represented by visual objects and the links between pages are represented by lines or arrows connecting the visual objects" (p. 2). Figure 14.7 shows three different formats for course maps.

Figure 14.7. Three Map Layouts.

From Potelle and Rouet, 2003.

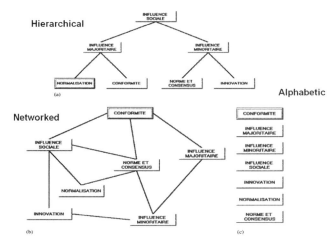

Research has been mixed on the contribution of course maps to learning. Neiderhauser, Reynolds, Salmen, and Skolmoski (2000) included a topic map containing a graphic representation of the hierarchical structure of the hypertext. Learners could access any screen in the hypertext from the topic map. A trace of user paths found that many learners did access the topic map frequently but rarely used it to navigate. Most would access the map, review the levels, and return to where they were reading. A few participants never accessed the topic map. In correlating map use with learning, the research team found only a slight benefit.

Potelle and Rouet (2003) compared comprehension of a hypertext between novice and content specialists for the three menu layouts shown in Figure 14.7: a hierarchical map, a network map, and an alphabetical list. Low knowledge participants learned most from the hierarchical map whereas the type of map made no difference to high prior knowledge participants. It may be that course maps are less important for navigational control than for providing learners, especially novice learners, with an orientation to the content structure. Novice learners may benefit most from such an orientation.

Shapiro (2005, 2008) compared learning from two versions of site maps for hypertext on a fictitious world of animals. One map version focused on animal categories. For example, a main menu item of reptiles included a submenu of desert shark, fat tail lizard, and so forth. The other map version focused on ecosystems. For example, a main menu item of desert included a submenu of long plume quail, fin lizard, and so forth. Half of the students were given learning goals pertaining to animal categories, whereas the other half were given goals pertaining to ecosystems. The focus of the map had a strong effect on learning, whereas the learning goals did not.

Shapiro (2008) suggests that site maps allow "learners to see the global structure of a hypermedia system, which is useful in that it provides a bird's eye view of the landscape" (p. 35). She recommends that site maps be organized according to the learner's goals. If the multimedia will include materials potentially relevant to many goals, a flexible site map could allow access from several different perspectives.

For example, the site map on the right-hand side of the screen in Figure 14.8 allows access according to eras, technologies, and social impact. It also illustrates link annotations in the lower left that will help learners know the content of a link destination.

We recommend the following guidelines regarding site maps:

- Consider using course maps or site maps for resources that are lengthy and complex and/or for learners who are novice to the content.

- Use a simple hierarchical structure.

- If your content will apply to learners with different tasks and instructional goals, consider multiple versions of a site map adapted to the instructional goals.

Figure 14.8. A Flexible Site Map with Link Explanations.

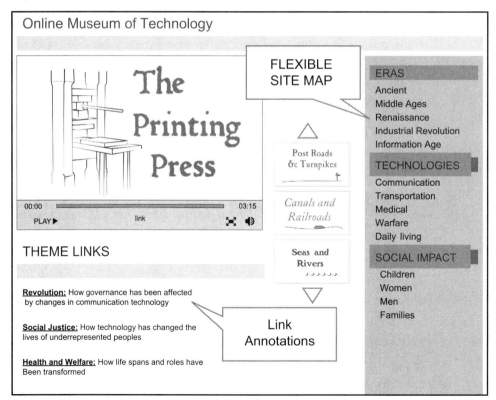

Provide Basic Navigation Options

In asynchronous e-learning, make elements for forward and backward movement, replay of audio and video, course exit, and menu reference easily accessible from every display. In courses that use scrolling pages, navigation should be accessible from both the top and bottom of the page to avoid overloading learners with unnecessary mouse work (having to scroll back to the top of the page to click "next"). Additionally, some sort of a progress indicator such as "Page 1 of 10" or a progress bar is useful to learners so that they know where they are in a topic and how far they have to go to complete it.

What We Don't Know About Learner Control

Although we have seen evidence that learners low in prior knowledge or metacognitive skills benefit from program control, we need to know more about the relationship between prior knowledge, metacognitive skills, and various navigational control options. For example, do high metacognitive skills override low prior knowledge? Do learners with high metacognitive skills benefit from a different type of navigational support than those with low metacognitive skills?

Although adaptive e-learning seems to have advantages compared to program control or learner control, we need more information on the cost benefit of dynamic adaptation. Under what circumstances will the resource investment made in adaptive designs pay off in more efficient learning outcomes?

How should navigational elements such as site maps, lesson menus, or lesson topics be displayed? Is a left or right screen display more effective? Will a drop-down course map be as effective as an on-screen menu? Are on-screen tabs that chunk topics but still maintain context more effective than placing topics on separate screens?

DESIGN DILEMMA: RESOLVED

Ben and Reshmi's disagreement about the amount and type of learner control to use in the spreadsheet lesson led to the following options:

A. Ben is correct. Millenials are experienced with high levels of learner control and will be turned off by excessive guidance.

B. Reshmi is correct. Learners do not make good decisions about what to study and what to skip. Program control will result in better learning.

C. Reshmi and Ben can evaluate the background knowledge of their audience and determine whether adaptive control would be a cost-effective option.

If the learners have a mixed background and budget is low, we recommend providing learner control but ensuring that the default navigation leads to important instructional elements. In addition, frequent knowledge checks with feedback can help learners monitor their progress and make appropriate decisions. Alternatively, if budget and time allow, providing personalized adaptive lessons based on responses to self-explanation questions might lead to more efficient learning. However, if the learners will be primarily novice to the topic, the most cost-effective approach is a program-controlled design.

WHAT TO LOOK FOR IN e-LEARNING

Consider high learner control when:

☐ Your content is relatively low in complexity and topics are not logically interdependent

☐ Your audience is likely to have high metacognitive or learning self-regulation skills

☐ Your audience is likely to have prior knowledge of the content

☐ Your lessons or courses are advanced so that learners have built a knowledge base

☐ You are designing the pacing options such as moving forward or backward or exiting the course

☐ You can easily add generic advisement such as "If you are new to these skills, take the lessons in the sequence shown"

☐ You can include important instructional elements such as examples and practice in the default navigational path

☐ You are using an animation and can pause it at logical breaks giving the learner the option to replay or continue

Consider adaptive designs when:

☐ Your audience has a mix of background knowledge and skills related to the desired learning outcomes

☐ Saving learning time is a high priority and there are sufficient numbers of highly paid staff to cost justify the resources required

☐ Reaching high levels of skill and knowledge proficiency for all learners is a high priority

☐ Resources are available to create the assessments, decision logic, and alternative instructional methods that characterize adaptive systems

Consider program control when:

☐ Your audience is primarily novice and a high level of proficiency is a priority

COMING NEXT

In Chapter 1 we distinguished between instructional goals that are procedural (near transfer) and those that are strategic or require problem solving (far transfer). Many perform e-learning courses currently in use are designed to teach procedural skills—especially computer skills such as the Excel lesson we have used in this book. What is the potential of e-learning to teach more complex problem-solving skills such as consultative selling? In the next chapter we look at this question.

Suggested Readings

Corbalan, G., Kester, L., & van Merrieonboer, J.J.G. (2008). Selecting learning tasks: Effects of adaptation and shared control on learning efficiency and task involvement. *Contemporary Educational Psychology, 33,* 733–756.

DeRouin, R.E, Fritzsche, B.A., & Salas, E. (2004). Optimizing e-learning: Research-based guidelines for learner-controlled training. *Human Resource Management, 43*(2–3), 147–162.

Kalyuga, S. (2008). When less is more in cognitive diagnosis: A rapid online method for diagnosing learner task-specific expertise. *Journal of Educational Psychology, 100,* 603–612.

Moos, D.C. & Azevedo, R. (2008). Self-regulated learning with hypermedia: The role of prior domain knowledge. *Contemporary Educational Psychology, 33*(2), 270–298.

National Research Council. (1994). Illusions of comprehension, competence, and remembering. In D. Druckman & R.A. Bjork (Eds.), *Learning, remembering, believing*. Washington, DC: National Academy Press.

Rouet, J.F., & Potelle, H (2005). Navigational principles in multimedia learning. In R.E. Mayer (Ed.), *The Cambridge handbook of multimedia learning.* New York: Cambridge University Press.

Salden, R.J.C.M, Aleven, V., Schwonke, R., & Renkl, A. (2010). The expertise reversal effect and worked examples in tutored problem solving. *Instructional Science, 38,* 289–307.

Shapiro, A.M. (2008). Hypermedia design as learner scaffolding. *Educational Technology Research & Development, 56,* 29–44.

CHAPTER OUTLINE

15

e-Learning to Build Thinking Skills

WHEN YOU HELP LEARNERS BUILD thinking skills, you enable the workforce to quickly adapt to changing conditions. For example, in the military, Chatham (2009) observes: "Today's missions now require that we also train each soldier to be a little bit of a linguist, anthropologist, city manager, arbitrator, negotiator, engineer, contract specialist, ambassador, and a consummate bureaucrat within the Army system. As if that weren't enough, each soldier must be ready instantly to shift into a shooting mode and then an hour later calmly negotiate with the brother-in-law of the man he shot" (p. 29). How many job roles in your organization rely on flexible problem-solving skills? From managerial skills to consultative sales and customer service, nearly all organizations rely on multiple competencies that require thinking skills to achieve bottom-line performance goals.

In the second edition of *e-Learning and the Science of Instruction,* we provided evidence and guidelines for using e-learning to build job-specific thinking or problem-solving skills. We emphasized some unique features of e-learning that can make mental problem-solving skills explicit. We recommended against using a broad approach to thinking skills training in favor of a job- or domain-specific focus. These recommendations are still valid. To update this chapter, we expand our discussion of domain-specific whole-task multimedia learning environments as well as offer more details on cognitive task analysis to identify job-specific thinking processes.

DESIGN DILEMMA: YOU DECIDE

"I wish our employees were better thinkers! Too much of our training involves soporific decks of PowerPoint or classes that teach step-by-step tasks in a rote manner. We need a workforce that can adapt quickly to new technology, new products, changing economic conditions—well, to a changing world in general. Our success relies on flexibility. I want everyone to take thinking skills training!"

That was the message from senior management. Your team leader led the kick-off meeting: "Management wants training on problem-solving skills and they want it for everyone, including operations, marketing, sales, engineers, and supervisors. We've got two weeks to report back with either a design for the training or with recommendations for off-the-shelf courseware that would do the job."

Back at your desk, you do a Google search on thinking skills training. You are amazed to get over nine million hits! As you access websites like the one in Figure 15.1, you are surprised to see the number and diversity of different classes and books that promise to make people more creative and better problem solvers. After reviewing some of the options, you end up with more questions than you had originally. Can thinking skills be trained? Are there some general thinking skills that can apply to most of the jobs in your organization? Shouldn't thinking skills be taught in a face-to-face learning environment rather than e-learning?

Based on your own experience or intuition, which of the following options would you select:

A. Money can be saved by purchasing an off-the-shelf course that includes techniques like the ones listed in Figure 15.1.

B. Thinking skills training would be most effective in a face-to-face environment.

C. Thinking skill training should be job specific; no one general thinking course will translate into improved work performance.

D. There is no way to improve thinking through training; it's like intelligence—you either have it or you don't.

Figure 15.1. A Website Promoting Thinking Skills Resources.

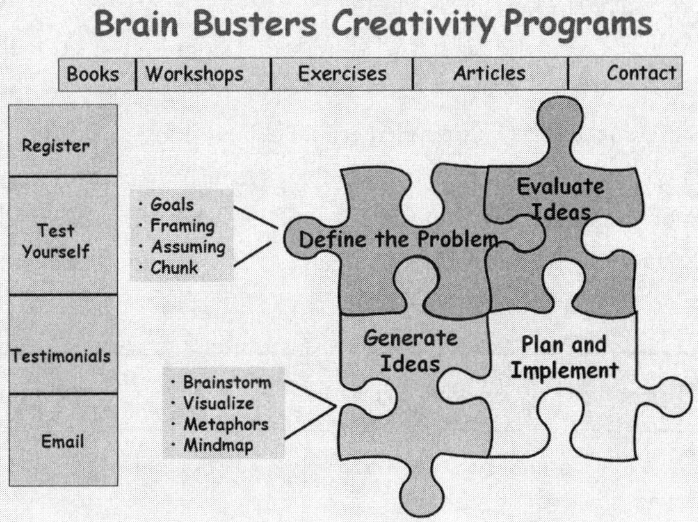

Three Types of Thinking Skills

Thinking skills training programs are popular. Over 25 percent of organizations with more than one hundred employees provide some form of thinking or creativity skills training (Scott, Leritz, & Mumford, 2004). But what do we mean by thinking skills? In Table 15.1. we summarize three types of thinking skills: creative thinking, critical thinking, and metacognition. By creative thinking we refer to the skill of generating novel and useful ideas. Most design work, such as creation of a new website, training course, or marketing plan, relies on creative thinking. Critical thinking involves evaluation of products or ideas. For example, when doing Internet research, a critical thinker considers the credibility of the resources. She might review the expertise of the author, consider the credibility of the publication, and determine when the information was posted.

Metacognition is the super-ordinate thinking skill of planning, monitoring, and evaluating new products or ideas. In Chapter 14, we defined metacognition as the skill that sets goals, plans an approach, monitors progress, and makes adjustments as needed. People with good metacognitive skills focus not only on the outcome of the task, but on the rationale or process behind the decisions made to achieve that outcome. When working in a team, the person with high metacognitive skills will be the one to say: "Wait—let's stop and see whether we're making progress. Will our individual efforts come together?" When working on a problem alone, he might say: "I'm hitting some dead ends here. Where can I get some help?" When a mission or project is completed, she will organize a debriefing session in which lessons learned are articulated and documented. In other

Table 15.1. Three Types of Thinking Skills.

Type	Description	Examples
Creative Thinking	Generating novel and useful ideas	Design an e-learning course Create a marketing campaign Draft an architectural plan
Critical Thinking	Evaluation of products and ideas	Evaluate validity of Internet resource Consider pros and cons of a new marketing campaign
Metacognition	Your mind's operating system responsible for setting goals, monitoring progress, adjusting approaches	Assessment of what you do and do not know Identify skills you are not learning Monitor progress in a team setting

words, the metacognitive worker or team is mindful of his or her specific thinking processes.

Can thinking skills be trained? Which of the three thinking skills listed in Table 15.1 would be most important to achieve specific outcomes? What training methods are best? In what ways can technology support the acquisition of thinking skills? Can practice with techniques like the ones shown in Figure 15.1 build better thinkers? How can we best identify the thinking skills of our expert performers? These are some of the issues we consider in this chapter.

Can Thinking Skills Be Trained?

Before considering specific guidelines for building thinking skills, it makes sense to first ask whether there is any evidence that they can be enhanced through training at all and, if so, what types of training work best. Because a number of wide-scale thinking skill programs have been evaluated, we have data on the outcomes from thinking skills training. Reviews of both educational and organizational thinking skills programs by Mayer (2008), Ritchhart and Perkins (2005), and Scott, Leritz, and Mumford (2004) conclude that thinking skills programs do have positive effects with some degree of transfer to tasks similar to those included in the programs. However, "this is not to say that such results demonstrate overwhelming success. Impacts on learners' thinking are typically moderate rather than huge" (Ritchhart & Perkins, p. 780).

A comparison of more successful with less successful thinking skills programs helps us identify the features of effective programs. Mayer (2008) notes that successful programs (1) focus on a few well-defined skills, (2) contextualize those skills within authentic tasks, and (3) incorporate social learning strategies, including instructor modeling and student collaboration. We conclude that thinking skills programs can be effective but, as with other skill training, job-specific thinking skills must be defined and trained using many of the proven techniques we have reviewed throughout this book. You will obtain greatest transfer when you integrate job-specific thinking skills into training on job tasks rather than create or implement stand-alone generic thinking skills courses.

To help you design or select programs that are likely to give you a return on investment, we offer the following guidelines:

Principle 1: Focus on job-specific cognitive and metacognitive skills

Principle 2: Consider a whole-task course design

Principle 3: Make thinking processes explicit

Principle 4: Define job-specific thinking processes

Thinking Skills Principle 1: Focus on Job-Specific Cognitive and Metacognitive Skills

It would be wonderful if training on general problem-solving techniques, such as those illustrated in Figure 15.1, could boost thinking skills across a spectrum of jobs. If this were the case, the thinking skills that underlie problem solving would be *general*, with applicability to many different career fields. A general thinking skills training approach like the one in Figure 15.1 would be quite efficient, since one training course on a set of generic problems would suffice for all employees in all work roles.

What's wrong with this approach? We know that successful training must transfer back to the job after the learning event, and transfer has proven to be a thorny problem. Our goal in improving worker thinking skills is to enable them to solve non-routine problems, that is, novel problems for which they do not have a standardized response. We know that work-related problems are encountered in a specific job context, such as sales, military threat assessment, patient care, or automotive troubleshooting. It is unlikely that the general skills derived from broad thinking skills training will transfer effectively to these diverse settings.

Throughout this book we have focused on instructional modes and methods primarily designed to help learners build knowledge and skills that underlie performance of specific tasks. In this chapter, we look at complementary thinking skills, including job-specific creative thinking skills, critical thinking skills, and metacognitive skills. Rather than teach a one-size fits-all list of generic thinking skills in dedicated training events, we recommend that you identify job role-specific skills and integrate these skills into the technical training designed for those work roles.

Thinking Skills Principle 2: Consider a Whole-Task Course Design

In Chapter 1 we defined three types of instruction for e-learning courses: teaching by show-and-tell (receptive), teaching by show-and-do (directive), and teaching by problem solving (guided discovery). Directive training is a type of *part-task instruction* in which content is broken into small segments, prerequisite knowledge is usually taught first, and frequent practice with feedback helps learners build skills gradually.

In contrast, *whole-task instruction* begins the lesson with an authentic work assignment and integrates the needed knowledge and skills in the context of working on that assignment. Whole-task instruction is one form of guided discovery also called *scenario-based learning*, *case-base learning*, or *immersive learning*. Because whole-task instruction teaches skills in context of a realistic work task, it offers opportunities to teach thinking skills along with cognitive skills. Compare the lesson outlines for an Excel course shown in Figure 15.2. Which outline reflects a part-task design and which a whole-task approach?

Figure 15.2. A Part- and Whole-Task Lesson Design for Excel.

Excel Outline Part Task
I.   What is a cell
II. Cell references
III. What is a formula
IV. Formats
V.   Operators
VI. Input a formula
VII. Chart types
VIII. Chart procedures

Excel Outline Whole Task
I.   Add data in column
  • What is a cell
  • Cell references
II. Average sales
  • What is a formula
  • Formats
  • Operators
III. Make a sales chart
  • Type of charts

If you identified the outline on the left as a part-task design, you are correct! Let's get a tangible feeling for whole-task lesson designs by looking at three examples and using them to summarize the key features of whole-task instruction.

Example 1: Problem-Based Learning

About forty years ago, McMaster's University in Canada initiated a major change in their medical school curriculum which subsequently has been widely adopted as an alternative to a traditional science-focused curriculum. In problem-based learning (PBL), the science lectures that predominated the first two years of medical school are replaced by small team reviews of medical cases such as the example we show in Figure 15.3. Typically, a team of five to seven students facilitated by a faculty member reviews a case together and reaches a common understanding of the case followed by individualized self-study to learn more about the issues in the case. After a period of time, the team reconvenes to debrief lessons learned. Most PBL programs follow a structured process such as:

1. Clarify unknown terms and concepts.

2. Define the problem in the case.

3. Brainstorm to analyze the problem by identifying plausible explanations (creative thinking).

4. Critique explanations produced and draft a coherent description of the problem (critical thinking).

5. Define the learning issues (metacognitive thinking).

6. Engage in self-directed study to fill the gaps specified by the learning issues (metacognitive thinking).

7. Reconvene to debrief the case and share lessons learned.

Many evaluation efforts have been directed at PBL, often comparing learning and motivation between PBL and the traditional curriculum. We will review this research later in this chapter.

Figure 15.3. A Case Problem Used in PBL.

From Schmidt and Moust, 2000.

The Miserable Life of a Stomach

The protagonist of our story is the stomach of a truck driver who used to work shifts and who smokes a lot. The stomach developed a gastric ulcer and so the smoking stopped. Stomach tablets are not a regular part of the intake.

While on the highway in Southern Germany, our stomach had to digest a heavy German lunch. Half an hour later, a severe abdominal pain developed. The stomach had to expel the meal. Two tablets of acetylsaliclic acid were inserted to relieve the pain.

A second extrusion some hours later contained a bit of blood. In a hospital in Munich an endoscope was inserted. The stomach needed to be operated upon in the near future. Explain.

Example 2: Automotive Troubleshooting

In Figure 15.4 you see the interface for a multimedia whole-task practice environment for automotive troubleshooting. The task assignment begins

Figure 15.4. A Multimedia Interface for Automotive Troubleshooting.

With permission from Raytheon Professional Services.

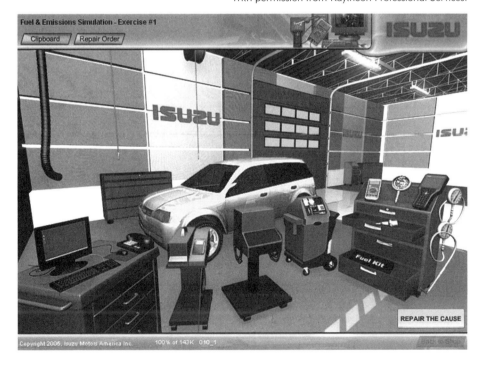

with a work order that states the symptoms of a malfunction, such as high idle. The learners can conduct tests using the virtual shop equipment to identify the source of the failure. Once they believe they have identified the fault, they can select their answer from a list of about fourteen different failures. When they have completed the case and resolved the failure, the learners compare their diagnostic decisions and repair actions with those of an expert, as shown in 15.5.

Figure 15.5. A Comparison of Learner with Expert Problem-Solving Actions During Automotive Troubleshooting.

With permission from Raytheon Professional Services.

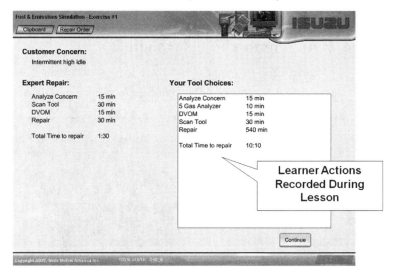

Example 3: BioWorld

BioWorld is a multimedia environment designed to teach scientific reasoning processes, including evidence gathering and analysis. Originally designed for high school students, BioWorld is currently being adapted for medical students (Lajoie, 2009). As shown in Figure 15.6, BioWorld displays a text description of a patient case. The learner begins by selecting relevant phrases mentioned in the case description and dragging them into the evidence table located in the left frame. For example, in this case involving a complaint of abdominal discomfort, the learner has selected patient age, complaint, and recent dietary changes. After identifying relevant evidence, learners select an initial hypothesis from the "Select Hypothesis" pull-down menu located in the upper left-hand corner. In this example, the learner selected Salmonella and can then order diagnostic tests from a pull-down menu to support the hypothesis. Learners can access resources from the online library at any time, including information on biological terms, diagnostic tests, and symptoms. At the conclusion of a case, learners prioritize the evidence supporting their diagnoses and can compare their priorities to those of an expert. As we write this chapter, an animated demonstration of BioWorld is located at www.education.mcgill.ca/cognitionlab/bioworld/en/BWTutorialsmall/BWTutorialsmall.html.

BioWorld includes many elements of an effective thinking skills program. First, it is domain specific—focusing on teaching of medical case reasoning. Second, it is case-based. The learning is contextualized within the process

---

Figure 15.6. The Learner Moves Relevant Data into the Evidence Table in BioWorld.

www.education.mcgill.ca/cognitionlab/bioworld/en/BWTutorialsmall/BWTutorialsmall.html.
Accessed September 2010.

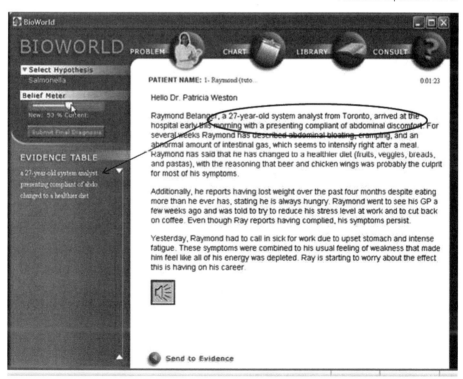

of gathering evidence about a patient and forming diagnostic hypotheses. Third, it makes scientific reasoning explicit by requiring learners to select a hypothesis and build and prioritize evidence to support it. Fourth, it offers instructional support in the form of library resources. Fifth, BioWorld provides feedback on the accuracy of the hypotheses as well as the prioritization of evidence.

Features of Whole-Task Instruction

Now that we have taken a quick tour of three whole-task learning environments, let's summarize the main features that distinguish a whole-task from a part-task design:

1. *Problem-Centered.* Learning starts with a job-realistic scenario or problem, as shown in Figures 15.3 and 15.6. Case studies are not new to training. However, in part-task designs, the case study is sequenced at the end of a lesson or series of lessons. In contrast, in whole-task learning, the lesson is initiated by a case scenario that serves as the context for learning.

2. *Guided Learning.* Learners are supported during the problem-solving episode to avoid mental overload. In part-task instruction, component lesson topics are sequenced one at a time in a building block fashion to avoid mental overload. To minimize overload in whole-task learning, the design must manage the complexity of the scenarios as well as the amount of help available. Early lessons begin with a simple scenario the solution for which might be demonstrated by an expert. Later lessons include complex scenarios with more variables and require the learner to do most of the work.

3. *Inductive Learning.* Learners have freedom to try different actions and reflect on outcomes. Part-task lessons take a directive approach in which learners view examples and complete short practice exercises similar to those we showed in Chapters 11 and 12. The practice exercises are followed by immediate explanatory feedback. In contrast, whole-task designs use a more inductive approach in which the learners can try a number of actions and may not receive feedback until

they submit a case resolution. The feedback may be intrinsic. By that we mean that, after taking an action, the learners may see the consequence of their action and infer the accuracy of their action from that consequence. For example, in the automotive troubleshooting lesson, an incorrect response results in the feedback you see in Figure 15.7. At the end of the case, a summary of their problem-solving actions to promote reflection is displayed next to the actions of an expert, as shown in Figure 15.5.

Figure 15.7. Intrinsic Feedback Given to an Incorrect Response During Automotive Troubleshooting.

With permission from Raytheon Professional Services.

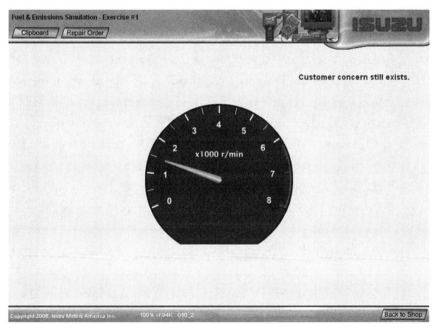

Evidence for Whole-Task Instruction

Although there is a lot of enthusiasm for whole-task learning, evidence of its effectiveness has been mixed. In this section, we review a sampling of research studies comparing learning from various forms of whole-task instruction with an alternative approach.

Evidence from Problem-Based Learning

Because problem-based learning has become a widely adopted alternative in medical education, many studies have compared outcomes among medical students who studied in a PBL curriculum with medical students who studied in a traditional lecture science-based curriculum. Conclusions have varied. For example, Schmidt, Van der Molen, te Winkel, and Wijnen (2009) reported a meta-analysis of 270 research studies comparing outcomes between PBL and traditional medical students in a single medical school. They conclude that medical knowledge and diagnostic reasoning were generally equivalent between the two groups. In contrast, interpersonal skills, practical medical skills, and student satisfaction ratings favored the problem-based learning approach. Koh, Khoo, Wong, and Koh (2008) reviewed thirteen studies involving post-graduate assessment of medical competencies comparing physicians who studied via PBL with those who studied under a traditional program. Assessment scores showed that the social dimension, including teamwork skills, appreciation of social and emotional aspects of health care, and communication skills were higher among PBL graduates. There were no differences for other competencies.

In contrast, Albanese (2010) concludes: "Research on the effectiveness of PBL has been somewhat disappointing to those who expected PBL to be a radical improvement in medical education. Several reviews of PBL over the past twenty years have not shown the gains in performance that many had hoped for" (p. 42).

Although the effects of PBL on learning and medical competencies have been mixed, most reviews agree that, overall, students rate PBL more favorably than the traditional curriculum. Perhaps learning in the context of real-world patient cases makes the relevance of the lesson more salient and hence increases motivation. However, keep in mind that medical students are a unique population whose learning preferences may not match your audience.

Evidence from Sherlock

Sherlock is a computer-coached whole-task practice environment focused on troubleshooting realistic failures in the F-14 electronic test station. Sherlock was designed to provide automated apprenticeship-like training for airpersons who completed their technical school training. Similar to the automotive troubleshooting example we described previously in this chapter, the Sherlock environment emulated the real shop and provided a practice environment in the context of realistic troubleshooting assignments. An Air Force evaluation of Sherlock found that trainees who were on the job for six months and spent twenty to twenty-five hours working with Sherlock were as proficient in troubleshooting the test station as technicians who had been on the job four years (Lajoie, 2009).

This acceleration of expertise stems no doubt from the compressed experience that Sherlock offered. In the real-world troubleshooting environment, failures were infrequent and occurred in no specific order of complexity. In other words, the real world did not provide the optimal frequency and sequence of problems for learning. An important lesson learned from Sherlock is the opportunity to accelerate expertise through experience with digital cases that in the real world could take months or years to accumulate.

Evidence from Excel Training

Lim, Reiser, and Olina (2009) compared several learning measures from part-task and whole-task learning environments teaching how to use Excel to prepare a grade book. Student teachers were randomly assigned to a face-to-face class that used either a part-task or whole-task design. In the part-task version, twenty-two component Excel skills, such as entering data, merging cells, or copying a formula, were described and demonstrated followed by immediate student practice of each component skill at the learner's workstation. At the end of the second lesson in the part-task program, learners were assigned to complete a grade book.

In contrast, the whole-task lesson started with an instructor demonstration of how to use Excel to create a simple grade book. Immediately after the demonstration, learners completed the same grade book just demonstrated. Then they created a second grade book using different data. In the second class session, the same pattern was followed constructing a more complex grade book that involved weighted averages. In summary, learners in the part-task version practiced many small component Excel skills and had one opportunity to practice setting up a grade book. In contrast, the whole-task group had the opportunity to set up four grade books: two simple grade books in Session 1 and two complex grade books in Session 2.

Three different tests taken by learners in both groups evaluated learning. A part-task test measured the ability to perform sixteen separate small Excel tasks. A whole-task test required learners to prepare a grade book different from the one they prepared in class. Finally, a transfer test asked learners to use Excel for an entirely new task—to prepare a budget. As you can see in Figure 15.8, both groups performed about the same on the part-task test. However, learners in the whole-task group did significantly better than learners in the part-task group on the grade book test, with an effect size of .71. Since the whole-task group had four opportunities to practice setting up a grade book compared to one opportunity in the part-task group, this is not a surprising outcome. The transfer test showed much better performance among the whole-task group than the part-task group, with a large effect size of 1.14. The research team points to the opportunities for varied context practice in the whole-task group, which may have helped these learners build a more flexible Excel skill set.

A lesson we can take from the Excel research is that well-designed whole-task learning may better prepare learners to apply new skills to different

Figure 15.8. Learning from Part- Versus Whole-Task Excel Lessons.
Based on data from Lim, Reiser, and Olina, 2009.

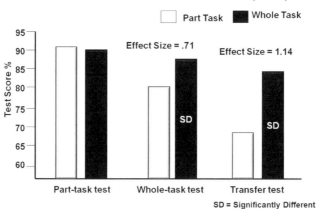

problems than those faced during training. Therefore, whole-task learning might be an effective design to achieve far-transfer learning goals.

A Summary of Evidence for Whole-Task Instruction

Taken together, there is mixed evidence regarding the benefits of a whole-task approach over a part-task design. Rather than compare whole-task designs with alternative designs, a more productive path is to (1) define the situations under which whole-task designs are more effective than part-task designs and (2) to isolate elements of whole-task designs requisite for optimal learning. Whole-task lessons may be best suited for more experienced learners who are not as easily overloaded and for learning of far transfer tasks that benefit from a more flexible mental model of the skills involved.

Thinking Skills Principle 3: Make Thinking Processes Explicit

Whether you adopt a part-task a whole-task or some combination design, it will be important to use instructional methods that make invisible thinking processes explicit. In BioWorld, for example, learners identify, post, and prioritize relevant evidence to support their diagnostic hypothesis. At the end of each case, they compare their evidence priorities with those of an expert.

Effective problem-solving training must include both the cognitive *and* the thinking skills of the job—including approaches to creative, critical, and meta-cognitive thinking. Most job training today concentrates on knowledge of job facts, concepts, and procedures. The emphasis is on cognitive skills, along with associated knowledge. Rarely are the processes, especially the invisible mental processes involved in solving job problems, explicitly incorporated into the learning environment. For example, you may recall from your mathematics classes a focus on the calculation procedures needed to solve a problem. The mental processes underlying problem solution were typically not included. The result may have been that you knew what to do to solve a problem but you did not know when to do it or how to tell whether your approach was working.

Teach Metacognitive Skills

One important component of thinking involves planning, monitoring, and revising—in other words, metacognitive skills. In the last twenty years, educators have designed programs with the explicit goal of building metacognitive skills in their learners. Alan Schoenfeld, a mathematics professor, noted that his graduate students were quite adept at specific mathematical techniques taught in their classes, but they lacked problem-solving skills (1987). In studying the thinking processes of students, he noted that about 60 percent would read a problem, start down a solution path, and continue down that path, whether it was productive or not. Schoenfeld characterizes this as the "read the problem, make a decision to do something, and then pursue it come hell or high water" approach (p. 207). In contrast, experts solving the same problem were more reflective. In Figure 15.9 you can see Schoenfeld's visual representations of problem-solving activities of experts compared to novices. He gathered this data by recording and analyzing the dialog of experts and novices who talked aloud while they solved problems over a ten- to twenty-minute period. Unlike the novices who stuck to one approach, the expert problem solvers moved iteratively among planning, implementing, and evaluating problem-solving actions.

Figure 15.9. Different Problem-Solving Activities in Novice and Expert Mathematicians Over Time.

From Schoenfeld, 1987.

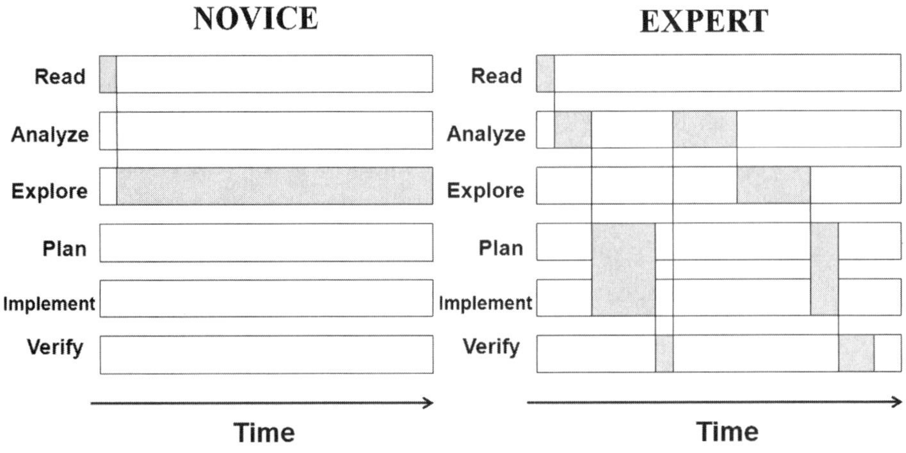

Schoenfeld designed training to help students build more expert-like problem-solving skills. He used worked examples and practice as his main instructional methods. He solved demonstration problems in class, during which he would voice aloud his thoughts—including his monitoring and adjusting thoughts. On occasion he might deliberately go down an unproductive path. After a bit he would stop and say something like, "Wait—is this getting me anywhere? What other alternatives might I consider?" In this way he provided examples not only of problem solutions but *also of the thinking processes* behind them. Second, he assigned problems to small student groups. As they worked together, he would visit the groups and ask "metacognitive questions" such as, "What are you doing now?" "Why are you trying that approach?" "What other approaches might you consider?" By first demonstrating and then holding learners responsible for applying these problem-solving process skills, they soon learned to incorporate this kind of thinking in their problem-solving sessions.

We recommend two techniques for making problem-solving processes explicit in e-learning:

- Engage learners with models of expert problem-solving actions and thinking.

- Require learners to interact not only to take the actions needed to resolve a problem but also to identify or generate the rationale behind those actions.

Display Expert Thinking Models

Similar to the Schoenfeld techniques described in the previous section, e-learning can make expert thinking processes explicit. Take a look at Figure 15.10 from our pharmaceutical consultative sales course. The sales expert is modeling the best responses to the physician's statements and questions. In this example, the learner can see into the expert's thinking process. The on-screen bubble displays her thoughts as she frames her answers. Pressing the "continue" button will display the remainder of the dialog. Expert thoughts could include consideration of alternative responses, as in this example, a rationale for a response, and/or responses to avoid.

Figure 15.10. The Thought Bubble Makes Expert Thinking Explicit.

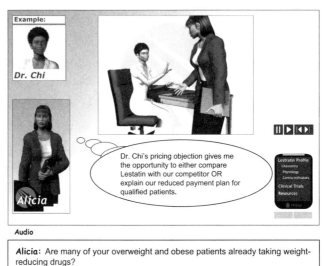

Focus Learner Attention to Behaviors of Expert Models

Moreno (2009) compared learning of teaching principles such as techniques to maintain attention, promote active learning, and prevent cognitive overload from animated teacher models that did or did not add focusing statements. Sixty-one student teachers were assigned to a multimedia lesson that explained teaching principles, followed by an animated classroom model of an expert teacher applying the principles. In one lesson version, a narrative statement from the teacher summarizing the principle to be shown in the animation was placed just prior to the scene modeling that principle. For example, "To maintain students' attention, I called them randomly by name though out the lesson" would be heard just prior to seeing the animated model calling on various students. The comparison lesson version used the same animation but omitted the focusing narration. Moreno (2009) found that the group lacking the focus statements took significantly longer to study the animated models and scored substantially lower on a transfer test. She concludes that "virtual classroom exemplars should be carefully designed to include narrated guidance that can help prospective teachers make

Figure 15.11. The Sales Representative Tells the Learner What to Watch for in the Video Example.

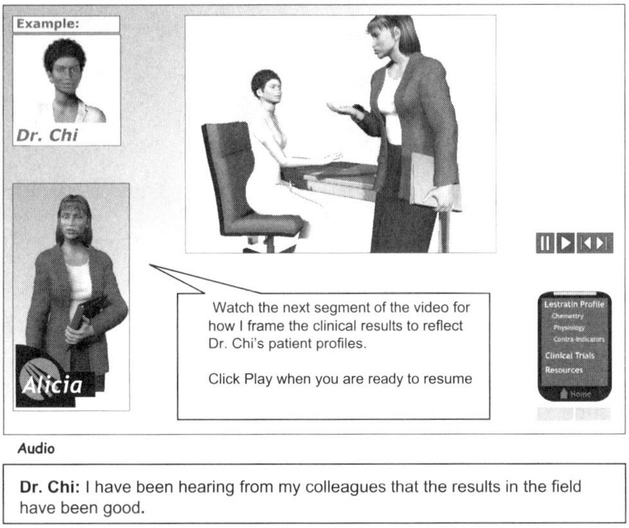

meaningful connections between the theory learned and the rich classroom information contained in the exemplars" (p. 499). In Figure 15.11 you can see how we applied this technique to our sales lesson.

Promote Active Observation of Expert Models

Van Gog, Sluijsmans, Joosten-ten Brinke, and Prins (2010) describe a pilot teacher-training online program in which learners select a professional situation such as handling groups of learners, conducting parental consultations, or asking effective questions. For each scenario reflecting a specific situation, learners are assigned to: observe, analyze, describe, and act. In the observe task, the learner watches a video example of a teacher responding to the situation and writes summaries of the main actions taken. The analyze task uses the same video but requires the learners to evaluate the actions they identified during the observation. For the describe task, learners observe the start of a new scenario related to the same professional situation and describe how they would respond. The learner receives feedback by comparing an expert response for the observation, analysis, and description assignments. The final act assignment requires the learner to respond to a similar situation on the job and receive feedback from a peer or mentor.

A lesson learned from the research on video modeling of teaching skills is that novices especially may not know where to direct their attention and may benefit from focusing guidance such as a statement just prior to the modeled behavior or a requirement to identify specific behaviors in the video.

Promote Learner Reflection on Their Own Thinking Processes

In e-learning you have some unique opportunities to provide learners with feedback on their problem-solving processes and promote reflection on those processes. For example, in Figure 15.5 an end-of-lesson screen from the troubleshooting lesson displays the path of the learner's testing actions next to those of an expert. By asking learners to articulate their own lessons learned from this type of comparison, a reflection assignment focuses on the problem-solving process—not just the final solution. In the same way, in BioWorld, as shown in Figure 15.6, the learner is asked to select a hypothesis and also to prioritize the evidence or the rationale for the hypothesis.

Thinking Skills Principle 4: Define Job-Specific Thinking Processes

As you plan e-learning to build problem-solving skills in your workforce, build in case scenarios, research tools, data sources, activities, and thinking processes that reflect job-specific expert approaches to problem resolution. You identify these job-specific thinking skills during the analysis phases of the design process. Because, when asked, most experts cannot articulate their rationale, you will often need to use special techniques called *cognitive task analysis* (CTA) to define the scenarios to be solved in the training as well as the thinking skills experts use to solve them.

In Table 15.2 we summarize a few different cognitive task analysis techniques. Which technique will work best for you will depend on the nature of the problems being solved as well as the work environment.

Table 15.2. Some Cognitive Task Analysis Methods.

Method	Description	Tradeoffs
Concurrent reporting	Subjects asked to verbalize all of their thoughts at the same time that they are solving a problem or working on a task	Not practical with verbal tasks such as sales Obtrusive May provide high amount of relevant data
Retrospective reporting	Subjects asked to verbalize all of their thoughts immediately or soon after solving a problem or working on a task	Relies on memory Unobtrusive
Cued retrospective reporting	Subjects asked to verbalize all of their thoughts after solving a problem or working on a task while viewing a record (video recording, eye-tracking data) of their work.	Provides memory support Obtrusive
Critical decision method	Expert identifies and reports on a past incident in which they solved a problem or worked on a task. Probing questions asked throughout several interview iterations.	Relies on memory Unobtrusive
Structured expert interview	Several experts independently describe three situations of diverse complexity in which they resolved a given professional situation and list the factors that influence their complexity rating. A consensus meeting identifies complexity factors and most appropriate response to situations.	Relies on memory Leverages multiple sources of expertise Unobtrusive

For example, concurrent reporting, which requires the workers to talk aloud while they resolve a task, cannot be used for a task that requires talking such as sales or customer service or for tasks that cannot be observed such as a combat situation. For tasks such as these, a retrospective approach that asks experts to later recall their actions and thoughts may be more appropriate. In the next paragraphs we summarize two cognitive task-analysis projects that relied on reflective interviews of experts describing problem situations they resolved in the past.

Two Cognitive Task Analysis Interviews

In one interview, Van Gog, Sluijsmans, Joosten-ten Brinke, and Prins (2010) summarize a method called structured expert sessions, used as the basis for the teacher training program described in the preceding section. To begin, a team of five to ten expert professionals is given a specific professional situation and each member individually describes from his or her own experience three specific instances of resolving that situation at different levels of complexity. For example, a team of five experienced teachers write out how they managed a parent-teacher conference. As part of the pre-work phase, each expert reviews her descriptions and abstracts specific factors that distinguish a less complex from a more complex situation. Following the pre-work, a team meeting of approximately two hours first gains agreement on the complexity factors, followed by consensus on the most appropriate actions to address situations that involve those factors.

In a second interview, Lajoie, Azevedo, and Fleiszer (1998) used expert interviews to plan an intensive care nursing problem-solving training. The development team interviewed three head nurses from the intensive care unit to determine the most difficult aspects of their jobs. These were used to define the job competencies that distinguish expert from beginning practitioners.

Following the interviews, the team worked with expert nurses to identify specific case problems that would incorporate those key competencies. Once some cases were developed on paper, the actions that experienced nurses would take to solve them were defined by asking three nurses unfamiliar with the case to talk aloud as they solved the problem. These problem-solving interviews followed a specific sequence. For every action that a nurse would mention, the interviewer would ask the reason for the action. Then the interviewer would state the outcome of the action and the respondent would state his or her interpretation of the outcome. The transcripts collected from these problem-solving sessions were coded into thinking skills categories, including hypothesis generation, planning of medical interventions, actions performed, results of evidence gathering, and interpretation of results, along with overall solution paths.

In summary, since expert job practitioners can rarely articulate their thinking process in a direct way, these must be inferred through a cognitive task analysis technique. Through the cognitive task analysis, you define: (1) scenarios to serve as learning cases, (2) criteria that distinguish scenarios of more or less complexity, (3) the normal tools and resources available to the worker, and (4) alternative solution paths and rationale.

Teaching Thinking Skills: The Bottom Line

In this chapter we have seen evidence and examples for the design of job-specific e-learning that builds thinking skills integrated with technical knowledge and skills. We suggest a domain- or job-specific approach that uses a real-world context for learning the thinking skills unique to a discipline. e-Learning offers: (1) unique opportunities to provide simulated experience in a compressed time frame and (2) a vehicle to make thinking processes explicit as well as to promote practice applying those skills.

Your training plan may reflect either a part-task or whole-task learning design. A part-task approach that ends with a case study might be appropriate for novice learners, who may be overloaded in a whole-task lesson. In contrast, a whole-task approach might benefit apprentice-level staff when effectively designed to offer a sequence of cases of increasing complexity with an appropriate level of learning support. With either design, keep in mind the considerable resources you will need to identify the relevant thinking and cognitive skills that will serve as the foundation for your program.

What We Don't Know About Teaching Thinking Skills

Based on evidence to date, we recommended some specific instructional approaches for helping learners build job-relevant thinking skills. However, many questions remain:

1. For what kinds of learners and work tasks will a whole-task versus a part-task learning design be most appropriate?

2. How can whole-task learning environments accommodate evolving expertise of a learner?

3. How will design of whole-task learning differ for relatively well structured problems such as automotive troubleshooting, compared to more open problems that have multiple approaches and solutions?

4. What is the potential return on investment (ROI) for the time invested in cognitive task analysis and design of thinking-skills e-learning? How will ROI be influenced by the stability of the cognitive and metacognitive skills involved?

5. How can cognitive load be best managed during whole-task learning?

6. How important is collaboration (among learners and between learners and instructors) to optimizing learning in whole-task problem solving environments?

DESIGN DILEMMA: RESOLVED

Your training department was charged with providing courses that would improve workforce thinking skills. In reviewing the many courses claiming to improve creative thinking, you wondered which of the following options were correct:

A. Money can be saved by purchasing an off-the-shelf course that includes techniques like the ones listed in Figure 15.1.

B. Thinking skills training would be most effective in a face-to-face environment.

C. Thinking skills training should be job specific; no one general thinking course will translate into improved workplace performance.

D. There is no way to improve thinking ability through training; it's like intelligence—you either have it or you don't.

Based on evidence to date, we believe that Option C offers the greatest promise for performance results from thinking skills training. However, this option requires customized training focusing on specific job-cognitive and metacognitive skills. Effective training may require considerable effort first to define the important thinking skills and then to create a learning environment to help learners acquire those skills.

To be most cost-effective, the training department might recommend a needs analysis to define which job roles involve thinking skills that most directly lead to organizational competitive advantage. Once identified, the complexity of problems involved in those roles and the stability of the underlying knowledge and skills should be evaluated. Such an analysis might help pinpoint work roles for which thinking skills training will give a maximum return on investment.

WHAT TO LOOK FOR IN e-LEARNING

☐ Lessons that allow learners to observe and apply job-specific thinking skills

☐ Interactions that require learners to make their reasoning process and products explicit

☐ Lessons that model thinking processes and assign practice that reflect expert strategies derived from cognitive task analysis

☐ Lessons that offer sufficient instructional guidance to ensure successful case resolution and learning of problem-solving skills

☐ Lessons that include several diverse problem scenarios to foster a more robust set of problem-solving skills

COMING NEXT

Games and simulations are one of the hottest topics in e-learning today. But before you jump on the bandwagon, you might wonder what evidence we have for the instructional value of games and simulations. In the next chapter we define the key elements of games and simulations, show some examples, and review what lessons we have learned from these environments so far.

Suggested Readings

Albanese, M.A. (2010). Problem-based learning. In W.B. Jeffries & K.N. Huggett (Eds.), *An introduction to medical teaching.* New York: Springer.

Crandall, B., Klein, G., & Hoffman, R.R. (2006). *Working minds.* Cambridge, MA: MIT Press.

Lajoie, S.P. (2009). Developing professional expertise with a cognitive apprenticeship model: Examples from avionics and medicine. In K.A. Ericsson (Ed.), *Development of professional expertise.* New York: Cambridge University Press.

Lajoie, S.P., & Nakamura, C. (2005). Multimedia learning of cognitive skills. In R.E. Mayer (Ed), *The Cambridge handbook of multimedia learning.* New York: Cambridge University Press.

Lim, J., Reiser, R.A., & Olina, Z. (2009). The effects of part-task and whole-task instructional approaches on acquisition and transfer of a complex cognitive skill. *Educational Technology Research & Development, 57,* 61–77.

Mayer, R.E. (2008). *Learning and instruction* (2nd ed.). Upper Saddle River, NJ: Pearson Merrill Prentice Hall. See Chapter 12: Teaching by Fostering Problem-Solving Strategies.

Ritchhart, R., & Perkins, D.N. (2005). Learning to think: The challenges of teaching thinking. In K.J. Holyoak & R.G. Morrison (Eds.), *The Cambridge handbook of thinking and reasoning,* New York: Cambridge University Press.

Schoenfeld, A.H. (1987). What's all the fuss about metacognition? In A. Schoenfeld (Ed.), *Cognitive science and mathematics education.* Mahwah, NJ: Lawrence Erlbaum Associates.

Scott, G., Leritz, L.E., & Mumford, M.D. (2004). The effectiveness of creativity training: A quantitative review. *Creativity Research Journal, 16*(4), 361–388.

Van Gog, T., Sluijsmans, D.M.A., Joosten-ten Brinke, D., & Prins, F.J. (2010). Formative assessment in an online learning environment to support flexible on-the-job learning in complex professional domains. *Educational Technology Research and Development, 58*, 311–324.

CHAPTER OUTLINE

The Case for Simulations and Games

What Are Simulations and Games?
   What Are Simulations?
   What Are Games?

Do Games and Simulations Teach?
   What Research (Fails to) Tell Us About Games and Simulations

Games and Simulations Principle 1: Match Game Types to Learning Goals

Games and Simulations Principle 2: Make Learning Essential to Game Progress

Games and Simulations Principle 3: Build in Proven Instructional Strategies
   Incorporate Explanatory Feedback
   Add Self-Explanation Questions

Games and Simulations Principle 4: Build in Guidance and Structure
   Avoid Discovery Learning
   Design Guidance Appropriate for Inquiry Simulations
   Incorporate Visualization Support
   Incorporate Instructional Explanations

Games and Simulations Principle 5: Manage Complexity
   Move from Simple to Complex Goals
   Provide Training Wheels
   Align Pace to Instructional Goals
   Ensure Ease of Use
   Adapt Complexity to Learner Expertise

Games and Simulations Principle 6: Make Relevance Salient

16

Simulations and Games in e-Learning

WILL ONLINE LEARNING GAMES replace books, lectures, and traditional step-by-step e-learning? Are younger generations better served by experiential multimedia? Do educational games and simulations offer a more effective and more motivational learning alternative than other interactive formats such as case studies? Are there proven principles to guide design of effective learning games? Unfortunately, when it comes to learning, there is quite a bit *we don't know* about simulations and games. However, we are beginning to accumulate new evidence published since the second edition of *e-Learning and the Science of Instruction* about how games and simulations can be designed to promote learning. In this chapter we take an evidence-based approach to help you define tradeoffs and leverage proven techniques when considering simulations and games to achieve your learning goals.

In Chapter 1 we introduced the activity matrix shown in Figure 16.1. Since by definition games and simulations involve high degrees of overt learner engagement, they will fall into the right-hand side of the matrix. Your challenge is to maintain their entertainment or motivational features while at the same time to foster learning. Games and simulations that fall into the lower-right quadrant promote a lot of behavioral activity, but fail to support cognitive processes that require deliberation and reflection. If your goal is learning of cognitive skills, your game or simulation will need to effectively support *both* psychological and behavioral activity and fall into the upper-right quadrant.

Figure 16.1. The Psychological-Behavioral Activity Matrix.

Adapted from Stull and Mayer, 2007.

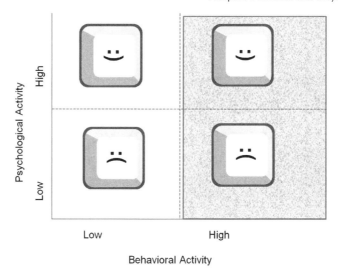

games. The workforce of today—those who have been playing online games for years—have different brains! Their nervous systems are attuned to high engagement rich multimedia. These Millennials are turned off by anything that even looks like traditional training!

Let's leverage the popularity of games with a spreadsheet adventure theme. We could design a fantasy scenario where spreadsheet solutions open doors to new worlds that offer clues and tools. Take a look at the storyboard our graphic artist created. The visuals alone make you want to jump into the game!"

Figure 16.2. A Fantasy Theme for a Learning Game.

Credit: Mark Palmer.

Matt: "OK. This sounds exciting. . . . but how long will it take to develop this game? And how will it affect our production budget? And what about learning time? How long do you think it will take to play the game compared to completing a traditional tutorial? If we invest in this game, will they learn how to use spreadsheets as effectively and efficiently as if we used a traditional lesson that just shows them how? And will their new spreadsheet skills transfer to the kinds of spreadsheets they need to develop in their work roles?"

Sandy is excited about teaching spreadsheet concepts and tasks in a highly interactive game-type environment, but Matt has some questions. Based on your own experience or intuition, which of the following options would you select:

A. Sandy is correct. Raised on games, the younger workforce will learn more effectively from game-type lessons.

B. More participants will complete a game-type course than will complete a traditional tutorial.

C. Learning by exploration and discovery is more effective than learning by explanations and traditional practice exercises.

D. Constructing a gaming environment will be more expensive than developing a traditional course; however, the investment will pay off in higher completion rates and better transfer of skills.

The Case for Simulations and Games

According to the Entertainment Software Association's annual report (2010), video and computer games are ubiquitous in American households—and not just among the young. Sixty-seven percent of American households play computer or video games. The average age of game players is thirty-four, with 26 percent over the age of fifty. Males outplay females, making up 60 percent of the gaming population. You can see in Figure 16.3 that the most popular types of digital games have not changed since the 2006 data we reported in the second edition of this book. Action and sports remain the most popular video games, and strategy and family/children's games capture the greatest market share among computer games. Since 1996, there has been a steady increase in the annual dollar sales of computer and video games, which peaked at $11.7 billion in 2008.

Figure 16.3. Sales of Video and Computer Game Types.
Source: Entertainment Software Association, 2010.
Accessed from www.theesa.com/, September 2010.

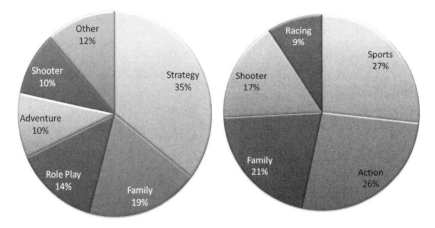

Best-Selling Computer Game Types   Best-Selling Video Game Types

Enthusiasts hope to leverage the popularity of entertainment games and simulations to improve learning outcomes. Some argue that the Millennial generation, raised on games and simulations, has different neurological requirements and expectations that demand highly interactive media-intensive learning environments.

In medical education high-fidelity simulations are recommended because (1) managed health care has resulted in shorter patient stays with consequent fewer clinical teaching opportunities than in the past, (2) patient safety is enhanced when procedures can be learned and practiced on simulators, (3) new medical procedures such as sigmoidoscopy, laparoscopy, and robotics involve motor and perceptual skills that can be effectively practiced via simulators, and (4) deliberate practice involving repetitive performances leads to improved skills (Issenberg, McGaghie, Petrusa, Gordon, & Scalese, 2005).

Instructional games (also called serious games) are popular among some adult learners. In a review of research on computer simulations used in many business school settings, Anderson and Lawton (2009) found that, with a few exceptions, learners prefer simulation exercises more than either lectures or case discussions. Not all games, however, are equally embraced. In a survey evaluation of two games designed for new hire orientation, Carson (2009) attributed a relatively low participation in the game to usability issues and perceived lack of relevance.

Given that at least some games and simulations are highly popular with a sizable population segment, what evidence do we have about their instructional effectiveness and efficiency? Will a simulation or game result in higher e-learning completion rates compared to standard tutorials? Will learning be faster? Will learners feel more positive about the instructional experience as well as about the knowledge and skills learned? Do the Millennials benefit more from games than from traditional training methods? What is the cost/benefit of simulations and games? How can you tell an effective game or simulation from an ineffective one? Our goal in this chapter is to look beyond the hyperbole on multimedia games and simulations to see what controlled evidence tells us about their learning potential.

What Are Simulations and Games?

Suppose you wanted to teach the basics of genetics. You could develop a structured linear interactive tutorial. Alternatively, you could opt for a more experiential environment like the genetics simulation in Figure 16.4. In this simulation, learners can change the genes on the chromosomes and immediately see how the dragon features are altered. In Figure 16.5, the simulation has been converted into a game by giving learners a goal to change the lower-left dragon to match the one in the upper left.

What Are Simulations?

A simulation is a model of a real-world system. Simulated environments respond in dynamic and rule-based ways to user responses. For example, in

Figure 16.4. Simulation of Laws of Genetics.

From Biologica Project, http://biologica.Concord.org.

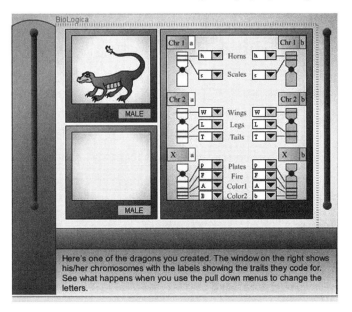

Figure 16.5. Game Based on Simulation of Laws of Genetics.

From Biologica Project, http://biologica.Concord.org.

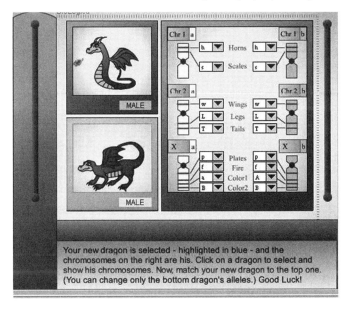

the genetics simulation in Figure 16.4, when the user changes the h gene on chromosome 1 to a dominant gene H, horns appear on the dragon, reflecting the laws of genetics. De Jong (2011) defines computer simulations as "computer programs that have as their core a computational model of a system or process. The system or process that is modeled normally has a natural world origin and the model that is created is usually a simplification of the real world phenomenon" (p. 446).

There are two basic types of simulations: operational and conceptual. Operational simulations are designed primarily to teach procedural skills, whereas conceptual simulations focus on learning of domain-specific concepts and strategic knowledge. In workforce learning, operational simulations have been used for training of software applications, medical procedures, and safety-related skills, such as aircraft piloting and industrial control operations. In contrast, conceptual simulations, such as the one shown in Figure 16.4, are primarily designed to build *far transfer* knowledge of a specific domain as well as associated inquiry or problem-solving skills. Conceptual simulations in the educational arena have modeled principles of physics, genetics, chemistry, botany and ecology, to name a few. In professional and workforce learning, conceptual simulations have been designed to teach business management strategies, military combat decision making, bank loan analysis, medical diagnostics, and equipment troubleshooting, among others.

What Are Games?

From PacMan to Jeopardy to Doom, online games reveal a diverse array of formats and features. In Table 16.1 we summarize some of the major genres of commercial online video games. If you don't agree with our categories, you are probably correct, as games are in a constant state of evolution and many could be classified as hybrids of two or more of these classes. Mayer and Johnson (2010) list four common features of games: (1) rule-based, allowing players to understand the environment, (2) responsive, allowing the learner to experience control, (3) challenging, and (4) cumulative so that the current state of the environment reflects the player's previous actions and shows progress toward goals. In contrast to most games built for entertainment, educational games are designed to help learners achieve

Table 16.1. Some Genres of Video Games.

Based on Wikipedia, http://en.wikipedia.org/wiki/Video_game_genres September 6, 2010

Genre	Description	Examples
Action	Use quick reflexes, accuracy, and timing to overcome obstacles. Often emphasis on combat.	Pong, Street Fighter, Donkey Kong
Shooter	Combat with projectile weapons such as guns and missiles	Doom, Halo Series, Call of Duty: Modern Warfare Series, Space Invaders
Action-Adventure	Focus on exploration and usually involve item gathering, simple puzzle solving, and combat.	Adventure Myst, Resident Evil 4
Role Play	Assume role of one or more "adventurers" who specialize in specific skill sets while progressing through a predetermined storyline.	Final Fantasy Series, Grand Theft Auto, World of Warcraft
Simulation	Designed to emulate aspects of a real or fictional reality including simulations involving construction, vehicle operations, biology, pet management, etc.	SimCity, Flight Simulator, The Sims
Strategy	Focus on game play requiring careful and skillful thinking and planning in order to achieve victory	Civilization Series, Empire Earth, Master of Orion
Music	Challenge the player to follow sequences of movement or develop specific rhythms.	Guitar Hero, Rock Band
Sports	Emulate playing of traditional sports	Madden NFL Series

specific learning objectives while at the same time providing a motivational environment.

For example, in Figure 16.6 we show a screen shot from a business management game. Lemonade Tycoon 2 sets different goals in different modes: time mode (make as much money as possible in a given time frame) or money mode (be the first team to attain a set amount of money). Players control their marketing budget, stock levels, recipes, and prices and make decisions regarding hiring employees, investing in equipment, and so forth. The Lemonade Tycoon game involves a simulation. However, not all learning games incorporate simulations. For example, quiz games such as Jeopardy are not simulation based.

Figure 16.6. Lemonade Tycoon—A business Simulation Game.
From Ncube, 2010. Reprinted with permission.

Do Games and Simulations Teach?

Yes, simulations and games teach, but the lesson learned is not always the intended one. For example, Rieber (2005) tested the effectiveness of the simulation shown in Figure 16.7 for teaching physics principles of velocity and acceleration. The player manipulates the ball's acceleration by clicking on the large arrows. To add a motivational element to the simulation, some participants were given a game goal to earn points by making the ball flip-flop as many times as possible inside the small box in the center of the overhead view.

Figure 16.7. The Flip Flop Game Interface.
From Rieber, 2005. Reprinted with permission of Cambridge University Press and L. Rieber.

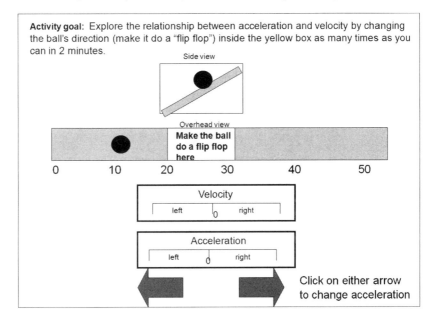

Participants using the game version reported much higher enjoyment than those who worked with the simulation without the game goals. However, when tested on physics principles, the gaming group scored significantly *lower* than those who explored the simulation without a game goal! The flip-flop game players focused exclusively on improving their scores and in the process failed to reflect on the physics principles underlying the model.

In this experiment, we see that a gaming environment can be a lot of fun and at the same time depress learning. Why? The game goals generated behaviors that were antagonistic to the instructional goals. We would classify this game in the lower-right quadrant of our Activity Matrix in Figure 16.1. The game prompted a lot of behavioral activity that did not translate into the psychological activity needed to achieve the instructional goals.

Games must be designed in ways that promote learning. That way we can get the best of both worlds—fun and learning! Later in this chapter we will focus on design guidelines to optimize learning from simulations and games.

What Research (Fails to) Tell Us About Games and Simulations

In the second edition of this book, we summarized reviews of the effectiveness of games and simulations, concluding that better quality research studies were needed. For example, Gosen and Washbush (2004) reported that of 155 studies reviewed, *not one* met all of the criteria for sound research.

Six years later, we don't see major changes among the reviews scholars have published on simulations and games. For example, in 2008, Hannafin and Vermillion note: "Games are very motivating and have tremendous potential in education, but despite a rapidly growing research base, there is yet insufficient evidence to draw definitive conclusions" (p. 215). In a review of computer-based business simulations, Anderson and Lawton (2009) draw three main conclusions: (1) students like business simulation exercises more than either lectures or case discussion, (2) there is little correlation between learner ratings of the simulation and actual performance in the simulation, and (3) there is little objective evidence for the relative educational merits of simulations versus case studies or lectures. Specifically, they observe: "We have continued to be very disappointed with how little we can objectively demonstrate regarding what students learn from participating in simulation exercises" (p. 200). Van Eck (2007) summarizes the challenges facing digital game-based learning: "We do not yet have the theoretical and research base we need to establish guidelines for practice, and, while we have everyone's attention now, we do not yet know what to say"(p. 31).

Fortunately, the most recent research has refocused the general question: "*Are games and simulations effective*? to ask "*What features of games and simulations lead to learning?*" Mayer (2011b) calls this research perspective a *value-added approach.* In a value-added study, different versions of a game or simulation are tested and conclusions drawn regarding how to design games and simulations that are both motivating and educational. For example, we summarized research in Chapter 9 showing better learning from a botany game when the script was conversational using first and second person than when the language was more formal (See Figures 9.6 and 9.7).

In the remainder of this chapter we review the following evidence-based principles to maximize the learning potential of games and simulations:

Principle 1: Match game types to learning goals

Principle 2: Make learning essential to game progress

Principle 3: Build in proven instructional strategies

Principle 4: Build in guidance and structure

Principle 5: Manage complexity

Principle 6: Make relevance salient

Games and Simulations Principle 1: Match Game Types to Learning Goals

To be effective, the goals, activities, feedback, and interfaces of simulations and games must align with the desired instructional outcomes. The flip-flop game illustrated in Figure 16.7 included elements that were antagonistic to the learning objectives. Learning occurred, but it was not the intended learning. Specifically, the rapid-fire response requirements of the flip-flop game were counterproductive to the deeper reflection needed to learn physics principles.

In Table 16.1 we summarized the most common genres of commercial video games. Which genres are best suited for various learning outcomes? Van Eck (2007) suggests that "depending on what kinds of skills one wants to foster in digital game-based learning practice, different forms and styles of games will be required. Card games, Jeopardy-style games, action games, and adventure games can all be digital in form, yet each will have its own characteristics that make it more or less suited to different instructional uses" (p. 41).

Based on evidence to date, we recommend that, for cognitive learning outcomes, games with time goals that require fast responses are not a good match. However, rapid response games may be well suited for skills that must become automated through extensive drill and practice. Train engineers, for example, must be able to rapidly identify the meaning of a track signal and quickly respond. It is easy to see how a gaming environment could make the drill and practice involved in this skill more fun. We look to future research to validate the match between game types, game features, and learning.

Games and Simulations Principle 2: Make Learning Essential to Game Progress

Ensure that game progress and success translate into learning. In other words, the learning required to succeed in a game should be the same learning required by your instructional objectives. Belanich, Sibley, and Orvis (2004) evaluated learning of twenty-one individuals who played the America's Army game with questions assessing information presented during the game. Participants completed four sections of the game, including marksmanship training, an obstacle course, weapons familiarization, and an operational training mission. The research team compared learning of information that was relevant to playing the game with information that did not impact progress in the game. For example, a relevant question asks: "During basic rifle marksmanship qualifying, how many rounds are in a magazine?" In contrast, "What is written on the lane posts of the obstacle course?" is irrelevant to game progress. As you can see in Figure 16.8, learning of relevant information was greater with an effect size of .65, which is moderate. The research team recommends that "instructional objectives should be integrated into the game's storyline so that the training material is relevant to the progression of the game" (p. 17).

Games and Simulations Principle 3: Build in Proven Instructional Strategies

Throughout this book we have highlighted instructional strategies that are proven to accelerate learning. We've discussed the benefits of worked examples, self-explanation questions, audio narration, explanatory feedback, pretraining, relevant visuals, and personalization techniques, to name just a

Figure 16.8. Players Recognized More Game-Relevant Information
Than Game-Irrelevant Information.

Based on data from Belanich, Sibley, and Orvis, 2004.

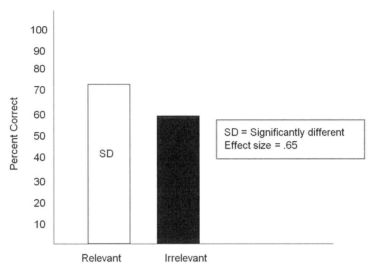

few. Rather than start at ground zero, why not integrate these proven features into games and simulations in ways that maintain their motivational benefits? Mayer (2011b) has summarized a number of multimedia principles we have reviewed in this book that have proven beneficial in games with high effect sizes, including modality, personalization, and pretraining. In this section we review a sampling of research studies that compared learning from versions of the same game or simulation environment that varied one or more of these proven instructional strategies.

Incorporate Explanatory Feedback

Knowledge of results that incorporates guidance is one of the most important instructional elements in any simulation or game. Feedback was the single most commonly mentioned success factor among research studies on the effectiveness of medical simulations (Issenberg, McGaghie, Petrusa, Gordon, & Scalese, 2005). Feedback may be built into a simulator, provided by an instructor, or provided in a video replay reviewed after a simulator session. The source of the feedback is less important than its presence and quality. Controlled comparisons of different versions of the Design-A-Plant and Circuit games summarized in the following paragraphs support the value of incorporating feedback into games or simulations.

Moreno (2004) evaluated learning and efficiency of two versions of a botany game called Design-A-Plant. See Figure 9.9 to review the Design-A-Plant interface. In Design-A-Plant, learners are given a goal to construct a plant with the best combinations of roots, leaves, and stems to survive in planets of different environmental features. The game goal is to design a plant that succeeds in a specific environment. The instructional goal is to learn how plant features are adaptive to various environmental conditions.

In one version of Design-A-Plant, a learning agent provided explanatory feedback to learner responses. A comparison version offered only "correct–incorrect" feedback. In the explanatory feedback version, when the learner makes a correct selection, the agent confirms the choice with a statement such as: "*Yes, in a low sunlight environment, a large leaf has more room to make food by photosynthesis.*" For an incorrect choice, the agent responds with a statement such as: "*Hmmmm, your deep roots will not help your plant collect the scarce rain that is on the surface of the soil.*" This feedback is followed by the correct choice.

The explanatory feedback version resulted in better learning and was also rated as more helpful than the versions that only provided correct or incorrect feedback. There were no differences in student ratings of motivation or interest for the two versions. Adding explanations to the feedback improved learning, but did not detract from the enjoyment of the game.

In a follow-up experiment, Moreno and Mayer (2005) confirmed these findings. Learners working with versions that provided explanatory feedback scored twice as much on a transfer post-test, with an effect size of 1.87, which is very high.

Mayer and Johnson (2010) compared learning from different versions of an arcade game designed to teach basic principles of how an electric circuit works. Learning from a version of the Circuit game with explanatory feedback improved performance during the game as well as on a transfer test, with effect sizes of 1.31 and .68, respectively.

Add Self-Explanation Questions

In Chapter 11, we reviewed evidence showing that adding a self-explanation question to a worked example boosted the instructional benefits of the example. Mayer and Johnson (2010) tested the benefits of adding self-explanation questions to the Circuit game. In Figure 16.9 you can compare one screen from the basic game to a screen that added a checklist of explanations to each game problem. For example, two of the checklist options are: "If you add a battery in serial, you increase flow rate of the current" or "If you add a battery in parallel with another battery, you do not change the flow rate of the current." As you can see in Figure 16.10, the game version with the

Figure 16.9. A Screen Shot from the Circuit Game Without and with Self-Explanation Questions.

From Mayer and Johnson, 2010.

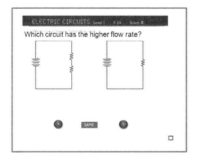

A. Base Version   B. Self-Explanation Version

Figure 16.10. Better Learning with Self-Explanation Questions Added to a Game.

Based on data from Mayer and Johnson, 2010.

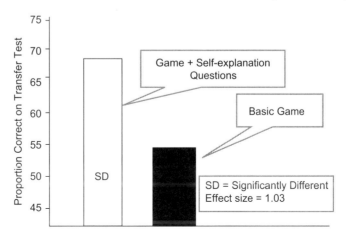

self-explanation checklist improved performance during the game as well as on a transfer test, with high effect sizes. In a recently published follow-up study, Johnson and Mayer (2010) replicated the results of their first study, finding that the self-explanation groups achieved scores on a transfer test of about 74 percent, compared to 53 percent from the game version without self-explanations.

Games and Simulations Principle 4: Build in Guidance and Structure

Perhaps one of the most important guidelines we can offer is to design simulations and games that offer structure and learning support. In fact, much recent research focuses on strategies you can use to guide experiential learning. Here we review several techniques that have emerged from this research.

Avoid Discovery Learning

If there is one thing we do know about experiential learning, it's that pure discovery learning, whether by an individual alone or with a group, does not pay off. The assumption that mental activity must be predicated on physical activity is a teaching fallacy (Mayer, 2004). "Instructional programs evaluated over the past fifty years consistently point to the ineffectiveness of pure discovery. Activity may help promote meaningful learning, but instead of behavioral activity per se, the kind of activity that really promotes meaningful learning is cognitive activity" (p. 17).

Judge the value of any simulation or game not on the activity but rather on the degree to which the activity promotes appropriate cognitive processing. "Guidance, structure, and focused goals should not be ignored. This is the consistent and clear lesson of decade after decade of research on the effects of discovery methods" (Mayer, 2004, p. 17).

We *discourage* the creation of games and simulations that are highly exploratory—environments that at best are inefficient for learning and at worst defeat learning completely. One way to mitigate these unintended consequences is to incorporate guidance into simulations and games.

Design Guidance Appropriate for Inquiry Simulations

An inquiry simulation is a simulation designed to teach scientific investigation skills such as the Genetics simulation we show in Figure 16.4. In a review of research on inquiry simulations, De Jong (2011) concludes that the following types of guidance benefit learning: (1) help learners identify relevant variables, (2) provide hypotheses in a "ready-made" manner such as in a menu rather than asking learners to derive hypotheses on their own, (3) offer a domain-specific structure for the inquiry process through a set of concrete assignments, and (4) require learners to reflect on their activities and the results of their activities. For example, in the genetics simulation shown in Figures 16.4 and 16.5, the program might suggest a specific strategy such as:

> "Change one gene on a single chromosome, record the change observed in the dragon, then change the corresponding gene on the paired chromosome. What do you notice when one of the chromosomes contains a dominant (capital letter) gene? What happens when both chromosomes contain a recessive (small letter) gene? Based on your observations, write a hypothesis about dominant and recessive genes. Next plan a dragon experiment to test your hypotheses."

Incorporate Visualization Support

Success in some simulations or games may rely on spatial skills. For these types of games, instructional aids can promote learning by providing external spatial representations as guides. For example, Mayer, Mautone, and Prothero (2002) evaluated different types of support for a geology simulation game called the Profile Game. In the game learners collect data from a planet whose surface is obscured by clouds. Players draw a line on the interface and the computer shows a profile line indicating how far above and below sea level the surface is at each point on the line. By drawing many lines, learners can determine whether the section contains a mountain, trough, island, or other feature.

Participants were provided with strategy aids in text, visual aids diagramming the various geological features, or no aids. Figure 16.11 shows a sample of the visual aid. The visual aids led to best game performance. The research team concludes that "students need support in how to interact with geology simulations, particularly support in building and using spatial representations" (p. 181).

Figure 16.11 This Visual Aid Helped Learners Identify Geological Features in a Geology Simulation Game.

From Mayer, Mautone, and Prothero, 2002.

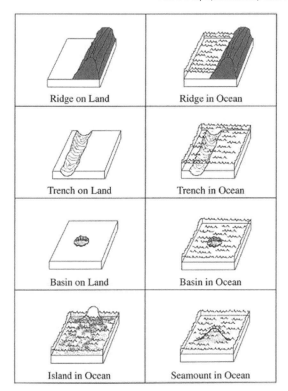

Incorporate Instructional Explanations

An instructional explanation is a brief tutorial that states the principles or concepts being illustrated in the simulation or game. We have evidence that learning from games or simulations with explanations is better than from games and simulations without explanations. There are two main ways to integrate explanations. They can be included as feedback to learner responses, as we described previously in this chapter. Additionally, explanations can be offered in the form of hints appearing between simulation rounds. When using a simulation or game lacking explanations, learners try to achieve the goals of the game and learn at the same time. These two activities may lead to mental overload and it's usually the game—not the learning—that takes precedence.

Rieber, Tzeng, and Tribble (2004) evaluated learning of laws of motion from a game in which learners clicked to kick a ball to position it on a target on the screen. The game score was based on the time needed to reach the goal. Learning was measured with a multiple-choice test that assessed understanding of the physics principles. Some participants received hints between game rounds such as:

> "This simulation is based on Newton's laws of motion. Newton's second law says that the speed of an object depends on size of the force acting upon it. Therefore, an object kicked two times to the right would move at a speed twice as fast as a ball kicked only once."
> (p. 314)

Those who received hints had an average pretest-posttest gain of 32 points compared to 13 points for those who did not receive hints!

The research team concluded that "Discovery learning within a simulation can be very inefficient, ineffective, and frustrating to students, but providing students with short explanations at just the right time can offset these limitations" (p. 319). A brief and succinct instructional explanation incorporated into a simulation can improve learning and at the same time not detract from the game experience.

Taken together, the research we have reviewed in this section recommends that you design *guided* experiential environments. No doubt there are many techniques for effective guidance and we will expand our list as research accumulates on this important issue.

Games and Simulations Principle 5: Manage Complexity

In 2007 a major technology firm commissioned two adventure games for new hire orientation. In one of the games, Rise of the Shadow Specters, the player assumes the role of a new employee on a fantasy planet and finds that Shadow Specters have attacked the network, thereby threatening the planet. The goal is to defeat the specters by answering questions and opening secret doors to learn about the business. In a survey evaluation, Carson (2009) reported that relatively low participation in the game among new workers was due to poor usability, perceived lack of relevance, and the time commitment required to play the game.

These results likely reflect two issues: cognitive overload due to interface design complexity and failure to motivate, reflecting a perceived lack of game relevance to the job. In this section we summarize several techniques you can use to manage complexity in games and simulations.

Move from Simple to Complex Goals

Begin a game or simulation with a relatively low challenge task or goal and move gradually to more complex environments. For example, in the genetics simulation game shown in Figure 16.5, the challenge of the game can be adjusted by changing the number of genes needed to match the test dragon to the target dragon or by the complexity of the genetic relationships required to achieve a given match. Game complexity can be controlled by asking learners to select a game difficulty level based on their relevant experience or by dynamically adapting game complexity based on accuracy of responses during the game.

Provide Training Wheels

Carroll (2000) described a "training wheels" principle for software simulations. He recommended that learners work with a simulation in which only some of the functionality is enabled. Although the full interface may be visible, only relevant elements of it work. In that way, learners cannot go too far astray during early trials. As more tasks are learned, the constraints are gradually relaxed until the user is working with a highly functional system. For example, when initially working with a software simulation, only a few commands or icons are functional. As the learner gains experience, greater functionality is added.

Align Pace to Instructional Goals

According to some, the new generation of gamers is not patient. They have learned to multitask and to respond to multiple digital information sources quickly. Slow game pace was one complaint of players of an Indiana Jones adventure game (Ju & Wagner, 1997). While fast-paced games may be more popular, they are also likely to lead to greater overload and to fewer opportunities for reflection. For example, in comparing learning from a paper-based explanation of wave formation to a multimedia animated, narrated version, Mayer and Jackson (2005) found better learning from the paper group because learners could interact with the material at their own pace and were less likely to experience cognitive overload.

Games that rely on rapid responses to win may benefit learning of skills that require responses based on speed and accuracy. If your instructional goals require application of concepts and rules, games that proceed under learner control of pacing and do not reward speed will be more effective.

Ensure Ease of Use

Previously in this chapter, we reviewed findings by Mayer and Johnson (2010) showing the benefits of encouraging reflection by requiring learners to select self-explanations during playing of a Circuit game. You can review the game interface and results in Figures 16.9 and 16.10. In a recent follow-up study, Johnson and Mayer (2010) compared learning among three versions of the Circuit game: the base game shown in Figure 16.9 A, the base game with a checklist of self-explanation questions shown in Figure 16.9 B, and the base game in which the learners were required to generate their own self-explanations by typing them into a window to the right of each circuit problem (not shown in Figure 16.9). The research team found that requiring learners to select an explanation from a list improved learning, whereas requiring them to type in their own explanations gave no better results than the base-game. Asking game players to generate and type in their own explanations apparently added too much cognitive load and/or disrupted the game flow.

Holzinger, Kickmeier-Rust, Wassentheurer, and Hessinger (2009) compared learning of arterial blood flow principles from a simulation called HAEMOSIM. Learning was compared from three instructional versions. One group studied a traditional text description. Group 2 used HAEMOSIM unaided, while Group 3 used HAEMOSIM preceded by a thirty-second video that explained how to use the simulation and described the main parameters involved. Learning was much better from HAEMOSIM *only when preceded by the explanatory video.* The research team concludes that "It is essential to provide additional help and guidance on the proper use of a simulation *before* beginning to learn with the simulation" (p. 300).

Similar findings were reported by Lazonder, Hagemans, and De Jong (2010), who compared simulation performance among three groups. One group was provided pretraining on the different variables in the simulation and also had access to the information during the simulation. A second group received no pretraining but had access to the information during the simulation. A third group worked with the simulation without any help. Participants who had access to simulation information outperformed those who had no help, with the group that received information both before and during the task scoring highest.

A lesson learned from these experiments is the importance of making the interface user-friendly with techniques such as providing a checklist rather than requiring typing. In addition, performance of novice learners benefits from pretraining as well as embedded help that explains how the game or simulation works and/or provides domain-specific background knowledge.

Adapt Complexity to Learner Expertise

Interface complexity is a function of the type and display of images used in a game or simulation. Lee, Plass, and Homer (2006) created a conceptual simulation of Boyles and Charles Laws that describe the relationships between gas pressure and gas volume (Boyles Law) and gas temperature and gas volume (Charles Law). The research team created high- and low-complexity simulations by varying the visual representations and the number of variables learners could manipulate at once. A simple version used concrete imagery such as a weight to represent pressure or a flame to represent temperature and only allowed manipulation of one variable at a time—either pressure or temperature. A complex version used abstract imagery in the form of a slider bar and allowed manipulation of two variables (heat and temperature) at once. In Figure 16.12 we compare the concrete and abstract imagery versions. Learners with minimal background in science benefited from the concrete version. In contrast, high prior knowledge students learned equally well from the concrete and abstract representations.

Figure 16.12. A Simple and Complex Simulation Interface for Ideal Gas Laws.

From Lee, Plass, and Homer, 2006.

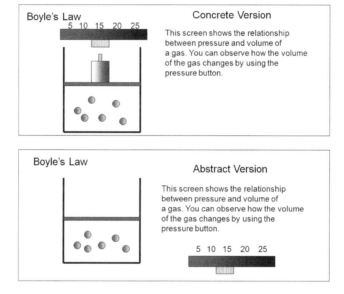

Games and Simulations Principle 6: Make Relevance Salient

Consider the context and genre of the game or simulation to ensure that its relevance to job roles is immediately clear. Workforce learners are subject to many demands, have limited time, and will often discard learning environments that do not immediately appear relevant.

Although fantasy game interfaces such as Figure 16.1 may be visually stimulating, their lack of correspondence with the work environment may actually detract from the motivational potential of the game. High-fantasy elements are considered motivational in games and simulations designed for entertainment (Malone & Lepper, 1987). However, the fantasy features may not always motivate workforce learners.

The relevance of any game can be enhanced by providing learning objectives, pretraining explanations, embedded explanations, and/or interfaces that either mirror or are analogous to work role demands. We will need additional research to define features that optimize learning and motivation in games and simulation environments designed for workforce learners.

What We Don't Know About Games and Simulations

Although our knowledge base is growing, there remains much to learn. We do know that, for some, games are motivational and, when well designed, can improve learning. We are also confident that well-designed simulations can offer instructional environments for practice and learning that are unavailable or unsafe in the workplace. The research of the next few years should give more guidance about how to design simulation and game features that effectively balance motivational and learning elements. Here is a list of some important questions for which we need empirical data:

1. *Guidance for guidance.* We reviewed accumulating evidence that guidance is an essential ingredient of an effective learning simulation or game. However, we need more information on the most appropriate format, source, and type of guidance to use for different instructional goals at different learning stages.

2. *Simulation and game taxonomies for different learning outcomes.* We know it's important to match the simulation or game goal, actions, feedback, and interface to the instructional goals. However, we have only general guidelines for making an appropriate match, most of which lack empirical verification. Will arcade games with rapid response features be most effective for visual discrimination

or motor skills? Will adventure or strategy games be best aligned to learning cause-and-effect relationships? Are memory goals such as learning product knowledge best supported by game-show-type formats? An empirically based taxonomy of game formats aligned to learning outcomes should help game and simulation designers make optimal matches.

3. *Cost/benefit of games and simulations.* To design and implement a computer game or simulation of any complexity requires an investment of time and resources. In addition to development costs, participant time is invested in interacting with the simulation or game. What are the efficiencies of games? How does the time to achieve an instructional goal from a game compare with achieving the same goal from a book or tutorial? When does the motivational appeal of a game offset the investment in development and learning time? For example, will an embedded game result in higher completion of e-learning as well as equal or better learning contrasted to traditional methods? In most commercial settings, there is a cost attached to the development and use of learning environments, and we have much to learn about the cost/benefit tradeoffs of games and simulations.

4. *Collaboration in games.* In Chapter 13 we reviewed the benefits of collaborative learning, which are realized when the collaborative assignment and incentives are optimized. A promising new area of research involves comparison of learning from games played solo with collaborative play.

5. *Value-added research on games.* How can we add proven instructional methods to enhance learning to games and simulations in ways that do not appreciably detract from the motivational elements of the game? Some examples of value-added research that we reviewed in this chapter revealed the benefits of adding explanatory feedback and self-explanation questions to games. A promising avenue of research is to identify other proven strategies that can be integrated into games and simulations.

DESIGN DILEMMA: RESOLVED

We started this chapter with a debate between Sandy and Matt on embedding the spreadsheet lesson content into an adventure game context. The options included:

A. Sandy is correct. Raised on games, the younger workforce will learn more effectively from game-type lessons.

B. More participants will complete a lesson based on a game than will complete a traditional tutorial.

C. Learning by exploration and experience is more effective than learning by explanations and traditional practice exercises.

D. Constructing a gaming environment will be more expensive than developing a traditional course; however, the investment will pay off in higher course completion rates and better learning.

While we would like to select Option D, at this time we do not have sufficient evidence to support it. Rather than ask whether games are a good idea or a bad idea, a better question is What kinds and features of games will offer cost/benefit for a given learner population and instructional goal. We look forward to additional research that specifies instructional methods that improve learning from simulations and games in workforce learning.

WHAT TO LOOK FOR IN e-LEARNING GAMES AND SIMULATIONS

☐ Goals, rules, activities, feedback, and consequences are aligned to desired learning outcomes.

☐ Sufficient structure and guidance are included to help learners reach instructional goals.

☐ Feedback to learner responses includes explanations.

☐ Explanations are incorporated between play rounds.

☐ Self-explanation questions require learners to review and reflect on choices and consequences.

☐ Visual support is included for games or simulations that rely on visualization skills.

☐ Unguided exploration is avoided.

☐ Simulation or game goal complexity and interface are managed in ways that adapt to learner prior knowledge.

☐ The game or simulation is easy to use via simple interface design and pretraining.

☐ The interface and goals make relevance to the workplace salient.

☐ Games and simulations are matched to learners who are motivated to initiate or complete learning goals in simulation or game formats.

COMING NEXT

In the previous chapters we have provided guidelines and examples based on evidence regarding a number of important issues e-learning designers and developers must address. In the next and final chapter, we summarize all of the guidelines to end our book with a comprehensive review of evidence-based principles of e-learning design.

Suggested Readings

Anderson, P.H., & Lawton, L. (2009). Business simulations and cognitive learning: Developments, desires, and future directions. *Simulation & Gaming, 40,* 193–216.

De Jong, T. (2011). Instruction based on computer simulations. In R.E. Mayer & P.A. Alexander (Eds.), *Handbook of research on learning and instruction.* New York: Routledge.

Hays, R.T. (2005). The effectiveness of instructional games: A literature review and discussion. Technical Report 2005–004. Orlando, FL: Naval Air Warfare Center Training Systems Division.

Mayer, R.E. (2008). Multimedia learning and games. In S. Tobias & D. Fletcher (Eds.), *Computer games and instruction.* Greenwich, CT: Information Age Publishers, pp. 127–147.

Mayer, R.E., & Johnson, C.I. (2010). Adding instructional features that promote learning in a game-like environment. *Journal of Educational Computing Research, 42,* 241–265.

Rieber, L.P. (2005). Multimedia learning in games, simulations, and micro-worlds. In R.E. Mayer (Ed.), *The Cambridge handbook of multimedia learning.* New York: Cambridge University Press.

CHAPTER OUTLINE

17

Applying the Guidelines

THIS CHAPTER consolidates all the guidelines we have discussed by describing how they apply or are violated in three e-learning lessons. Here you have the opportunity to consider all of the guidelines in concert as you evaluate them yourself and read our comments. In our update to this chapter, we added new guidelines to our checklist based on the new research we reported in this third edition. Finally, we reflect on our previous predictions about the future directions of e-learning for workforce learning and make some new predictions for digital learning beyond 2011.

Applying Evidence-Based Guidelines to e-Courses

The goal of our book is to help consumers and designers make e-learning decisions based on empirical research and on the psychological processes of learning. In an ideal world, e-courseware effectiveness would be based on measurement of how well and how efficiently learners achieve the learning objectives. This evaluation requires a validation process in which learners are formally tested on their skills after completing the training. In our experience, formal course validation is rare. More often, consumers and designers look at the features rather than the outcomes of an e-learning course to assess its effectiveness. We recommend that, among the features assessed, you include the research-based guidelines we have presented. We recognize that decisions about e-learning alternatives will not be based on evidence alone. A variety of factors shape e-learning decisions, including the desired outcome of the training, the culture of the organization sponsoring the training, the technological constraints of the platforms and networks available to the learners, and pragmatic issues related to politics, time, and budget. That is why you will need to adapt our guidelines to your unique training settings.

Your technological constraints and development resources will determine whether you will develop and deliver courseware with low-memory-intensive media elements like text and simple graphics or whether you can include media elements that require greater resources such as video, audio, animation, and simulations. If you are planning an Internet or intranet course, you can use collaborative facilities, including discussion boards, chats, and other social media to extend the learning environment.

Taken together, we can make a couple of general statements about the best use of media elements to present instruction to novice learners who are most susceptible to mental overload. In situations that support audio, best learning will result from *concise informal narration of relevant graphics.* In situations that preclude audio, best learning will result from *concise informal textual explanations of relevant graphics in which the text and graphic are integrated on the screen.* In all cases, learning of novices is best promoted by *dividing content into short segments,* allowing learners *to control the rate at which they access each segment.* In addition, in lessons of any complexity, the pre-training principle recommends *sequencing supporting concepts prior to the process or procedure* that is the focus of the lesson.

Table 17.1 compares the average effect sizes and number of experimental tests for the multimedia principles described in Chapters 4 through 10. Recall from Chapter 3 that effect sizes tell us the proportion of a standard

Table 17.1. Summary of Research Results from the Eight Multimedia Principles.

From Mayer, 2001, 2005a, b, c, d.

Principle	Median Effect Size	Number of Tests with Effects Greater than .5
Multimedia	1.50	9 of 9
Contiguity	1.11	8 of 8
Coherence	1.32	10 of 11
Modality	.97	20 of 21
Redundancy	.69	8 of 10
Personalization	1.30	10 of 10
Segmenting	.98	3 of 3
Pretraining	.92	7 of 7

deviation of test score improvement you gain when you apply that principle. For example, if you apply the multimedia principle, you can expect an over-all test score improvement of one and one half standard deviations greater than a comparable lesson without visuals. For our purposes, we suggest that any effect size greater than .5 indicates a practical difference worth applying. Principles with larger effect sizes based on more experimental tests indicate greater potential practical applicability than principles based on fewer experiments and/or experiments with low effect sizes.

Because the research underlying the multimedia principles was conducted in the same laboratory and used similar instructional materials (Mayer, 2001a; Mayer, 2005b, c, d), we can make these comparisons among the results. Regarding the principles summarized in Chapters 11 and beyond, however, the data comes from diverse experiments and researchers. Therefore we have not summarized the median effect sizes for those guidelines.

e-Lesson Reviews

In this section we offer three brief examples of how the most important guidelines might be applied (or violated) in e-learning courses. Two of the samples reflect a directive architecture for teaching Excel skills—one asynchronous and the other synchronous. The third sample is a simulation based on a guided discovery architecture designed to give automotive technicians practice in troubleshooting.

We do not offer these guidelines as a "rating system." We don't claim to have included all the important variables you should consider when evaluating e-learning alternatives. Furthermore, which guidelines you will apply will depend on the goal of your training and the environmental considerations mentioned previously. Instead of a rating system, we offer these guidelines as a checklist of research-based features you should consider in your e-learning design and selection decisions.

We have organized the guidelines in a checklist in Exhibit 17.1 by chapters and according to the technological constraints and training goals for e-learning as summarized in Table 17.2.

Table 17.2. Organization of Guidelines in Exhibit 17.1.

Guidelines	Apply To
1 to 23	All forms of e-learning
24 to 34	e-Learning designed to teach job tasks
35 to 40	e-Learning with collaborative facilities
41 to 44	Design of asynchronous e-learning navigation
45 to 56	e-Learning to build problem-solving skills and simulations and games

Feel free to make a copy of Exhibit 17.1 for easy reference as you review the samples to follow.

Exhibit 17.1. A Summary of e-Learning Guidelines.

Three Types of e-Learning

Type	Best Used for	Examples
Inform	Communicating information	New hire orientation Product updates
Perform Procedural Tasks	Building near-transfer skills	Computer end-user training
Perform Strategic Tasks	Building strategic skills for far transfer	Troubleshooting Sales skills

Chapters 4 through 10. Multimedia Guidelines for All Types of e-Learning

If Using Visual Mode Only:

1. Use relevant graphics and text to communicate content—Multimedia Principle.
2. Use animations to demonstrate procedures; use a series of stills to illustrate processes—Multimedia and Coherence Principles.
3. Use simpler visuals to promote understanding—Coherence Principle.
4. Use explanatory visuals that show relationships among content topics to build deeper understanding—Multimedia Principle.
5. Integrate text nearby the graphic on the screen—Contiguity Principle.
6. Allow learners to play an animation before or after reviewing a text description   Contiguity Principle.
7. Avoid covering or separating information that must be integrated for learning—Contiguity Principle.
8. Avoid irrelevant graphics, stories, and lengthy text—Coherence Principle.
9. Write in a conversational style using first and second person—Personalization Principle.
10. Use virtual coaches (agents) to deliver instructional content such as examples and hints—Personalization Principle.
11. Break content down into small topic chunks that can be accessed at the learner's preferred rate—Segmentation Principle.
12. Teach important concepts and facts prior to procedures or processes—Pretraining Principle.

13. When teaching concepts and facts prior to procedures or processes, maintain the context of the procedure or process—Pretraining Principle.

If Using Audio and Visual Modes:

14. Use relevant graphics explained by audio narration to communicate content—Multimedia and Modality Principles.
15. Maintain information the learner needs time to process in text on the screen, for example, directions to tasks, new terminology—Exception to Modality Principle.
16. Do not allow separation of visuals and audio that describes the visual—Temporal Contiguity Principle.
17. Do not present words as both onscreen text and narration when there are graphics on the screen—Redundancy Principle.
18. Avoid irrelevant videos, animations, music, stories, and lengthy narrations—Coherence Principle.
19. Script audio in a conversational style using first and second person—Personalization Principle.
20. Script virtual coaches to present instructional content such as examples and hints via audio—Modality and Personalization Principles.
21. Break content down into small topic chunks that can be accessed at the learner's preferred rate using a continue or next button—Segmentation Principle.
22. Use a continue and replay button on animations that are segmented into short logical stopping points—Segmentation Principle.
23. Teach important concepts and facts prior to procedures or processes—Pretraining Principle.

Chapters 11 and 12—Guidelines for e-Learning Designed to Teach Job Tasks
In addition to the above guidelines:

24. Transition from full worked examples to full practice assignments using fading—Worked Example Principle.
25. Insert questions next to worked steps to promote self-explanations—Self-Explanation Principle.
26. Add explanations to worked out steps in some situations—Guidance Principle.
27. Provide several diverse worked examples for far transfer skills—Varied Context Principle.
28. Promote active comparisons of varied context worked examples—Transfer Principle.

29. Provide job-relevant practice questions interspersed throughout and among the lessons—Spaced vs. Massed Practice Principle.
30. For more critical skills and knowledge, include more practice questions—Practice Principle.
31. Mix practice types throughout lessons rather than grouping similar types together—Distributed Practice Principle.
32. Provide explanatory feedback in text for correct and incorrect answers—Feedback Principle.
33. Design space for feedback to be visible close to practice answers—Contiguity Principle.
34. Avoid praise or negative comments in feedback that direct attention to the self rather than to the task—Feedback Attention Focus Principle.

Chapter 13—Guidelines for Use of Collaboration in Internet/Intranet e-Learning

35. Assign collaborative projects or problem discussions to heterogeneous small groups or pairs.
36. Use asynchronous communication tools for projects that benefit from reflection and independent research.
37. Use synchronous communication tools for projects that benefit from group synergy and social presence.
38. Make group assignments and assign participant roles that promote deeper processing.
39. Provide structured assignments such as structured controversy to minimize extraneous cognitive load.
40. Ensure social interdependence by giving a group reward based on the sum of individual achievements.

Chapter 14—Guidelines for Navigational Options—Learner Control Principles

41. Allow learners choices over topics and instructional methods such as practice when:
    • They have related prior knowledge and skills and/or good self-regulatory learning skills
    • Courses are designed primarily to be informational rather than skill-building
    • Courses are advanced rather than introductory
    • The content topics are not logically interdependent so sequence is not critical
    • The default option leads to important instructional methods such as practice

42. Limit learner choices over topics and instructional options when:
    - Learners are novice to the content, skill outcomes are important, and learners lack good self-regulatory skills
43. Use adaptive diagnostic testing strategies when:
    - Learners lack good self-regulation skills and the instructional outcomes are important
    - Learners are heterogeneous regarding background and/or instructional needs and the cost to produce tests and decision logic gives a return on investment
44. Always give learners options to progress at their own pace, replay audio or animation, review prior topics/lessons, and quit the program.

Chapter 15—Guidelines for e-Learning to Build Problem-Solving Skills

45. Use realistic job tools and cases to teach job-specific problem-solving processes.
46. Provide worked examples of experts' problem-solving actions and thoughts—Worked Examples Principle.
47. Use techniques such as a video commentary or self-explanation questions to ensure that learners attend to and process specific behaviors of expert models.
48. Provide learners with a map of their problem-solving steps to compare with an expert map—Feedback and Reflection Principles.
49. Provide sufficient guidance to ensure productive case work in whole-task lesson designs—Guidance Principle.
50. Base lessons on an analysis of actions and thoughts of expert practitioners through cognitive task analysis—Job Validity Principle.

Chapter 16—Guidelines for Games and Simulations

51. Align the goals, rules, activities, feedback, and consequences of the game or simulation to desired learning outcomes.
52. Provide structure and guidance to help learners reach instructional goals—Guidance Principle.
53. Avoid open-ended games and simulations that require unguided exploration—Guidance Principle.
54. Integrate proven instructional strategies such as explanatory feedback and self-explanation questions into games and simulations.
55. Manage goal and interface complexity to minimize extraneous cognitive load—Coherence Principle.
56. Design interface and activities to make the relevance of the activity salient.

Review of Sample 1: Asynchronous e-Lesson on Excel for Small Business

Figures 17.1 through 17.6 are screen captures from an asynchronous directive Excel lesson. The course is designed to help small business owners use spreadsheets. The course design assumes that learners are new to spreadsheets and Excel. Some of the learning objectives include:

- To identify and name cells
- To construct formulas for common calculations
- To use Excel functions

Take a look at Figure 17.1 on the topic of functions in Excel, review guidelines 1 through 23 from Exhibit 17.1, and make a list of which guidelines you feel are violated. Then look at Figures 17.2 and 17.3. Put a check beside the violations in your list that are remedied in the revisions shown in Figures 17.2 and 17.3. When you are finished, compare your analysis to ours.

Figure 17.1. What's Wrong Here?

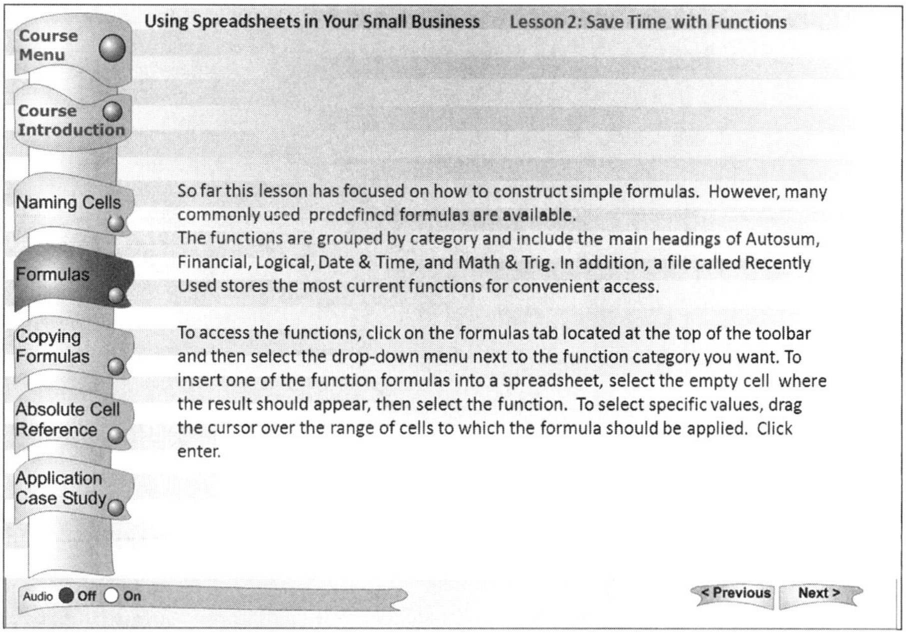

Figure 17.2. What Guidelines Are Applied in This Revision of Figure 17.1?

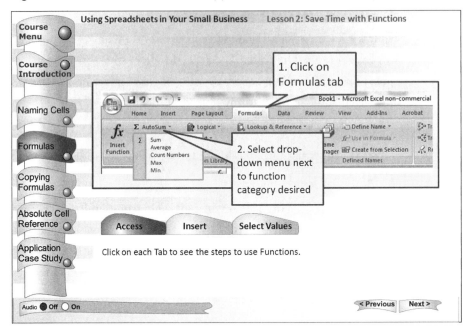

Figure 17.3. What Guidelines Are Applied in This Revision of Figure 17.1?

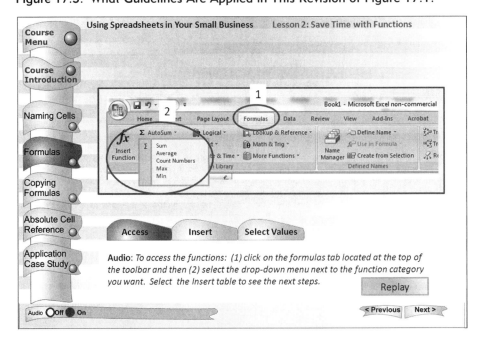

As you can see, the screen in Figure 17.1 includes a lot of text presenting an introduction to and procedure for using functions in Excel. Clearly, it violates the multimedia and coherence principles. The revision in Figure 17.2 applies the multimedia principle by incorporating a visual of the relevant tool bar as well as coherence by presenting only a small amount of text on the screen. The procedure is broken into a few steps organized with the tabs for *Access, Insert,* and *Select Values.* Steps are displayed with callouts to maximize contiguity between text and graphics. The revision in Figure 17.3 applies the modality principle by using audio rather than text to present a few steps at a time. It also helps direct attention to the relevant portion of the visual through the use of cueing circles and numbers corresponding to the steps. As with any audio, controls allow the learner to replay as desired. Since audio and text are not combined, the redundancy principle is not violated.

Next take a look at Figure 17.4 and refer to guidelines 24 through 34 from the exhibit. Make a list of ways you think this practice exercise could be improved.

Figure 17.4. What's Wrong Here?

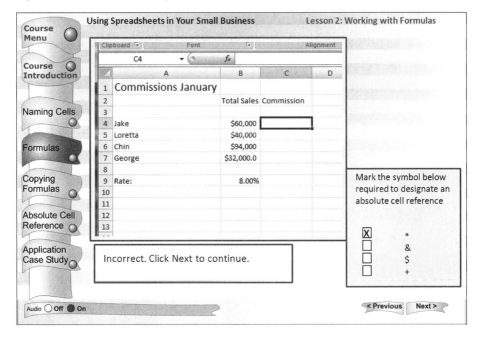

Figure 17.5. What Guidelines Are Applied in This Revision of Figure 17.4?

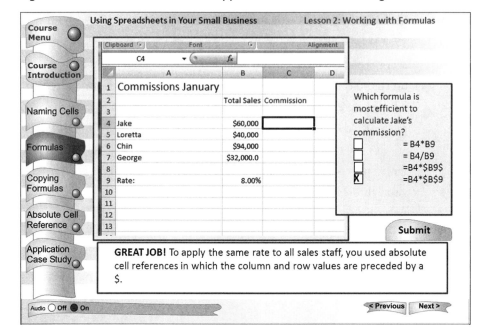

Next, look at a revision in Figure 17.5 and note which violations in your list have been remedied. Are there any further improvements you would make to the revision in Figure 17.5?

Figure 17.4 shows a practice exercise with feedback. We note the following major problems. First, the practice question is a recall or regurgitate question. While recall is needed on occasion, we recommend that for most workforce learning applications, you rely on higher-level application questions. Second, the practice directions and input boxes are separated from the spreadsheet, requiring the learner to expend mental effort integrating the two. We recommend better layout contiguity. Third, note that the feedback tells the learner that his answer is correct but does not give an explanation. Even correct answers may be the result of guessing, so providing an explanation for all response options improves learning. Some of these shortcomings are improved in Figure 17.5. The question is at an application level, is more contiguous with the spreadsheet, and explanatory feedback is provided. However, the feedback statement "Great Job" may draw attention to the ego rather than the task. Research on feedback recommends that praise be avoided.

Our final screen sample from the asynchronous Excel course in Figure 17.6 shows a worked example with a self-explanation question. The lesson has demonstrated inputting an incorrectly formatted formula in Cell E6 to calculate February profit. The self-explanation question requires the learner to evaluate the demonstration by identifying the error in the formula. This lesson uses the responses to the self-explanation questions as the basis for adaptive control. If the learner responds incorrectly to a self-explanation question, the program will provide another example illustrating a similar concept. In contrast, if the learner responds correctly, the program will branch to a more difficult question such as a partially worked example that the learner must complete or to a different topic. In Chapter 1 we identified customized training as one of the unique promises of digital learning environments. This example illustrates one technique to implement adaptive learning. See Chapter 14 to review additional alternatives.

Figure 17.6. Use of Self-Explanation Questions to Adapt Instruction.

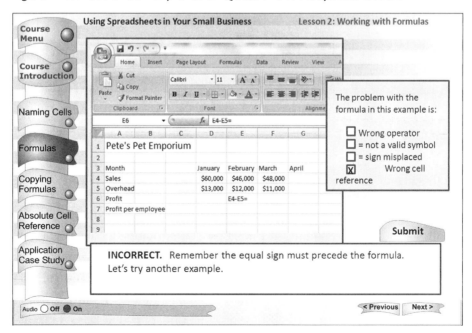

Review of Sample 2: Synchronous e-Lesson on Excel

Figures 17.7 through 17.10 are taken from a virtual classroom lesson on How to Use Excel Formulas. Synchronous e-learning has become a major player in e-learning solutions since our second edition and you can apply the principles in this book to virtual classroom lessons. The goal of the sample lesson is to teach end-user spreadsheet procedures. The lesson objectives are:

- To construct formulas with valid formatting conventions

- To perform basic calculations using formulas in Excel

Figure 17.7 shows a content outline. In applying guideline 12 based on the pretraining principle, the procedural part of the lesson is preceded by important concepts. Before learning the steps to input a formula in Excel, the lesson teaches the concept of a formula, including its formatting conventions. When teaching the procedures, the lesson applies guidelines for worked examples by starting with a full worked example accompanied by self-explanation questions and fades to a full practice exercise.

Figure 17.7. Content Outline of Synchronous Excel Lesson.

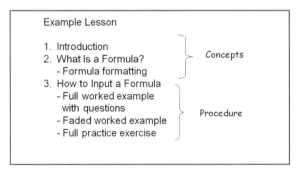

Although virtual classroom tools can project a video image of the instructor, in this lesson the instructor used audio alone. Research we reviewed in Chapter 9 showed that it was *the voice of a learning agent* —not the image— that was most instrumental in promoting learning. Since the main instructional message is contained on the whiteboard slides, the instructor decided to minimize the potential for split attention caused by a second image. The introductory slide is shown in Figure 17.8. The instructor places her photo on this slide to implement guideline 10 based on the personalization principle. In addition, the instructor builds social presence by inviting participants to use their audio as they join the session. One of the advantages of the virtual classroom is the opportunity to leverage social presence during learning through chat and audio participation of the learners.

Figure 17.8. Introduction to Synchronous Excel Lesson.

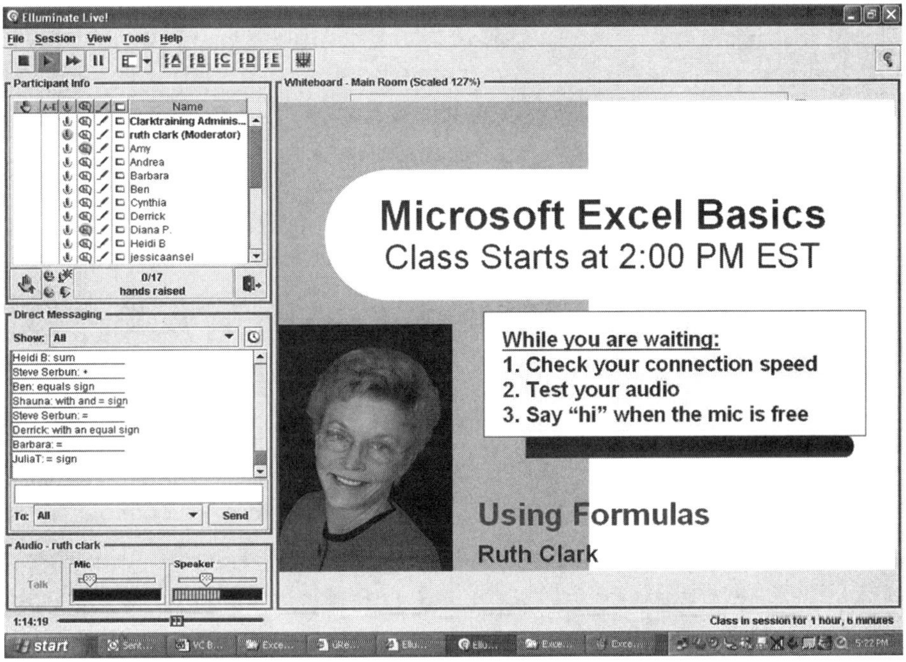

In Chapter 1 we identified customized training as one of the promises inherent in digital learning. Figure 17.9 shows a simple form of adaptive learning in which a pretest helps learners define which virtual classroom session they should attend. As we saw in Figure 17.6, asynchronous e-learning can dynamically tailor training to individual needs and progress. However, virtual classrooms are instructor-led and therefore offer fewer opportunities for dynamic learner control. A pretest administered prior to the event should help ensure a good match between learner prior knowledge and lesson objectives.

Figure 17.9. Adaptive Control in Synchronous Excel Lesson.

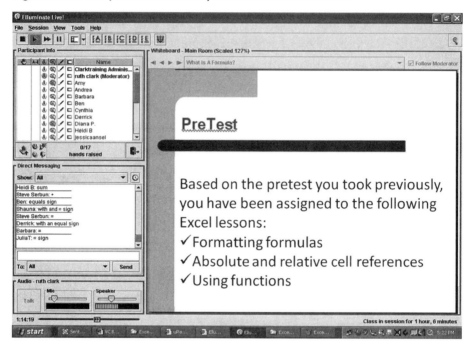

Figure 17.10 illustrates guidance in the form of example fading and memory support in the virtual classroom. The spreadsheet window in the center of the virtual classroom interface is being projected to the learners through application sharing. The instructor has completed the first step in the procedure by typing the equal sign and the first cell reference into the correct spreadsheet cell. The instructor asks participants to finish the example by typing the rest of the formula in the chat window. Note that in applying guideline 15, the directions are displayed on the screen in text because participants need to refer to them as they work the exercise. Additional memory support is provided in the left-hand box on the spreadsheet, which displays the valid operator syntax. The amount of guidance in this example should be faded as the lesson progresses.

Figure 17.10. Guidance from Faded Worked Example and Memory Support.
From Clark and Kwinn, 2007.

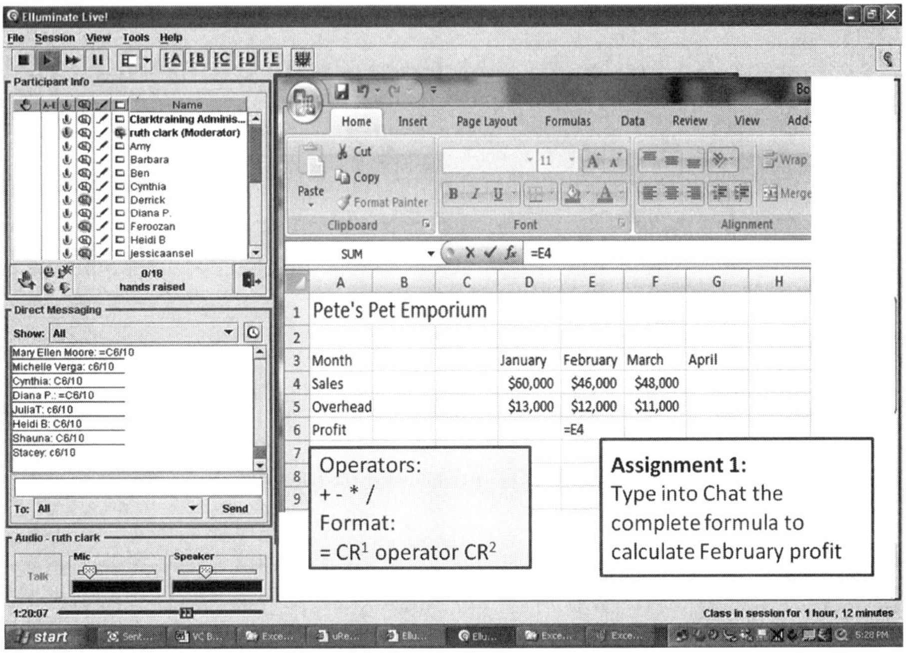

From this brief look at some virtual classroom samples, you can see that just about all of the principles we describe in the book apply. Because the class proceeds under instructor rather than learner control, it is especially critical to apply all guidelines that reduce extraneous mental load. Lesson designers should create effective visuals to project on the whiteboard that will be described verbally by the instructor applying the multimedia and modality principles. The instructor should use a conversational tone and language and incorporate participant audio to apply personalization. Skill-building classes can apply all of our guidelines for faded worked examples and effective practice exercises. The presence of multiple participants in the virtual sessions lends itself to collaborative projects. Most virtual classroom tools offer breakout rooms in which small teams can carry out assignments. Apply guidelines 35 through 40 as you plan collaborative activities. As with asynchronous e-learning, instructors should minimize irrelevant visual effects, stories, themes, or audio in accordance with the coherence principle.

Review of Sample 3: Automotive Troubleshooting Simulation

In Chapter 1 we identified the opportunity to accelerate expertise as one of the unique promises of digital learning environments. Figures 17.11 through 17.14 are from a simulation designed to give experienced automotive technicians compressed opportunities to practice unusual faults. The learner starts with a point of view perspective in the auto shop that includes all common troubleshooting tools. In Figure 17.11 you see the trigger event for the case in the form of a work order. Typical of guided discovery learning environments, the learner is free to use various tools in the shop to diagnose and

---

Figure 17.11. Work Order Triggers Automotive Troubleshooting Case.
With Permission from Raytheon Professional Services.

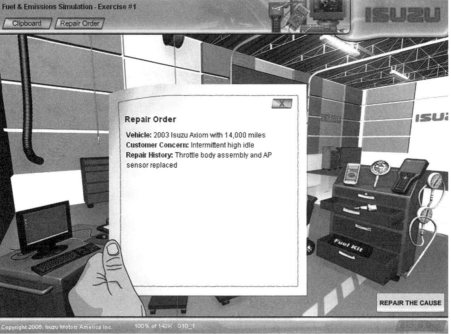

repair the failure. There are several sources of guidance. First, as you can see in Figure 17.12, a telephone offers technical advice. In addition, to the left of the telephone the computer opens to the actual reference system the technician uses on the job. Third, if the learner clicks on a tool that is irrelevant to the current problem, the system responds that the test is not relevant to this problem. This response constrains the environment in order to guide learners to the specific tests relevant to the case.

If the learner selects an incorrect failure and repair action, the high idle shown in Figure 17.13 shows the learner that the failure has not been resolved. Once the case is correctly resolved, the learner receives feedback and an opportunity for reflection by comparing his or her own activities in the right window with those of an expert shown in the left window in Figure 17.14.

Figure 17.12. Telephone and Computer Offer Technical Guidance During Troubleshooting Case.

With Permission from Raytheon Professional Services.

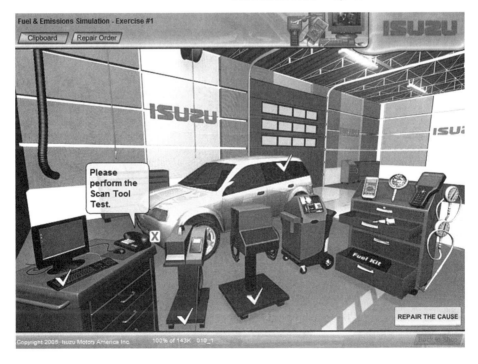

Figure 17.13. Continuing High Idle Shows that the Correct Diagnosis Was Not Selected.

With Permission from Raytheon Professional Services.

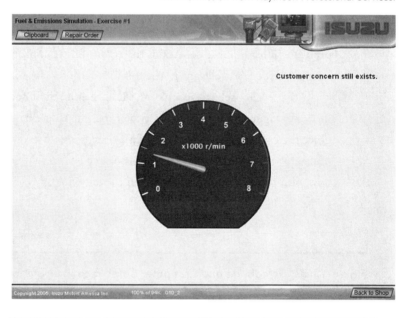

Figure 17.14. End of Troubleshooting Simulation Allows Student-Expert Solution Comparisons.

With Permission from Raytheon Professional Services.

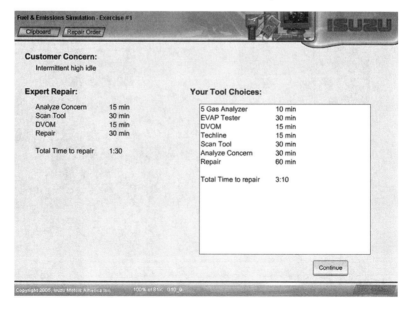

This lesson applies guidelines 45 through 56 applicable to e-learning to build problem-solving skills and to simulations. By situating the learner in a typical automotive shop, she has virtual access to the tools and resources she would have on the job. The goal, rules, activities, and feedback of the simulation are all aligned to the desired learning outcome, that is, to promote an efficient troubleshooting process to identify and correct the failure. Learners can see a map of their steps and compare it with an expert approach. Thus the lesson focuses not only on finding the correct answer but on how the answer is derived. There are several sources of structure and guidance available congruent with guideline 52.

Because the structure of the case study is guided discovery, it emphasizes learning during problem solving. Regarding navigation, there is a high level of learner control. Overall, we feel this course offers a good model for simulation environments designed for workers with relevant background knowledge and experience.

Reflections on Past Predictions

What differences will we see in e-learning developed for organizational training in the next few years? In the following section, we review our predictions from our first edition followed by our observations ten years later.

Because e-learning developed for workers in organizations is an expensive commitment, we had predicted more examples of online training that apply guidelines proven to lead to return on investment. Specifically, we made the following predictions:

- Fewer Las Vegas–style courses that depress learning by over-use of glitz and games. Instead, the power of technology will be leveraged more effectively to support acquisition and transfer of job-related skills.

- More problem-centered designs that use job-realistic problems in the start of a lesson or course to establish relevance, in the body of the lesson to help learners build related knowledge and skills, and at the end of the lesson to provide practice and assessment opportunities.

- More creative ways to blend computer technology with other delivery media so that the features of a given medium are best used to support ongoing job-relevant skill requirements.

- More problem-centered designs that use job-realistic problems in the start of a lesson or course to establish relevance, in the body of the lesson to help learners build related knowledge and skills, and at the end of the lesson to provide practice and assessment opportunities.

Over the past ten years we have seen a gradual increase in the proportion of courses delivered digitally. Ten years ago only a little over one-tenth of all learning was delivered via digital devices. By 2010 digital learning accounted for well over one-third of all workforce delivery. This expansion reflects (1) cost savings during a time of economic retraction, (2) more pervasive technology in terms of bandwidth, digital devices, and authoring systems, and (3) growing familiarity with and reliance on technology in the workforce. Although we predict that the proportion of electronic delivery will continue to grow with the expansion of training on hand-held devices, at the same time face-to-face learning will continue to account for a substantial proportion of instructional delivery. Better learning through distributed practice will be supported by combinations of face-to-face and digital learning. e-Learning implementations will continue to expand beyond training to include knowledge management resources, including traditional online references, resources, and social media workers can access during job task completion. For example, if a salesperson is writing a first proposal, the company website will offer industry-specific information, sample proposal templates, social networks to mentors, and recorded mini lessons on proposal success.

The growth of games for learning continues to leave a residue of Las Vegas courseware—primarily because we are still learning how to design and develop games that are simultaneously instructive and entertaining. We predict games will become more effective instructionally as we accumulate and apply a growing research base on serious games.

In the past five years, we have seen many more examples of simulations and scenario-based courses designed to support problem-solving skills. This type of courseware will continue to expand as instructional professionals learn to design and develop effective whole-task learning environments.

Beyond 2011

Looking forward, we predict that the promise of digital technology will be realized in the following ways:

- e-Learning will increasingly make use of the unique technological features that can support simulations and guided opportunities to learn from them. Whole-task learning will be used to accelerate expertise through opportunities to practice job tasks that occur infrequently or are impractical in real work settings. The current receptive lesson designs that use text, audio, and graphics to present content will survive. However, these will be supplemented by a growing body of e-courses that encourage the building of deeper mental models and problem-solving skills.

- e-Learning will increasingly be used to make invisible processes and events visible. Learners will view maps of their own problem-solving activities and rationale and compare them to expert maps and rationale. Additionally, learners will be able to "see" and "experience" invisible processes such as how equipment works or what a customer is thinking. In three-dimensional worlds, learners will be able to explore molecular structures or the circulatory system. In simulations, learners will experience the results of their actions to test hypotheses or view how an invisible world might respond in order to infer its properties.

- Collaborative e-learning features will be used more extensively and more effectively as we learn to harness the Web 2.0 effectively. Teams of learners will work synchronously and asynchronously to solve case problems and contribute to repositories of ongoing corporate lessons learned about issues relevant to a specific industry.

- The use of hand-held devices will expand and offer a growing opportunity for digital learning and reference.

- Virtual world technologies will become easier to author and more end-user friendly. At the same time, instructional professionals will leverage these environments for learning goals that benefit from three-dimensional interactions among multiple workers and continue to use more traditional courseware for instructional goals that do not benefit from three-dimensional representations.

- Questions such as "Are games (or graphics or you-name-it) good for learning?" will be replaced by questions that focus on the features of games (or graphics or you-name-it) that will best achieve your specific instructional goals for a specific group of learners.

- Customized training through adaptive learning will become more prevalent with authoring systems that incorporate adaptive techniques into their infrastructure. Adaptive learning will require a resource investment to design and develop interactions that are predictive of learning levels acquired. However, a return on investment will be realized for audiences with widely distributed background knowledge and skills.

In Conclusion

We began this book in Chapter 1 with a summary of the unique promises and pitfalls inherent in digital technology for instruction. We hope that the guidelines and evidence that we have described in this third edition will be a resource that minimizes the pitfalls and optimizes the promise of multimedia learning in your instructional environments.

REFERENCES

Albanese, M.A. (2010). Problem-based learning. In W.B. Jeffries & K.N. Huggett (Eds.), *An introduction to medical teaching*. New York: Springer.

Alexander, P.A., & Winne, P.H. (Eds.). (2006). *Handbook of educational psychology* (2nd ed.). Mahwah, NJ: Lawrence Erlbaum Associates.

Anderson, P.H., & Lawton, L. (2009). Business simulations and cognitive learning: Developments, desires, and future directions. *Simulation & Gaming, 40,* 193–216.

ASTD. (2010). *State of the industry report*. Alexandria, VA: American Society for Training and Development.

Atkinson, R.K. (2000). Optimizing learning from examples using animated pedagogical agents. *Journal of Educational Psychology, 94,* 416–427.

Atkinson, R.K., & Derry, S. J. (2002). Computer-based examples designed to encourage optimal example processing: A study examining the impact of sequentially presented, subgoal-oriented worked examples. In B. Fishman & S.E. O'Connor-Divelbill (Eds.), *Proceedings of the Fourth International Conference of Learning Sciences* (pp. 132–133). Mahwah, NJ: Lawrence Erlbaum Associates.

Atkinson, R.K., Mayer, R.E., & Merrill, M.M. (2005). Fostering social agency in multimedia learning: Examining the impact of an animated agent's voice. *Contemporary Educational Psychology, 30,* 117–139.

Atkinson, R.K., Renkl, A., & Merrill, M.M. (2003). Transitioning from studying examples to solving problems: Effects of self-explanation prompts and fading worked out steps. *Journal of Educational Psychology, 95*(4), 774–783.

Ayres, P., Marcus, N., Chan, C., & Qian, N. (2009). Learning hand manipulative tasks: When instructional animations are superior to equivalent static representation. *Computers in Human Behavior, 25,* 348–353.

Ayres, P., & Sweller, J. (2005). The split-attention principle in multimedia learning. In R.E. Mayer (Ed.), *The Cambridge handbook of multimedia learning* (pp. 135–146). New York: Cambridge University Press.

Baggett, P. (1984). Role of temporal overlap of visual and auditory material in forming dual media associations. *Journal of Educational Psychology, 76,* 408–417.

Baggett, P., & Ehrenfeucht, A. (1983). Encoding and retaining information in the visuals and verbals of an educational movie. *Educational Communications and Technology Journal, 31,* 23–32.

Bahrick, H.P. (1987). Retention of Spanish vocabulary over 8 years. *Journal of Experimental Psychology: Learning, Memory, and Cognition, 13,* 344–349.

Beck, I., McKeown, M.G., Sandora, C., Kucan, L., & Worthy, J. (1996). Questioning the author: A year-long classroom implementation to engage students in text. *Elementary School Journal, 96,* 385–414.

Belanich, J, Sibley, D.E., & Orvis, K.L. (2004). Instructional characteristics and motivational features of a PC-based game. Washington, DC: U.S. Army Research Institute for the Behavioral and Social Sciences, Research Report 1822.

Bernard, R.M., Abrami, P.C., Lou, Y., Borokhovski, E., Wade, A., Wozney, L., Wallet, P.A., Fixet, M., & Huant, B. (2004). How does distance education compare with classroom instruction? A meta-analysis of the empirical literature. *Review of Educational Research, 74,* 379–439.

Betrancourt, M. (2005). The animation and interactivity principles in multimedia learning. In R.E. Mayer (Ed.), *The Cambridge handbook of multimedia learning* (pp. 287–296). New York: Cambridge University Press.

Bishop, M.J., Amankwatia, T.B., & Cates, W.M. (2008). Sound's use in instructional software to enhance learning: A theory-to-practice content analysis. *Educational Technology Research and Development, 56,* 467–486.

Brown, P., & Levinson, S.C. (1987). *Politeness: Some universals in language usage.* New York: Cambridge University Press.

Butcher, K.R. (2006). Learning from text and diagrams: Promoting mental model development and inference generation. *Journal of Educational Psychology*, *98,* 182–197.

Campbell, J., & Stasser, G. (2006). The influence of time and task demonstrability on decision making in computer-mediated and face-to-face groups. *Small Group Research*, *37*(3), 271–294.

Carroll, J.M. (2000). *Making use: Scenario-based design of human-computer interactions.* Cambridge, MA: MIT Press.

Carson, B. (2009). The effectiveness of learning games in an on-boarding program at Sun Microsystems: An evaluation. Downloaded December 2010 from http://www.clsllc.com/8080/brandon/documents/The%20Effectiveness%20of%20Learning%20Games%20for%20Onboarding.pdf.

Cassell, J., Sullivan, J., Prevost, S., & Churchill, E. (2000). *Embodied conversational agents.* Cambridge, MA: MIT Press.

Chandler, P., & Sweller, J. (1991). Cognitive load theory and the format of instruction. *Cognition and Instruction*, *8,* 293–332.

ChanLin, L. (1998). Animation to teach students of different knowledge levels. *Journal of Instructional Psychology*, *25,* 166–175.

Chatham, R.E (2009). The 20th-century revolution in military training. In K. A. Ericsson (Ed.), *Development of professional expertise.* New York: Cambridge University Press.

Chi, M.T.H, Bassok, M., Lewis, M.W., Reimann, P., & Glaser, R. (1989). Self-explanations: How students study and use examples in learning to solve problems. *Cognitive Science, 13*, 145–182.

Chi, M.T. H., Roy, M., & Hausmann, R.G.M. (2008). Observing tutorial dialogues collaboratively: Insights about human tutoring effectiveness from vicarious learning. *Cognitive Science*, *32,* 301–341.

Clark, R.C. (2008). *Building expertise: Cognitive methods for training and performance improvement* (2nd ed.). San Francisco: Pfeiffer.

Clark, R.C. (2008). *Developing technical training* (3rd ed.). San Francisco: Pfeiffer.

Clark, R.C. (2010). *Evidence-based training methods.* Alexandria, VA: ASTD Press.

Clark, R.C., & Kwinn, A. (2007). *The new virtual classroom.* San Francisco: Pfeiffer.

Clark, R.C., & Lyons, C. (2011). *Graphics for learning* (2nd ed.). San Francisco: Pfeiffer.

Clark, R.C., & Mayer, R.E. (2008). Learning by viewing versus learning by doing: Evidence-based guidelines for principled learning environments. *Performance Improvement, 47,* 5–13.

Clark, R.C., Nguyen, F., & Sweller, J. (2006). *Efficiency in learning.* San Francisco: Pfeiffer.

Clark, R.C., & Nguyen, F. (2008). Behavioral, cognitive, and technological models for performance improvement. In J.M. Spector, M.D. Merrill, J.J.G. van Merrienboer, & M.P. Driscoll (Eds.), *Handbook of research on educational communications and technology* (3rd ed.). Mahwah, NJ: Lawrence Erlbaum Associates.

Clark, R.E. (1994). Media will never influence learning. *Educational Technology Research and Development, 42*(2), 21–30.

Cohen, J. (1988). *Statistical power analysis for the behavioral sciences* (2nd ed.). Mahwah, NJ: Lawrence Erlbaum Associates.

Corbalan, G., Kester, L., & van Merrienboer, J.J.G. (2008). Selecting learning tasks: Effects of adaptation and shared control on learning efficiency and task involvement. *Contemporary Educational Psychology, 33,* 733–756.

Corbalan, G., Paas, F.G.W.C., & Cuypers, H. (2010). Computer-based feedback in linear algebra: Effects on transfer performance and motivation. *Computers & Education, 55,* 692–703.

Craig, S.D., Chi, M.T.H., & VanLehn, K. (2009). Improving classroom learning by collaboratively observing human tutoring videos while problem solving. *Journal of Educational Psychology, 111,* 779–789.

Craig, S.D., Gholson, B., & Driscoll, D.M. (2002). Animated pedagogical agents in multimedia learning environments: Effects of agent properties, picture features, and redundancy. *Journal of Educational Psychology, 94,* 428–434.

Crandall, B., Klein, G., & Hoffman, R.R. (2006). *Working minds.* Cambridge, MA: MIT Press.

Crossman, E.R.F.W. (1959). A theory of the acquisition of speed skill. *Ergonomics, 2,* 153–166.

Cuban, L. (1986). Teachers and machines: *The classroom use of technology since 1920.* New York: Teachers College Press.

De Jong, T. (2011). Instruction based on computer simulations. In R.E. Mayer & P.A. Alexander (Eds.), *Handbook of research on learning and instruction.* New York: Routledge.

De Koning, B.B., Tabbers, H.K., Rikers, R.M.J.P., & Paas, F.G.W.C., (2007). Attention cueing as a means to enhance learning from an animation. *Applied Cognitive Psychology*, pp. 731–746.

DeRouin, R.E., Fritzsche, B.A., & Salas, E. (2004). Optimizing e-learning: Research-based guidelines for learner-controlled training. *Human Resource Management, 43*(2–3), 147–162.

De Wever, B., Van Winckel, M., & Valcke, M. (2008). Discussing patient management online: The impact of roles on knowledge construction for students interning at the paediatric ward. *Advances in Health Sciences Education, 13,* 25–42.

Dewey, J. (1913). *Interest and effort in education.* Cambridge, MA: Houghton Mifflin.

Dillon, A., & Gabbard, R. (1998). Hypermedia as an educational technology: A review of the quantitative research literature on learner comprehension, control, and style. *Educational Psychology, 81,* 240–246.

Druckman, D., & Bjork, R.A. (1991). *In the mind's eye: Enhancing human performance.* Washington, DC: National Academy Press.

Duncker, K. (1945). On problem solving. *Psychological Monographs, 58,* 270.

Ebbinghaus, N. (1913). *Memory* (N.R. Ruger & C.E. Bussenius, Trans.). New York: Teacher's College. (Original work published 1885).

Entertainment Software Association. (2010). Video games in the 21st century. Accessed from www.theesa.com/ September 2010.

Erhel, S., & Jamet, E. (2006). Using pop-up windows to improve multimedia learning. *Journal of Computer Assisted Learning, 22*, 137–147.

Ericsson, K.A. (2006). The influence of experience and deliberate practice on the development of superior expert performance. In K.A. Ericsson, N. Charness, P.J. Feltovich, & R.R. Hoffman (Eds.), *The Cambridge handbook of expertise and expert performance.* New York: Cambridge University Press.

Eva, K.W., Cunnington, J.P.W., Reiter, H.I., Keane, D.R., & Norman, G.R. (2004). How can I know what I don't know? Poor self-assessment in a well-defined domain. *Advances in Health Sciences Education, 9,* 211–224.

Fletcher, J.D., & Tobias, S. (2005). The multimedia principle. In R.E. Mayer (Ed.), *The Cambridge handbook of multimedia learning* (pp. 117–134). New York: Cambridge University Press.

Florax, M., & Ploetzner, R. (2010). What contributes to the split-attention effect? Role of text segmentation, picture labeling, and spatial proximity. *Learning and Instruction, 20,* 216–224.

Fonseca, B.A., & Chi, M.T.H. (2011). Instruction based on self-explanation. In R.E. Mayer & P.A. Alexander (Eds.), *Handbook of research on learning and instruction.* New York: Routledge.

Garner, R., Gillingham, M., & White, C. (1989). Effects of seductive details on macroprocessing and microprocessing in adults and children. *Cognition and Instruction, 6,* 41–57.

Gay, G. (1986). Interaction of learner control and prior understanding in computer-assisted video instruction. *Journal of Educational Psychology, 78*(3), 225–227.

Gentner, D., Loewenstein, J., & Thompson, L. (2003). Learning and transfer: A general role for analogical encoding. *Journal of Educational Psychology, 95*(2), 393–408.

Gick, M.L., & Holyoak, K.J. (1980). Analogical problem solving. *Cognitive Psychology, 12,* 306–355.

Ginns, P. (2005). Integrating information: A meta-analysis of spatial contiguity and temporal contiguity effects. *Learning and Instruction, 16,* 511–525.

Ginns, P. (2005). Meta-analysis of the modality effect. *Learning and Instruction, 15,* 313–331.

Glenberg, A.M., Sanocki, T., Epstein, W., & Morris, C. (1987). Enhancing calibration of comprehension. *Journal of Experimental Psychology: General, 116*(2), 119–136.

Gosen, J., & Washbush, J. (2004). A review of scholarship on assessing experiential learning effectiveness. *Simulation and Gaming, 35*(2), 270–293.

Graesser, A.C., Jeon, M., & Duffy, D. (2008). Agent technologies designed to facilitate interactive knowledge construction. *Discourse Processes, 45,* 298–322.

Hall, W.E., & Cushing, J.R. (1947). The relative value of three methods of presenting learning material. *Journal of Psychology,* 24, 57–62.

Halpern, D.F., Graesser, A., & Hakel, M. (2007). *25 Learning principles to guide pedagogy and the design of learning environments.* Washington, DC: Association of Psychological Science Taskforce on Lifelong Learning at Work and at Home.

Hannafin, R.D., & Vermillion, J.R. (2008). Technology in the classroom. In T.L. Good (Ed.), *21st century education: A reference handbook* (Vol. 2, pp. 209–218). Thousand Oaks, CA: Sage.

Harp, S.F., & Mayer, R.E. (1997). The role of interest in learning from scientific text and illustrations: On the distinction between emotional interest and cognitive interest. *Journal of Educational Psychology, 89,* 92–102.

Harp, S.F., & Mayer, R.E. (1998). How seductive details do their damage: A theory of cognitive interest in science learning. *Journal of Educational Psychology, 90,* 414–434.

Harskamp, E.G., Mayer, R.E., & Suhre, C. (2007). Does the modality principle for multimedia learning apply to science classrooms? *Learning and Instruction, 17,* 465–477.

Hattie, J. (2009). *Visible learning: A synthesis of over 800 meta-analyses relating to achievement.* New York: Routledge.

Hattie, J., & Gan, M. (2011). Instruction based on feedback. In R.E. Mayer & P.A. Alexander (Eds.), *Handbook of research on learning and instruction.* New York: Routledge.

Hays, R.T. (2005). The effectiveness of instructional games: A literature review and discussion. *Technical Report 2005–004.* Washington, DC: Naval Air Warfare Center Training Systems Division.

Hegarty. M., Carpenter, P.A., & Just, M.A. (1996). Diagrams in the comprehension of scientific texts. In R. Barr, M.L. Kamil, P. Mosenthal, & P.D. Pearson (Eds.), *Handbook of reading research* (Vol. II; pp. 641–668). Mahwah, NJ: Lawrence Erlbaum Associates.

Hegarty, M., Kriz, S., & Cate, C. (2003). The role of mental animations and external animations in understanding mechanical systems. *Cognition and Instruction, 21,* 325–360.

Hegarty, M. (2004). Dynamic visualizations and learning: Getting to the difficult questions. *Learning and Instruction, 14,* 343–351.

Hidi, S., & Renninger, K.A. (2006). The four-phase model of interest development. *Educational Psychologist, 41,* 111–127.

Hilbert, T., Renkl, A., Kessler, S., & Reiss, K. (2008). Learning to prove in geometry: Learning from heuristic examples and how it can be supported. *Learning and Instruction, 18,* 54–65.

Holzinger, A., Kickmeier-Rust, M.D., Wassertheurer, S., & Hessinger, M. (2009). Learning performance with interactive simulations in medical education: Lessons learned form results of learning complex physiological models with the Haemodynamics Simulator. *Computers & Education, 52,* 292–301.

Holsanova, J., Holmberg, N., & Holmqvist, K. (2009). Reading information graphics: The role of spatial contiguity and dual attention guidance. *Applied Cognitive Psychology, 23,* 1215–1226.

Industry Report. (2006). *Training, 38*(12), 20–32. Accessed December 8, 2006, from www.Trainingmag.com.

Inglese, T., Mayer, R.E., & Rigotti, F. (2007). Using audiovisual TV interviews to create visible authors that reduce the learning gap between native and non-native speakers. *Learning and Instruction, 17*, 67–77.

Issenberg, S.B., McGaghie, W.C., Petrusa, E.R., Gordon, D.L., & Scalese, R.J. (2005). Features and uses of high fidelity medical simulations that lead to effective learning: A BEME systematic review. *Medical Teacher, 27*(1), 10–29.

Jamet, E., & Le Bohec, O. (2007). The effect of redundant text in multimedia instruction. *Contemporary Educational Psychology, 32,* 588–598.

Johnson, D.W., Johnson, R.T., & Smith, K. (2007). The state of cooperative learning in postsecondary and professional settings. *Educational Psychology Review, 19,* 15–29.

Johnson, D.W., & Johnson, R.T. (1992). *Creative controversy: Intellectual challenge in the classroom.* Edina, MN.: Interaction Book Company.

Jonassen, D.H., Lee, C.B., Yang, C-C., & Laffey, J. (2005). The collaboration principle in multimedia learning. In R.E. Mayer (Ed.), *The Cambridge handbook of multimedia learning.* New York: Cambridge University Press.

Johnson, C.I., & Mayer, R.E. (2010). Applying the self-explanation principle to multimedia learning in a computer-based game-like environment. *Computers in Human Behavior, 26*, 1246–1252.

Ju, E., & Wagner, C. (1997). Personal computer adventure games: Their structure, principles, and applicability for training. *The DATA BASE for Advances in Information Systems, 28*(2), 78–92.

Kalyuga, S. (2005). Prior knowledge principle in multimedia learning. In R.E. Mayer (Ed.), *The Cambridge handbook of multimedia learning* (pp. 325–337). New York: Cambridge University Press.

Kalyuga, S. (2007). Expertise reversal effect and its implications for learner-tailored instruction. *Educational Psychology Review, 19*, 509–539.

Kalyuga, S. (2008). When less is more in cognitive diagnosis: A rapid online method for diagnosing learner task-specific expertise. *Journal of Educational Psychology, 100,* 603–612.

Kalyuga, S., Ayres, P., Chandler, P., & Sweller, J. (2003). Expertise reversal effect. *Educational Psychologist, 38,* 23–31.

Kalyuga, S., Chandler, P., & Sweller, J. (1998). Levels of expertise and instructional design. *Human Factors, 40,* 1–17.

Kalyuga, S., Chandler, P., & Sweller, J. (1999). Managing split attention and redundancy in multimedia instruction. *Applied Cognitive Psychology, 13,* 351–372.

Kalyuga, S., Chandler, P., & Sweller, J. (2000). Incorporating learner experience into the design of multimedia instruction. *Journal of Educational Psychology, 92,* 126–136.

Kalyuga, S., Chandler, P., & Sweller, J. (2004). When redundant on-screen text in multimedia technical instruction can interfere with learning. *Human Factors, 46,* 567–581.

Kartel, G. (2010). Does language matter in multimedia learning? Personalization principle revised. *Journal of Educational Psychology, 102,* 615–624.

Kellogg, R.T., & Whiteford, A.P. (2009). Training advanced writing skills: The case for deliberate practice. *Educational Psychologist, 44,* 250–266.

Knez, I., & Hygge, S. (2002). Irrelevant speech and indoor lighting: Effects of cognitive performance and self-reported affect. *Applied Cognitive Psychology, 15,* 709–718.

Kester, L., Kirschner, P.A., & Van Merrienboer, J.J.G. (2006). Just-in-time information presentation: Improving learning a troubleshooting skill. *Contemporary Educational Psychology,* 31, 167–185.

Kiewra, K.A., & Creswell, J.W. (2000). Conversations with three highly productive educational psychologists: Richard Anderson, Richard Mayer, and Michael Pressley. *Educational Psychology Review, 12*(1), 135–159.

Kirschner, F., Paas, F.G.W.C., & Kirschner, P.A. (2009). A cognitive load approach to collaborative learning: United brains for complex tasks. *Educational Psychology Review, 21,* 31–42.

Kirschner, P., Strijbos, J., Kreijns, K., & Beers, P.J. (2004). Designing electronic collaborative learning environments. *Educational Technology Research and Development, 52*(3), 47–66.

Kluger, A.N., & DeNisi, A. (1996). The effects of feedback interventions on performance: A historical review, a meta-analysis, and a preliminary feedback intervention theory. *Psychological Bulletin, 119,* 254–284.

Koh, G.C.H., Khoo, H.E., Wong, M.L., & Koh, D. (2008). The effects of problem-based learning during medical school on physician competency: a systematic review. *Canadian Medical Association Journal, 178,* 34–41.

Krause, U.M., Stark, R., & Mandl, H. (2009). The effects of cooperative learning and feedback on e-learning in statistics. *Learning and Instruction, 19,* 158–170.

Lajoie, S.P. (2009). Developing professional expertise with a cognitive apprenticeship model: Examples from avionics and medicine. In K.A. Ericsson (Ed.), *Development of professional expertise.* New York: Cambridge University Press.

Lajoie, S.P., Azevedo, R., & Fleiszer, D.M. (1998). Cognitive tools for assessment and learning in a high information flow environment. *Journal of Educational Computing Research, 18,* 205–235.

Lazonder, A.W., Hagemans, M.G., & De Jong, T. (2010). Offering and discovering domain information in simulation-based inquiry learning. *Learning and Instruction, 20,* 511–520.

Lee, H., Plass, J.L., & Homer, B.C. (2006). Optimizing cognitive load for learning from computer-based science simulations. *Journal of Educational Psychology, 98*(4), 902–913.

Lee, S., & Lee, Y.H.K. (1991). Effects of learner-control versus program control strategies on computer-aided learning of chemistry problems: For acquisition or review? *Journal of Educational Psychology, 83,* 491–498.

LeFevre, J.A., & Dixon, P. (1986). Do written instructions need examples? *Cognition and Instruction, 3,* 1–30.

Leahy, W., Chandler, P., & Sweller, J. (2003). When auditory presentations should and should not be a component of multimedia instruction. *Applied Cognitive Psychology, 17,* 401–418.

Lehman, S., Schraw, G., McCrudden, M.T., & Hartley, K. (2007). Processing and recall of seductive details in scientific text. *Contemporary Educational Psychology*, *32,* 569–587.

Lester, J.C., Towns, S.G., Callaway, C.B., Voerman, J.L., & Fitzgerald, P.J. (2000). Deictic and emotive communication in animated pedagogical agents. In J. Cassell, J. Sullivan, S. Prevost, & E. Churchill (Eds.), *Embodied conversational agents* (pp. 123–154). Cambridge, MA: MIT Press.

Lim, J., Reiser, R.A., & Olina, Z. (2009). The effects of part-task and whole-task instructional approaches on acquisition and transfer of a complex cognitive skill. *Educational Technology Research & Development*, *57,* 61–77.

Linek, S.B., Gerjets, P., & Scheiter, K. (2010). The speaker/gender effect: Does the speaker's gender matter when presenting auditory text in multimedia messages? *Instructional Science, 38*, 503–521.

Lorch, R.F., Jr., Lorch, E.P., Ritchey, K., McGovern, L., & Coleman, D. (2001). Effects of headings on text summarization. *Contemporary Educational Psychology, 26,* 171–191.

Lou, Y., Abrami, P.C., & d'Apollonia, S. (2001). Small group and individual learning with technology: A meta-analysis. *Review of Educational Research*, *71, 449–521.

Louwerse, M.M., Graesser, A.C., McNamara, D.S., & Lu, S. (2009). Embodied conversational agents as conversational partners. *Applied Cognitive Psychology*, *23*(9), 1244–1255.

Low, R., & Sweller, J. (2005). The modality effect in multimedia learning. In R.E. Mayer (Ed.), *The Cambridge handbook of multimedia learning* (pp. 147–158). New York: Cambridge University Press.

Lusk, M.M., & Atkinson, R.K. (2007). Animated pedagogical agents: Does the degree of embodiment impact learning from static or animated worked examples? *Applied Cognitive Psychology, 21*, 747–764.

Malone, T.W., & Lepper, M.R. (1987). Making learning fun: A taxonomy of intrinsic motivations for learning. In R.E. Snow & M.J. Farr (Eds.), *Aptitude, learning and instruction.* Mahwah, NJ: Lawrence Erlbaum Associates.

Mautone, P.D., & Mayer, R.E. (2001). Signaling as a cognitive guide in multimedia learning. *Journal of Educational Psychology, 81,* 240–246.

Mayer, R.E. (1989a). Models for understanding. *Review of Educational Research,* 59, 43–64.

Mayer, R.E. (1989b). Systematic thinking fostered by illustrations in scientific text. *Journal of Educational Psychology, 81,* 240–246.

Mayer, R.E. (1993). Illustrations that instruct. In R. Glaser (Ed.), *Advances in instructional psychology* (Vol. 4; pp. 253–284). Mahwah, NJ: Lawrence Erlbaum Associates.

Mayer, R.E. (2001a). *Multimedia learning.* New York: Cambridge University Press.

Mayer, R.E. (2001b). Cognitive constraints on multimedia learning: When presenting more material results in less learning. *Journal of Educational Psychology, 93,* 187–198.

Mayer, R.E. (2003). *Learning and instruction.* Upper Saddle River, NJ: Merrill Prentice Hall.

Mayer, R.E. (2004). Should there be a three-strikes rule against pure discovery learning: The case for guided methods of instruction. *American Psychologist, 59*(1), 14–19.

Mayer, R.E. (Ed.). (2005a). *The Cambridge handbook of multimedia learning.* New York: Cambridge University Press.

Mayer, R.E. (2005b). Principles for reducing extraneous processing in multimedia learning: Coherence, signaling, redundancy, spatial contiguity, and temporal contiguity. In R.E. Mayer (Ed.), *The Cambridge handbook of multimedia learning* (pp. 183 200). New York: Cambridge University Press.

Mayer, R.E. (2005c). Principles for managing essential processing in multimedia learning: Segmenting, pretraining, and modality principles.

In R.E. Mayer (Ed.), *The Cambridge handbook of multimedia learning* (pp. 147–158). New York: Cambridge University Press.

Mayer, R.E. (2005d). Principles based on social cues: Personalization, voice, and image principles. In R.E. Mayer (Ed.), *The Cambridge handbook of multimedia learning* (pp. 201–212). New York: Cambridge University Press.

Mayer, R.E. (2007). *Learning and instruction* (2nd ed.). Upper Saddle River, NJ: Pearson Merrill Prentice Hall.

Mayer, R.E. (2008). Research-based guidelines for multimedia instruction. In D.A. Boehm-Davis (Ed.), *Review of human factors and ergonomics* (Vol. 3; pp. 127–147). Santa Monica, CA: Human Factors and Ergonomics Society.

Mayer, R.E. (2009). *Multimedia learning* (2nd ed.). New York: Cambridge University Press.

Mayer, R.E. (2011a). *Applying the science of learning.* Upper Saddle River, NJ: Pearson.

Mayer, R.E. (2011b). Multimedia learning and games. In S. Tobias & D. Fletcher (Eds.), *Computer games and instruction.* (pp. 281–305). Greenwich, CT: Information Age Publishers.

Mayer, R.E., & Alexander, P.A. (2011). *Handbook of research on learning and instruction.* New York: Routledge.

Mayer, R.E., & Anderson, R.B. (1991). Animations need narrations: An experimental test of a dual-processing systems in working memory. *Journal of Educational Psychology, 90,* 312–320.

Mayer, R.E., & Anderson, R.B. (1992). The instructive animation: Helping students build connections between words and pictures in multimedia learning. *Journal of Educational Psychology, 84,* 444–452.

Mayer, R.E., Bove, W., Bryman, A., Mars, R., & Tapangco, L. (1996). When less is more: Meaningful learning from visual and verbal summaries of science textbook lessons. *Journal of Educational Psychology, 88,* 64–73.

Mayer, R.E., & Chandler, P. (2001). When learning is just a click away: Does simple user interaction foster deeper understanding of multimedia messages? *Journal of Educational Psychology, 93,* 390–397.

Mayer, R.E., Deleeuw, K.E., & Ayres, P. (2007). Creating retroactive and proactive interference in multimedia learning. *Applied Cognitive Psychology, 21,* 795–809.

Mayer, R.E., Dow, G., & Mayer, S. (2003). Multimedia learning in an interactive self-explaining environment: What works in the design of agent-based microworlds? *Journal of Educational Psychology, 95,* 806–813.

Mayer, R.E., Fennell, S., Farmer, L., & Campbell, J. (2004). A personalization effect in multimedia learning: Students learn better when words are in conversational style rather than formal style. *Journal of Educational Psychology, 96,* 389–395.

Mayer, R.E., & Gallini, J.K. (1990). When is an illustration worth ten thousand words? *Journal of Educational Psychology, 88,* 64–73.

Mayer, R.E., Griffin, E., Jurkowitz, I.T., & Rothman, D. (2008). Increased interestingness of extraneous details in a multimedia science presentation leads to decreased learning. *Journal of Experimental Psychology: Applied, 14,* 329–339.

Mayer, R.E., Hegarty, M., Mayer, S., & Campbell, J. (2005). When static media promote active learning: Annotated illustrations versus narrated animations in multimedia instruction. *Journal of Experimental Psychology: Applied, 11,* 256–265.

Mayer, R.E., Heiser, J., & Lonn, S. (2001). Cognitive constraints on multimedia learning: When presenting more material results in less understanding. *Journal of Educational Psychology, 93,* 187–198.

Mayer, R.E., & Jackson, J. (2005). The case for coherence in scientific explanations: Quantitative details can hurt qualitative understanding. *Journal of Experimental Psychology: Applied, 11,* 13–18.

Mayer, R.E., & Johnson, C.I. (2010). Adding instructional features that promote learning in a game-like environment. *Journal of Educational Computing Research, 42,* 241–265.

Mayer, R.E., & Johnson, C.I. (2008). Revising the redundancy principle in multimedia learning. *Journal of Educational Psychology, 100,* 380–386.

Mayer, R.E., Johnson, L., Shaw, E., & Sandhu, S. (2006). Constructing computer-based tutors that are socially sensitive: Politeness in educational software. *International Journal of Human Computer Studies, 64, 36–42.*

Mayer, R.E., & Johnson, C.I. (2010). Adding instructional features that promote learning in a game-like environment. *Journal of Educational Computing Research, 42,* 241–265.

Mayer, R.E., Mathias, A., & Wetzell, K. (2002). Fostering understanding of multimedia messages through pretraining: Evidence for a two-stage theory of mental model construction. *Journal of Experimental Psychology: Applied, 8,* 147–154.

Mayer, R.E., Mautone, P., & Prothero, W. (2002). Pictorial aids for learning by doing in a multimedia geology simulation game. *Journal of Educational Psychology, 94*(1), 171–185.

Mayer, R.E., & Moreno, R. (1998). A split-attention effect in multimedia learning: Evidence for dual coding hypothesis. *Journal of Educational Psychology, 83,* 484–490.

Mayer, R.E., & Moreno, R. (2003). Nine ways to reduce cognitive load in multimedia learning. *Educational Psychologist, 38,* 43–52.

Mayer, R.E., Moreno, R., Boire, M., & Vagge, S. (1999). Maximizing constructivist learning from multimedia communications by minimizing cognitive load. *Journal of Educational Psychology, 91,* 638–643.

Mayer, R.E., & Sims, V. (1994). For whom is a picture worth a thousand words? Extensions of a dual-coding theory of multimedia learning. *Journal of Educational Psychology, 86,* 389–401.

Mayer, R.E., Sims, V., & Tajika, H. (1995). A comparison of how textbooks teach mathematical problem solving in Japan and the United States. *American Educational Research Journal, 32,* 443–460.

Mayer, R.E., Sobko, K., & Mautone, P.D. (2003). Social cues in multimedia learning: Role of speaker's voice. *Journal of Educational Psychology, 95,* 419–425.

Mayer, R.E., Steinhoff, K., Bower, G., & Mars, R. (1995). A generative theory of textbook design: Using annotated illustrations to foster meaningful learning of science text. *Educational Technology Research and Development, 43,* 31–43.

McCrudden, M.T., Schraw, G., & Lehman, S. (2009). The use of adjunct displays to facilitate comprehension of causal relationships in expository text. *Instructional Science, 37,* 65–86.

McCrudden, M.T., Schraw, G., Lehman, S., & Poliquin, A. (2007). The effect of causal diagrams on text learning. *Contemporary Educational Psychology, 32,* 367–388.

McGill, L., Nicol, D., Littlejohn, A., Gierson, H., Juster, N., & Ion, W.J. (2005). Creating an information-rich learning environment to enhance design student learning: Challenges and approaches. *British Jounal of Educational Technology, 36*(4), 629–642.

McLaren, B.M., DeLeeuw, K.E., & Mayer, R.E. (2011). A politeness effect in learning with web-based intelligent tutors. *International Journal of Human Computer Studies, 69,* 70–79.

Micas, I.C., & Berry, D. (2000). Learning a procedural task: Effectiveness of multimedia presentations. *Applied Cognitive Psychology, 14,* 555–575.

Moos, D.C., & Azevedo, R. (2008). Self-regulated learning with hyper-media: The role of prior domain knowledge. *Contemporary Educational Psychology, 33*(2), 270–298.

Moreno, R. (2004). Decreasing cognitive load for novice students: Effects of explanatory versus corrective feedback in discovery-based multimedia. *Instructional Science, 32,* 99–113.

Moreno, R. (2005). Multimedia learning with animated pedagogical agents. In R.E. Mayer (Ed.), *The Cambridge handbook of multimedia learning* (pp. 507–524). New York: Cambridge University Press.

Moreno, R. (2007). Optimizing learning from animations by minimizing cognitive load: Cognitive and affective consequences of signaling and segmentation methods. *Applied Cognitive Psychology, 21,* 765–781.

Moreno, R. (2009). Learning from animated classroom exemplars: The case for guiding student teachers' observations with metacognitive prompts. *Educational Research and Evaluation, 15,* 487–501.

Moreno, R., & Flowerday, T. (2006). Students' choice of animated pedagogical agents in science learning: A test of the similarity-attraction hypothesis on gender and ethnicity. *Contemporary Educational Psychology, 31,* 186–207.

Moreno, R., & Mayer, R.E. (1999a). Cognitive principles of multimedia learning: The role of modality and contiguity. *Journal of Educational Psychology, 91,* 358–368.

Moreno, R., & Mayer, R.E. (1999b). Multimedia-supported metaphors for meaning making in mathematics. *Cognition and Instruction, 17,* 215–248.

Moreno, R., & Mayer, R.E. (2000a). A coherence effect in multimedia learning: The case for minimizing irrelevant sounds in the design of multimedia instructional messages. *Journal of Educational Psychology, 92,* 117–125.

Moreno, R., & Mayer, R.E. (2000b). Engaging students in active learning: The case for personalized multimedia messages. *Journal of Educational Psychology, 93,* 724–733.

Moreno, R., & Mayer, R.E. (2002a). Verbal redundancy in multimedia learning: When reading helps listening. *Journal of Educational Psychology, 94,* 156–163.

Moreno, R., & Mayer, R.E. (2002b). Learning science in virtual reality multimedia environments: Role of methods and media. *Journal of Educational Psychology, 94,* 598–610.

Moreno, R., & Mayer, R.E. (2004). Personalized messages that promote science learning in virtual environments. *Journal of Educational Psychology, 96,* 165–173.

Moreno, R., & Mayer, R.E. (2005). Role of guidance, reflection, and interactivity in an agent-based multimedia game. *Journal of Educational Psychology, 97,* 117–128.

Moreno, R., & Mayer, R.E. (2007). Interactive multimodal learning environments. *Educational Psychology Review, 19,* 309–326.

Moreno, R., & Mayer, R.E. (2005). Role of guidance, reflection, and interactivity in an agent-based multimedia game. *Journal of Educational Psychology, 97*(1), 117–128.

Moreno, R., Mayer, R.E., Spires, H., & Lester, J. (2001). The case for social agency in computer-based teaching: Do students learn more deeply when they interact with animated pedagogical agents? *Cognition and Instruction, 19,* 177–214.

Moreno, R., & Ortegano-Layne, L. (2008). Using cases as thinking tools in teacher education: The role of representation format. *Educational Technology Research and Development, 56,* 449–465.

Moreno, R., & Valdez, A. (2007). Immediate and delayed effects of using a classroom case exemplar in teacher education: The role of presentation format. *Journal of Educational Psychology, 99,* 194–206.

Nass, C., & Brave, S. (2005). *Wired for speech: How voice activates and advances the human-computer relationship.* Cambridge, MA: MIT Press.

National Research Council. (1994). Illusions of comprehension, competence, and remembering. In D. Druckman & R.A. Bjork (Eds.), *Learning, remembering, believing.* Washington, DC: National Academy Press.

NCube, L.B. (2010). A simulation of lean manufacturing: The lean lemonade tycoon 2. *Simulation & Gaming, 41,* 568–586.

Niederhauser, D.S., Reynolds, R.E., Salmen, D.J., & Skolmoski, P. (2000). The influence of cognitive load on learning from hypertext. *Journal of Educational Computing Research, 23,* 237–255.

Nilsson, R.M., & Mayer, R.E. (2002). The effects of graphic organizers giving cues to the structure of a hypertext document on users' navigation strategies and performance. *International Journal of Human-Computer Studies, 57,* 1–26.

Nolen, S. (1995). Effects of a visible author in statistical texts. *Journal of Educational Psychology, 87,* 47–65.

Nussbaum, E.M. (2005). The effect of goal instructions and need for cognition on interactive argumentation. *Contemporary Educational Psychology, 30*(3), 286–313.

Nussbaum, E.M., & Kardash, C.M. (2005). The effects of goal instructions and text on the generation of counter-arguments during writing. *Journal of Educational Psychology, 97*(2), 157–169.

Ollerenshaw, A., Aidman, E., & Kidd, G. (1997). Is an illustration always worth ten thousand words? Effects of prior knowledge, learning style, and multimedia illustrations on text comprehension. *International Journal of Instructional Media, 24,* 227–238.

O'Neil, H.F., & Perez, R.S. (2008). *Computer games and team and individual learning.* Oxford, UK: Elsevier.

O'Neil, H.F. (2005). *What works in distance learning: Guidelines.* Greenwich, CT: Information Age Publishing.

O'Neil, H.F., Mayer, R.E., Herl, H.E., Niemi, C., Olin, K., & Thurman, R.A. (2000). Instructional strategies for virtual aviation training environments. In H.F. O'Neil & D.H. Andrews (Eds.), *Aircrew training and assessment* (pp. 105–130). Mahwah, NJ: Lawrence Erlbaum Associates.

Paas, F.G.W.C., & van Merrienboer, J.J.G. (1994). Instructional control of cognitive load in the training of complex cognitive tasks. *Educational Psychology Review, 6,* 351–371.

Pashler, H., Bain, P., Bottage, B., Graesser, A., Koedinger, K., McDaniel, M., & Metcalfe, J. (2007). *Organizing instruction and study to improve student learning.* Washington, DC: National Center for Educational Research, Institute of Education Sciences.

Pashler, H., McDaniel, M., Rohrer, D., & Bjork, R. (2008). Learning styles: Concepts and evidence. *Psychological Science in the Public Interest, 9,* 105–119.

Paxton, R. (2002). The influence of author visibility on high school students solving a historical problem. *Cognition and Instruction, 20,* 197–248.

Phye, G.D., Robinson, D.H., & Levin, J. (Eds.). (2005). *Empirical methods for evaluating educational interventions.* San Diego: Elsevier.

Plant, E.A., Ericsson, K.A., Hill, L., & Asberg, K. (2005). Why study time does not predict grade point average across college students: Implications of deliberate practice for academic performance. *Contemporary Educational Psychology, 30,* 96–116.

Pociask, F.D., & Morrison, G.R. (2008). Controlling split attention and redundancy in physical therapy instruction. *Educational Technology Research and Development, 56,* 379–399.

Pollock, E., Chandler, P., & Sweller, J. (2002). Assimilating complex information. *Learning and Instruction, 12,* 61–86.

Potelle, H., & Rouet, J.F. (2003). Effects of content representation and readers' prior knowledge on the comprehension of hypertext. *International Journal of Human Computer Studies, 58,* 327–345.

Prichard, J.S., Bizo, L.A., & Stratford, R.J. (2006). The educational impact of team-skills training: Preparing students to work in groups. *British Journal of Educational Psychology, 76,* 119–140.

Quilici, J.L., & Mayer, R.E. (1996). Role of examples in how students learn to categorize statistics word problems. *Journal of Educational Psychology, 88*(1), 144–161.

Ransdell, S.E., & Gilroy, L. (2001). The effects of background music on word proceeded writing. *Computers in Human Behavior, 17,* 141–148.

Rawson, K.A., & Kintsch, W. (2005). Rereading effects depend on time of test. *Journal of Educational Psychology, 97*(1), 70–80.

Reeves, B., & Nass, C. (1996). *The media equation: How people treat computers, television, and new media like real people and places.* New York: Cambridge University Press.

Renkl, A. (2011). Instruction based on examples. In R.E. Mayer & P.A. Alexander (Eds.), *Handbook of research on learning and instruction.* New York: Routledge.

Renkl, A. (2005). The worked-out examples principles in multimedia learning. In R.E. Mayer (Ed.), *The Cambridge handbook of multimedia learning.* New York: Cambridge University Press.

Renkl, A., Hilbert, T., & Schworm, S. (2009). Example-based learning in heuristic domains: A cognitive load theory account. *Educational Psychology Review, 21,* 67–78.

Renninger, K.A., Hidi, S., & Krapp. A. (1992). *The role of interest in learning and development.* Mahwah, NJ: Lawrence Erlbaum Associates.

Resta, P., & Laferriere, T. (2007). Technology in support of collaborative learning. *Educational Psychology Review, 19,* 65–83.

Rey, G.D. (2011). Interactive elements for dynamically linked multiple representations in computer simulations. *Applied Cognitive Psychology, 25,* 12–19.

Rickel, J., & Johnson, L.W. (2000). Task-oriented collaboration with embodied agents in virtual worlds. In J. Cassell, J. Sullivan, S. Prevost, & E. Churchill (Eds.), *Embodied conversational agents.* Cambridge, MA: MIT Press.

Ritchhart, R., & Perkins, D.N. (2005). Learning to think: The challenges of teaching thinking. In K.J. Holyoak & R.G. Morrison (Eds.), *The Cambridge handbook of thinking and reasoning.* New York: Cambridge University Press.

Rieber, L.P. (2005). Multimedia learning in games, simulations, and microworlds. In R.E. Mayer (Ed.), *The Cambridge handbook of multimedia learning.* New York: Cambridge University Press.

Rieber, L.P., Tzeng, S.C., & Tribble, K. (2004). Discovery learning, representation, and explanation within a computer-based simulation: finding the right mix. *Learning and Instruction, 14,* 307–323.

Robinson, D.H. (2002). Spatial text adjuncts and learning: An introduction to the special issue. *Educational Psychology Review, 14,* 1–3.

Rohrer, D., & Taylor, K (2006). The effects of over-learning and distributed practice on the retention of mathematics knowledge. *Applied Cognitive Psychology, 20,* 1209–1224.

Rosenbaum, D.A., Carlson, R.A., & Gilmore, R.O. (2001). Acquisition of intellectual and perceptual motor skills. *Annual Review of Psychology, 52,* 453–470.

Rouet, J.F., & Potelle, H. (2005). Navigational principles in multimedia learning. In R.E. Mayer (Ed.), *The Cambridge handbook of multimedia learning.* New York: Cambridge University Press.

Rourke, A., & Sweller, J. (2009). The worked-example effect using ill-defined problems: Learning to recognize designers' styles. *Learning and Instruction, 19,* 185–199.

Sanchez, C.A., & Wiley, J. (2006). An examination of the seductive details effect in terms of working memory capacity. *Memory & Cognition, 34,* 344–355.

Salden, R.J.C.M., Aleven, V., Schwonke, R., & Renkl, A. (2010). The expertise reversal effect and worked examples in tutored problem solving. *Instructional Science, 38,* 289–307.

Salden, R.J.C.M., Paas, F.G.W.C., Broers, N., & Van Merrienboer, J.J.G. (2004). Mental effort and performance as determinants for the dynamic selection of learning tasks in air traffic control training. *Instructional Science, 32,* 153–172.

Schar, S.G., & Zimmerman, P.G. (2007). Investigating means to reduce cognitive load from animations: Applying differentiated measures of knowledge representation. *Journal of Research on Technology in Education, 40,* 64–78.

Scheiter, K., Gerjets, P., Huk, T., Imhof, B., & Kammerer, Y. (2009). The effects of realism in learning with dynamic visualizations. *Learning and Instruction, 19,* 481–494.

Schmidt, H.G., Van der Molen, H.T., te Winkel, W.W.R., & Wijnen, W.H.F.W. (2009). Constructivist, problem-based learning does work: A meta-analysis of curricular comparisons involved a single medical school. *Educational Psychologist, 44,* 227–249.

Schmidt-Weigand, F., Kohnert, A., & Glowalla, U. (2010a). A closer look at split attention in system- and self-paced instruction in multimedia learning. *Learning and Instruction, 20,* 100–110.

Schmidt-Weigand, F., Kohnert, A., & Glowalla, U. (2010b). Explaining the modality and contiguity effects: New insights from investigating students' viewing behavior. *Applied Cognitive Psychology, 24,* 226–237.

Schmidt, H.E., & Moust, J.H.C. (2000). Factors affecting small-group tutorial learning: A review of research. In D.H. Evensen & C.E. Hmelo (Eds.), *Problem-based learning.* Mahwah, NJ: Lawrence Erlbaum Associates.

Schnackenberg, H.L., Sullivan, H.J., Leader, L.R., & Jones, E.E.K. (1998). Learner preferences and achievement under differing amounts of learner practice. *Educational Technology Research and Development, 46,* 5–15.

Schnackenberg, H.L., & Sullivan, H.J. (2000). Learner control over full and lean computer based instruction under differing ability levels. *Educational Technology Research and Development, 48,* 19–35.

Schoenfeld, A.H. (1987). What's all the fuss about metacognition? In A. Schoenfeld (Ed.), *Cognitive science and mathematics education.* Mahwah, NJ: Lawrence Erlbaum Associates.

Schneider, B., Carnoy, M., Kilpatrick, J., Schmidt, W.H., & Shavelson, R.J. (2007). *Estimating causal effects.* Washington DC. American Educational Research Association.

Schworm, S., & Renkl, A. (2007). Learning argumentation skills through the use of prompts for self-explaining examples. *Journal of Educational Psychology, 99,* 285–296.

Scott, G., Leritz, L.E., & Mumford, M.D. (2004). The effectiveness of creativity training: A quantitative review. *Creativity Research Journal, 16*(4), 361–388.

Seabrook, R., Brown, G.D., & Solity, J.E. (2005). Distributed and massed practice: From laboratory to classroom. *Applied Cognitive Psychology, 19,* 107–122.

Seufert, T., Schutze, M., & Brunken, R. (2009). Memory characteristics and modality in multimedia learning: An aptitude-treatment interaction study. *Learning and Instruction, 19,* 28–42.

Shapiro, A.M. (2005). The site map principle in multimedia learning. In R.E. Mayer (Ed.), *The Cambridge handbook of multimedia learning.* New York: Cambridge University Press.

Shapiro, A.M. (2008). Hypermedia design as learner scaffolding. *Educational Technology Research & Development, 56,* 29–44.

Shute, V.J. (2008). Focus on formative feedback. *Review of Educational Research, 78*(1), 153–189.

Shavelson, R.J., & Towne, L. (Eds.). (2002). *Scientific research in education.* Washington, DC: National Academy Press.

Sitzmann, T., Brown, K.G., Casper, W.J., Ely, K., & Zimmerman, R.D. (2008). A review and meta-analysis of the nomological network of trainee reactions. *Journal of Applied Psychology, 93,* 280–295.

Slavin, R.E. (2011). Instruction based on cooperative learning. In R.E. Mayer & P.A. Alexander (Eds.), *Handbook of research on learning and instruction.* New York: Routledge.

Slavin, R.E., Hurley, E.A., & Chamberlain, A. (2003). Cooperative learning and achievement: Theory and practice. In W.M. Reynolds & G.E. Miller (Eds.), *Handbook of psychology: Volume 7, Educational psychology* (pp. 177–198). Hoboken, NJ: John Wiley & Sons.

Slobada, J.A., Davidson, J.W., Howe, M.J.A., & Moore, D.G. (1996). The role of practice in the development of performing musicians. *British Journal of Psychology, 87,* 287–309.

Spector, J.M., Merrill, M.D., van Merrienboer, J.J.G., & Driscoll, M.P. (Eds.). (2008). *Handbook of research on educational communications and technology* (3rd ed.). Mahwah, NJ: Lawrence Erlbaum Associates.

Steinberg, E.R. (1989). Cognition and learner control: A literature review, 1977–1988. *Journal of Computer-Based Instruction, 16*(4), 117–121.

Stone, N.J. (2000). Exploring the relationship between calibration and self-regulated learning. *Educational Psychology Review, 4,* 437–475.

Stull, A., & Mayer, R.E. (2007). Learning by doing versus learning by viewing: Three experimental comparisons of learner-generated versus author-generated graphic organizers. *Journal of Educational Psychology, 99,* 808–820.

Suomala, J., & Shaughnessy, M.F. (2000). An interview with Richard E. Mayer: About technology. *Educational Psychology Review, 12*(4), 477–483.

Suthers, D.D., Vatrapu, R., Medina, R., Joseph, S.M., & Dwyer, N. (2008). Beyond threaded discussion: Representational guidance in asynchronous collaborative learning environments. *Computers & Education, 50,* 1103–1127.

Svetcov, D. (2000). The virtual classroom vs. the real one. *Forbes, 166,* 50–54.

Sweller, J. (2004). Instructional design consequences of an analogy between evolution by natural selection and human cognitive architectures. *Instructional Science, 32,* 9–31.

Sweller, J., & Chandler, P. (1994). Why some material is difficult to learn. *Cognition and Instruction, 12,* 185–233.

Sweller, J., Chandler, P., Tierney, P., & Cooper, M. (1990). Cognitive load and selective attention as factors in the structuring of technical material. *Journal of Experimental Psychology: General, 119,* 176–192.

Sweller, J., & Cooper, G.A. (1985). The use of worked examples as a substitute for problem solving in learning algebra. *Cognition and Instruction, 2,* 59–89.

Tabbers, H.K., & de Koeijer, B. (2010). Learner control in animated multimedia instructions. *Instructional Science, 38,* 441–453

Tallent-Runnels, M.K., Thomas, J.A., Lan, W.Y., Cooper, S., Ahern, T.C., Shaw, S.M., & Liu, X. (2006). Teaching courses online: A review of the research. *Review of Educational Research, 76*(1) 93–135.

Taylor, K., & Rohrer, D. (2010). The effects of interleaved practice. *Applied Cognitive Psychology, 24,* 837–848.

Tuffiash, M., Roring, R.W., & Ericsson, K.A. (2007). Expert performance in Scrabble: Implications for the study of the structure and acquisition of complex skills. *Journal of Experimental Psychology: Applied, 13,* 124–134.

Tutty, J.I., & Klein, J.D. (2008). Computer-mediated instruction: A comparison of online and face-to-face collaboration. *Educational Technology Research and Development, 56*, 101–124.

Tversky, B., Morrison, J.B., & Betrancourt, M. (2002). Animation: Can it facilitate? *International Journal of Human-Computer Studies, 57*, 247–262

Uribe, D., Klein, J.D., & Sullivan, H. (2003). The effect of computer-mediated collaborative learning on solving ill-defined problems. *Educational Technology Research and Development, 51*(1), 5–19.

Van Eck, R. (2007). Six ideas in search of a discipline. In B.E. Shelton & D. Wiley (Eds.), *The design and use of simulation computer games in education* (pp. 31–60). Rotterdam, The Netherlands: Sense Publishers.

Van Merrienboer, J.J.G., & Kester, L. (2005). The four-component instructional design model: Multimedia principles in environments for complex learning. In R.E. Mayer (Ed.), *The Cambridge handbook of multimedia learning*. New York: Cambridge University Press.

Van Gog, T., Paas, F.G.W.C., & van Merrienboer, J.J.G. (2008). Effects of studying sequences of process-oriented and product-oriented worked examples on troubleshooting transfer efficiency. *Learning and Instruction, 18*, 211–222.

Van Gog, T., Sluijsmans, D.M.A., Joosten-ten Brinke, D., & Prins, F.J. (2010). Formative assessment in an online learning environment to support flexible on-the-job learning in complex professional domains. *Educational Technology Research and Development, 58*, 311–324.

Verkoeijen, P., & Tabbers, H. (2009). When quantitative details impair qualitative understanding of multimedia lesson. *Educational Psychology, 29*, 269–278.

Violato, C., & Lockyer, J. (2006). Self and peer assessment of pediatricians, psychiatrists, and medicine specialists: Implications for self-directed learning. *Advances in Health Sciences Education, 11, 235*–244.

Walczyk, J.J., & Hall, V.C. (1989). Effects of examples and embedded questions on the accuracy of comprehension self-assessments. *Journal of Educational Psychology, 81, 435*–437.

Wang, N., Johnson, W.L., Mayer, R.E., Rizzo, P., Shaw, E., & Collins, H. (2008). The politeness effect: Pedagogical agents and learning outcomes. *International Journal of Human Computer Studies, 66,* 98–112.

Wang, N., Johnson, L., Mayer, R.E., Rizzo, P., Shaw, E., & Collins, H. (2008). The politeness effect: Pedagogical agents and learning gains. In C. Looi, G. McCalla, B. Bredeweg, & J. Breuker (Eds.), *Artificial intelligence in education: Supporting learning through intelligent and socially informed technology* (pp. 868–693). Amsterdam: IOS Press.

Wong, A., Marcus, N., Ayres, P., Smith, L., Cooper, G.A., Paas, F.G.W.C., & Sweller, J. (2009). Instructional animations can be superior to statics when learning human motor skills. *Computers in Human Behavior, 25,* 339–347.

Wouters, P., Paas, F.G.W.C., & Van Merrienboer, J.J.G. (2008). How to optimize learning from animated models: A review of guidelines based on cognitive load. *Review of Educational Research, 78,* 645–675.

Yeh, K.H., & She, H.C. (2010). Online synchronous scientific argumentation learning: Nurturing students' argumentation ability and conceptual change in science context. *Computers and Education, 55,* 586–602.

Yetter, G., Gutkin, T.B., Saunders, A., Galloway, A.M., Sobansky, R.R., & Song, S.Y. (2006). Unstructured collaboration versus individual practice for complex problem solving: A cautionary tale. *Journal of Experimental Education, 74*(2), 137–159.

Young, J.D. (1996). The effect of self-regulated learning strategies on performance in learner controlled computer-based instruction. *Educational Technology Research and Development, 44,* 17–27.

GLOSSARY

Active Observation	Learning by watching a human tutor explain a problem to a student. Most effective when observing an explanation of an assigned problem with a partner. Encourages self-explanations and deeper processing.
Active Processing	A psychological principle stating that learning occurs when people engage in appropriate mental processing during learning, such as attending to relevant materials, responding to practice exercises, or reflecting on examples.
Adaptive Control	A process in which learners are directed or branched to different instructional materials in a lesson based on the program's evaluation of their responses to lesson exercises. Also called *personalized instruction* or *user modeling*.
Advance Organizer	A device placed in the start of a learning event designed to provide an overview or big picture of the lesson content. May take the form of a graphic or table.
Agents	Onscreen characters who help guide the learning process during an e-learning episode. Also called *pedagogical agents*.
Animation	A graphic that depicts movement, such as a video of a procedure or a moving sequence of line drawings
Architecture	A course design that reflects a theory of learning. Architectures vary regarding the amount and type of structure and interactivity included in the lesson.
Argumentation	A process of defining various propositions or hypotheses for a position, identifying supporting data for those propositions, and presenting a rational case for the position.

Arousal Theory	The idea that adding entertaining and interesting material to lessons stimulates emotional engagement that promotes learning.
Asynchronous Collaborations	Opportunities for learners and/or instructors to interact with each other via computer at different times, such as in a discussion board or email.
Asynchronous e-Learning	Digitized instructional resources intended for self-study. Learners can access training resources any time and any place.
Auditory Channel	Part of the human memory system that processes information that enters through the ears and is mentally represented in the form of sounds.
Automaticity	A stage of learning in which new knowledge or skills can be applied directly from long-term memory without using working memory capacity. Some common examples of automatic tasks are driving a car, typing, and reading. Knowledge becomes automatic only after many practice repetitions.
Behavioral Engagement	A visible response by a learner during an instructional episode such as clicking an on-screen object, pressing the forward button, typing a response, responding verbally. Contrast with *Psychological Engagement*.
Blocked Practice	The grouping of practice exercises in or among lessons according to the concept or skill being learned. Blocked practice leads to easier learning during the lesson but poorer long-term learning compared with mixed practice.
Blogs	A website on which individuals write commentaries on an ongoing basis. Visitors can comment or link to a blog.
Borrowing and Reorganizing Principle	An instructional principle proposed by John Sweller that emphasizes the role of imitation of others in learning.
Breakout Rooms	An online conferencing facility that usually supports audio, whiteboard, polling, and chat used for small groups in conjunction with a virtual classroom event.

Boundary Conditions	The situations in which an instructional method or principle is or is not effective. For example, one boundary condition for the effectiveness of graphics is the background experience of the learner.
Calibration	The accuracy of self-estimates of knowing. If a learner estimates low knowledge and scores low on a test he or she has good calibration; likewise if someone estimates high knowledge and scores high on a test that person has good calibration.
Chats	Two or more participants communicating online at the same time via text.
Clinical Trials	Research comparing the learning outcomes and/or processes of people who learn in a test e-learning course versus people who learn in another venue such as a competing e-learning course. Also called *controlled field testing*.
Cognitive Learning Theory	An explanation of how people learn based on the idea of dual channels (information is processed in visual and auditory channels), limited capacity (only a small amount of information can be processed in each channel at one time), and active learning (meaningful learning occurs when learners pay attention to relevant information, organize it into a coherent structure, and integrate it with what they already know). Also called *cognitive theory* and *cognitive theory of multimedia learning*.
Cognitive Load	The amount of mental resource in working memory required by a task.
Cognitive Interest	A source of motivation stemming from a learner's ability to make sense of the instructional materials. As a result of understanding the lesson, the learner experiences enjoyment. Contrast with *Emotional Interest*.

Cognitive Models	A type of modeled example in which a person shows how to perform a technical task such as setting up a spreadsheet or solving a math problem.
Cognitive Task Analysis	Techniques used to define the thinking processes used by experts during real-world problem solution.
Coherence Principle	Avoid extraneous audio, graphics, or graphic treatments and words to minimize irrelevant load imposed on memory during learning.
Collaborative Learning	A structured instructional interaction among two or more learners to achieve a learning goal or complete an assignment.
Computer-Supported Collaborative Learning (CSCL)	Any instructional program in which two or more individuals work together (synchronously or asynchronously) on an instructional activity or assignment using digital technology to communicate.
Concurrent Reporting	A form of cognitive task analysis in which experts verbalize their thoughts at the same time that they are solving a problem or completing a task. Contrast with *Retrospective Reporting*.
Concept	Lesson content that refers to a category that includes multiple instances, for example, web page, spreadsheet, software, e-learning.
Content Analysis	Research to define content and content relationships to be included in an educational course. See also *Task Analysis*.
Contiguity Principle	People learn more deeply when corresponding printed words and graphics are placed close to one another on the screen or when spoken words and graphics are presented at the same time.
Control	A comparison lesson that does not include the variable being studied in the treatment lesson. For example, a

	text-only lesson is a control being compared with a lesson with both text and graphics.
Controlled Studies	Research comparing the learning outcomes and/or processes of two or more groups of learners; the groups are the same except for the variable(s) being studied. Also called *experimental comparison*.
Conversational Style	A writing style that uses first- and second-person constructions, active voice, and speech-like phrases.
Cooperative Learning	See *Collaborative Learning*.
Corrective Feedback	Instructional responses to answers to a practice exercise that tells the learner whether they answered corrected or incorrectly. Contrast with *Explanatory Feedback*.
Course Map	A type of menu or concept map that graphically represents the structure of an online course or lesson. Course maps have been shown to influence how learners organize learning content.
Creative Thinking	The production of novel and useful ideas such as designing an e-learning course or solving novel, ill-defined problems.
Critical Decision Method	A form of cognitive task analysis in which an expert describes in detail an incident he or she resolved in the past.
Critical Thinking	Evaluation of products and ideas, such as critiquing an e-learning course or preparing an argument for a position.
Decorative Graphics	Visuals used for aesthetic purposes or to add humor, such as a picture of a person riding a bicycle in a lesson on how bicycle pumps work.
Dependent Measure	The outcome measure in an experimental study. In many learning experiments, a test score is the dependent variable.
Design	One of the stages in e-learning development in which the content is defined and summarized in the form of outlines, learning objectives, and storyboards

Development	One of the stages in e-learning development in which the course is created, including graphics, text, programming, etc.
Deliberate Practice	Exercises that fall just outside the learner's level of competence that focus on specific skill gaps and demand focus and reflection. The type of practice that leads to continued performance improvement.
Directive Architecture	Training that primarily asks the learner to make a response or perform a task and then provides feedback. Also called *show-and-do method.* Based on a response-strengthening view of learning.
Discovery Learning	Experiential exploratory instructional interfaces that offer little structure or guidance.
Disruption	A process that interferes with the organization of new content in memory as a result of irrelevant content getting in the way.
Distraction	A process that interferes with the selection process by taking learner focus away from important instructional content or methods.
Distributed Practice	Exercises that are placed throughout a lesson rather than all in one location. Long-term learning is better under conditions of distributed practice. Compare to *Massed Practice.*
Drag and Drop	A facility that allows the user to move objects from one part of the screen to another. Often used in e-learning practice exercises.
Dual channels	A psychological principle stating that humans have two separate channels for processing visual/pictorial material and auditory/verbal material.
Dynamic Adaptive Control	A form of learner control based on a continuous assessment of learner skills during the lesson, followed by

	immediate branching to needed instructional methods, topics, or lessons. Contrast with *Static Adaptive Control*.
Effect Size	A statistic indicating how many standard deviations difference there is between the mean score of the experimental group and the mean score of the control group. A useful metric to determine the practical significance of research results. Effect sizes greater than .5 indicate an outcome of practical significance worthy of implementation.
e-Learning	A combination of content and instructional methods delivered by media elements, such as words and graphics on a computer or mobile device intended to build job-transferable knowledge and skills linked to individual learning goals or organizational performance. May be designed for self-study or instructor-led training. See *Asynchronous* and *Synchronous e-Learning*.
Emotional Interest	A source of motivation stemming from treatments that induce arousal in learners such as dramatic visuals or stories. See also *Seductive Details*. Contrast with *Cognitive Interest*.
Encoding	Integration of new information entering working memory into long-term memory for permanent storage.
Encoding Specificity	A principle of memory stating that people are better able to retrieve information if the conditions at the time of original learning are similar to the conditions at the time of retrieval. For example, to enable learning of a new computer system, learners should practice in training with the same system they will use on the job so they encode memories that are identical to the performance environment.
Engagement Matrix	A two-by-two model that crosses psychological engagement (high and low) with behavioral engagement (high and low). Deeper learning stems from high

	psychological engagement with or without high behavioral engagement.
Essential Processing	Mental work during learning directed at representing the content, which is created by the inherent complexity of the content. More complex content requires greater amounts of essential processing.
Evidence-Based Practice	Basing instructional techniques on research findings and research-based theory.
Experimental Control	The test group and the comparison (control) group receive identical treatments except for the one feature being tested. For example, the control group studies from a lesson using text and the test group studies from the same lesson that adds graphics.
Experimental Studies	See *Controlled Studies*.
Expertise Reversal Effect	Instructional methods that are helpful to novice learners may have no effect or even depress learning of high-knowledge learners.
Explanatory Feedback	Instructional responses to student answers to practice exercises that tell the learners whether they are correct or incorrect and also provide the rationale or a hint guiding the learners to a correct answer.
Explanatory Visual	A graphic that helps learners build relationships among content elements. Includes the organizational, relational, transformational, and interpretive types of visuals.
Exploratory Lessons	Lessons that are high in learner control and rely on the learner to select instructional materials they need.
Extraneous Processing Load	Irrelevant mental work during learning that results from ineffective instructional design of the lesson.
Eye Tracking	A physiological indicator of attention involving tracing eye movements as an individual reviews pages or screens of content.

Fact	Lesson content that includes unique and specific information or data. For example, the codes to log into a system or a specific application screen.
Factorial Experimental Comparison	A controlled experiment that compares learning among subjects who did or did not experience the instructional feature and that also varies another factor such as the type of learner, type of learning objective, or type of learning environment. For example, learning from a lesson with and without graphics is compared among experienced and novice learners.
Fading	An instructional technique in which learners move from fully worked examples to full practice exercises through a series of worked examples in which the learners gradually complete more of the steps.
Far Transfer Tasks	Tasks that require learners to use what they have learned in a novel situation, such as adjusting a general principle for a new problem. For example, how to troubleshoot an unusual system failure or how to write a sales proposal. See also *Strategic Knowledge*.
Feedback	Information concerning the correctness of one's performance on a learning task or question. Should include an explanation for correct and incorrect responses and should direct attention to the task rather than the ego.
Formative Evaluation	The evaluation of courseware based on learner responses (test results or feedback) during the development and initial trials of the courseware.
Game	An online environment that involves a competitive activity with a challenge to achieve a goal, a set of rules and constraints, and a specific context. Game features vary dramatically, including games of chance, games based on motor skills (also called *twitch games*), and games of strategy. Games for learning are called *instructional games* or *serious games*.

Generative Processing	Relevant mental work during learning directed at deeper understanding of the content that stems from the motivation of the learner to make sense of the material.
Graphic	Any iconic representation, including illustrations, drawings, charts, maps, photos, organizational visuals, animation, and video. Also called *picture*.
Guided Discovery	An instructional architecture in which the learner is assigned an authentic job task or case study, along with guidance from the instructor about how to process the incoming information. Based on a knowledge construction view of learning.
Heterogeneous Groups	Learners who differ regarding prior knowledge, job background, culture, or other significant features. Contrast with *Homogeneous Groups*.
Homogeneous Groups	Learners who are similar regarding prior knowledge, job background, culture, or other significant features. Contrast with *Heterogeneous Groups*.
Independent Variable	The feature that is studied in an experiment. For example, in a lesson that uses visuals that is compared to a lesson that uses text alone, visuals are the independent variable.
Inductive Learning	Learning that comes from experience rather than direct explanations.
Inform Programs	Lessons designed primarily to communicate information rather than build skills.
Informal Studies	Research in which conclusions are based on observing people as they learn or asking them about their learning. Also called *observational studies*.
Information Acquisition	A metaphor of learning that assumes that learners absorb information that is provided to them by the instructor. This metaphor is the basis for receptive architectures of learning.

Information Delivery	An explanation of how people learn based on the idea that learners directly absorb new information presented in the instructional environment. Also called the *transmission view* or the *information acquisition view*. See also *Information Acquisition*.
Ill-Defined Tasks	Problems for which there is no one correct answer or approach, for example, designing a website or developing a patient treatment plan.
Inquiry Simulation	An online simulation designed specifically to teach skills of the scientific method such as identifying hypotheses, setting up experiments to test hypotheses, etc.
Instruction	The training professional's manipulation of the learner's experience to foster learning.
Instructional Method	A technique in a lesson intended to facilitate cognitive processing that underlies learning, for example, a demonstration, a practice exercise, feedback to practice responses.
Interaction	See *Practice*.
Interdependence	A condition in collaborative group work in which the rewards of each individual member depend to some degree upon the outcomes of all group members. Has been shown to be an important condition for successful collaborative learning.
Interpersonal Model	A type of worked example in which a person demonstrates a social skill. For example, a video of an experienced teacher showing how to teach or a computer animation of an experienced salesperson demonstrating how to present a new product.
Integration Process	A cognitive process in which visual information and auditory information are connected with each other and with relevant memories from long-term memory.

Interpretive Graphics	Visuals used to depict invisible or intangible relationships such as an animation of a bicycle pump that uses small dots to represent the flow of air.
Knowledge Construction	A metaphor of learning that holds that learners are active participants in the building of new knowledge by integrating new content into existing knowledge structures. Cognitive approaches to learning are based on this metaphor.
Knowledge Map	A two-dimensional graphic representation of content. A *concept map* is one example.
Learning	A change in the learner's knowledge due to experience.
Learner-Centered	An instructional approach that adapts technological features to psychological events of learning.
Learner Control	A condition in which the learner can select or manage elements of the lesson, such as the pacing, topics, sequencing, and instructional methods. Asynchronous e-learning can provide various types of learner control. Contrast with *Program Control*.
Learning Styles	The idea that individuals process information in different ways based on some specific mental differences. For example, some learners may have an auditory style and learn better from narration, while others have a visual style and learn better from graphics. There is little evidence to support most learning styles.
Limited Capacity	A psychological principle stating that humans have a small capacity in working memory, allowing them to actively process only a few pieces of information in each channel at one time. See also *Cognitive Load*.
Link	An object on a screen (text or graphic) that when double-clicked leads to additional information on the same or on different web pages.

Long-Term Memory	Part of the cognitive system that stores memories in a permanent form.
Massed Practice	Practice exercises that are placed all in one location in a lesson. Compare to *Distributed Practice*.
Media	Devices used to deliver instruction, including computers, smart phones, books, and instructors.
Media Element	Text, graphics, or sounds used to convey lesson content.
Message Boards	A communication facility in which a number of participants type comments at different times that remain on the board for others to read and respond to.
Meta-Analysis	A computation of average effect sizes among many experiments. Data based on a meta-analysis give us greater confidence in the results because they reflect many research studies.
Metacognition	Awareness and control of one's learning or thinking processing, including setting goals, monitoring progress, and adjusting strategies as needed. Also called *metacognitive skill* and *self-regulatory skill*.
Mixed Practice	Incorporating practice exercises on multiple concepts or skills together rather than organizing them by type. Mixed practice can make learning more difficult during the lesson but often leads to better learning. Use mixed practice when learners must discriminate among different categories of concepts or problems. Contrast with *Blocked Practice*.
Modality Principle	People learn more deeply from multimedia lessons when graphics are explained by audio narration rather than onscreen text. Exceptions include situations when learners are familiar with the content, are not native speakers of the narration language, or when only printed words appear on the screen.

Modeling Example	A demonstration of how to solve a problem or perform a task that incorporates a human. For example, an expert may demonstrate how to solve a technical problem while explaining her rationale or a video may show a sales expert working with a customer.
Mouse-Over	A technique in which new information appears on the screen when the user places his or her mouse over a designed screen area. Also see *Roll-Over*.
Multimedia Presentation	Any presentation containing words (such as narration or onscreen text) and graphics (such as illustrations, photos, animation, or video).
Multimedia Principle	People learn more deeply from words and relevant graphics than from words alone. Also called the *multimedia effect*.
Near Transfer Tasks	Tasks that require the learner to apply a well-known procedure in the same way as it was learned. For example, how to access your email, how to complete a routine customer order. Contrast with *Far Transfer*.
Operational Goals	Bottom-line indicators of organizational success, such as increased sales, decreased product errors, or increased customer satisfaction.
Organizational Graphics	Visuals used to show qualitative relationships among lesson topics or concepts, for example, a tree diagram.
Over Learning	Practice that continues after learners can accurately complete the task or solve a problem.
Pacing Control	Allowing learners to proceed in a lesson at their own rate, usually by pressing a next or continue button.
Part-Task Instruction	A form of directive instructional architecture in which content is broken into small logical chunks and taught in a sequential manner. Also known as rule, example, practice, or stair-step training. Contrast with *Whole-Task Instruction*.
Pedagogical agent	See *Agents*.

Performance Analysis	Research to determine that training will support organizational goals and that e-learning is the best delivery solution.
Perform Programs	Lessons designed primarily to build job-specific skills.
Personalization Principle	People learn more deeply from multimedia lessons when learners experience heightened social presence, as when a conversational script or learning agents are used.
Polite Speech	Narration that includes courteous phrases.
Pop-Up	A window or message that appears on the screen when the mouse touches an active object on the screen. Also see *Roll-Over*.
Power Law of Practice	Learners become more proficient at a task the more they practice, although the improvement occurs at a logarithmic rate. Greatest improvements occur during initial practice, with diminishing improvements over time.
Practice	Structured opportunities for the learner to engage with the content by responding to a question or taking an action to solve a problem. Also called *interaction.*
Pre-Training Principle	People learn more deeply when lessons present key concepts prior to presenting the processes or procedures related to those concepts.
Principle-Based Lessons	Lessons based on guidelines that must be adapted to various job situations. These lessons teach strategic knowledge, for example, how to close a sale, how to design a web page. See also *Strategic Knowledge* or *Far Transfer*.
Procedural Lessons	Lessons designed to teach step-by-step skills that are performed the same way each time. See also *Near Transfer*.

Process	Lesson content that refers to a flow of events such as in a business or scientific process, for example, how new staff are hired, how lightning is formed.
Probability	A statistic indicating the chances that we would be incorrect in concluding that there is a difference between the mean scores of the experimental and control groups. Most instructional experiments use a probability of less than .05 as an indicator of statistical significance.
Problem-Based Learning (PBL)	A type of collaborative whole-task instruction in which groups define and research learning issues based on their discussion of a case problem. Has been broadly adopted in medical education.
Program Control	A condition when the topics, sequencing, instructional methods, and pacing are managed by the instructional environment and not the learner. Instructor-led sessions generally are presented under program control. Also called *instructional control*. Contrast with *Learner Control*.
Psychological Engagement	A mental response by a learner during an instructional event that promotes learning. Contrast with *Behavioral Engagement*.
Random Assignment	A condition of experimental research in which the subjects are allocated to test and control conditions on a random basis. Random assignment assures that there are no systematic differences among the students in the different groups.
Rapid Verification Method	A method for dynamic adaptive control in which learners indicate whether a given solution step is correct or incorrect.
Receptive Instruction	An instructional architecture that primarily presents information without explicit guidance to the learner for how to process it. Also called the *show-and-tell method*. See also *Inform Programs*.

Redundant Onscreen Text	Onscreen text that contains the same words as corresponding audio narration.
Redundancy Principle	People learn more deeply from a multimedia lesson when graphics are explained by audio narration alone rather than audio narration and on-screen text. This principle applies most when the lesson is fast-paced, the words are familiar to the learners, and many words are presented on the screen. Some exceptions to the redundancy principle include: screens with no visuals, learners who are not native speakers of the course language, and placement of only a few key words on the screen.
Regurgitative Interactions	Practice questions that require learners to repeat content provided in the lesson. Will not generally lead to deep understanding.
Rehearsal	Active processing of information in working memory, including mentally organizing the material. Effective rehearsal results in integration of new content with existing knowledge structures.
Relational Graphics	Visuals used to summarize quantitative relationships such as bar charts and pie graphs.
Representational Graphics	Visuals used to show what an objective looks like, such as a computer screen or a piece of equipment.
Retrieval	Transferring information stored in long-term memory to working memory. Also called *retrieving process.*
Retrospective Reporting	A form of cognitive task analysis in which experts verbalize their thoughts immediately or soon after solving a problem or completing a task.
Response Strengthening	A learning metaphor that focuses on strengthening or weakening of associations based on rewards or punishments provided during the learning event. Is the basis of directive instructional architectures.

Roll-Over	A technique in which new content appears on the screen when the learner's mouse contacts on-screen objects. For example, when you place the mouse cursor over an on-screen icon, the name or function of the icon appear in a small text box. Also see *Mouse-Over.*
Scenario-Based Learning	Instructional method that uses realistic case studies as the primary basis for learning. Also called *whole-task* or *immersive instruction.*
Seductive Details	Text or graphics added to a lesson in order to increase the learner's interest but which is not essential to the learning objective.
Segmenting Principle	People learn more deeply when content is broken into small chunks and learners can control the rate at which they access the chunks. A good strategy for managing complex content that imposes considerable essential processing.
Selecting Process	A cognitive process in which the learner pays attention to relevant material in the lesson.
Self-Explanations	The mental process involved in reviewing and making sense of instructional content such as a worked example or a graphic.
Self-Explanation Questions	An instructional technique designed to promote processing of worked examples in which the learner responses to questions asking about worked-out steps in a worked example.
Sensory Memory	Part of the cognitive system that briefly stores visual information received by the eyes and auditory information received by the ears.
Signaling	An instructional technique used to draw attention to critical elements of the instruction. Common techniques include use of arrows, circles, bolding of text, or emphasis in narration.

Simulation	An interactive environment in which features in the virtual environment behave similarly to real-world events. Simulations may be conceptual, such as a simulation of genetic inheritance, or operational, such as a flight simulator.
Site Map	A menu or concept map that graphically represents topics included in a course or online reference resource.
Split Attention	When learners must divide mental resources unnecessarily between two or more media elements. For example, when a graphic is explained by text that is located far from the graphic, the learner must divide his or her attention between the two.
Social Media	Software allowing learners to upload content and connect with others through the Internet. Some well-known applications include Facebook and Twitter. See also *Social Software*.
Social Presence	The extent to which a delivery medium can communicate face-to-face human interactions, including speech, body language, emotions, etc.
Social Interdependence	A collaborative learning arrangement in which the achievement of each individual team member depends on the achievements of other team members.
Social Software	Computer applications that allow individuals to correspond or collaborate with others. Some examples include wikis, blogs, discussion boards, Facebook, and online conferencing.
Spacing Effect	Practice exercises distributed within and among lessons result in better long-term retention. This principle is the basis for the benefits of distributed practice.
Standard Deviation	The amount of dispersal among test scores or other outcome results. A larger standard deviation indicates greater spread among test scores, while a smaller standard deviation indicates greater consistency among scores.

Static Adaptive Control	A form of learner control based on a one-time assessment of learner skills followed by branching to needed topics or lessons such as in a pretest. Contrast with *Dynamic Adaptive Control.*
Statistical Significance	A measure of the probability that the differences in the outcome results in the test and control groups are real and are not a chance difference.
Storyboard	A layout that outlines the content and instructional methods of a lesson, typically used for preview purposes before programming.
Strategic Knowledge or Skills	Guidelines that help in problem solving or completion of tasks that require judgment and reflection. For example, developing a sales proposal, writing an analytic report. See also *Far Transfer.*
Structured Controversy	A structured collaborative learning design involving team argumentation and synthesis of perspectives.
Structured Expert Interview	A type of cognitive task analysis in which experts work independently and then together to identify situations of diverse complexity in a domain.
Summative Evaluation	Evaluation of the impact of the courseware conducted at the end of the project; may include cost-benefit analysis.
Synchronous Collaboration	Opportunities for learners and/or instructors to interact with each other via computer at the same time.
Synchronous e-Learning	Electronic delivery of instructor-led training available to geographically dispersed learners at the same time. Delivered through specialized software such as WebEx, Elluminate, Adobe Connect. Synchronous sessions can be recorded and accessed for asynchronous review after the event. Also called *Virtual Classrooms* or *Webinars*
Task Analysis	Research to define the knowledge and skills to be included in training, based on observations of performance and interviews of performers.

Technophile	An individual or group that is enamored with technological features and may overload training with more sensory stimuli than learners can process.
Technostic	An individual or group that fails to exploit the potential of a new learning technology by transferring previous instructional techniques from older media to new technology with little or no adaptation, for example, books transferred to screens.
Transfer	Application of previously learned knowledge and skills to new situations encountered after the learning event. Relies on retrieval of new knowledge and skills from long-term memory during performance.
Training Wheels	A technique introduced by John Carroll in which learners work with software simulations that are initially of limited functionality and progress to higher fidelity simulations as they master lower-level skills.
Transfer Appropriate Interactions	Activities that require the learners to perform during training as they would on the job. For example, when learning a new computer system, learners practice with case examples and software interfaces that are identical or very similar to the job. See *Encoding Specificity*.
Transformational Graphics	Visuals used to show changes in time or space such as a weather cycle diagram or an animated illustration of a computer procedure.
Treatment	A variable or factor incorporated in an experimental lesson to determine its impact on learners.
Twitch Games	Online games that rely on fast and accurate motor responses on a game device such as a joy stick for success. Various arcade games are typical examples.
Value-Added Research	Experiments in which different versions of games or simulations are tested to derive the conditions under which a game or simulation is most effective for learning.

Varied Context Examples	A series of examples with different surface features but that illustrate the same principles. For example, a series of examples illustrating correlations use rainfall and crop growth, age and weight, and practice time and speed. See also *Deep Structure*.
Virtual Classroom	See *Synchronous e-Learning*.
Virtual World	A digital three-dimensional environment in which participants assume an avatar persona and explore and/or engage with the on-screen objects. Second Life is one early example of a virtual world.
Visible Author	A personal style of writing in which the author reveals information about him- or herself or about personal perspectives regarding the content.
Visual Channel	Part of the human memory system that processes information received through the eyes and mentally represented in pictorial form.
Web 2.0	The name attributed to two-way Internet capability for users to both upload and download content.
Webinar	See *Synchronous e-Learning*.
Whole-Task Instruction	A form of guided discovery instruction in which the lesson begins with and learning is driven by a realistic work assignment or problem. Also called *scenario-based learning*, *case-based learning*, or *immersive learning*. Contrast with *Part-Task Instruction*.
Wiki	A website that allows visitors to edit its contents. Can be controlled for editing/viewing by a small group or by all.
Worked Example	Step-by-step demonstration of how to solve a problem or accomplish a task.
Working Memory	Part of the cognitive system in which the learner actively (consciously) processes incoming information from the environment and retrieves information from long-term memory. Working memory has two channels (visual and auditory) and is limited in capacity.

LIST OF TABLES AND FIGURES

Introduction

Chapter 1

Chapter 5

Chapter 6

Chapter 8

Chapter 9

Chapter 10

Chapter 11

Chapter 12

Chapter 13

Chapter 14

Chapter 16

Chapter 17

NAME INDEX

A

Abrami, P.C., 283, 289
Ahern, T.C., 13
Aidman, E., 83
Albanese, M.A., 352
Aleven, V., 326
Alexander, P.A., 51, 61
Amankwatia, T.B., 155
Anderson, P.H., 374, 380
Anderson, R.B., 79, 109
Asberg, K., 273
Association of Psychological Science, 81
ASTD, 14–15, 19, 74, 286
Atkinson, R.K., 188, 192, 193, 194, 195, 196, 233, 238
Ayres, P., 83, 86, 105, 108, 171
Azevedo, R., 318, 362

B

Baggett, P., 109
Bahrick, H.P., 268
Bain, P., 16, 67, 82
Beck, I., 184, 198
Belanich, J., 382
Bernard, R.M., 12
Berry, D., 109
Betrancourt, M., 84
Bishop, M.J., 155
Bjork, R., 137
Bjork, R.A., 268
Bjorn, B., 173
Boire, M., 109
Bottage, B., 16, 67, 82
Bove, W., 79, 170, 171
Bower, G., 106, 108
Brave, S., 188, 189
Broers, N., 324
Brown, G.D., 268
Brown, K.G., 289, 317

Brown, P., 190
Brunken, R., 127
Bryman, A., 79, 170, 171
Butcher, K.R., 81, 164

C

Callaway, C.B., 193
Campbell, J., 84, 166, 186, 187, 295
Carlson, R.A., 259
Carnoy, M., 53
Carpenter, P.A., 108
Carroll, J.M., 390
Carson, B., 374, 390
Casper, W.J., 289, 317
Cassell, J., 191, 193
Cate, C., 84
Cates, W.M., 155
Chan, C., 86
Chandler, P., 83, 107, 139, 140, 211, 218, 236, 327, 328
ChanLin, L., 86
Chatham, R.E., 339
Chi, M.T.H., 231, 233, 234, 283
Churchill, E., 191, 193
Clark, R.C., 16, 51, 74
Clark, R.E., 12
Cohen, J., 60
Coleman, D., 329
Collins, H., 190
Cooper, G.A., 86, 227
Cooper, M., 107
Cooper, S., 13
Corbalan, G., 266, 324
Craig, S.D., 123, 139, 195, 234
Crossman, E.R.F.W., 259
Cuban, L., 32
Cunningham, J.P.W., 316
Cushing, J.R., 12
Cuypers, H., 266

SUBJECT INDEX

A

Accelerated learning: acceleration of expertise through scenarios, 18

Active comparison of varied context examples, 243–245

Active observing, 234; applying to workforce learning, 246; promoting active observation of expert models, 359–360. *See also* observational learning; self-explanations

Active processing, 35, 36

Activity matrix, *370*

Adaptive control, 323–324; accuracy of self-explanations for, 326–327; evidence for dynamic adaptive control vs. program control, 324–325; rapid verification method for dynamic adaptive control, 325–326; when to consider adaptive e-learning, 327

Animations: avoiding simultaneous display with text, 101; changing static illustrations to, 84–86

Appropriate measures, 56–57

Architectures, 22–23

Asynchronous e-learning, 9

Asynchronous learning, 10; customized training, 15–16; navigational techniques used in, 314; sample e-lesson on Excel for small business, 409–413

Audio: presenting steps with audio not audio and text, 236–237. *See also* extraneous audio

Auditory learning styles, 137

Author: evidence for the visible author, 200–201; making the author visible, 197–199; psychological reasons for using a visible author, 200

Automotive troubleshooting, 347–348; simulation, 418–421. *See also* whole-task instruction

B

Background music. *See* extraneous audio

Behavioral engagement, 16–17

BioWorld, 348–350. *See also* whole-task instruction

Blocked practice, 270. *See also* practice

Blogs, 284

Boundary conditions: and the coherence principle, 164; for conversational style, 187–188; and instructional explanations of worked examples, 234–235; and the personalization principle, 179; for politeness theory, 190–191; and the redundancy principle, 133, 141; for the visible author, 201

Breakout rooms, 284

C

Calibration accuracy, 315–317

Captions: avoiding displaying at the bottom of screens, 99

Case-based learning. *See* whole-task instruction

Chats, 285

Cognitive interest, 174

Cognitive learning theory, 39

Cognitive load, 41

Cognitive models, 226

Cognitive overload, 105

Cognitive processing capacity, 37–39

Cognitive skills, 344–345, 355

Cognitive task analysis, 360–362; interviews, 362–363; methods, 361

Cognitive theory of multimedia learning, 138–139; and extraneous audio, 156–157; and extraneous graphics, 161

Coherence principle, 151; applying to practice interactions, 273; avoiding e-lessons with extraneous audio, 153–156; avoiding e-lessons with extraneous words, 166–168; avoiding extraneous graphics, 159–160; evidence for omitting extraneous audio, 157–159; evidence for omitting extraneous graphics, 161–164; evidence for omitting extraneous words, 168–172; evidence for using simpler visuals, 164–166; psychological reasons for avoiding extraneous graphics, 160–161; psychological reasons to avoid extraneous audio, 156–157;

RUTH COLVIN CLARK is a recognized specialist in instructional design and technical training. She holds a doctorate in educational psychology and instructional technology from the University of Southern California. Prior to founding Clark Training & Consulting, she served as a training manager at Southern California Edison. Dr. Clark is a past president of the International Society for Performance Improvement and was honored in 2006 with the Thomas F. Gilbert Award for Distinguished Professional Achievement. Dr. Clark has authored six books that translate instructional research into guidelines for practitioners, including the best-selling *e-Learning and the Science of Instruction* and *Building Expertise*, both of which were bestowed the Best Communication Award from ISPI. She lives in Arizona and Colorado.

RICHARD E. MAYER is a professor of psychology at the University of California, Santa Barbara. His research interests are in applying the science of learning to education, with a focus on multimedia learning. He has served as president of Division 15 (Educational Psychology) of the American Psychological Association and vice president of Division C (Learning and Instruction) of the American Educational Research Association. He is the winner of the Thorndike Award for career achievement in educational psychology and the Distinguished Contribution of Applications of Psychology to Education and Training Award, and is ranked number one as the most productive educational psychologist in the world in Contemporary Educational Psychology. He serves on the editorial boards of fourteen journals, mainly in educational psychology. He is the author or editor of more than four hundred publications, including twenty-five books, including the *Handbook of Research on Learning and Instruction* (editor, with P. Alexander, 2011), *Applying the Science of Learning* (2010), *Multimedia*

Learning (2nd ed.) (2009), *Learning and Instruction* (2nd ed.) (2008), and *The Cambridge Handbook of Multimedia Learning* (2005). He lives in Goleta, California.

The authors can be reached at Ruth@Clarktraining.com or Mayer@Psych. ucsb.edu.

Pfeiffer Publications Guide

This guide is designed to familiarize you with the various types of Pfeiffer publications. The formats section describes the various types of products that we publish; the methodologies section describes the many different ways that content might be provided within a product. We also provide a list of the topic areas in which we publish.

FORMATS

In addition to its extensive book-publishing program, Pfeiffer offers content in an array of formats, from fieldbooks for the practitioner to complete, ready-to-use training packages that support group learning.

FIELDBOOK Designed to provide information and guidance to practitioners in the midst of action. Most fieldbooks are companions to another, sometimes earlier, work, from which its ideas are derived; the fieldbook makes practical what was theoretical in the original text. Fieldbooks can certainly be read from cover to cover. More likely, though, you'll find yourself bouncing around following a particular theme, or dipping in as the mood, and the situation, dictate.

HANDBOOK A contributed volume of work on a single topic, comprising an eclectic mix of ideas, case studies, and best practices sourced by practitioners and experts in the field.

An editor or team of editors usually is appointed to seek out contributors and to evaluate content for relevance to the topic. Think of a handbook not as a ready-to-eat meal, but as a cookbook of ingredients that enables you to create the most fitting experience for the occasion.

RESOURCE Materials designed to support group learning. They come in many forms: a complete, ready-to-use exercise (such as a game); a comprehensive resource on one topic (such as conflict management) containing a variety of methods and approaches; or a collection of like-minded activities (such as icebreakers) on multiple subjects and situations.

TRAINING PACKAGE An entire, ready-to-use learning program that focuses on a particular topic or skill. All packages comprise a guide for the facilitator/trainer and a workbook for the participants. Some packages are supported with additional media—such as video—or learning aids, instruments, or other devices to help participants understand concepts or practice and develop skills.

- *Facilitator/trainer's guide* Contains an introduction to the program, advice on how to organize and facilitate the learning event, and step-by-step instructor notes. The guide also contains copies of presentation materials—handouts, presentations, and overhead designs, for example—used in the program.

• *Participant's workbook* Contains exercises and reading materials that support the learning goal and serves as a valuable reference and support guide for participants in the weeks and months that follow the learning event. Typically, each participant will require his or her own workbook.

ELECTRONIC CD-ROMs and web-based products transform static Pfeiffer content into dynamic, interactive experiences. Designed to take advantage of the searchability, automation, and ease-of-use that technology provides, our e-products bring convenience and immediate accessibility to your workspace.

METHODOLOGIES

CASE STUDY A presentation, in narrative form, of an actual event that has occurred inside an organization. Case studies are not prescriptive, nor are they used to prove a point; they are designed to develop critical analysis and decision-making skills. A case study has a specific time frame, specifies a sequence of events, is narrative in structure, and contains a plot structure—an issue (what should be/have been done?). Use case studies when the goal is to enable participants to apply previously learned theories to the circumstances in the case, decide what is pertinent, identify the real issues, decide what should have been done, and develop a plan of action.

ENERGIZER A short activity that develops readiness for the next session or learning event. Energizers are most commonly used after a break or lunch to stimulate or refocus the group. Many involve some form of physical activity, so they are a useful way to counter post-lunch lethargy. Other uses include transitioning from one topic to another, where "mental" distancing is important.

EXPERIENTIAL LEARNING ACTIVITY (ELA) A facilitator-led intervention that moves participants through the learning cycle from experience to application (also known as a Structured Experience). ELAs are carefully thought-out designs in which there is a definite learning purpose and intended outcome. Each step—everything that participants do during the activity—facilitates the accomplishment of the stated goal. Each ELA includes complete instructions for facilitating the intervention and a clear statement of goals, suggested group size and timing, materials required, an explanation of the process, and, where appropriate, possible variations to the activity. (For more detail on Experiential Learning Activities, see the Introduction to the *Reference Guide to Handbooks and Annuals,* 1999 edition, Pfeiffer, San Francisco.)

GAME A group activity that has the purpose of fostering team spirit and togetherness in addition to the achievement of a pre-stated goal. Usually contrived—undertaking a desert expedition, for example—this type of learning method offers an engaging means for participants to demonstrate and practice business and interpersonal skills. Games are effective for team building and personal development mainly because the goal is subordinate to the process—the means through which participants reach decisions, collaborate, communicate, and generate trust and understanding. Games often engage teams in "friendly" competition.

ICEBREAKER A (usually) short activity designed to help participants overcome initial anxiety in a training session and/or to acquaint the participants with one another. An icebreaker can be a fun activity or can be tied to specific topics or training goals. While a useful tool in itself, the icebreaker comes into its own in situations where tension or resistance exists within a group.

INSTRUMENT A device used to assess, appraise, evaluate, describe, classify, and summarize various aspects of human behavior. The term used to describe an instrument depends primarily on its format and purpose. These terms include survey, questionnaire, inventory, diagnostic, survey, and poll. Some uses of instruments include providing instrumental feedback to group members, studying here-and-now processes or functioning within a group, manipulating group composition, and evaluating outcomes of training and other interventions.

Instruments are popular in the training and HR field because, in general, more growth can occur if an individual is provided with a method for focusing specifically on his or her own behavior. Instruments also are used to obtain information that will serve as a basis for change and to assist in workforce planning efforts.

Paper-and-pencil tests still dominate the instrument landscape with a typical package comprising a facilitator's guide, which offers advice on administering the instrument and interpreting the collected data, and an initial set of instruments. Additional instruments are available separately. Pfeiffer, though, is investing heavily in e-instruments. Electronic instrumentation provides effortless distribution and, for larger groups particularly, offers advantages over paper-and-pencil tests in the time it takes to analyze data and provide feedback.

LECTURETTE A short talk that provides an explanation of a principle, model, or process that is pertinent to the participants' current learning needs. A lecturette is intended to establish a common language bond between the trainer and the participants by providing a mutual frame of reference. Use a lecturette as an introduction to a group activity or event, as an interjection during an event, or as a handout.

MODEL A graphic depiction of a system or process and the relationship among its elements. Models provide a frame of reference and something more tangible, and more easily remembered, than a verbal explanation. They also give participants something to "go on," enabling them to track their own progress as they experience the dynamics, processes, and relationships being depicted in the model.

ROLE PLAY A technique in which people assume a role in a situation/scenario: a customer service rep in an angry-customer exchange, for example. The way in which the role is approached is then discussed and feedback is offered. The role play is often repeated using a different approach and/or incorporating changes made based on feedback received. In other words, role playing is a spontaneous interaction involving realistic behavior under artificial (and safe) conditions.

SIMULATION A methodology for understanding the interrelationships among components of a system or process. Simulations differ from games in that they test or use a model that depicts or mirrors some aspect of reality in form, if not necessarily in content. Learning occurs by studying the effects of change on one or more factors of the model. Simulations are commonly used to test hypotheses about what happens in a system—often referred to as "what if?" analysis—or to examine best-case/worst-case scenarios.

THEORY A presentation of an idea from a conjectural perspective. Theories are useful because they encourage us to examine behavior and phenomena through a different lens.

TOPICS

The twin goals of providing effective and practical solutions for workforce training and organization development and meeting the educational needs of training and human resource professionals shape Pfeiffer's publishing program. Core topics include the following:

> Leadership & Management
> Communication & Presentation
> Coaching & Mentoring
> Training & Development
> e-Learning
> Teams & Collaboration
> OD & Strategic Planning
> Human Resources
> Consulting

What will you find on pfeiffer.com?

• The best in workplace performance solutions for training and HR professionals

• Downloadable training tools, exercises, and content

• Web-exclusive offers

• Training tips, articles, and news

• Seamless on-line ordering

• Author guidelines, information on becoming a Pfeiffer Partner, and much more

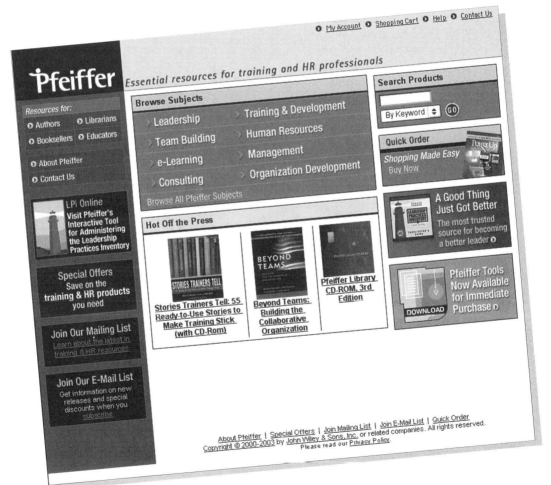

Discover more at www.pfeiffer.com